THE VAJRA ESSENCE

Düdjom Lingpa's Visions of the Great Perfection

This three-volume series presents English translations of Düdjom Lingpa's five visionary teachings on *Dzokchen*, the Great Perfection, along with three essential commentaries by his disciples.

Volume 1. Heart of the Great Perfection

The Sharp Vajra of Conscious Awareness Tantra, Düdjom Lingpa

Essence of Clear Meaning, Pema Tashi

The Foolish Dharma of an Idiot Clothed in Mud and Feathers, Düdjom Lingpa

The Enlightened View of Samantabhadra, Düdjom Lingpa

Volume 2. Buddhahood Without Meditation

Buddhahood Without Meditation, Düdjom Lingpa

The Fine Path to Liberation, Sera Khandro

Garland for the Delight of the Fortunate, Sera Khandro

Volume 3. The Vajra Essence

The Vajra Essence, Düdjom Lingpa

The Vajra Essence

Düdjom Lingpa's Visions of
The Great Perfection,
Volume 3

Foreword by Sogyal Rinpoche

Translated by B. Alan Wallace
Edited by Dion Blundell

Wisdom

Wisdom Publications
199 Elm Street
Somerville, MA 02144 USA
wisdompubs.org

Library of Congress Cataloging-in-Publication Data
Bdud-'joms-glin-pa, Gter-ston, 1835–1904.
[Works. Selections. English]
Dudjom Lingpa's visions of the Great Perfection / Translated by B. Alan Wallace ; Edited by Dion Blundell.
volumes cm
Includes bibliographical references and index.
Contents: Volume 1. Heart of the Great Perfection — volume 2. Buddhahood without meditation — volume 3. The Vajra essence.
ISBN 1-61429-260-4 (pbk. : alk. paper)
1. Rdzogs-chen. I. Wallace, B. Alan. II. Title.
BQ942.D777A25 2016
294.3'420423—dc23
2014048350

ISBN 978-1-61429-347-7 ebook ISBN 978-1-61429-276-0

20 19 18 17 5 4 3 1

Cover and interior design by Gopa & Ted2, Inc.
Set in Garamond Premier Pro 10.6/13.16.
Hūṃ syllable calligraphy by Lama Chönam.

Wisdom Publications' books are printed on acid-free paper and meet the guidelines for permanence and durability of the Production Guidelines for Book Longevity of the Council on Library Resources.

This book was produced with environmental mindfulness.
For more information, please visit wisdompubs.org/wisdom-environment.

Printed in the United States of America.

MIX
Paper from responsible sources
FSC® C011935

Please visit fscus.org.

Contents

TASHI CHOLING

CENTER FOR BUDDHIST STUDIES

TASHICHOLING.ORG

P.O BOX 64
ASHLAND. OR 97520

VEN. GYATRUL RINPOCHE
SPIRITUAL DIRECTOR

The revelations of the great treasure revealer, enlightened master, and fearless conduct yogi from eastern Tibet Heruka Düdjom Lingpa are treasure troves of teaching, advice, and insights into the human mind's true nature of wisdom awareness. For those who connect to the lineage through empowerment, transmission, and instruction under the guidance of qualified lineage masters, these teachings hold the key to understanding the true meaning of permanent happiness and benefit. Having known Alan for many years and observed his enthusiastic devotion and passion for Dharma in general and especially for the teachings of the Great Perfection as transmitted through Heruka Düdjom Lingpa's revelations, I am certain that he has done his very best to make these translations as accurate as possible and I rejoice in this effort from the bottom of my heart. This trilogy of English translations is a wondrous gift for disciples of the tradition. May there be great waves of benefit for countless sentient beings!

Gyatrul Rinpoché
Tashi Choling

Dhomang Gyatrul

Foreword

TWELVE HUNDRED YEARS AGO, one of the most dramatic and daring spiritual undertakings in history took place in Central Asia. The entire teaching of the Buddha, as it existed at the time in India and the Himalayan region, was imported and transplanted in Tibet. Sometimes I try to imagine what it must have been like to be there at that spectacular moment. To see the unforgettable, awe-inspiring figure of Guru Rinpoché, Padmasambhava, whose protection and inspiration enabled this whole revolutionary endeavor to unfold. To witness the great Madhyamaka scholar and abbot Śāntarakṣita, who brought with him the vast heritage of Nālandā Monastery, and the Tibetan king Trisong Detsen, the thirty-seventh in his line, who sponsored this massive and imaginative program. Or to gaze in wonder as Guru Rinpoché stood atop Mount Hepori and bound the spirits of Tibet under his command, and to watch the first monastic university, called Samyé "The Inconceivable," gradually take shape. If you had been there, you would have caught sight of scores of realized and learned paṇḍitas, who had made the arduous journey across the Himalayas and were working with translators to render the sutras, tantras, and treatises into Tibetan. Transmissions of various kinds were taking place, the first seven Tibetan monastics were being ordained, and Guru Padmasambhava was opening the maṇḍala of the Secret Mantrayāna teachings at Chimpu for his twenty-five disciples. They were the first saints and siddhas of Tibet, headed by Guru Rinpoché's closest disciple and consort, Yeshé Tsogyal, the king himself, and the virtuoso translator Vairocana. What a glorious and momentous time this must have been! And although history tells us that this did not happen without opposition and resistance, both human and nonhuman, as Kyapjé Düdjom Rinpoché explains, "Because the kingdom was protected by the true Dharma, Tibet is known to have enjoyed the happiness of paradise."

For about fifty-five years, it is said, the Great Guru stayed in Tibet and the Himalayan regions, sowing his blessings into the environment and the psyche of the Tibetan people. Foreseeing the needs of future generations and the limits of people's understanding at the time, Padmasambhava concealed countless *terma* treasure teachings in the landscape and in the unchanging pure awareness of his realized disciples. The terma teachings remain concealed until the precise moment in time when they will be of maximum benefit and relevance, and they are then revealed by a continuing series of incarnations of the same twenty-five disciples whom Padmasambhava had entrusted with his teachings and his blessings. As a result, the ancient Nyingma tradition of early translations that follows Padmasambhava's vision comprises both the long, unbroken *kama* lineage of canonical teachings and the close lineage of terma treasures. And at the heart of the Nyingma tradition flows the deepest current of wisdom within the Buddhist teachings of Tibet, the pinnacle of all spiritual vehicles—the Great Perfection, *Dzokpachenpo*, with its living lineage of realization stretching from the Primordial Buddha Samantabhadra down to the present day.

One of Guru Rinpoché's twenty-five disciples showed remarkable aptitude at a very early age. He learned Sanskrit with ease and was quickly chosen to be part of the group of Tibetan translators. Drokpen Khyeuchung Lotsawa lived as a *ngakpa*, a lay mantric practitioner, wearing his hair long and dressing in white. He mastered all the secret Mantrayāna teachings Padmasambhava conferred on him and became a great siddha. His realization and power were such that he could summon birds from the sky through his mere gaze or a gesture of his hand, and then, it is said, give them teachings. Like others among the twenty-five disciples, Khyeuchung Lotsawa reincarnated over the centuries as a series of realized masters who spread and deepened the teachings of the Buddha and brought enormous benefit to beings. In the nineteenth century he appeared as the great treasure revealer, visionary, and powerful mystic Düdjom Lingpa.

I first came to learn about this amazing master after meeting his incarnation, Kyapjé Düdjom Rinpoché, who became one of my most beloved teachers. I discovered that everything about Düdjom Lingpa was extraordinary: his birth in 1835 in the Serta Valley of the Golok region on Guru Rinpoché's day, the tenth day of the waxing moon; his amazing life story, which was a continuous stream of visions, dreams, and prophecies starting at the age of three; the way in which he received visionary teachings of the greatest depth and clarity directly from enlightened beings of every kind; his mastery of earth termas, mind termas, and pure visions; the sheer profundity of his revelations, such as those contained in these volumes; his visits to pure lands, including Sukhāvatī and the Copper Colored Mountain paradise of Guru Rinpoché—a visit that spanned one human day but for him lasted twelve years; and his continuous perception of enlightened beings and pure realms.

No less astounding was the way in which he predicted his own incarnation, Düdjom Rinpoché Jikdral Yeshé Dorjé. Having spent most of his life in eastern Tibet and the Golok area, Düdjom Lingpa received a number of visionary instructions that he should go to Pemakö, perhaps the most famous of the "hidden lands" of Padmasambhava and one that had been opened by Düdjom Lingpa's earlier incarnation, Rikzin Düdul Dorjé (1615–72). It lay far to the southeast and was a region of legendary, majestic beauty and sacred significance. There, Guru Rinpoché said, "All the mountains open like blossoming flowers, all the rivers naturally resound mantras and flow with nectar, and rainbows arch across the trees and bushes." During his lifetime, Düdjom Lingpa was unable to travel to Pemakö. Yet he knew of the devastation that within decades would ravage Tibet, and not long before he passed away in 1904, he called his disciples together and told them to pack up and leave for Pemakö: "Now in this final age of degeneration, it's time to go to the hidden land of Pemakö. Anyone who puts his or her trust in me should go there as well. But this old man will get there before you youngsters arrive!"

Just as he predicted, when his disciples eventually made their way to Pemakö, they discovered a three-year-old child who called them by name, spoke not in the local language but in the Golok dialect, and had already asked his parents to prepare for a party of guests. The young boy was Düdjom Lingpa's reincarnation. It is said that Düdjom Rinpoché was conceived while Düdjom Lingpa was still alive, for there are no limits that can possibly impede the enlightened mind.

As I pay homage here to Düdjom Lingpa, I would like to take this opportunity to share a few of my memories of Kyapjé Düdjom Rinpoché, whom I had the privilege and blessing of knowing personally. I first met him thanks to my master Jamyang Khyentsé Chökyi Lodrö. He always used to talk about what a wonderful and realized master Düdjom Rinpoché was, and how he was the living representative of Guru Padmasambhava. They held each other in the highest esteem. In Lhasa, where they met in the 1950s, Düdjom Rinpoché confided to Trulshik Rinpoché that he considered Jamyang Khyentsé the holiest master they could ever hope to find. Düdjom Rinpoché moved to Kalimpong in India in around 1957, and my master took me to meet him and receive his blessing. Jamyang Khyentsé told him he had never had the privilege of receiving the entire transmission of his terma revelations and asked him for a special blessing. Düdjom Rinpoché gave him the "seal of authorization" for all of his own terma treasures. He also conferred on Jamyang Khyentsé the empowerments and instructions for his mind treasure of Dorjé Drolö, the wild, wrathful aspect of Guru Padmasambhava. They wrote long-life prayers for each other. My master spoke of Düdjom Rinpoché as "the authentic great Sovereign Lord of the extraordinary and profound secret terma treasures." Düdjom Rinpoché called him "the sole champion in our time of the great and supreme path of the Vajra Heart Essence, the magical wisdom manifestation of the lotus-born lord Padmasambhava and Vimalamitra."

Some years later, I went to visit Düdjom Rinpoché in Kalimpong and by coincidence found myself translating for one of his American disciples. It was then that I realized just how extraordinary he was. By the end of his teaching, a pointing-out instruction on the nature of mind, tears were running down my face, and I understood what Jamyang Khyentsé had meant when he said this was an exceptional master. I instantly felt enormous faith in him, and there and then I requested Düdjom Rinpoché to be my master and grant me teachings.

Düdjom Lingpa's revelations and Düdjom Rinpoché's terma cycles are together known as the *Düdjom Tersar*, the "New Treasures of Düdjom," which are new in the sense that they are still fresh with the warm breath of the ḍākinīs, and because there is only one master in the lineage between Guru Rinpoché and the practitioners of the treasures. Although I see these two great masters as one and the same, their outward characters were quite different. Düdjom Lingpa was a commanding and unpredictable figure, well known for his wrathful demeanor and behavior. Düdjom Rinpoché describes how to visualize him: "His body is red in color, his beard reaching as far as his heart, and his eyes are open wide, staring steadily straight ahead. His long hair is mostly tied up in a knot on top of his head with a small sacred book, while the rest tumbles loosely over his shoulders. He wears a gown of reddish brown silk, a shawl of white cotton, and conch-shell earrings, with a sword of wisdom thrust through his belt. His right hand wields a vajra in the sky, and his left hand rolls a *purba* dagger of meteoric iron. He sits with his left leg stretched out slightly in the posture of royal play."

In marked contrast, Düdjom Rinpoché had about him an air of captivating kindness, gentleness, and serenity. In fact, he used to tell a story about his predecessor that always brought a twinkle to his eye. When Düdjom Lingpa was about to pass away and leave this world, some of his disciples approached him timidly and begged him to return in a more peaceful form. He chuckled and said, "Well, all right. But don't complain if I am *too* peaceful."

Like his previous incarnation, Düdjom Rinpoché was a very great Dzokchen master. It is said of him that he was the body emanation of Khyeuchung Lotsawa, the speech emanation of Yeshé Tsogyal, and the mind emanation of Guru Padmasambhava. In *The Tibetan Book of Living and Dying*, I tried to sum up some of his characteristics: "He was small, with a beautiful and gentle face, exquisite hands, and a delicate, almost feminine presence. Like a yogin, he wore his hair long and tied up in a knot; his eyes always glittered with secret amusement. His voice seemed the voice of compassion itself, soft and a little hoarse." One of Padmasambhava's terma prophecies captured his qualities with remarkable prescience: "In a noble family there will appear an emanation of Khyeuchung Lotsawa bearing the name Jñāna, keeping the yogic discipline of a master of mantras, his appearance not fixed in any way, his behavior spontaneous like a child, and endowed with piercing wisdom. He will reveal new termas and safeguard the ancient ones, and he will guide whoever has a connection with him to the Glorious Copper Colored Mountain in Ngayab Ling."

Düdjom Rinpoché, I learned, began receiving termas when he was a young boy, and he met Guru Rinpoché and Yeshé Tsogyal in a vision when he was only thirteen. Although he revealed his own powerful terma treasures, he decided to prioritize maintaining, protecting, and spreading the older termas as well as the kama tradition of the Nyingmapas. While still quite young, he was regarded as a supreme master of the Great Perfection, and by the time he was in his thirties he had already accomplished an enormous amount. When other lamas saw his famous prayer *Calling the Lama from Afar*, which he composed at the age of thirty and which captured completely his profound realization, they immediately recognized him as a great tertön and Dzokchen master. Chökyi Nyima Rinpoché told me that his father, Tulku Urgyen Rinpoché, one of the greatest teachers of Dzokchen and Mahāmudrā in recent times, used to say that if anyone ever wondered what a true Dzokchen master and practitioner was like, they only had to look at Düdjom Rinpoché. His eyes always sparkled with a kind of freshness and vibrant clarity. Unencumbered by opinions of good or bad, and ever carefree, spacious, and relaxed, Düdjom Rinpoché had about him a child-like innocence—you could call it an enlightened purity.

His work in compiling the Nyingma kama, which he began at the age of seventy-four, paralleled the achievement of Jamgön Kongtrul in compiling the treasure teachings in the *Precious Treasury of Termas*. He saved many precious texts and sacred relics from loss, and with meticulous care, he compiled, preserved, emended, and annotated the older texts and practices, to the extent that there seems hardly anything he did not have a hand in perfecting. In fact Düdjom Rinpoché's achievements for the Nyingma tradition as a whole were monumental. He gave the transmission of the *Precious Treasury of Termas* ten times, and he transmitted the kama and *The Hundred Thousand Tantras of the Nyingmapas* as well as countless treasure cycles and priceless teachings. Unanimously requested to become the supreme head of the Nyingma tradition, his own revelations and writings fill twenty-five volumes, among which his *History of the Nyingmapas* and *Fundamentals of the Nyingmapas* are classics. His compositions were amazing, his scholarship famous, his calligraphy much copied, his poetry lucid yet profound, and his detailed knowledge of every aspect of Vajrayāna practice and ritual truly phenomenal.

Düdjom Rinpoché also played a huge part in reestablishing Tibetan culture and education in exile, and he composed his *History of Tibet* at the request of His Holiness the Dalai Lama. On occasion, His Holiness has expressed his regret at not having been able to receive transmissions directly from Düdjom Rinpoché, although when he embarked on a retreat on the Kagyé—Eight Great Practice Maṇḍalas—according to the *sangwa gyachen* pure visions of the Great Fifth Dalai Lama, Düdjom Rinpoché wrote a practice guide for him that he found outstanding. Among Düdjom Rinpoché's countless disciples were the most eminent lamas of the last century, including the most senior masters of Mindröling and Dorjé Drak monasteries, and he had innumerable followers all over Tibet and the Himalayas, Europe, America, Taiwan, and Hong Kong. When he gave the transmission of the *New Treasures of Düdjom* at Boudhanath in Nepal in 1977–78, thousands upon thousands flocked to attend.

After my master Jamyang Khyentsé passed away, Düdjom Rinpoché held me with all his care and compassion, and I had the great privilege of serving as his translator for a number of years. I quickly discovered that he had a unique way of inspiring the realization of the innermost nature of mind. It was through the very way he spoke. The words he used were simple and down to earth, and yet they had a way of penetrating right into your heart. As the instructions on the nature of mind flowed effortlessly from his wisdom mind, it seemed as if he became the teaching of Dzokpachenpo itself, and his words served to gather you into the actual experience. Through his presence, and through his gaze, he created a subtle but electrifying atmosphere, enveloping you in his wisdom mind, so that you could not help but feel the pure awareness that he was pointing out. I can only compare it to sitting in front of a blazing, open fire—you cannot help but feel warm. It was as simple as that.

Düdjom Rinpoché demonstrated, again and again, that when a great master directs the blessing of his wisdom mind, something extraordinary and very powerful can take place. All your ordinary thoughts and thinking are disarmed, and you arrive face to face with the deeper nature—the original face—of your own mind. In Düdjom Rinpoché's words, "all the stirrings of discursive thoughts melt, dissolve, and slip into the expanse of *rigpa*, your pure awareness, which is like a cloudless sky. All their power and strength is lost to the rigpa awareness." At that moment everything drops, a completely different dimension opens up, and you glimpse the sky-like nature of mind. With Düdjom

Rinpoché I came to understand that what the master does, through the power and blessing of his realization, is to make the naked truth of the teaching come alive in you, connecting you to your buddha nature. And you? You recognize, in a blaze of gratitude, that there is not, and could never be, any separation between the master's wisdom mind and the nature of your own mind. Düdjom Rinpoché said just this in his *Calling the Lama from Afar*:

> Since pure awareness of nowness is the real buddha,
> in openness and contentment I found the lama in my heart.
> When we realize this unending natural mind is the very nature
> of the lama,
> then there is no need for attached, grasping, or weeping prayers
> or artificial complaints.
> By simply relaxing in this uncontrived, open, and natural state,
> we obtain the blessing of aimless self-liberation of whatever
> arises.

At the same time, Düdjom Rinpoché wore his realization and learning with such simplicity and ease. I sometimes felt that his outward appearance was so subtle and understated that it would have been easy for a newcomer to miss who he really was. Once in 1976 I traveled with him from France to the United States. I shall never forget that flight for as long as I live. Düdjom Rinpoché was always very humble, but now and then he would say something that betrayed what an incredible master he was. At one point I was sitting next to him and he was gazing out the window at the Atlantic Ocean when he said quietly, "May I bless all those I fly over, all the beings living in the ocean down below." It was the way he said it that struck me and sent a shiver down my spine. I could feel that there was simply no question: He actually did possess the power to bless and relieve the suffering of countless living beings. And beyond any shadow of doubt, there and then, they were receiving his blessing. In that moment I realized what a great master he was—and not just a master, but a buddha.

To tell the truth, even now, thirty years or so since he left this world, Düdjom Rinpoché's greatness still continues to dawn on me, day after day. The gratitude I feel toward him is boundless, and not a day goes by when I do not think of his words:

> Having purified the great delusion, the heart's darkness,
> the radiant light of the unobscured sun continuously rises.
> This good fortune is the kindness of the lama, our only father
> and mother;

Lama of unrepayable kindness, I only remember you.

I must also mark my gratitude to Düdjom Rinpoché's spiritual wife, Sangyum Kushok Rikzin Wangmo, who was one of the greatest ḍākinīs I have ever known. She played a unique and crucial role in Rinpoché's life. With her extraordinary love, care, and magnetic charm, she provided the perfect environment for Rinpoché, so that the teachings and revelations could pour from his wisdom mind. She lengthened his life and enabled him to stay among us for as long as he did, longer in fact than had been predicted by his masters, so as to teach, guide, and bless so many disciples and benefit countless sentient beings. Not only do I have the greatest devotion and respect for her but also a deep feeling of love, and I feel honored that both she and Rinpoché made me truly feel like part of their family.

How impossible it seems to try to measure in words the qualities and realization of masters like Düdjom Lingpa and Düdjom Rinpoché! Even their contributions to the future of the Dharma, I feel, are fathomless and not widely known. The longer I live, the more convinced I am that the Dzokchen teachings have enormous potential at this time to touch and awaken people *all over the world*, people from any country and any kind of background. I have heard a number of prophecies about these teachings and how powerful, transformative, and relevant they are at critical points in our history—at times such as this. One prophecy says, "In this dark age, the heart essence of Samantabhadra will blaze like fire." If these predictions are to come true, I know it will have a lot to do with the two great masters Düdjom Lingpa and Düdjom Rinpoché and their epic contributions to the Dharma, to sentient beings, and to the world.

Just look at the impact of their work: Düdjom Lingpa's prolific treasures have spread all over Tibet, east and west, the Himalayan lands like Bhutan, and now the Western world as well. His revelations, edited by Düdjom Rinpoché himself, fill twenty large volumes. Then, Düdjom Lingpa's eight sons were all incarnations of great masters, perhaps the most renowned being Jikmé Tenpé Nyima, the Third Dodrupchen Rinpoché, who was my master Jamyang Khyentsé's root lama, and whose writings on Dzokchen are treasured by H. H. the Dalai Lama. Düdjom Lingpa's daughters were considered to be ḍākinīs. It was not only his children who were exceptional but his students as well. In the prayer that Düdjom Rinpoché composed celebrating Düdjom Lingpa's extraordinary life story, there is this verse:

Your eight sons, holders of the family line, were the eight great bodhisattvas,

thirteen supreme disciples accomplished the body of light,
and one thousand attained the stage of vidyādhara—
to you, who established this victorious line of realized beings, I pray.

Thirteen of Düdjom Lingpa's disciples attained the rainbow body, and in his prophecies Düdjom Lingpa was told that a hundred might even attain the great transference rainbow body. As Düdjom Rinpoché wrote, "In this precious lineage of ours, this is not just ancient history. For today, just as in the past, there are those who through the paths of *trekchö* and *tögal* have attained the final realization and have dissolved their gross material bodies into rainbow bodies of radiant light." In his *History*, he wrote, "It is impossible to estimate the number of those who passed into the rainbow body by following the paths of the profound treasures of the Great Perfection..." and he lists a number of those who attained the rainbow body, including the father of my own tutor Lama Gyurdrak, a simple man called Sönam Namgyal whose body dissolved into light, leaving nothing behind but his nails and hair. These were offered to Jamyang Khyentsé, who verified it as an actual case of a rainbow body. Even today we continue to hear of instances of the rainbow body, for example the well-known case of Khenpo Achö in eastern Tibet in 1998.

There is a story about Düdjom Lingpa that I find fascinating. In the mid 1850s he had a dream in which he was given a conch shell and asked to blow it in each of the four directions. The loudest sound was in the west, and he was told in the dream that this was a sign that disciples particularly suited to him were to be found in the western regions, where his renown would spread and where he would have countless followers in the future.

Something uncannily similar happened to Düdjom Rinpoché, and he told us the story many years later, in France. One of the lamas who had traveled to Pemakö to find Düdjom Lingpa's incarnation was Ling Lama Orgyen Chöjor Gyatso, an accomplished Dzokchen master who had been a disciple of Patrul Rinpoché before becoming a close student of Düdjom Lingpa. He was one of Düdjom Rinpoché's first teachers. He told Düdjom Rinpoché that Patrul Rinpoché had asked Düdjom Lingpa's son Jikmé Tenpé Nyima, the Third Dodrupchen, to give a teaching on the *Guide to the Bodhisattva Way of Life* at the age of eight. Orgyen Chöjor Gyatso reasoned that if the son could do so at eight, then the father—in other words Düdjom Lingpa's reincarnation—should do so by the age of seven and a half at the latest. So he requested Düdjom Rinpoché to teach from the first chapters of Śāntideva's great work. When the teaching had finished, Orgyen Chöjor Gyatso was overjoyed, and he invited Düdjom Rinpoché to go outside and sound a conch in each of the four directions. In the south there was a beautiful tone, but in the west an even louder and sweeter sound rang out. Orgyen Chöjor Gyatso told him that his work would be of immeasurable benefit in the south and in the west.

Thinking of this, how meaningful it is that Düdjom Rinpoché came and taught and blessed so many people in the West. And how moving it is that he chose to pass away in Europe, in France, thereby blessing the Western world with the power of his enlightenment and confirming the arrival of these teachings in lands that had not known them before. The fact that Sangyum Kushok Rikzin Wangmo also chose to leave this world in the United States points to the same truth. It is as if they were placing their seal on Düdjom Rinpoché's celebrated aspiration:

> May the living tradition of Guru Padmasambhava, Bodhisattva Śāntarakṣita, and the Dharma-king Trisong Detsen
> spread throughout the world in all directions.
> May the Buddha, Dharma, and Saṅgha be present in the minds of all,
> inseparably, at all times, bringing peace, happiness, and well-being.

Just as Düdjom Rinpoché's life covered most of the twentieth century, Düdjom Lingpa's spanned the nineteenth century, a time when a number of great masters were pioneering a far-reaching renewal of Buddhism in Tibet, in the open-minded, ecumenical spirit of *Rimé*. They included masters such as Jamyang Khyentsé Wangpo, Jamgön Kongtrul Lodrö Thayé, Chokgyur Dechen Lingpa, and Jamgön Mipam Rinpoché. Interestingly, it was Jamyang Khyentsé Wangpo who sent his own close disciple, the incarnate lama Gyurmé Ngedön Wangpo, to Düdjom Lingpa. He told him: "You have a karmic link with Düdjom Lingpa from past lives, so meeting him will be enormously useful to the teachings and to beings." Gyurmé Ngedön Wangpo became the great treasure revealer's heart son and custodian of his treasures, and he stayed with him until he passed away. He then traveled to Pemakö, where he recognized Kyapjé Düdjom Rinpoché as the reincarnation of Düdjom Lingpa, became his root lama, and gave him many of the most important transmissions, including Düdjom Lingpa's revelations.

My own predecessor, the treasure revealer Lerab Lingpa, who was born in 1856, was somewhat younger than Düdjom Lingpa, and I know of no record of their having met. And yet their lives were mysteriously entwined. Lerab Lingpa was a very close confidant, student, and teacher of Dodrupchen

Jikmé Tenpé Nyima, Düdjom Lingpa's eldest son, and he was also the master of Düdjom Lingpa's youngest son, Dorjé Dradul, as well as three of Düdjom Lingpa's grandsons, Terchen Kunzang Nyima, Sönam Deutsen, and Tenzin Nyima. In fact, Lerab Lingpa composed and gave to Dorjé Dradul a guru yoga practice that focuses on the lama as embodying the Primordial Buddha Samantabhadra, Guru Padmasambhava, Dorjé Drolö, Düdul Dorjé, Düdjom Lingpa, Jikmé Tenpé Nyima and himself. On another occasion, one day in 1923, Lerab Lingpa experienced a vision of Guru Rinpoché and a throng of ḍākinīs, who gave him a five-part *ladrup*—a sādhana practice for accomplishing the lama—in which Düdjom Lingpa, Khanyam Lingpa, Jamyang Khyentsé Wangpo, Kusum Lingpa, and Jamgön Kongtrul each appear in the form of a deity. Düdjom Lingpa manifests as Dorjé Drolö. In the vision, Lerab Lingpa was told how urgent it was that he accomplish this practice.

The more we look, the more it seems that Düdjom Lingpa's impact on the spread of the Buddha's teachings is endless, and we can detect his traces everywhere. There is one more intriguing link between Düdjom Lingpa and Terchen Lerab Lingpa, one that had a momentous significance for the flourishing of the Dharma. In 1980, the great Khenchen Jigmé Phuntsok Rinpoché (1933–2004), one of the incarnations of Lerab Lingpa, founded his Buddhist Academy in the Larung Valley in Serta. He built his own residence on the very same site as Düdjom Lingpa's hermitage, a place also associated with the thirteen disciples who attained the rainbow body. One of Düdjom Lingpa's prophecies had in fact predicted that after a hundred years, when only the name of the Buddhadharma remained, in this very place a master would come to fan the flames of the embers and make the Nyingma teachings blaze once more. It was there that the truly remarkable Larung Gar Five Sciences Buddhist Academy developed, a center of excellence setting the highest standards of study and practice, seeing six hundred fully trained khenpos graduate in the first twenty years, and putting in motion a renaissance of Buddhist teaching and practice in eastern Tibet.

I am deeply touched to be asked to write this foreword to a collection of translations of Düdjom Lingpa's Dzokchen teachings, and I do so out of my deep and undying devotion to Kyapjé Düdjom Rinpoché and Sangyum Rikzin Wangmo, to his lineage, and to all the masters who hold it. This is a major achievement, as these teachings are legendary because of their profundity and completeness. As Düdjom Rinpoché wrote: "Even if you were to actually meet Samantabhadra, I swear that he would not say a single word other than these." Alan Wallace has made a great contribution in translating these precious teachings, and I am moved by the fact that he is not simply a very experienced translator but also someone who is a deeply conscientious and dedicated practitioner, one who has a knowledge of many Buddhist traditions but has found his home in these extraordinary treasures of the lineage of Düdjom Lingpa. How wonderful as well that he has translated the brilliant clarifications provided by the great Sera Khandro and Pema Tashi.

The profound teachings in these volumes speak for themselves, and there is no need to elaborate on their contents. But to highlight a few crucial points, I believe that the teachings of Dzokpachenpo need to be approached with great care, reverence, and maturity. First, we need to recognize just how rare, how precious, and how deep they are, as they actually possess the capacity to bring realization and even liberation in one lifetime. As Düdjom Rinpoché wrote, "Don't throw away such a precious jewel as this and then look around for semiprecious stones. Now that you have had such great good fortune as to have met this profound teaching, the very heart blood of the ḍākinīs, your mind should be uplifted and you should practice with tremendous inspiration and joy."

As we can see, Düdjom Lingpa's revelations explicitly spell out the qualities we need in order to embrace this path and practice these teachings. They include devotion and pure perception, trust and faith, a keen understanding of impermanence and cause and effect, contentment and disenchantment with mundane distractions, compassion and bodhicitta motivation, honesty and courage, commitment and single-minded enthusiasm, and the ability to see the appearances of this life as dreamlike and integrate the practice into everyday life.

Düdjom Rinpoché would always encourage students to embrace the *ngöndro* practice, saying how profound and important it is: "A full understanding and realization of the true essence of Dzokpachenpo depends *entirely* on these preliminary practices. In particular it is vital to put all your energy into the practice of guru yoga, holding on to it as the life and the heart of the practice." In these remarkable teachings, Düdjom Lingpa gives direct instructions about how to consider the master as Guru Padmasambhava in person, see him as the nature of our own clear-light rigpa awareness, and through the practice of guru yoga, unite our mind with his wisdom mind. "By merging your mind with his," he says, "you will experience the nonconceptual primordial consciousness of ultimate reality, and extraordinary realizations will arise in your mindstream."

And so I encourage you from the bottom of my heart, if you have not already done so, to seek out qualified lamas of this lineage and receive the necessary empowerments, oral transmissions, and instructions for these sacred and profound teachings so that you can put them into practice and proceed along the sublime path of Dzokpachenpo. It is our great good fortune that the New Treasure lineage of Düdjom Lingpa and Düdjom Rinpoché thrives today, thanks to the kindness and enlightened vision of their own incarnations, their family lineages, and the masters who hold these precious teachings, allowing them to resound all over the world. The prophecy of the conch shell is playing out before our very eyes.

Finally, let me take this opportunity to pray that this great Nyingma lineage and the tradition of the two extraordinary masters Düdjom Lingpa and Düdjom Rinpoché may continue in the future, going from strength to strength, touching countless sentient beings, and awakening them to their own enlightened nature—the indestructible heart essence. May all the visions and aspirations of Düdjom Lingpa and Düdjom Rinpoché be accomplished, as fully and as quickly as possible. I believe that these two great masters continue to bless the whole world. Freed from physical form, they abide in the unconditioned timeless splendor of the dharmakāya, benefitting all beings beyond the limitations of time and space, and I know that if we call upon them now with all our hearts, we will find them with us instantly. So I pray that with their blessings the lives of all the great masters may be safe and strong, and that the precious teachings of the Buddha may flourish and spread, to pacify conflict, suffering, and negativity all over the world, to bring peace and tranquility, and to ensure the welfare and happiness of living beings everywhere. And may all of us who are striving to follow and practice the sublime teachings of the clear-light Dzokpachenpo progress in our realization, overcome all obstacles, and finally seize the stronghold of Samantabhadra!

Sogyal Rinpoche

Publisher's Acknowledgment

THE PUBLISHER gratefully acknowledges the generous contribution of the Hershey Family Foundation toward the publication of this book.

Preface

HERUKA DÜDJOM LINGPA (1835–1904) was one of the foremost tantric masters of nineteenth-century Tibet. His written works include five visionary texts describing the path to perfect enlightenment from the unexcelled perspective of the Great Perfection, or Dzokchen. This series includes these five seminal texts, along with three essential commentaries by his disciples. They all reveal the same path to realizing the rainbow body in this very lifetime, but each one offers different degrees of detail and highlights different aspects of the path. Dzokchen's essential terminology and practices are clearly explained while potential misunderstandings and errors are systematically eliminated. Together they constitute a vast wealth of practical guidance and pith instructions concerning the view, meditation, and conduct of Dzokchen, the pinnacle of the Nyingma school of Tibetan Buddhism. These revered teachings have inspired generations of Tibetans, yet only one has become well known to English speakers, thanks to Richard Barron's popular translation of *Buddhahood Without Meditation*.[1]

These translations were developed and refined over many years. I served as interpreter for Venerable Gyatrul Rinpoché and translated several Dzokchen texts under his guidance beginning in 1990. In 1995, while living with him in the hills above Half Moon Bay, California, I asked whether he would like me to translate any other text. "How about the *Vajra Essence*?" he replied. "Sure!" I said, without knowing anything about these teachings received by Düdjom Lingpa in pure visions (Tib. *dag snang*) of the "Lake-Born Vajra" manifestation of Padmasambhava. Reading the text for the first time, I knew that I had found my heart's desire: a presentation of the entire path to enlightenment that was coherent, integrated, and richly informative. I was profoundly inspired—I felt that if I were marooned alone on a proverbial desert island with only one book to read, this would be it! Between 1995 and

1. Dudjom Lingpa, *Buddhahood Without Meditation: A Visionary Account Known as Refining One's Perception (Nang-jang)*, trans. Richard Barron and Susanne Fairclough (Junction City, CA: Padma Publishing, 2006).

1998, I translated it under his guidance. Then I served as his interpreter as he explained the text line by line to a hand-picked group of his close disciples, enabling me to correct errors in my translation and clear up points of lingering uncertainty in my comprehension.[2]

In 1972, Gyatrul Rinpoché was chosen by His Holiness the Dalai Lama and His Holiness Düdjom Rinpoché, Jikdral Yeshé Dorjé (1904–87), to be the Nyingmapa representative accompanying the first group of Tibetans resettling in Canada. In 1976, Düdjom Rinpoché appointed him as his spiritual representative for America and as director of Pacific Region Yeshe Nyingpo, his network of Dharma centers. For decades Gyatrul Rinpoché has taught students, established Dharma centers, and trained teachers and translators according to traditional methods and with deep understanding of the needs of his Western disciples. Gyatrul Rinpoché received the oral transmission of the *Vajra Essence* three times from three of Düdjom Lingpa's emanations: In Tibet he received it from his root guru, Jamyang Natsok Rangdröl (1904–58), recognized as the enlightened activity emanation of Düdjom Lingpa, and from Dzongter Kunzang Nyima (1904–58), Düdjom Lingpa's enlightened speech emanation and grandson. Later in Nepal he received it from Düdjom Rinpoché, the enlightened mind emanation of Düdjom Lingpa.

In 1998 I served as Rinpoché's interpreter as he gave the oral transmission and his commentary to the *Foolish Dharma of an Idiot Clothed in Mud and Feathers* to a small group of his close disciples. He asked that this be translated and made available to sincere, qualified Dharma students.[3] Rinpoché authorized me to teach all the texts he taught me, and several years later I taught the opening section of the *Vajra Essence* to a small group of students in Wales. Between teaching sessions, I began reading the text immediately following the *Vajra Essence* in Düdjom Lingpa's collected works, his *Enlightened View of Samantabhadra*. I had already concluded from the *Vajra Essence* that among the wide range of meditations explained in that text, only four were absolutely indispensable on the Dzokchen path: śamatha, vipaśyanā, cutting through, and direct crossing over. The *Enlightened View of Samantabhadra*,

2. This resulted in the publication of the first edition of the *Vajra Essence* a few years later: Düdjom Lingpa, *The Vajra Essence: From the Matrix of Pure Appearances and Primordial Consciousness, a Tantra on the Self-Originating Nature of Existence*, trans. B. Alan Wallace (Alameda, CA: Mirror of Wisdom, 2004).

3. This was published as the first text in Dudjom Rinpoche and Dudjom Lingpa, *Sublime Dharma: A Compilation of Two Texts on the Great Perfection*, trans. Chandra Easton and B. Alan Wallace (Ashland, OR: Vimala Publishing, 2012), 17–52.

presenting the entire path to enlightenment in one lifetime, focused on just those four practices, which reaffirmed my conclusion from the *Vajra Essence.*

Not long afterward, while teaching the opening section of the *Enlightened View of Samantabhadra* to a small group of students gathered for a retreat in the high desert of eastern California, I described how I had been deeply moved by my first encounter with this text—the very heart of the *Vajra Essence* presented with great clarity and brevity. A student then asked, "What comes next in that volume?" When I checked, I discovered the *Sharp Vajra of Conscious Awareness Tantra* and its commentary. This is the most quintessential and concise of Düdjom Lingpa's visionary texts, summarizing each of the four essential stages of the path with breathtaking clarity. I felt I had no choice but to translate the *Enlightened View of Samantabhadra* and the *Sharp Vajra of Conscious Awareness Tantra* and its commentary, and with Rinpoché's encouragement I did so.

In the summer of 2005, in Ojai, California, Gyatrul Rinpoché gave the oral transmission and a brief commentary on *Buddhahood Without Meditation*, for which I served as interpreter. With his encouragement I translated the text along with Sera Khandro's commentary, enabled by a generous grant from Dzongsar Khyentse Rinpoché, the son of Thinley Norbu Rinpoché and grandson of Düdjom Rinpoché.

Acknowledgments

The mission of transmitting the authentic Buddhadharma to the modern world has been led by H. H. the Dalai Lama, and the dissemination of the Nyingma tradition in particular was the lifelong work of Düdjom Lingpa's incarnation His Holiness Düdjom Rinpoché, who blessed us with his scholarship and wisdom, established Dharma centers, and taught many of today's lamas. The present translations were inspired by Venerable Gyatrul Rinpoché, who transmitted and explicated these peerless teachings. Lama Tharchin Rinpoché kindly granted me permission to listen to his oral commentary on the *Sharp Vajra of Conscious Awareness Tantra* given during his 2013 retreat on the practice of cutting through at Pema Osel Ling in California. I gratefully received the oral transmissions of the *Sharp Vajra of Conscious Awareness Tantra* and the *Enlightened View of Samantabhadra* from Tulku Orgyen Phuntsok.

I have received much help and guidance from many Dharma friends and mentors as I prepared these translations, and I have done my best to render these sacred texts in English. I am deeply grateful to Dion Blundell, who has tirelessly devoted himself with sincere faith and altruism to editing my translations. His assistance has been invaluable. However, flaws in the translation may well remain, and I ask that scholars, translators, and contemplatives who identify any errors bring them to my attention so that they can be corrected in any future editions of these works.

Technical Notes

My goal in translating these sublime treasure teachings has been to render them as accurately and clearly as possible, without omitting or adding anything. In discussing the profound nature of reality, the Great Perfection literature presents significant challenges for the translator. It employs its own special vocabulary in addition to the highly developed general lexicon of Buddhism. Because these are early days in the translating of the Dharma into English, many terms have not yet become standardized. I have noted the Tibetan and Sanskrit equivalents of key terms to assist readers familiar with other translation choices. Many Sanskrit terms that were translated into Tibetan have become well known, and I have used these original terms where their English equivalents are unsettled or awkward: for example, *kāya* instead of "enlightened body" to refer to embodiments of enlightenment.

As a further challenge, it is not uncommon for a single Tibetan term to refer to both the ultimate and the relative natures of its referent—ultimate truth and relative truth—depending on the context. One example is the Tibetan term *rigpa* (*rig pa*, Skt. *vidyā*), which sometimes refers to ordinary awareness, or cognizance. In other contexts it refers to pristine awareness, which is none other than the *primordial consciousness* (Tib. *ye shes*, Skt. *jñāna*) that is transcendently present in the ground of being. The Sanskrit term *jñāna*, in turn, also has ultimate and relative meanings, depending on the context. On the ultimate level, *jñāna* is primordial consciousness, but at the level of relative truth it simply means "knowledge," as in the two accumulations of merit and knowledge. In Buddhist psychology it simply refers to the basic knowing function of the mind.

Similarly, the Sanskrit term *dhātu* carries multiple meanings, with both ultimate and relative senses. It can mean "space" (Tib. *dbyings*) or "domain" (Tib. *khams*), but more typically in these works it is an abbreviation of *dharmadhātu*, translated as the *absolute space of phenomena*, the ground of being that is inseparable from primordial consciousness. In other cases, however, *dharmadhātu* has a more mundane meaning as the relative *space of awareness*, which is synonymous with "element of phenomena" throughout these translations. This dharmadhātu is the range of phenomena that can be perceived by mental consciousness and is one of the eighteen elements (Tib. *khams*, Skt. *dhātu*) commonly cited in Buddhist phenomenology.

Definitions of key terms are embedded throughout these texts as *contextual etymologies* (Tib. *nges tshig*), which gloss each component of the Tibetan term, unlike the linguistic etymologies commonly found in dictionaries. The term being etymologized is given in a footnote because it manifests in Tibetan only as a sequence of marked components, whose English equivalents are italicized in the text. The results in English may not be as elegant as the Tibetan constructions, but the core vocabulary of Dzokchen is defined succinctly and powerfully, in a variety of ways, throughout our texts.

Tibetan compositions are often endowed with brief or extensive outlines (Tib. *sa bcad*), but they don't always appear explicitly. Topics are simply listed as they come up. Lacking the typographical features English readers expect, a Tibetan text can be very difficult to peruse without first understanding its outline. The *Sharp Vajra of Conscious Awareness Tantra* may be considered the root text of these revealed teachings not only for its brevity and profundity but also for its outline, consisting of eight progressive *phases* (Tib. *skabs*) in the unsurpassed path of the Great Perfection. Pema Tashi's commentary includes a detailed outline built around these eight phases. But the longer explanations in the *Enlightened View of Samantabhadra* and the more elaborate *Vajra Essence* have come to us as transcripts with no divisions whatsoever. As an aid to navigation, we have indicated the phase headings of the root text in these two longer texts, where they are implicit. In the *Vajra Essence*, additional headings were suggested by the text itself or taken from *Essence of Clear Meaning*. Furthermore, many of that commentary's key passages clearly derive from the *Enlightened View of Samantabhadra* and the *Vajra Essence*; such quotations are not cited in the Tibetan, but many have been noted here. Comparisons between the parallel sections and passages in our texts will clarify understanding and drive home the essential points.

Our texts are found in the *Collected Works of the Emanated Great Treasures, the Secret Profound Treasures of Düdjom Lingpa.*[4] My translations are based on the computer-input edition of that collection published in 2004 by Lama Kuenzang Wangdue of Bhutan, known as Lopon Nikula, who was Düdjom Rinpoché's senior disciple and personal secretary for many years. The colophons of several of our texts show that Düdjom Rinpoché himself edited them for publishing. The process of converting texts from woodblock prints into digital form is critical for the accurate preservation of the vast and profound literature of Tibetan Buddhism. We are fortunate beneficiaries of the many lamas, monks, and laypeople who are engaged in this mission. In particular, Gene Smith, who founded the Tibetan Buddhist Resource Center, established an extensive library of scanned and computer-input editions

4. The Tibetan Buddhist Resource Center (www.tbrc.org) identifies this as W28732.

of Tibetan Buddhist works, making them available online to current and future generations of scholars and practitioners.

Tibetan names and terms are spelled phonetically in the body of the texts, with Wylie transliteration given in parentheses. Sanskrit terms include diacritics to give readers an appreciation for the correct pronunciation of this beautiful language, whose roots are often visible in English. Foreign terms are italicized on first appearance in each volume; most can be found in the glossary, which appears at the end of volume 1. Tibetan readers may consult the source texts via the folio references to Kuenzang Wangdue's edition in square brackets. Source notes, appearing as smaller characters in the original Tibetan, have been included here in parentheses, whereas my own clarifications appear in brackets. Cross-references between our texts are given using the following abbreviations followed by the folio references:

SV The Sharp Vajra of Conscious Awareness Tantra
CM Essence of Clear Meaning
MF The Foolish Dharma of an Idiot Clothed in Mud and Feathers
VS The Enlightened View of Samantabhadra
BM Buddhahood Without Meditation
FP The Fine Path to Liberation
GD Garland for the Delight of the Fortunate
VE The Vajra Essence

Requirements

These texts clearly reveal the most sublime of all Dharmas—secret mantra, Vajrayāna, or the Vajra Vehicle. The Sanskrit term *vajra* signifies the nature of ultimate reality, with its seven attributes of invulnerability, indestructibility, reality, incorruptibility, stability, unobstructability, and invincibility; and *yāna* means a vehicle for spiritual practice. Such profound instructions are guarded as secrets due to their potential for being dangerously misunderstood and to protect the teachings from disparagement. However, these texts also maintain their own secrecy, as Düdjom Lingpa states:

> Only those who have stored vast collections of merit in many ways, over incalculable eons, will encounter this path. They will have aspired repeatedly and extensively to reach the state of perfect enlightenment, and they will have previously sought the path through other yānas, establishing propensities to reach this path. No others will encounter it.

> Why not? Although people lacking such fortune may be present where this yāna is being explained and heard, because they are under the influence of their negative deeds and the strength of the powerful, devious *māras*[5] of mental afflictions, their minds will be in a wilderness five hundred *yojanas*[6] away.

If you wish to put the meaning of these sacred texts into practice, you must seek out a qualified guru to guide you in your understanding and practice. Düdjom Lingpa continues by stating that you must have "belief in the Dharma and your guru; unwavering trust in the path; earnest mindfulness of death and the conviction that all composite phenomena are impermanent, so that you have little attraction to mundane activities; contentment with respect to food, wealth, and enjoyments; insatiability for the Dharma due to great zeal and determination; and integration of your life and spiritual practice, without complaining." Rather than merely striving to accumulate virtues that might benefit you in some future lifetime, you should seize this precious opportunity—a human life in which you can practice the sublime Dharma—and generate the aspiration to achieve enlightenment in this present lifetime. He continues:

> If you arrive with that aspiration at the gateway of secret mantra—and you have firm faith and belief in it and strong, unflagging enthusiasm—the time has come to practice. . . . Once you have obtained a human life and encountered a guru and the secret-mantra Dharma, if this is not the time to practice the Great Perfection, then there will never be a better time than this in another life—this is certain.[7]

Gyatrul Rinpoché has authorized the publication of these translations with the stipulation that they should be restricted to suitable readers, specifically those who earnestly aspire to achieve liberation and enlightenment. Such people will not be fixated on material success, but due to understanding the first noble truth of suffering, they will have turned away from the allures of saṃsāra. Suitable readers will honor the fundamental Buddhist teachings

5. Tib. *bdud.* A demonic force or being that manifests as all kinds of grasping involving hopes and fears.

6. A *yojana* is an ancient Indian measure of a day's range for an ox cart, about five miles.

7. VE 14–18.

included in the Śrāvakayāna, and they will revere the Mahāyāna as well, including the cultivation of the four immeasurables, the six perfections, and the insights presented in the Yogācāra and Madhyamaka views. In addition, they will value all the outer, inner, and secret classes of the tantras and have a genuine desire to practice the cutting through and direct crossing over stages of the Great Perfection. Finally, suitable readers will treat these volumes with reverence and care. This is Gyatrul Rinpoché's sincere request for those interested in *Düdjom Lingpa's Visions of the Great Perfection.*

While those who devote themselves to the practice of these Dzokchen teachings should receive the appropriate empowerments, oral transmissions, and explanations of the lineage masters, the texts themselves do not restrict their readership to those who have completed certain preliminary practices, such as a hundred thousand recitations of the Vajrasattva mantra and so on. So I do not feel that it is appropriate for me as the translator of these texts to impose such restrictions. This is a decision to be made by individual qualified lamas of this lineage. The teachings translated in this series describe in detail the qualities needed on the part of disciples following the path of the Great Perfection, without mentioning empowerments. In fact, the *Vajra Essence* states that ultimately, through the realization of emptiness and pristine awareness, one spontaneously receives all four empowerments:

> Establishing saṃsāra and nirvāṇa as great emptiness is the *vase empowerment.* Recognizing precious spontaneous actualization as the self-emergent kāyas and facets of primordial consciousness is the *secret empowerment.* The revelation of pristine awareness, the nonconceptual primordial consciousness of ultimate reality, is the *wisdom empowerment.* Mastering the fruition in yourself is called the *word empowerment.* These are the actual four empowerments, devoid of a bestower and a recipient.[8]

May these translations be of great benefit to all those who study and practice them, resulting in their swift realization of śamatha, vipaśyanā, cutting through, and direct crossing over!

B. Alan Wallace
Santa Barbara, California
April 17, 2015

8. VE 248–49.

Introduction

PLEASE REFER TO the volume 1 introduction for brief overviews of the life of Düdjom Lingpa and the path of the Great Perfection.

The Vajra Essence

> In earlier times, the teachings of the Great Perfection shone like the sun. When sublime, supreme teachers explained them to people with good karma and fortune, first they would gain certainty by way of the view. Then they would identify pristine awareness and dispel their flaws by means of meditation. And finally, by practicing, remaining inactive, they all became siddhas and experienced the state of omniscient enlightenment. This is the unsurpassed quality of the profound path of the *Vajra Essence*.
> —DÜDJOM LINGPA, VE 504

Nowadays, our supreme guide continues, meditators lack the view, teachers cannot reveal the path, and the Great Perfection teachings are becoming like a drawing of a butter lamp—incapable of illumination. In revealing his most extensive visionary text that presents the ultimate path, Düdjom Lingpa compares it to the sun appearing briefly through a break in the clouds. He calls it a synthesis of all the sūtras and the tantras and expresses his wish that we fortunate recipients will practice these teachings correctly, maintain the lineage of the Great Perfection, and become fully enlightened.

If the root of these visionary teachings on the unsurpassed path is the *Sharp Vajra of Conscious Awareness Tantra*, and the *Enlightened View of Samantabhadra* may be regarded as an elaboration on that text, then the *Vajra Essence* constitutes an extensive commentary on both of them. Even though Düdjom Lingpa included no headings or divisions in its hundreds of pages, the *Vajra Essence* clearly sets forth the same phases as these more concise texts. The phases have been marked with chapter breaks in the translation in order to help readers navigate the wealth of explanatory material found here. Additional headings have been taken from the text itself and from the corresponding sections in *Essence of Clear Meaning*.

This remarkable testament begins with Düdjom Lingpa's account of his vision of the direct perception of ultimate reality: the moment when he became a matured vidyādhara, at the age of twenty-seven.[9] He describes his vision of the true Teacher, Samantabhadra, manifesting as the Lake-Born Vajra surrounded by an illusory display of bodhisattvas—appearing clearly, yet nonexistent. The Teacher explains that this gathering will reveal an entrance to the mind of all the buddhas, primordial consciousness, which is appearing to itself in these illusory forms. The disciples, who are his own emanations, address a series of questions to the Teacher, who responds generously with detailed teachings concerning each stage of the path of the Great Perfection.

At each step of spiritual development, the disciples questioning the Teacher are our surrogates, voicing our misunderstandings, exposing our doubts, and humbly asking for quintessential teachings that will bring us all to enlightenment. Because we are facing Samantabhadra, the essence of naked awareness, nothing is left unanswered. In the process, all provisional interpretations, relative meanings, and conventional explanations are shown to be pervaded by the sublime truth of the nature of existence, the Great Perfection. All ordinary Dharma practices are subsumed within the practice of the Great Perfection. And the result of this path contains the results of all other spiritual paths.

In the colophon, Düdjom Lingpa reports that his vision remained secret for eighteen years until the circumstances were appropriate for it to be written down. Later, due to errors that had crept in, our text was edited by Düdjom Lingpa's mind emanation, H. H. Düdjom Rinpoché, who calls it "the ever-so-profound essence of the awareness of Samantabhadra," which "descends as a rain of Dharma that is the essence of a hundred thousand classes of tantras." We are truly fortunate to hold this embodiment of the Dharma in our hands.

9. Düdjom Lingpa dates this vision to the first lunar month of the male water dog year (1862), five days after his twenty-seventh birthday.

The Vajra Essence

From the Matrix of Pure Appearances and Primordial Consciousness, a Tantra on the Self-Emergent Nature of Existence

by
Düdjom Lingpa

Introduction

[2] Homage to the manifest face of Samantabhadra himself, the Omnipresent Lord, the original, primordial ground.[10]

The Enlightened View Lineage of the Buddhas[11] is so designated because the minds of all the *jina*s of the three times are of one taste in the absolute space of phenomena.[12] The Symbolic Lineage of the Vidyādharas is so designated because the symbolic signs of ultimate reality,[13] the treasury of space, are spontaneously released, without reliance upon the stages of spiritual training and practice. The Aural Lineage of Ordinary Individuals is so designated because these practical instructions naturally arise in verbal transmission as an entrance to the disciples' paths, [3] like filling a vase. These instructions were revealed by themselves, not by human beings, as the illusory display of primordial consciousness. May I, the guru of the world, embodying these three lineages, being blessed with the inexhaustible ornamental wheels[14] of the three secrets of the jinas and *jinaputra*s, and holding the permission of the Three Roots[15] and the oceanic, *samaya*-bound[16] guardians, bring this to perfection.

10. This homage is immediately preceded by the series of syllables *rba, thta thnya rna, rtra, thta khka bdhaḥ*, which is said to be a Tibetan transliteration from the ḍākinī script.

11. Tib. *rgyal ba dgongs pa'i brgyud pa*. The term *dgongs pa* is the honorific form of *bsam pa*, which means "thought" or "intention." However, according to Gangteng Tulku Rinpoché, in the context of these teachings it is the honorific form of *lta ba*, which means "view" or "perspective."

12. Tib. *chos kyi dbyings*; Skt. *dharmadhātu*. The ultimate ground of all phenomena in saṃsāra and nirvāṇa, also called *absolute space*.

13. Tib. *chos nyid*; Skt. *dharmatā*. The ultimate nature of all phenomena, which is emptiness.

14. The qualities of the jinas and jinaputras are inexhaustible ornaments of reality, which continue forever like revolving wheels.

15. The Three Roots are the guru, personal deity, and ḍākinī.

16. Tib. *dam tshig*. A samaya is a commitment or vow made to the buddhas as represented by one's vajra guru.

The primordial, originally pure[17] nature of existence, which is great, intellect-transcending ultimate reality, free of conceptual elaboration, is obscured by conceiving of a self and dualistic grasping. Because of this, individuals are bound by clinging to the true existence of the three delusive realms of *saṃsāra*. Still, there are those who have accumulated vast merit over many eons [4] and who have the power of pure aspirations. Therefore, for the sake of those with the fortune to master ultimate reality, the treasury of space—by awakening the karmic momentum[18] of engaging in the action of nonaction in great, self-emergent primordial consciousness—I shall present this fundamental king of tantras, spontaneously arisen from the nature of existence of the *sugatagarbha*.[19]

Here is how this tantra originated: On the evening of the fifteenth day of the first month of the male water dog year,[20] by the power of the profound, swift path of direct crossing over,[21] the vision of the direct perception of ultimate reality arose. Because I had practiced the path of skillful means of the stage of generation a little, [5] I reached the ground of a matured vidyādhara. Through that power, all appearances and mindsets dissolved into originally pure ultimate reality, absolute space free of conceptual elaboration. Then the very face of the *dharmakāya*[22] manifested.

After some time, the following spontaneous appearances arose in the form of a buddhafield:

> On that very occasion of self-emergent, originally pure great bliss, my environment naturally arose as the actual Akaniṣṭha.[23] This illusorily displayed buddhafield was vast and spacious, and its sur-

17. The Tibetan term *ka dag* also connotes a transcendence of time: *ka* refers to the beginning of time, and *dag* implies transcendence over the very concept of a beginning.

18. Tib. *las 'phro.* The carryover into this life of one's karma from previous lifetimes.

19. Tib. *bde gshegs snying po*. The essence, or womb, of the sugatas, synonymous with buddha nature.

20. This was the year 1862.

21. Tib. *thod rgal*; Skt. *vyutkrāntaka*. Direct crossing over is the second of the two phases of practice of the Great Perfection, aimed at realizing the spontaneous manifestations of the dharmakāya.

22. Tib. *chos kyi sku.* The "enlightened embodiment of truth," which is the mind of the buddhas.

23. Tib. *'Og min*. Lit. "unsurpassed," the buddhafield of Samantabhadra, in which every being finally achieves supreme enlightenment.

face was smooth, level, and pliant to the touch. Verdant hills of medicinal herbs [6] were fragrant with mists of pleasing aromas. The whole ground was completely covered with various radiant, luminous, clear, sparkling, shimmering, lovely flowers in shades of white, yellow, red, green, and blue and variegated hues. In the four directions were four oceans of ambrosia imbued with eight excellent qualities.[24] On the shores of those great oceans were pebbles of jewels, sands of gold, turquoise meadows, and overarching halos of rainbows.

Forests of wish-fulfilling trees flourished in the four cardinal directions, billowing forth clouds of sensory offerings. Various types of beautiful apparitional birds voiced the sounds of Dharma with gentle, soothing calls. Various lovely emanated animals frolicked about and appeared to be contentedly listening to the Dharma. The whole sky was covered with checkered patterns of lattices[25] of rainbow light. Everywhere the sky was filled with singing and dancing *vīras*[26] and *vīrās*,[27] while many goddesses made sensory offerings and expressed their devotion.

In the center of this region, in a great, delightful garden, resting against a tree covered with foliage and flowers, [7] a vast and lofty jeweled throne was supported by eight lions. The branches of the tree were draped with various silk hangings, jeweled latticework and pendants, and many tinkling miniature bells ringing with the natural sounds of the holy Dharma.

Upon this lion-supported throne was a seat composed of a lotus, sun, and moon, upon which sat the true Teacher, Samantabhadra, the Lake-Born Vajra, appearing naturally with the inner glow of the ground of reality. His body was dark blue in color, bearing the features of an eight-year-old youth. His right hand was in the *mudrā* of expounding the Dharma, and his left hand

24. The eight excellent qualities (Tib. *yan lag brgyad*) are cool, sweet, soothing, light, clear, pure, not harmful to the throat, and beneficial to the stomach.

25. Tib. *drva ba*; Skt. *jāla*. A lattice, web, or matrix of looping garlands decorating the walls of a temple or celestial palace.

26. Tib. *dpa' bo*. Lit. "heroic being," one who shows great courage in not succumbing to mental afflictions and in striving diligently in spiritual practice. A highly realized male bodhisattva who manifests in the world in order to serve sentient beings.

27. Tib. *dpa' mo*. A female counterpart to a vīra.

was in the mudrā of meditative equipoise. He was adorned with the signs and symbols of enlightenment and all the *saṃbhoga-kāya*[28] apparel. Within the realm of his oceanic, radiant, transparent body, all the peaceful and wrathful buddhas and myriads of buddhafields and emanations naturally appeared, like planets and stars reflected brightly in a lake. Innumerable rays of blazing light emanated from him, and from their tips appeared various symbolic syllables.

Gathered around the Teacher, an illusorily displayed retinue of 84,000 disciples was assembled, including these bodhisattvas: Vajra of Pristine Awareness, [8] Faculty of Wisdom, Vajra of Primordial Consciousness, Boundless Great Emptiness, Faculty of Pervasive Luminosity, Spontaneous Display, Lord of Outer Appearances, Faculty of Vision, Faculty of Hearing, Faculty of Smell, Faculty of Taste, Faculty of Touch, and others. They were all looking at the Teacher while sitting silently, bowed in reverence. The Teacher was also silent as he gazed into the expanse of the sky. At that moment, the natural sound of ultimate reality emerged from the absolute domain of pristine space:

Āḥ!
All of saṃsāra and *nirvāṇa* is groundless and rootless.
The Vajra Queen is great space.
The great emptiness of space is the Great Mother.
All phenomena are apparitions
of ultimate reality and the One Being. [9]
Everything arises from the unborn.
The emerging apparitions cease.
Causes and conditions are extinguished right where they are.
Thus, in ultimate reality, the Teacher and the teaching,
the path and its fruition, are devoid of signs and words.
The many avenues of skillful means and wisdom
appear as a great natural occurrence and natural arising.
The space of nonobjectivity and great openness
is lucid, clear, and free of contamination.
All displays of the buddhafield, Teacher, and retinue

28. Tib. *longs spyod rdzogs pa'i sku*. The "enlightened embodiment of perfect enjoyment," a subtle form accessible only to āryabodhisattvas and buddhas.

are nonexistent, but from nonexistence they appear as existent.
How we praise this with great wonder!

As soon as this sound arose, the entire assembled retinue spoke with one voice to the Bhagavān: "O Teacher, Bhagavān, Omnipresent Lord and Immutable Sovereign, please listen to us and consider our words! Please, Teacher, explain why this entire buddhafield is here, with Teacher and assembled disciples, and tell us how this arose."

The Teacher replied, "O apparitional disciples who have appeared and gathered here, listen: You ask why these illusory displays of primordial consciousness—the buddhafield, Teacher, and disciples—have arisen. They are for the sake of revealing an entrance to the nonconceptual primordial consciousness of the mind of all the *sugatas*[29] of the three times, [10] who manifest in accordance with the faculties of all the beings wandering in the three realms of saṃsāra. By the great power of wisdom and primordial consciousness, the natural emergence of the actual Akaniṣṭha as a buddhafield is revealed in the great vision of ultimate reality. As for myself, the Teacher is the primordial ground, which naturally appears to itself from the innate radiance of the sugatagarbha. The natural radiance of empty awareness, free of conceptual elaboration, appears as Vajra of Pristine Awareness. The natural radiance of the wisdom of identitylessness appears as Faculty of Wisdom. The natural radiance of the eight aggregates of consciousness, together with the mental factors, appears as the assembled retinue."

Then Bodhisattva Faculty of Wisdom rose from his seat and asked the Bhagavān, "O Teacher, Bhagavān, you appear as the natural radiance of the sugatagarbha. I, Faculty of Wisdom, appear as the natural radiance of wisdom. Vajra of Pristine Awareness appears as the natural radiance of pristine awareness. The assembly of male and female bodhisattvas appears as the eight aggregates of consciousness,[30] together with the mental factors. But if this is

29. Tib. *bde bar gshegs pa*. Lit. "well-gone one," an epithet of a buddha meaning one who has gone to the far shore of liberation, fulfilling one's own and others' needs by achieving perfect enlightenment.

30. The eight aggregates of consciousness are the five types of sensory consciousness, mental consciousness, the substrate consciousness, and afflictive mentation.

so, we should appear in that way [11] to all the beings of the three realms. Therefore, why do they carry on in the midst of the delusive appearances of joys, sorrows, friends, and enemies in the three realms of existence, where miseries occur and pure appearances do not? Teacher, please explain!"

He replied, "O son of the family, beings who have slipped into the ethically neutral[31] ground do not see pure appearances. Impure, delusive mental states and appearances of friends, enemies, joys, and sorrows are characteristic of ordinary sentient beings. By the great power of wisdom and primordial consciousness, inconceivable pure appearances arise here to individuals who have previously sat in the presence of the nonhuman, self-appearing Teacher, the perfect Buddha, Lake-Born Vajra of Orgyen. These people have attained the supreme *siddhi*[32] after entering the gateway of Vajrayāna[33] Dharma and applying themselves diligently to its practice. From then until the myriad realms of beings are empty, due to the power of their pure aspirations, they repeatedly appear as teachers for the sake of the world, teaching in accordance with the individual needs of disciples. When their previous karmic momentum is aroused, they directly see the truth of ultimate reality, and they emerge from the expanse of wisdom. Pure appearances arise for them, but these are neither the mind nor mental processes. [12] Rather, these appearances are by nature displays of manifest absolute space. They are not the eight aggregates of consciousness, but they are not otherwise, so they are called by these names. These appearances arise in numerous ways from the nondual Teacher and retinue. Those known as bodhisattvas have gone well beyond mundane existence, even though they have not become buddhas—that is why they are so known."

Again Bodhisattva Faculty of Wisdom spoke, "Yes, O Teacher, Bhagavān. If the apparitionally displayed Teacher and the entire retinue are nondual and not different, as you have said, there is no purpose for all the teaching and listening on the part of the Teacher and the assembly of disciples. Since there is no difference in the quality of everyone's primordial consciousness, what is the point in putting on a show of teaching and listening? Teacher, please explain!"

He replied, "O Faculty of Wisdom, the self-appearing Teacher known as

31. Tib. *lung ma bstan*. Characteristic of all phenomena that are by nature neither virtuous nor nonvirtuous.

32. Tib. *dngos sgrub*. A supernormal ability or achievement, the supreme siddhi being perfect enlightenment.

33. Tib. *rdo rje'i theg pa*. The vehicle (Skt. *yāna*) of esoteric Buddhist teachings and practices aimed at bringing one swiftly to the state of enlightenment.

Śākyamuni arose as an emanation for disciples in the past, like light from the sun. The Teacher, those who sought teachings from him, and the retinue, acting as listeners, appeared to be teaching or listening [13] to individual kinds of spiritual paths and *yāna*s for training disciples. Although the Teacher and the retinue were nondual, for the sake of the disciples, various expressions of skillful means were displayed, like an illusionist and his illusions."

Then Bodhisattva Boundless Great Emptiness reverently bowed to the Bhagavān and asked, joining his palms, "O Teacher, Bhagavān, so that all beings may be liberated from the ocean of miseries of mundane existence and reach the state of liberation, please grant us the profound pith instructions to actually achieve the state of the fully perfected Buddha Samantabhadra in one lifetime and with one body."

The Teacher replied, "O Boundless Great Emptiness and the rest of you assembled here, listen! The great, sublime path that brings all sentient beings to the grounds and paths[34] of liberation is called the *swift path of the clear-light Great Perfection*. This is the most sublime of all Dharmas. It is a general synthesis of all the paths, the goal of all yānas, and an expansive treasury of all secret mantras. [14] However, only those who have stored vast collections of merit in many ways, over incalculable eons, will encounter this path. They will have aspired repeatedly and extensively to reach the state of perfect enlightenment, and they will have previously sought the path through other yānas, establishing propensities to reach this path. No others will encounter it.

"Why not? Although people lacking such fortune may be present where this yāna is being explained and heard, because they are under the influence of their negative deeds and the strength of the powerful, devious *māra*s of mental afflictions, their minds will be in a wilderness five hundred yojanas away. Such unfortunate servants of māras, with their perverse aspirations, act contrary to this profound Dharma and respond to it with abuse, false conjecture, repudiation, envy, and so on.

"On the other hand, those who enter the gateway of this Dharma and implement its meaning will appear as rarely as stars appear during the daytime. Some, when entering the path, will hear and understand a little, then

34. Tib. *sa lam*; Skt. *bhūmimārga*. The stages of attainment and the paths that lead to them. There are five sequential paths culminating in the liberation of a śrāvaka, five sequential paths culminating in the liberation of a pratyekabuddha, and five bodhisattva paths culminating in the perfect enlightenment of a buddha. According to the sūtra tradition, there are ten āryabodhisattva grounds. According to the Great Perfection tradition, there are twenty āryabodhisattva grounds, followed by the culmination of the twenty-first ground.

abandon it and casually go astray. Not engaging in spiritual practice, they will face death as ordinary beings, and they will not achieve liberation.

"In general, to enter this yāna and put it into practice, [15] you must have all the following characteristics:

- Belief in the Dharma and in your guru
- Unwavering trust in the path
- Earnest mindfulness of death and the conviction that all composite phenomena are impermanent, so that you have little attraction to mundane activities
- Contentment with respect to food, wealth, and enjoyments
- Insatiability for the Dharma due to great zeal and determination
- Integration of your life and spiritual practice, without complaining

"When such people with stable minds—without being boastful about the mere number of months or years they have spent practicing in retreat—see this entrance and undertake the practice, they will definitely achieve the supreme state of Buddha Vajradhara in this very lifetime. In other yānas, it is said that after collecting the accumulations[35] and purifying obscurations for three countless eons, finally you manifestly become perfectly enlightened. Nevertheless, because of karma,[36] mental afflictions, and habitual propensities gathered over eons, through the course of many lifetimes, the influences of various thoughts and actions make it difficult to encounter the path of accumulation and purification. Think carefully about this situation and you will become clear and certain of it.

"Be that as it may, due to excellent karmic connections from the past, now you have obtained a precious human life [16] with freedom and opportunity, and you have encountered the most sublime of Dharmas, the secret mantra, Vajrayāna. This is no time to hold on to the hope of accumulating merit over a long period until you finally attain enlightenment. Rather, you must apprehend the ground of your own being for yourself, by experiencing the intrinsic nature of the sugatagarbha, the primordial ground that is the path to liberation in this lifetime. Apart from this, the teachings that say that the state of liberation arises from accumulating much karma from one life to another are effective for bringing about temporary happiness in the minds

35. Tib. *tshogs bsags*. The twofold accumulations of merit (*bsod nams*), which culminates in the achievement of the form (*rūpakāya*) of a buddha, and of wisdom (*ye shes*), which culminates in the achievement of the mind (*dharmakāya*) of a buddha.

36. Tib. *las*. Actions defiled by mental afflictions, especially the delusion of self-grasping.

of beings, but enlightenment in this way is extremely difficult. Consider that such teachings may have a merely provisional meaning."

Bodhisattva Boundless Great Emptiness commented, "O Teacher, Bhagavān, one can achieve liberation by striving in this present human life for good thoughts that expand the mind and for bodily and verbal virtues, and then, at some future time, by practicing the view and meditation of the clear-light Great Perfection, the vajra essence of secret mantra. But it is said that it is difficult to achieve liberation by practicing in this lifetime alone. Moreover, it is said that small-minded beings, such as *śrāvakas*[37] and *pratyekabuddhas*,[38] [17] cannot fathom the vast and profound Vajrayāna Dharma. Is this true or not? If it is true, and the quality and capacity of the minds of beings differ, then the small-minded would have to expand their minds to become beings of the Mahāyāna class, and some beings would not be able to expand their minds sufficiently. If this were so, they would have to acquire some secret mantra from somewhere other than their own mindstreams. If this were the case, I don't know what it would mean. Teacher, please explain!"

He replied, "O Boundless Great Emptiness, in this present lifetime, if you arrive with that aspiration at the gateway of secret mantra—and you have firm faith and belief in it and strong, unflagging enthusiasm—the time has come to practice. When fortunate beings come to the gateway of the profound secret mantra, apart from simply having strong faith and belief, there is never anything else—such as clairvoyance, omens, or auspicious circumstances—to make them think that the time has come to practice secret mantra. Once you have obtained a human life and [18] encountered a guru and the secret mantra Dharma, if this is not the time to practice the Great Perfection, then there will never be a better time than this in another life—this is certain.

"It is not that the minds of śrāvakas, pratyekabuddhas, ordinary beings, and so forth are too small. Rather, due to their previous karma, they do not reach the gateway of secret mantra. Or even if they do, they have no faith and no belief, and because of spiritual sloth and distraction, they don't practice.

"Understand that this has nothing to do with the specific capacities of beings' minds. Don't think that there are any differences in the capacities of the minds of beings. To those fettered by selfishness, I teach that by opening their hearts to all beings throughout space, without concern for their own welfare, they will see the truth of the nonduality of self and other."

37. Tib. *nyan thos*. Lit. "hearer," a person who is committed to his own individual liberation by following the Buddha's path.

38. Tib. *rang sangs rgyas*. Lit. "solitary buddha," a person who is committed to his own individual liberation by solitary practice.

Boundless Great Emptiness continued, "O Teacher, Bhagavān, if so, is it impossible for them to expand their minds by meditating on the profound mystery of the Great Perfection? Or even if they meditate on the Great Perfection, do they need to develop *bodhicitta*[39] in some other way? Teacher, please explain!" [19]

He replied, "O son of the family, this Great Perfection is the yāna of the unsurpassed fruition. That which manifests the great reality that pervades all of saṃsāra and nirvāṇa is called *bodhicitta of the ultimate ground*—you need apprehend only this. Apart from this, intellectually fabricating so-called bodhicitta with effort entails generating a mental state in which you view yourself as the meditator and other sentient beings as objects of meditation—an attitude that is as limited as a teacup.

"In the expanse of the Great Perfection—the original nature of the great equality of saṃsāra and nirvāṇa—the mode of existence of the ground itself is known, just as it is, by means of great, omniscient primordial consciousness. To speak of having bodhicitta greater than the vision of great, all-seeing primordial consciousness would be like saying you must seek moisture elsewhere, even though you already have water.

"The primordial, originally pure ground, the great reality that pervades all of saṃsāra and nirvāṇa, is bodhicitta. Without knowing this, even the benign sense of love and compassion that parents have for their children is a conceptual, object-focused state of mind. With that alone, you might aspire for a fortunate rebirth; [20] but hoping it will lead to enlightenment is as senseless as hoping that the son of a barren woman will become a householder."

39. Tib. *byang chub kyi sems*. In the context of the Great Perfection, this is the primordial, originally pure ground, which pervades all of saṃsāra and nirvāṇa. The nominal cultivation of bodhicitta entails bringing forth the motivation to liberate all sentient beings of the three realms from the ocean of suffering of mundane existence and bring them to the state of omniscience.

Phase 1: Taking the Impure Mind as the Path

Identifying the Creator of All Phenomena as the Mind

Bodhisattva Boundless Great Emptiness requested, "O Teacher, Bhagavān, please teach us the profound path that liberates disciples!"

He replied, "O son of the family, entrances to the city of great liberation appear as many avenues of skillful means and wisdom. But ultimately, taking the mind as the path is the quest for the true way. Then, once you have determined the ground, you may take ultimate reality as the path. Between these two options, first, here is the way to take the mind as the path.

"At the outset, disciples who maintain their samayas initially train their minds by way of the common outer preliminaries—namely, the four thoughts that turn the mind[40]—and the seven uncommon inner preliminaries.[41] Subsequently, the way to follow the progressive path of the main practice is like this: First, retreat to a secluded forest, pray to your guru, and, merging your mind with your guru's, relax for a little while.

"O Boundless Great Emptiness, among your body, speech, [21] and mind, which is most important? Which is the main agent? Tell me, which is the immutable, autonomous sovereign? Then, to the great benefit of disciples, the acts of teaching and listening and the nature of the instruction will become perfectly clear."

Bodhisattva Boundless Great Emptiness responded, "O Teacher, Bhagavān, the body is created by the mind. When matter and awareness separate at death, the mind follows after one's karma, and then it delusively grasps at the appearance of a body once again. Moreover, one's body in the waking state, one's body while dreaming, and one's bodies following this life are all

40. Tib. *blo ldog rnam bzhi.* Contemplations of (1) the preciousness and rarity of a human life of freedom and opportunity, (2) death and impermanence, (3) the faults of saṃsāra, and (4) actions and their consequences.

41. Tib. *nang gi sngon 'gro bdun.* These are (1) taking refuge, (2) cultivating bodhicitta, (3) offering the maṇḍala, (4) practicing the purificatory meditation and mantra of Vajrasattva, (5) guru yoga, (6) the transference of consciousness, and (7) the severance of māras.

created by the self-grasping mind. They are temporary transformations that have never existed except as mere appearances to the mind. Therefore, since the mind is the all-creating sovereign, it is of the utmost importance.

"A mindless body is nothing more than a corpse, so it has no power. When the body and mind separate, experiences of joy and sorrow—reaching up to the state of enlightenment or down to the three realms of saṃsāra—are all due to mental consciousness delusively engaging with objects.[42] Therefore the mind is certainly the agent.

"Likewise for speech: Whatever appears to be voiced is nothing more than appearances [22] to the mind. Speech has no existence other than the conceptualizing mind's creation of the appearance of vocal expressions, so the mind is most important. When the body, speech, and mind are separated, one by one, the mind continues, the body becomes a corpse, and the speech vanishes altogether. Therefore the mind is definitely the most important.

"Here is the way the body, speech, and mind are established as indistinguishable: In the practice of the stage of generation, your own body, speech, and mind are regarded as displays of the vajra body, speech, and mind of your personal deity. In this way, you purify them and attain liberation. If they were separate, both the immutable vajra of the body and the unimpeded vajra of speech would be left behind when the mind was drawn away. Then, when the assembly of the three vajras disintegrated, wouldn't the deity perish? Therefore, rather than being separate, the many are determined to be of one taste. It follows that these three are none other than the mind: they are ascertained to be the mind alone, and this is the best and highest understanding."

Establishing the Mind as Baseless and Rootless

Again the Teacher asked, "Do you, as the all-creating sovereign, have form or not? If you do, what type of being's form does yours resemble? Do you, the sovereign, have eyes, ears, a nose, a tongue, and a mind [23] or not? If so, where do they presently exist? What are they? Moreover, is your form round, rectangular, semicircular, triangular, many sided, or some other kind of shape? Are you white, yellow, red, green, or variegated in color? If you are, by all means let me see this directly with my eyes or touch it with my hands!

"If you conclude that none of these exist, you may have fallen to the extreme of nihilism. So consider saṃsāra and nirvāṇa, joys and sorrows,

42. Although one does not reach the state of buddhahood by the mind deludedly engaging with objects, since awareness is primordially pure, the sense that it reaches a state of enlightenment is due solely to one's mental constructs.

appearances and the mind, and all their substantial causes, and show me their real nature."

Boundless Great Emptiness responded, "O Teacher, Bhagavān, the self has no form, so it is empty of form. Likewise, it has no sound, smell, taste, touch, or mind, so it is empty of each of these. It is devoid of shape and color, so it is empty of them. It is certain that the eyes, ears, nose, tongue, and mind have no existence apart from lucid, clear consciousness itself. Without nihilistically reducing them to nonexistence, the indeterminate manifestations of saṃsāra and nirvāṇa [24] appear like an illusionist and his illusions. Therefore, I have come to the conclusion that the agent has only the quality of being unimpeded."

The Bhagavān asked, "O Vajra of Mind, tell me, when you first arose, what was your source? Did you come from the earth and water, from fire, and from air and space, or did you originate from the four cardinal directions, from the eight directions, or from above or below? Investigate whence you arose and that which arises, and analyze! Likewise, investigate where you are now and what you are, and analyze!

"If this so-called mind were located in the head, when a thorn pierced the foot, for instance, there would be no reason to experience a sharp pain. If it were located in the feet, why would there be pain even if the head and limbs were amputated? Suppose it were located in the body as a whole. In that case, if unbearable regret or misery were to arise in the mind when an external item, such as an article of clothing, a cup, a house, or some other possession, was taken away or destroyed by others, the mind would have to be located in it. If it were located inside the body, there would be no one who identified with things outside. If it were located outside, [25] there would be no one inside to grasp at and cling to the body. If it is presently located in the body, where will it be located when it separates from the body? On what will it depend?

"Directly point out the body, face, and location of the being who is present. Investigate the location and environment, along with the size and so forth, of this being who is in charge. Look! Finally, you must investigate the act of going and the being who goes. So observe the destination, path, and point of departure of the mind—the being doing everything—and watch how it moves. If you see the act of going and the being who goes, show me the size, form, shape, and color of the being who goes."

Boundless Great Emptiness responded, "O Teacher, Bhagavān, I have no eyes, so there is nothing that appears to me as form. Likewise, I have no ears, so there is nothing that appears to me as sound. I have no nose, so there is nothing that appears to me as smell. I have no tongue, so there is nothing that appears to me as taste. I have no body, so there is nothing that appears to me as touch, either.

"Therefore, because I lack the five senses and their appearances, [26] there is no 'I' that arises. If the being who arises is not established as being real, then from this time onward, the so-called mind is not established as real either, and is therefore nonexistent. Until now, there should have been something bearing attributes called *this being*. Since I am unoriginated emptiness, the source of my origination is empty. As for seeking the source, earth is something I have created. Similarly, all phenomena, including water, fire, air, and space, are nothing other than apparitions of self-grasping alone. This implies that the 'I' that arises is nowhere to be found.

"I am the nonabiding nature of emptiness, so there is no place I dwell. As for the so-called body: Sores, swelling, goiters, ulcers, and so on may arise on the body that appears in the waking state, but they are not present on the dream body. And sores, swelling, goiters, and ulcers that appear to afflict the body and limbs in a dream are absent in the waking state. During the waking state, the body may be wounded or beaten as punishment by a king, but this does not appear on the dream body. If it happens in a dream, it is not present on the body in the waking state. Similarly, location, environment, and their possessor, whether they appear to be outside or are grasped as being inside, are all nothing more than my own appearances.

"Therefore, [27] I do not abide in either external or internal phenomena, nor do external or internal phenomena abide in me. They are apparitions of self-grasping, like conjury and illusions, but they are not created intentionally, as in the case of an illusionist and his illusions. The self arises, so external appearances arise automatically, but they have no location. Even if you investigate the agent and the destination, the being who moves and the destination have no objective existence, so they do not go with the nature of me and mine.

"All phenomena appear, yet they are not other than the domain of the self. Moreover, as the body, speech, and mind have never existed separately, their appearances are of the same taste. In all waking appearances, dream appearances, and appearances of the hereafter, the body, speech, and mind are indistinguishable from me. So this is certain: the being who goes and the destination are not established as real."

The Bhagavān commented, "O Vajra of Mind, investigate the dimensions of your so-called mind; then determine and recognize its essential nature. Are external space and the internal mind the same or different? If they are the same, the essential nature of the mind must be space. If they are different, [28] you would have to agree that space in a dream, space in the daytime, and space after this life are not the same but different. If the earlier space ceases and the latter types of space arise, one after the other, each space would be subject to transformation, creation, and destruction. In that case, determine the causes and conditions from which they arise. If space actually appears in the daytime due to the sun rising in the morning, doesn't the sun cause it to appear in a dream and after this life? Or is it the clear light of your own mind? Don't just give this lip service; instead, penetrate it with certainty."

Boundless Great Emptiness responded, "O Teacher, Bhagavān, the essential nature of my mind is definitely space. During the daytime, earth, water, fire, air, self, others, form, sound, smell, taste, touch, and mental objects are displayed in the domain of space, grasped by the conceptual mind. In dream appearances as well, the ground of the mind appears as space, and all physical worlds, their sentient inhabitants, and all sense objects are displayed as they were before. [29] In future lives, too, the essential nature of the mind appears as space, and in that domain all physical worlds, their sentient inhabitants, and all sense objects appear in the same way: they are held by the mind, and one is deluded over and over again.

"Therefore space, self, others, and all sense objects are of one taste—they are certainly not separate. Moreover, it is the luminosity of space itself, and nothing else, that makes appearances manifest. The essential nature of the mind and its ground is space itself. Various appearances occur in the realm of the mind—lucid, clear, ever-present consciousness. The displays of these appearances are like reflections in a mirror or images of planets and stars in a pool of lucid, clear water. Once lucid, clear consciousness has withdrawn into the central domain of pervasive, empty space, it has been directed inward. At that time, the mind and all appearances disappear as they completely dissolve into an ethically neutral, pervasive void. Through the power of self-grasping, the essential nature of this great, pervasive vacuity—the ground space of awareness—arises as the mind and mental factors. This is certain. Since space and luminosity are nothing other than the mind, the mind itself becomes self and others by the power of the contributing circumstance of its radiant luminosity." [30]

How Individuals with Specific Faculties May Enter the Path

"By taking the mind itself as the path, a person of superior faculties directly actualizes the nature of existence of suchness—ultimate reality—and realizes the consummation of saṃsāra and nirvāṇa, achieving liberation in the pristine domain of absolute space. A person of middling faculties achieves certainty in the formless realm, and a person of inferior faculties experiences joy in the form realm. For a person of the lowest faculties, the path is experienced as happiness in the desire realm. Please, Teacher, explain how this occurs."

He replied, "O Vajra of Mind, first merge this mind with external space[43] and remain in meditative equipoise for seven days. Then fix your attention on a pebble, a stick, a physical representation of the Buddha, or a syllable, and remain in meditative equipoise for seven days. Then imagine a clear, radiant, five-colored *bindu* at your heart, fix your attention on it, and remain in meditative equipoise for seven days. For some, this places the mind in a state of bliss, luminosity, and vacuity. This experience, devoid of thought, like an ocean unmoved by waves, is called *śamatha with signs*.

"Some cannot calm their thoughts because the mind is so agitated, [31] and they experience uncomfortable pains and maladies in the heart, the life-force channel, and so on. Those with unstable minds, with a wind constitution, or with coarse minds may fall unconscious or slip into a trance. Such people should relax and let thoughts be as they are, continually observing them with unwavering mindfulness and careful introspection.

"Stillness without thinking of anything is called *stillness in the domain of the essential nature of the mind*. The movements and appearances of various thoughts are called *fluctuations*. Not letting any thoughts go by unnoticed, but recognizing them with mindfulness and introspection, is called *awareness*. With that explanation, come to know these points.

"'Now, to remain for a long time in the domain of the essential nature of the mind, I shall be watchful, observing motion, keeping my body straight, and maintaining vigilant mindfulness.' When you say this and practice it, fluctuating thoughts do not cease; however, mindful awareness exposes them, so you don't get lost in them as usual. By applying yourself to this practice continuously at all times, both during and between meditation sessions, eventually all coarse and subtle thoughts will be calmed in the empty expanse of the essential nature of your mind. You will become still, in an unfluctuating state [32] in which you experience bliss like the warmth of a fire, luminosity like the dawn, and nonconceptuality like an ocean unmoved by waves. Yearning for this and believing in it, you will not be able to bear being separated from it, and you will hold fast to it.

"If you get caught up in bliss, this will cast you into the desire realm; if you

43. Sera Khandro in *Garland for the Delight of the Fortunate* says, "As for external space, all phenomena included in the vast outer physical worlds; the multitudes of inner, animate sentient inhabitants; the well-displayed intervening appearances of the five senses; your own body, aggregates, elements, and space bases; and all the appearances and mindsets of ordinary sentient beings are external space" (GD 87).

get caught up in luminosity, this will propel you into the form realm; and if you get caught up in nonconceptuality, this will launch you to the peak of mundane existence. Therefore, understand that while these are indispensable signs of progress for individuals entering the path, it is a mistake to get caught up in them indefinitely.

"This is called *ordinary śamatha of the path,* and if you achieve stability in it for a long time, you will have achieved the critical feature of stability in your mindstream. However, know that among unrefined people in this degenerate era, very few appear to achieve more than fleeting stability. Nowadays, deities appear to some people, who settle their attention on them. Visions of buddhafields appear to some, and they stabilize and settle their minds on these. Some particularly experience bliss, luminosity, or nonconceptuality, and they settle on this. To others, images of their guru, rainbows, lights, and bindus appear, so they settle on these, [33] and so forth. Understand that due to the functioning of the channels and elements of each individual, experiences are not the same for everyone."

How Meditative Experiences and Realizations Arise

Boundless Great Emptiness asked, "O Teacher, Bhagavān, please explain how meditative experiences and realizations arise as a result of such practice."

He replied, "O Vajra of Mind, awareness is nakedly revealed in all the tantras, oral transmissions, and pith instructions of the past. Among them, I will not describe more than a mere fraction of the ways the signs of experience occur. Because individuals' constitutions and faculties are unimaginably complex and their array of experiences is equally unimaginable, I know that there is no uniformity among them. So understand that I will speak only in the most general terms.

"The indeterminate, inconceivable range of experiences is inexpressible. But teachers with great experience, proficiency in the explanations of the grounds and paths, and extrasensory perception, owing to the strength of their great wisdom, are knowledgeable and clear. Also, although vidyādharas from matured vidyādharas to vidyādharas with mastery over life[44] [34] might not have firsthand knowledge of the ways experiences occur, they know them directly by means of extrasensory perception. Even without this, they can free others from their experiences by adapting and interpreting the instructions.

44. Nyingma tantras describe four levels of vidyādharas, which are, in ascending order of realization, the matured vidyādhara, the vidyādhara with mastery over life, the mahāmudrā vidyādhara, and the spontaneously actualized vidyādhara.

"For example, *devas*,[45] *ṛṣis*, *brāhmins*, *ācāryas*, and so on who practice *samādhi* cultivate it by focusing on various seed syllables. As a result, whatever purpose these syllables had in meditation, those who practice with them can recite them later while focusing on an illness to benefit men and women. Likewise, vidyādharas can intuitively identify all illnesses; or, by revealing techniques of meditation and recitation for that purpose, they can dispel all but a few diseases that are incurable due to past karma. This being the case, it goes without saying that they can guide a yogin's experiences on the path.

"If foolish teachers lacking any of these qualities give instruction to students and say that all these experiences will arise in the mindstream of a single individual, they are deceiving both themselves and others, and the life force of their students will fall prey to māras. Why? Outer upheavals such as illusory displays of gods and demons, inner upheavals including various physical illnesses, and secret upheavals of unpredictable experiences of joy and sorrow can all arise. [35]

"When giving instructions on the mind's nature, foolish, unintelligent teachers explain the causes for disturbing experiences; yet, when they occur, such teachers do not recognize them as such and mistake them for illnesses. Then they compound this by blaming these experiences on demons. They think anxieties portend death, and they insist that their students resort to divinations, astrology, and medical treatment. Then, if the students see the faces of demons and malevolent beings, they may turn to various rituals and other countermeasures. But whatever they do turns out to be completely detrimental, without bringing them an iota of benefit, and finally death is the only way out. In this way, the teacher becomes a māra for students, as if he or she had given them a deadly poison. Ponder this point carefully and apply skillful means!

"When meditation is introduced, with special terminology such as *vipaśyanā* and so forth, there are many explanations of the stages of the path. Here, on our own path, mindfulness is presented as being like a cowherd, with thoughts like cows. Their steady, vivid manifestation, without interruption by various expressions of hope, fear, joy, or sorrow, is called *enmeshed mindfulness*.

"In general, these are some of the signs of progress for individuals who take appearances and awareness as the path: [36]

45. Tib. *lha*. A "god" within saṃsāra, who experiences great joy, extrasensory perception, and paranormal abilities, but who suffers greatly when faced with death.

- The impression that all your thoughts are wreaking havoc in your body, speech, and mind, like boulders rolling down a steep mountain, crushing and destroying everything in their path
- A sharp pain in your heart as a result of all your thoughts, as if you had been pierced with the tip of a weapon
- The ecstatic, blissful sense that mental stillness is pleasurable but movement is painful
- The perception of all phenomena as brilliantly colored particles
- Intolerable pain throughout your body, from the tips of the hairs on your head down to the tips of your toenails
- The sense that even food and drink are harmful, as a result of being tormented by a variety of the 404 types of identifiable, complex disorders of wind, bile, phlegm, and so on
- An inexplicable sense of paranoia about meeting other people, visiting their homes, or being in town
- Compulsive hope in medical treatment, divinations, and astrology
- Such unbearable misery that you think your heart will burst
- Insomnia at night, [37] or fitful sleep like that of someone who is critically ill
- Grief and disorientation when you wake up, like a camel who has lost her beloved calf
- The conviction that there is still some decisive understanding or knowledge you must have, and yearning for it like a thirsty person longing for water
- The emergence, one after another, of all kinds of thoughts stemming from the mental afflictions of the five poisons, so that you must pursue them, as painful as this may be
- Various speech impediments and respiratory ailments

"All kinds of experiences can occur—called *meditative experiences* because all thoughts are expressions of the mind, where all appearances of joys and sorrows are experienced as such and cannot be articulated—yet all experiences of joys and sorrows are simultaneously forgotten and vanish:

- The conviction that there is some special meaning in every external sound you hear and form you see, thinking 'that must be a sign or omen for me,' and compulsively speculating about the chirping of birds and everything else you see and feel
- The sensation that [38] external sounds and the voices of humans, dogs, birds, and so on are all piercing your heart like thorns

- Unbearable anger due to having paranoid thoughts that everyone is gossiping about you and disparaging you
- Negative reactions when you hear and see others joking around and laughing, thinking that they are making fun of you, and retaliating verbally
- Compulsive longing for others' happiness when you watch them, due to your own experience of suffering
- Fear and terror about weapons and even your own friends, because your mind is filled with a constant stream of anxieties
- Everything around you leading to all kinds of hopes and fears
- Premonitions of others who will come the next day, when you get into bed at night
- Uncontrollable fear, anger, obsessive attachment, and hatred when images arise—seeing others' faces, forms, minds, and conversations, as well as demons and so forth, preventing you from falling asleep
- Weeping out of your admiration and reverence for your gurus, faith and devotion to the Three Jewels, sense of renunciation and disillusionment with saṃsāra, or heartfelt compassion for sentient beings [39]
- The vanishing of all your suffering and the saturation of your mind with radiant luminosity and ecstasy, like pristine space, although such radiant luminosity may be preceded by rough experiences
- The feeling that gods or demons are actually carrying away your head, limbs, and vital organs, leaving behind only a vapor trail, or merely having the sensation of this happening, or experiencing it in a dream

"Afterward, all your anguish vanishes, and you experience a sense of ecstasy as if the sky had become free of clouds. In the midst of this, the four types of mindfulness[46] and various pleasant and harsh sensations may occur.

"Spiritual mentors who teach this path properly must know and realize that these experiences are not the same for everyone, so bear this in mind! For a person with a fire constitution, a sense of joy is prominent; for one with an earth constitution, a sense of dullness is prominent; for one with a water constitution, a sense of luminosity is prominent; for one with an air constitution, harsh sensations are prominent; and for one with a space constitution, a sense of vacuity is prominent.

46. Tib. *dran pa rnam pa bzhi*. Single-pointed mindfulness, manifest mindfulness, the absence of mindfulness of the substrate, and the self-illuminating mindfulness of the substrate consciousness. See CM 354.

"After all pleasant and harsh sensations have disappeared into the space of awareness—by just letting thoughts be, without having to do anything with them— [40] all appearances lose their capacity to help or harm, and you can remain in this state. You may also have an extraordinary sense of bliss, luminosity, and nonconceptuality, visions of gods and demons, and a small degree of extrasensory perception. The channels and elements function differently from one person to the next, so those with dominant earth and air elements do not commonly experience extrasensory perception or visionary experiences. Extrasensory perception and visions are chiefly experienced by people with a prominent fire or water element.

"Now, to classify the different levels by name, superior vision with single-pointed mindfulness in which movement and mindfulness are united[47] is called *vipaśyanā*. If a sense of stillness predominates at this time, it is called *the union of śamatha and vipaśyanā*. In what way is this vision superior? Previously, even if you watched with great diligence, your mind was veiled by subconscious movement and by laxity and dullness, so thoughts were hard to see. But now, even without exerting yourself very much, all thoughts that arise become apparent, and you detect them very well.

"As for the visionary experiences at this stage, some yogins see everything, wherever they look, as forms of deities and as vibrant bindus. Some see different seed syllables, lights, [41] and various other forms. Some perceive buddhafields, unfamiliar lands, melodies, songs, and the speech of various unknown beings, and a multitude of all sorts of vīras and ḍākinīs dancing and displaying various expressions. To some, all sights, sounds, smells, tastes, and tactile sensations appear as signs and omens. Some have the sense of clairvoyantly observing many entities with and without form.

"After meditating deeply in this way, any sense of joy or sorrow may trigger a unification of mindfulness and conceptualization. Then, like the knots in a snake uncoiling, all appearances dissolve into the external environment. Subsequently, everything appears to vanish by itself, resulting in a natural release. Appearances and awareness become simultaneous, so that events seem to be released as soon as they are witnessed. Thus, emergence and release are simultaneous. As soon as things emerge from their own space, they are released back into their own space, like lightning flashing from the sky and vanishing back into the sky. Since this appears by looking within, it is called *liberation into the expanse*. All of these are in fact [42] the unification of mindfulness and appearances, entailing the single-pointed focus of attention.

47. This refers to the meditative state in which the conceptual movements of the mind are held constantly in the field of mindfulness.

"After all pleasant and unpleasant visionary experiences have dissolved into the space of awareness, consciousness rests in its own stainless, radiant luminosity. Whatever thoughts and memories arise, do not cling to these experiences; do not modify or judge them, but let them arise as they rove to and fro. In doing so, the effort involved in vivid, steady apprehension—as in the case of thoughts apprehended by tight mindfulness—vanishes of its own accord. Such effort makes the dissatisfied mind compulsively strive after mental objects. Sometimes, feeling dissatisfied, as if you're lacking something, you may compulsively engage in a lot of mental activity entailing tight concentration and so on.

"In this phase, consciousness comes to rest in its own state; mindfulness emerges, and because there is less clinging to experiences, consciousness settles into its own natural, unmodified state. In this way, you come to a state of naturally settled mindfulness. This experience is soothing and gentle, with clear, lucid consciousness that is neither benefited nor harmed by thoughts, and you experience a remarkable sense of stillness, without needing to modify, reject, or embrace anything.

"If you are not counseled by a good spiritual mentor at this time, you might think, 'Now an extraordinary, unparalleled view and meditative state [43] have arisen in my mindstream; this is difficult to fathom and can be shared with no one.' After placing your trust and conviction in this without discussing it with anyone, you may delude yourself for a while. Even if you discuss your situation with a spiritual mentor, unless that person knows how to listen critically and responds in a persuasive fashion, you will stray far from the path. If you get stuck here for the rest of your life, you will be tied down and prevented from transcending the realm of mundane existence. Therefore, be careful!

"In particular, the experience of luminosity may result in visions of gods and demons, and you may think that you are suddenly being assaulted by demons. At times this might even be true; however, by thinking you are clairvoyant and repeatedly fixating on gods and demons, eventually you will feel that you are being overcome by demons. In the end, by mentally conjuring up gods and demons and spreading the word that you are clairvoyant, your meditation will be all about demons, and your mind will be possessed by them. Then your vows and samayas will deteriorate and you will stray far from the Dharma, become lost in the mundane activities of this life, and befuddle yourself with magic rituals. As you pursue food and wealth without even a trace of contentment, your mind will be ensnared by clinging, attachment, and craving. [44] If you die in this state, you will be reborn as a malevolent demon. Having accumulated the causes of experiencing the environment and suffering of a sky-roving *preta*, your view and meditation will go awry, and you will remain endlessly deluded in saṃsāra.

"When people of middling or inferior faculties enter this path, the signs of the path will surely occur; but if they cling to anything, they will be trapped again by that clinging. Knowing that such experiences are highly misleading and unreliable, leave your awareness in its own state, with no clinging, hope, fear, rejection, or affirmation. By so doing, these experiences will be spontaneously released into their own nature, like mist disappearing into the sky. Know this to be true!

"O Vajra of Mind, there's no telling what specific types of good and bad experiences might arise. All techniques, from the achievement of śamatha until conscious awareness manifests, simply lead to experiences, so anything can happen. Therefore, understand that identifying all these as experiences is a crucial point and the quintessence of practical advice. Then realize this and bear it in mind!"

Why We Should Practice Meditation

Then Boundless Great Emptiness asked, "O Bhagavān, if all meditative experiences, whether pleasant or rough, are far from being the path to omniscience and bring no such benefit, why [45] should we practice meditation? Teacher, please explain!"

The Bhagavān replied, "O Vajra of Mind, when individuals with coarse, dysfunctional minds agitated by discursive thoughts enter this path, by reducing the power of their compulsive thinking, their minds become increasingly still, and they achieve unwavering stability. On the other hand, even if people identify conscious awareness but do not continue practicing, they will succumb to the faults of spiritual sloth and distraction. Then, even if they do practice, due to absent-mindedness they will become lost in endless delusion.

"The mind, which is like a cripple, and the vital energy, which is like a blind, wild horse, are subdued by tethering them to the stake of meditative experience and firmly maintained attention. Once people of dull faculties have recognized the mind, they control it with the reins of mindfulness and introspection. Consequently, as a result of their meditative experience and familiarization, they have the sense that all subtle and coarse thoughts have vanished. Finally they experience a state of unstructured consciousness devoid of anything on which to meditate. Then, when their awareness reaches the state of great nonmeditation, their guru points this out, so that they do not go astray. [46]

"For this to occur, first you undergo great struggles in seeking the path;

you take the movement of thoughts as the path; and finally, when consciousness settles upon itself, this is identified as the path. Until unstructured path awareness, or consciousness, manifests and rests in itself, because of the perturbations of your afflicted mind, you must gradually go through rough experiences like the ones discussed."

Bodhisattva Boundless Great Emptiness then asked, "O Bhagavān, are thoughts to be cleared away or not? If they are, must consciousness emerge again after the mind has been purified? Teacher, please explain!"

The Teacher replied, "O Vajra of Mind, the rope of mindfulness and firmly maintained attention is dissolved by the power of meditative experience, until finally the ordinary mind of an ordinary being disappears, as it were. Consequently, compulsive thinking subsides and roving thoughts vanish into the space of awareness. You then slip into the vacuity of the substrate, in which self, others, and objects disappear. By clinging to the experiences of vacuity and luminosity while looking inward, the appearances of self, others, and objects vanish. This is the *substrate consciousness*.[48] [47] Some teachers say that the substrate to which you descend is 'freedom from conceptual elaboration' or the 'one taste,'[49] but others say it is ethically neutral. Whatever they call it, in truth you have come to the essential nature [of the mind].[50]

"On the other hand, someone with enthusiastic perseverance may recognize that this is not the authentic path; and by continuing to meditate, all such experiences defiled by clinging to blankness, vacuity, and luminosity vanish into the space of awareness, as if you were waking up. Subsequently, outer appearances are not impeded, and the rope of inner mindfulness and firmly maintained attention is cut. Then you are not bound by the constraints of good meditation, nor do you fall back to an ordinary state through pernicious ignorance. Rather, ever-present, translucent, luminous consciousness shines through, transcending the conventions of view, meditation, and conduct. Without dichotomizing self and object, such that you can say 'this is consciousness' and 'this is the object of consciousness,' the primordial, self-emergent mind is freed from clinging to experiences.

"When you settle into a spaciousness in which there is no cogitation or referent of the attention, all phenomena become manifest, for the power of

48. Tib. *kun gzhi rnam shes*; Skt. *ālayavijñāna*. An ethically neutral, inwardly directed state of consciousness, free of conceptualization, in which appearances of self, others, and objects are absent.

49. These are the second and third of the four stages of mahāmudrā practice, the first being *single-pointedness*, and the fourth being *nonmeditation*.

50. These two sentences compare with CM 355.

awareness is unimpeded. Thoughts merge with their objects, disappearing as they become nondual with those objects, and they dissolve. Since not a single one has an objective referent, [48] they are not thoughts of sentient beings; instead, mentation shifts to wisdom, its creative power shifts to primordial consciousness, and stability is achieved there. Understand this to be like water that is clear of sediment."

Phase 2: Revealing Your Own Face as the Sharp Vajra of Vipaśyanā

The Path Pristine Awareness, Free of Conceptual Elaboration

THEN Bodhisattva Faculty of Luminosity rose from his seat and addressed the Bhagavān: "O Teacher, Bhagavān, Omnipresent Lord and Immutable Sovereign, please listen and consider me. Is the state of primordial, self-emergent liberation achieved solely by cultivating an inconceivable, ineffable, clear awareness, or not? If it is, how is this achieved? If not, what is the point of cultivating it? What kinds of good qualities arise? Please explain this for the sake of your disciples."

The Teacher replied, "O Faculty of Luminosity, listen and bear in mind what I say, and I shall fully explain this to you. Even though you achieve stability in this profound path free of conceptual elaboration in the state of conscious awareness, if the dharmakāya, primordial consciousness that is present in the ground of being, is not realized, as soon as you pass away from this life, you will be forcefully propelled to the form and formless realms.[51] [49] But with that alone it is impossible to achieve the omniscient state of buddhahood. Once you have identified this path for the first time through the power of intense meditation, when the dharmakāya, primordial consciousness that is present in the ground, is ascertained, this is the path wisdom and the creative power of primordial consciousness.

"Here are the excellent qualities that result from this: Just as there is no space that is different from the space inside a pot and no water that is different from the water that fills a cup, likewise, there is no path other than this path of manifest, conscious awareness. Even if you wander downward in impure saṃsāra, this is constructed by the stream of consciousness. And

51. The Tibetan reads *mu bzhi'i khams*, literally translated as "realm of the four alternatives," instead of the more common *gzugs med khams*. The "four alternatives" are the four meditative absorptions of the formless realm, namely, boundless space, boundless consciousness, nothingness, and neither-discernment-nor-nondiscernment, which is the peak of mundane existence.

upward, with the virtuous karma of fine merit, even if you generate deities and practice meditation and recitation, this is accomplished with the stream of consciousness. And even if you practice transforming the channels, bindus, and vital energies into displays of the three vajras, it is the stream of consciousness that liberates you. Moreover, it is the manifestation of this alone that is the originally pure ground—self-emergent, lucid, clear, nondual primordial consciousness.

"In general, whatever yāna you enter, there is no entrance other than the stream of ever-present primordial consciousness. Even when ordinary, deluded beings chant many prayers and count mantras with a virtuous motivation, [50] such practices are taught for the sake of the stream of the ground consciousness. Therefore, since the stream of consciousness is what accumulates all karma, this manifest consciousness itself is unrivaled by any tainted virtue.

"Moreover, the difference between practicing a mere technique *pertaining* to the stream of consciousness on the one hand and actually *manifesting* consciousness on the other is like the difference between the sky and the earth. That being the case, all extraordinary sublime qualities are wholly present in this manifestation of consciousness.

"O son of the family, ever-present primordial consciousness is the natural clear light of the minds of sentient beings. It does not objectify any appearances or mental states; rather, their manifestations are the external radiance of wisdom. The nature of these manifestations is the inner glow of wisdom. The greatness of this distinction is like the dawn appearing in the sky.

"If people with superior faculties and perseverance apply themselves continuously and single-pointedly to practice without distraction, the power of discerning primordial consciousness will ultimately blaze forth. As a result, the sublime qualities of the view and meditation of the clear-light Great Perfection, which is ultimate reality, the very nature of suchness,[52] will truly manifest; and those people will become enlightened in the original, primordial ground of Samantabhadra. [51]

"Even individuals who are not of that sort may identify this crucially important, unstructured, self-emergent consciousness, which manifests without meditation, and they may achieve a little stability in it. All the other physical and verbal virtues accumulated throughout a galaxy would not come close to the merit of even a hundredth, a thousandth, a ten-thousandth, or a hundred-thousandth of this. People who practice those [other virtues] are bound to achieve long-lasting stability in the peak of mundane existence."

52. Tib. *de bzhin nyid kyi gnas lugs.*

Phase 3: Revealing the Ground Dharmakāya

Determining the Identitylessness of Subjective Persons

AGAIN Bodhisattva Faculty of Luminosity asked, "O Teacher, Bhagavān, Omnipresent Lord and Immutable Sovereign, please listen and consider me. If taking the mind and consciousness as the path does not result in the fruitional state of liberation or enlightenment, no matter how much one meditates in that way, please show us a way to directly identify for ourselves the originally pure Great Perfection, sovereign awareness free of extremes, without having to resort to such a long and difficult path that yields various joys and sorrows but no accomplishment of that result. Reveal to us the stages of the path free of hardships, and give us profound teachings to prevent us from falling into error." [52]

He replied, "O son of the family, the great, universal ground of all yānas is profound emptiness. I shall explain the way to determine the reality of profound emptiness, so listen well! The basis for the delusion of all beings in the three realms is ignorance of one's self alone. Examine the basis and root of its origin, location, and destination.

"To investigate the basis and root of the initial arising of the 'I': It is a stream of consciousness that grasps at the fundamental, pervasive surrounding space as the self. All appearances and mindsets do not exist and are not established as anything other than mere appearances, so the source from which they emerge is empty.

"To investigate its location in the interim: The head is called the *head*, and it is not given the name 'I.' Likewise, hair is *hair* and not the 'I.' The eyes are *eyes* and not the 'I.' The ears are *ears* and not the 'I.' The nose is the *nose* and not the 'I.' The tongue is the *tongue* and not the 'I.' The teeth are *teeth* and not the 'I.' The shoulder blades are *shoulder blades* and not the 'I.' The upper arms are *upper arms* and not the 'I.' The lower arms are *lower arms* and not the 'I.' The palms, the backs of the hands, and the fingers are not the 'I.' The spine is not the 'I.' The ribs are not the 'I.' The lungs and [53] heart are not the 'I.' The liver and its lining are not the 'I.' The small intestine, spleen, and kidneys are not the 'I.' The thighs, hips, calves, ankles, and all the finger and toe joints each have their own names, and they are not the 'I.' The skin, fat, flesh, blood, lymph, ligaments, tendons, and body hair all have their own names, and they are not established as the 'I.'

"If the 'I' were located in the lower part of the body, there would be no pain if the head and the upper limbs were amputated, so it is not present there. If it were located in the upper body, there would be no pain if the lower portions of the body such as the legs were harmed. If it were located inside, there would be no reason why scraping off outer body hair and skin would cause searing pain.

"Consider whether it is located in the body. When all your clothes, jewelry, food, wealth, and possessions are taken away and used by someone else, misery and intolerable attachment and hostility arise, so the 'I' is not located within your body. If it were located in external objects, all physical worlds and their sentient inhabitants could be apprehended as being mine, but in fact all things have their own names, and they are not the 'I.'

"All phenomena of the physical worlds and their inhabitants other than the 'I' seem to exist separately from the self. Nevertheless, whether in a dream, the waking state, or the hereafter, the self and other appearances [54] always appear like a body and its shadow, like liquid and moisture, and like fire and heat. So the 'I' dominates all the physical worlds and their sentient inhabitants, but the 'I' is not located anywhere.

"Finally, to investigate and analyze where it goes: The entire phenomenal world is the basis and essential nature of the great phantasm of the 'I,' so its destination is naturally empty. All three realms arise as apparitions of grasping at the 'I,' so it has nowhere else to go. That which goes did not arise, and it is not located anywhere, which implies that it has no objective existence."

Again Faculty of Luminosity asked, "So if it is certain that the origin, location, and destination of the 'I' do not exist and are not established as real, how do you account for the continuity from one appearance to the next? Teacher, please explain!"

He replied, "O son of the family, after the consciousness that grasps at the 'I' has manifested, the 'I' and mind emerge from their own space, and they disappear back into their own space. They alternately emerge from and withdraw into the expanse of an ethically neutral, vacuous ground. Thus, dream phenomena, phenomena in the waking state, and all the phenomena of the three realms arise as mere appearances without existence. So know that the domain that is the place of movement and the agent who moves [55] are not established as being real."

Again Bodhisattva Faculty of Luminosity asked, "O Teacher, Bhagavān, when grasping at the 'I' vanishes into the space of awareness, isn't its continuum severed? Teacher, please explain!"

He replied, "O son of the family, even when the appearances and mindsets of grasping at the 'I' vanish into the space of awareness, an ethically neutral state, which is the ground in which your sublime qualities are not manifest, acts as the cause of self-grasping. So it is just this unimpeded continuum of the causal ignorance of self-grasping that is called *grasping at the identity of a person.*"

Determining the Identitylessness of Objective Phenomena

Faculty of Luminosity asked, "Teacher, Bhagavān, how are external objects empty? Teacher, please explain!"

He replied, "Let's investigate how, when you grasp at the identities of phenomena other than the 'I,' all these names, things, and signs are not established as being real. First, let's determine the emptiness of the names of the body by investigating the basis of designation of each name. To examine what is called the *head*: hair is *hair* and not the head. The eyes are *eyes* and not the head. [56] The ears are *ears* and not the head. The nose is the *nose* and not the head, and the tongue is the *tongue* and not the head. Likewise, the skin, flesh, bones, blood, lymph, ligaments, and so on all seem to have their own names, so they are not established as the head."

Faculty of Luminosity asked, "Teacher, Bhagavān, if you reduce the head to its components like that, it is not established as being real, but their assembly is still called the *head*, isn't it?"

He replied, "Son of the family, observe that in general there are many cases in which the collection of those components is not designated as a *head.* If you ground someone's head into particles and then collected them and showed them to others, they would not call them a *head*. Even if those particles were moistened and formed into a sphere, it would not be called a *head.*

"If your head that appears in a dream, your head that appears during the waking state, your head that appears in the past, and your head that appears in the future were all identical, whatever sores, swellings, goiters, moles, and warts you possessed would have to appear on all those occasions. [57] But they don't. If each of those heads were different, either you would have to get rid of all the prior heads, or it would become evident that they were never established as real. If you say something is called the *head* because it is seen to be on top, you should analyze the upper and lower regions of space. Thus, by investigating how the front, back, upper, and lower regions of space exist, you will determine that the head is not established as any of them.

"Likewise, upon what is the *eye* designated? Not all fluid spheres are known by the name *eye.* The skin, blood, fat, channels, and muscles are not given the name *eye*. As in the previous case, the eye does not exist as their assembly either. If you think that a fluid sphere that sees forms is called the *eye*, observe whether that which sees forms at all times—in the past, future, and present, while dreaming, and in the waking state—is this fluid sphere that exists now. Self-appearances are due to primordially present consciousness rather than this present fluid sphere. Even if a hundred million eyeballs were pointed in the same direction, they would not see form.

"Likewise, as for the *ears*, since the flesh, skin, channels, muscles, blood, lymph, and cavities each have their own names and not the name *ear*, what is called the *ear*? [58] If you say something is called the *ear* because it hears sounds, check whether that which hears sounds at all times, during and after this life, while dreaming and while awake, is the ear. By doing so, you will find that it is mental consciousness that hears, and not the form of the present ear. Even if you held countless attentive ears in your hands, they would not hear sounds. So the ear has never been established as something real.

"Similarly, by investigating and analyzing the name and actual characteristics of the *nose*, you find that the flesh, bones, blood, lymph, channels, muscles, and cavities all have their own different names, so they are not established as the *nose*, nor is it established as their assembly.

"If you think that that which smells odors is called the *nose* and that odors are sensed through this orifice, consider that this orifice is not needed in the dream state or in other lifetimes. Consciousness in the intermediate period detects odors as well. Therefore, since mental consciousness has no nose, the nose certainly has no objective existence.

"Likewise, the *tongue* is not established as any of the individual components of the flesh, blood, skin, channels, and muscles; nor is the name *tongue* given to their assembly. If you assert that that which experiences tastes is the tongue, check out whether or not it is this very tongue that experiences tastes in the dream state, the intermediate period, and in other lifetimes. Then it will become clear to you.

"By investigating the so-called body in terms of the skin, fat, flesh, [59] blood, marrow, bones, and all the channels and muscles, you will find that the body is not established as being real. If they were all reduced to minute particles and then massed together, the name of *body* would not apply. Even if they were moistened and formed into a lump, that would not be a *body*. If you say that that which experiences tactile sensations is designated as the *body*, check out what experiences tactile sensations while in a dream and the intermediate period. By doing so, you will see that it is mental consciousness itself, and since the name *body* is not applied to the mind, the body does not exist.

"Moreover, upon investigating the location of the so-called arm, you will recognize that the shoulder is not the arm, nor are the upper arm, the forearm, or the palm and fingers the arm. So I say, 'Identify what the arm is and tell me.' You may claim that whatever performs the functions of the arm is called the *arm*. But then, if you examine the appearance of an arm that performs the functions of an arm in a dream, and all such appearances in the intermediate period, and ask of them, 'Is this it?' you will find that it is not. Rather, you will determine that they are merely appearances to the mind. So the arm is not established except as something imputed upon the mind.

"Moreover, upon examining the *shoulder*, you will see that the flesh is not the shoulder, nor are the bones, channels, or muscles. [60] It is not established as any of those individual components, and it is not the assembly of the particles to which they can be reduced, even if you were to moisten them and form them into a lump. Likewise, carefully examining all the *joints* proves that the basis of designation of that name has no objective existence.

"Furthermore, to what do you give the name *person* for the appearance of a person over there? The head is not a person. The five sense faculties are not a person. The name *person* is not established as flesh, blood, bones, marrow, channels, muscles, major and minor limbs, or consciousness. Likewise, what is the basis of designation for a so-called house? The clay is not a house. As for the stones, they are called *stones*, not *house*. Nor are pillars, rafters, beams, or the foundation called *house*, and even if they were piled together, the name *house* would not apply.

"Take another example: a cup. Its exterior is not the cup, nor is its interior, its mouth, or its base the cup, nor is the wood the cup. Neither its individual components nor their assembly exist objectively as its basis of designation. Also in the case of a so-called mountain, earth is not a mountain, nor are grass or trees. Their assembly is not a mountain either, [61] so the word *mountain* is empty.

"To examine the basis of designation of a single stick, its tip is just a tip and not a stick. Its base is nothing other than its base, the wood is nothing other than wood, its burnt ashes are nothing more than ashes, and its pulverized particles are just particles and not a stick. So even that name simply vanishes, with no objective existence.

"Know that earth, water, fire, and air also do not exist in the realm of gross particles, tiny particles, or minute partless particles. The illusory nature of all kinds of names cannot even be established as an illusion, for it is nothing more than the mere name *illusion*. A *mirage* cannot be established as a mirage and is nothing more than a mere name. A *dream* cannot be established as a dream and is nothing more than a mere name. A *reflection* cannot be established as a reflection and is nothing more than a mere name. A *city of gandharvas* cannot be established as a city of gandharvas and is nothing more than a mere name. An *echo* has no objective existence apart from its mere name *echo*. The *moon in water* is nothing more than the mere words *moon in water*. A *water bubble* has no objective existence apart from the mere words *water bubble*. A hallucination has no objective existence apart from the mere name. [62] And an *emanation* has no existence apart from the mere utterance of the name.

"Like the utterances of the sounds of those names, all the bases of designation of the names and words that are uttered for all kinds of appearing phenomena are nonexistent. They are emptiness, which itself is not established as being real. Recognize that emptiness has no objective existence, for it is none other than the expanse of space. These are pith instructions."

Coarse and Subtle Considerations for Determining Emptiness

Again Bodhisattva Faculty of Luminosity asked, "O Teacher, Bhagavān, if all the deluded disciples, bound by clinging to true existence, cannot realize the essential nature of phenomena simply by recognizing the nonexistence of the basis of designation of a name, please, Teacher, reveal a way to determine the nature of emptiness by way of coarse and subtle considerations."

He replied, "O Faculty of Luminosity, it is like this: When a tree trunk appears to you, consider whether it is permanent or utterly nonexistent. The investigation and analysis go like this: If it were permanent, it would have to be invulnerable, indestructible, real, incorruptible, stable, unobstructable, and invincible. Since a gash occurs when it is chopped with an ax, [63] it is vulnerable, and when it is chopped many times, it is destroyed. Since the one becomes many, it is deceptive and not real; and since it can be stained with white and black dyes and powders, it is corruptible, not incorruptible. Since it is subject to change due to the seasons and other influences, it is not stable. Since there are objects that it cannot penetrate, it is obstructable. This wood can be demolished in any number of ways, so it is not invincible. Not having even one of the vajra qualities, it is proven not to exist."

Faculty of Luminosity asked, "O Teacher, Bhagavān, what is a vajra replete with all the seven vajra qualities? Please explain!"

He replied, "O Faculty of Luminosity, referring to the existence of a relative,[53] material vajra is like referring to the son of a barren woman. One can

53. Tib. *kun rdzob* [*bden pa*]; Skt. *saṃvṛti* [*satya*]. Lit. "totally obscurational [truth]," such conventional, provisional truths appear in a manner contrary to their mode of existence and thereby obscure the nature of ultimate truth.

show material vajras that are made of bone and stone, and by burning them they are destroyed. And iron vajras can be melted in fire. Not being truly existent, those relative vajras are destructible.

"The space vajra that appears everywhere (1) cannot be injured with weapons or anything else; (2) objects or circumstances cannot [64] destroy it; (3) devoid of faults or contamination, it is the great basis for the appearance of phenomenal existence, so it is real; (4) it cannot be corrupted by faults or virtues, so it is incorruptible; (5) it is free of change throughout the three times, so it is stable; (6) since it can penetrate everything, it is utterly unobstructable; and (7) it cannot be modified or changed by anything, so it is invincible.

"This is the space vajra that appears everywhere. For those who grasp at autonomous existence, it is a relative vajra, and for those who comprehend its nature as unadulterated liberation, it is the ultimate, indestructible vajra. If some other object replete with all seven vajra qualities were to exist, it would be permanent. But since there is no such thing, everything is definitely emptiness, which is not established in itself.

"Thus, substances that appear as things, such as tree trunks, earth, stones, buildings, or household goods, may be pounded, broken, and ground up. By grinding them down to particles, they are reduced to powder. By pulverizing such particles to one-seventh of their size, they are reduced to minute particles, and by disintegrating these to one-seventh of their size, they are reduced until they have no spatial dimension. They are obliterated and vanish into the nature of space.

"Moreover, the ashes of any substance that has been burned in fire naturally disappear into space, [65] and something that appears to be the form of a living being totally vanishes once it has been killed and burned up. By examining and analyzing all phenomena that appear in this way, you find that they all vanish completely, and not a single thing is established as being truly existent. Intensive inquiry into this topic is essential, so know this!"

How All Phenomena Arise and Appear

Faculty of Luminosity asked, "O Teacher, Bhagavān, if they are not established as being real but are deceptive in that way, from what do all phenomena arise and appear? May the Teacher explain!"

He replied, "O Faculty of Luminosity, self-grasping acts as the primary cause and conceptualization acts as the contributing condition due to which they emerge as mere appearances. When the initial consciousness moves to an object, appearances suddenly arise. With the thought that something is being eliminated and with the emergence of the thought that something is being destroyed, it shifts or vanishes altogether. All phenomena are mere appearances arising from dependently related events, and nothing more. There is certainly nothing whatsoever [66] that is truly existent from its own side.

"For example, with the convergence of the primary cause of another person's eyes, the basis of radiant, clear space, and the contributing condition of conjuring substances, mantras, and an illusionist's mind, the dependent event of an illusory apparition appears, even though it is nonexistent. Due to the assembly of the cause of lucid, clear space and the contributing condition of warmth and moisture, a mirage appears, yet it is not established as real. Due to the interaction of the cause of the lucid, clear substrate consciousness and the contributing condition of self-grasping, dream appearances arise that are nonexistent; and people are deluded by grasping at their reality and clinging to their true existence as if they were appearances in the waking state. With the interaction of the cause of a lucid, clear mirror and the contributing condition of someone's face, a reflection appears that is nonexistent.

"With the dependent relation of the conjunction of the causal samādhi of *dhyāna* and the contributing condition of a vessel and moisture, a city of gandharvas appears as an object. With the causes of a solid, high object, such as a boulder, and auditory consciousness, along with the contributing condition of making a noise such as shouting, an echo occurs from their dependent relation. With the cause of lucid, clear water and the contributing condition of planets and stars in the sky, reflections appear from their dependent relation of coming together. With the cause of water and the contributing condition of stirring or agitation, [67] bubbles emerge from their dependent relation of coming together. With the cause of the eyes and the contributing condition of pressure simultaneously applied to the nerves in the eyes, a hallucination takes place from their dependent relation. With the cause of mastery of emanation and the contributing condition of entering into the samādhi of producing emanations, nonexistent emanations appear from their dependent relation of coming together.

"Thus, for these ten analogies[54] there are said to be (1) a *dependence* because of a reliance upon causes, (2) a *relationship* because of the simultaneous presence of the causes and the contributing conditions, and (3) *origination* because of the emergence of nonexistent appearances. Likewise, in the displays of the all-encompassing expanse of the ground, the unimpededly free

54. These ten analogies of illusion indicate the illusory nature of all phenomena: an illusion, a dream, a mirage, a reflection, a city of gandharvas, an echo, the moon in water, a bubble, a hallucination, and an emanation. See GD 71–86.

expanse that is baseless, unceasing space without root, the ground is divided by the consciousness that is continually reifying the self. The self is maintained and the ground of space is externalized; and through the radiant clarity of the mirror-like ground, anything can arise, and the appearances of the three realms emerge.

"To give some examples of this: Foam is inseparable from the ocean, but its emergence sets it apart from the ocean. And rainbows, while inseparable from the sky, appear there, making the sky appear as something else.

"There are said to be (1) a *dependence* because of reliance upon the 'I,' [68] (2) a *relationship* because of the nonduality of the self and other phenomena, and (3) *origination* because of emergent phenomena that have no objective existence. So by investigating in this way the myriad appearances of all phenomena, recognize the crucial point that they are displays of the empty space of ultimate reality.

"Moreover, when you fall asleep, all objective appearances of waking reality—including the physical worlds, their sentient inhabitants, and all the objects that appear to the five senses—dissolve into the vacuity of the substrate, which is of the nature of space, and they infinitely pervade that vacuity. Once again, self-grasping consciousness is aroused by the apparitions of the movements of karmic energies.[55] Consequently, from the appearance of the self, as before, all inner and outer phenomena—including the physical worlds, their sentient inhabitants, and sensory objects—emerge as dream appearances within the ground space of awareness. Joy, sorrow, and indifference are held close and clung to as being truly existent. This is delusion, so recognize it!"

Then Bodhisattva Lord Displaying All Appearances[56] rose from his seat, bowed reverently, and said to the Bhagavān, "O Teacher, Bhagavān, I do not accept that all appearances dissolve like that. When I go to bed, wrap myself in warm bedding, [69] and fall asleep, this array of phenomena remains where it was."

The Bhagavān countered, "O Lord Displaying All Appearances, when you go to bed, wrap yourself in warm bedding, and fall asleep, if all waking appearances of the physical worlds, their sentient inhabitants, and all sensory objects stay where they are, where is the enormous physical world that objectively appears in the dream state? Where are the many beings who inhabit it?

55. Tib. *las rlung.*

56. Tib. *kun snang bkod pa'i dbang po.* He was introduced as Lord of Outer Appearances.

And where are those fine arrays of appearances to the five senses? Tell me, do those objects emerge outside or inside your body?"

Lord Displaying All Appearances replied, "I believe they manifest inside the body."

He replied, "O Vajra of Appearances, consider all the areas of the body from inside the head on down. Tell me, where do those vast and numerous phenomena, such as the many mountains and valleys, manifest?"

Lord of Appearances replied, "O Teacher, Bhagavān, if we examine and analyze in that way, the head is not large enough to hold such phenomena of the physical worlds and their sentient inhabitants, nor are the limbs or the torso. Perhaps consciousness [70] comes out of the body and perceives another realm."

He replied, "O Lord of Appearances, if your awareness and material body separate like that and consciousness goes outside, from what orifice does it emerge? And when it goes back into the body, by what orifice does it reenter? Identify this. Where is the location of objects in a dream: are they present in the cardinal directions, in the intermediate directions, above, or below? Tell me, do you think the objects that appear in a dream—including the physical worlds and their sentient inhabitants—are the same as those in daytime appearances, or are they different?"

The bodhisattva replied, "I see no such orifice, nor can I identify their presence in the east, south, west, or north. I think the objects that appear in a dream exist in some other dimension."

The Bhagavān continued, "Consider the possibility that consciousness passes through some aperture. In the waking state there are the appearances of doors that allow one to pass in and out of a house, and they can be identified. If you assert that consciousness goes somewhere in this world of the waking state, then since all the elements and everything animate and inanimate in the dream world would be of the same taste as phenomena in the waking state, they would not really be dream phenomena at all. Moreover, if it were possible for awareness to reenter the material body after having been separated from it, there would be no reason why all the dead couldn't reenter their own bodies. If your body at night does not grow cold [71] and lifeless due to the separation of awareness from matter, there would be no reason why it should grow cold at death, either. Therefore, if you believe that phenomena in the daytime and the nighttime are the same, are they differentiated by sleep or not? If you believe they are different, is there some hierarchy of higher versus lower, or outer versus inner? Tell me what you think."

He replied, "Teacher, Bhagavān, based on this kind of examination and analysis, if consciousness were to go elsewhere, the body would turn into a corpse, and all appearances of the physical worlds and their sentient inhabitants would have to be the same [during the waking and dream states]. So there would be no differentiation when sleeping, and at death there would have to be some way to reenter the body. If phenomena were different during the daytime and nighttime, one would have to be higher or lower than the other. If they were the same, there would be no distinction between phenomena in the states of waking and dreaming. So dream phenomena emerge after waking phenomena have disappeared into the space of awareness."

Again Lord Displaying All Appearances addressed the Bhagavān, "O Teacher, Bhagavān, for this body to exist, it must depend upon the causes and contributing conditions of one's parents. But since this implies that phenomena do not change [72] in the way you have described, in dependence on what do these parents and this body appear? Teacher, please explain."

He replied, "O Lord of Appearances, if you think both parents are necessary for the existence of a body, recall that a body in the intermediate period, a dream body, one that is born from heat and moisture, and one that is born spontaneously all arise without a mother or father. If you believe this body exists in dependence upon one's parents, before beings became embodied, where did the original father come from? Where did he live? Where did he finally go? Examine the mother similarly—how she was born, lived, and passed away. Investigate the evolution of parents up to this present body. Understand this."

Lord of Appearances responded, "All right, Teacher, Bhagavān—by establishing the nature of appearances, I suspect that the phenomenon of myself alone is a mere appearance and does not exist. Is that so or not? Teacher, please explain!"

He replied, "O great being, don't think like that! By establishing all appearances like that, [73] if your perception of everything as empty finally leads you to the conclusion that nothing is empty except the mere nonexistent phenomenon of yourself alone, you have conflated that which is not empty with that which is empty. That is merely setting yourself up to view that which is existent as being nonexistent. While regarding emptiness as relative and reifying existence as ultimately real, if you believe that you alone do not exist from your own side, then that understanding of the emptiness of yourself alone leaves you with the śrāvaka view of mere personal identitylessness. By regarding the entire phenomenal world as being like the ten analogies of illusion, understand that there are no objects that appear apart from the illusionist. From the very moment they appear, know that they vanish for the person to whom they appear, and they are not truly existent. Understand this as ultimate emptiness."

Lord of Appearances replied, "Here is what I think: They are not the appearances of one sentient being. If all the three realms were merely my own appearances, when just my appearances changed, all the appearances of the three realms should change accordingly—they would certainly have to pass away, vanish, and be extinguished with me. Since that's not so, I [74] don't think that due to my perception of external objects, the physical worlds and their sentient inhabitants in the three realms perish and vanish together with me. So, Teacher, please explain fully the meaning of this."

He responded, "O Lord of Appearances, such thoughts of yours are familiar to all beings who are deluded by grasping at true existence. But knowing how to act like others is not the way to realize emptiness. For beginningless lifetimes, you have apprehended your own appearances as being other than yourself, and by grasping at them, you have become deluded. The phenomena of a dream, with all its sensory objects, are not left behind and discarded when you wake up. Rather, they all vanish into the realm of the mind. Likewise, all appearances vanish into yourself. You must recognize that no autonomous physical worlds, sentient beings, or sense objects exist out there.

"Sentient beings become deluded by holding that for themselves alone there are no beings or appearances apart from themselves, and then mistakenly reifying appearances. So observe that tendency within your own mind! When the teachings of the Buddha degenerate, blind sentient beings establish emptiness [75] merely by coming to the conclusion that although the physical worlds and their sentient inhabitants do not exist from one's own perspective, they do exist autonomously from their own side. There are very few who identify the ultimate path of emptiness, so carefully examine the nature of this crucial point."

Again Lord of Appearances asked, "O Teacher, Bhagavān, if someone ascertains emptiness in terms of such nonexistence, doesn't that person still experience joy and sorrow and move from one place to another within the realms of the phenomenal world? Teacher, please explain!"

He replied, "O Lord of Appearances, throughout beginningless lifetimes, such a great being has never revolved within the three realms of saṃsāra. Although he may have traveled widely from one region to another, he does not exist. His eyes do not see the slightest trace of form. His ears have never heard even the sound of an echo, nor has his nose detected odors, his tongue experienced tastes, or his body felt tactile sensations. He has never taken even a single step in the three realms of saṃsāra. He has never exerted the slightest bit of effort toward making a living. [76] He does not sit or rise, nor does he ever move any of his limbs. Know with certainty that he has never been subject to the experiences of birth, youth, adulthood, old age, illness, death, and so forth."

Again Lord of Appearances asked, "O Teacher, Bhagavān, this beginningless and endless delusion certainly does exist, and there is surely much wandering about in saṃsāra. Moreover, countries are seen with the eyes, sounds and voices are heard with the ears, various odors are detected with the nose, and things that are experienced as tactile objects are also seen with the eyes. Ultimately, things are taken in hand, eaten, and tasted. All gentle and rough tactile sensations are experienced with the body. We do move around on the ground with our legs, and the phenomena of birth, aging, sickness, and death are incontrovertible. Moreover, people do try to make a living by moving about and exerting themselves. Why do you say that these don't exist? Teacher, please explain!"

He replied, "O Lord of Appearances, you do not travel from one region in a dream to somewhere else in the waking state. Rather, appearances simply shift, so to speak. Although you may have seen a country in a dream, [77] upon looking for it today, not even a trace of it can be seen. While a variety of sounds, voices, smells, tastes, and different sorts of tactile sensations may have appeared in the dream, if you look for them today, you find the ears hear their own sounds and the nose detects its own smells; and the tongue experiences its own tastes, other than which you have never tasted a single bite of food.

"Although you may dream of traveling around a country on foot, you never take a single step. Although it may seem that you have exerted yourself in various ways to make a living in a dream, by observing your situation today you will see that not even an instant's worth of such work was done. Likewise, all the appearances of birth, aging, sickness, death, walking, sitting, and movement are nonexistent. From the very moment that these delusive appearances arise, observe how they are nonobjective, nonabiding, baseless, never occurring, and unborn. Like these examples, all phenomena are mere appearances—they are empty and not established as real."

Lord of Appearances objected, "Dreams are not like phenomena in the waking state. Dreams seem to be delusive appearances, whereas phenomena in the waking state appear to be truly existent, stable, and incapable of being influenced by the mind. So how is that? [78] Teacher, please explain!"

He responded, "O Lord of Appearances, since this body of yours first appeared and was brought to mind, there have been all kinds of waking appearances of working, finding employment, acquiring things, striving, and perceiving sensory objects. Where are they all now? What aims and tasks have been accomplished? Identify what is truly existent! Likewise, examine the ways in which they are and are not comparable to dream appearances. See whether or not there are differences between these two in terms of their duration and quantity.

"There is no way to distinguish between saṃsāra and nirvāṇa apart from the presence and absence of delusion. If you take dreams to be delusive and unreal, and waking appearances to be nondelusive and real, do you think you are an undeluded buddha during the daytime and a deluded sentient being while dreaming? If so, saṃsāra and nirvāṇa would trade places in a single day, so there would certainly be no hope for either of them. On the other hand, if you think they are both delusive but there is truth and falsity within each delusion, there is no reason to distinguish between delusive appearances.

"Delusive appearances are so designated because something that is not so is taken to be so. In your dreams do you think, 'This is a dream [79] and this is delusive,' without making any distinction between truth and falsehood? Is there no hatred toward your enemies, attachment to your friends, hope for good things, or fear of bad things? On the contrary, if you grasp and cling to the reality of good and bad, joy and sorrow, and all sensory objects during the waking state, and do the same for dream appearances as if they were waking appearances, then you are deceiving yourself. Presented with misleading appearances and mindsets, you cling to their reality and deceive yourself. Examine how this happens!

"O Lord of Appearances, due to the power of conceptualization, when appearances of going in all directions arise, by merely appearing to take one step after another, various types of images of form and so on emerge from and simultaneously disappear back into the space of awareness. With regard to mountains and valleys, homes, possessions, and everything else—what appeared formerly vanishes as the latter arise, but the latter do not arrive by leaving the former behind somewhere. Know that simply by opening and closing the eyes, all appearances dissolve into absolute space and subsequent ones emerge."

Lord of Appearances responded, "I think these phenomena that appear right here [80] are none other than all the people, earth, water, and mountains that were already present, and they appear to the sense faculties. I don't think the latter ones emerged after the earlier ones had disappeared into the space of awareness. The manifestations and nature of all appearing phenomena invariably seem to be of one taste. What is that nature? Teacher, please explain!"

He replied, "O Lord of Appearances, it's not like that. Do you believe the rainbow that appeared in the sky earlier and the one that appears today are identical? Do you think the clouds, mist, thunder, rain, and wind that occurred in the sky previously are the same as such events today? Do you believe that your body and all sensory objects in a dream are identical to those in the waking state? If you do, examine where they all abide when they are not appearing. There would not be the slightest distinction in terms of the form, shape, color, or nature of any of them.

"Do you believe the people and animals that appear in the waking state are identical to, and thus in no way different from, those in a dream? [81] If you think they are the same, you should recognize the obvious signs of their dissimilarity. For instance, in the waking state people may appear to be ill, be struck by weapons, and perish, but not in the dream state; and the various appearances—land being destroyed, mountains crumbling—are also different.

"You are deluded in regarding as permanent all the nonexistent, unestablished phenomena that appear. In reality they are unestablished, impermanent, and mutable; and from the very moment they appear, they are empty and nonobjective. Knowledge of this state is the quintessence of all the tantras, oral transmissions, and pith instructions. So fathom this!"

The Point of Realizing the Emptiness of Phenomena

Lord of Appearances then commented, "In that case, all phenomena appear even though they are nonexistent. But I don't see any point in ascertaining that all appearing phenomena are primordially empty, for I think it is enough to realize the emptiness of oneself alone. How about that? Teacher, please explain!"

He replied, "O Lord of Appearances, the appearances and mindsets of all beings are identityless, nonobjective, and of the nature of emptiness. However, by failing to recognize this, beings wander endlessly in the three realms of saṃsāra, [82] clinging to true existence. Establishing such nonexistence as the nature of emptiness, realizing it as it is, and causing this state to become manifest is the supreme quintessence of the essential nature of meditation, the authentic path, and the teachings, oral transmissions, and pith instructions of the perfect Buddha. So know this! If it is not realized, emptiness is reduced to an ethically neutral state that neither benefits nor harms. Knowledge of the nature of emptiness is the great wisdom of realizing identitylessness, which is the essential nature of all the grounds and paths."

Lord of Appearances then asked, "Even though all phenomena are perfectly empty, the mere realization of this doesn't cause them to become nonexistent. So couldn't it be that physical or verbal virtues surpass this realization? Teacher, please explain the meaning here."

The Bhagavān replied, "Don't think like that. Even if you spent your entire life practicing relative virtues such as prostrations and circumambulations with your body and mere oral recitations with your mouth, how could liberation ever be achieved? Since you won't become liberated even by such mental virtues as meditating on a deity, cultivating the dhyānas, or merely recognizing your thoughts, [83] what's the point of frustrating yourself by thinking that liberation won't be attained simply by knowing emptiness? If you think that, you are obscured by a great darkness of stupidity and foolishness, and your eye of wisdom with which to investigate the nature of all phenomena is blinded."

Lord of Appearances asked, "Nowadays some people venture into meditation and strive in practice, and some masters acquire knowledge through the teachings, tantras, oral transmissions, and pith instructions of the Buddha and through their own training, yet they do not succeed in meditation or realization. Each must judge this for himself. After passing through many pleasant and difficult stages, there are people who finally identify some degree of knowledge and claim it to be authentic. Are such claims true or not? Teacher, please explain!"

He replied, "O Lord of Appearances, the buddhas have taught that all phenomena, ranging from form up to the omniscient mind, are of the nature of emptiness. They have taught the characteristics of all phenomena because yogins must know and realize them. The path of their followers accords [84] with this, so it is crucial for that path to conform to all the tantras, oral transmissions, and pith instructions as well. For beginningless eons, beings have failed to discover the path by themselves, and they have been deluded by clinging to the experiences of a constant stream of joyful and painful appearances. If they still fail to conform to the teachings, tantras, oral transmissions, and pith instructions of the buddhas, they will not discover the grounds and paths to liberation on their own. And the appearances of pleasant and painful sensations make the attainment of the state of omniscience as improbable as the horns of a hare. Know that their speech is very stupid and foolish, and their words indicate a lack of investigation, analysis, and realization."

Lord of Appearances then asked, "Even though I know that phenomena are empty due to their nonexistence, anxiety and fear still arise when things happen such as being attacked by others, falling over a cliff, or being assaulted with water, fire, or weapons; and experiences such as pain, illness, loss, and regret do occur. So it seems to me they must exist. Please explain how this happens."

He replied, "O Lord of Appearances, when appearances arise such as an attacker beating you with a weapon or a stick, or frightening situations occur involving water, fire, or a cliff, [85] sensations of suffering and pain certainly arise due to dualistic grasping. But in reality there is no injury or entity that inflicts harm. The fires of hell do not burn, pretas are not tormented by hunger or thirst, and *asuras* are not hacked up with weapons of war. Likewise, in terms of phenomena, all misery and pain merely appear; but in terms of emptiness, they are not established as being anything real at all.

"O son of the family, the primordial ground, appearing as space, is apprehended as something else. Once space appears as earth, earth is apprehended as being a real substance. Similarly, space appears as sensory objects such as water, fire, air, and sentient beings, and these appearances are taken to be real things. For example, various reflections of the sun, moon, planets, stars, and so on appear in the ocean, but they have no existence apart from the ocean. In this way, recognize that everything is subsumed in space itself."

Combating the Faults of Benefit and Harm

Lord of Appearances asked, "O Teacher, Bhagavān, in the nature of pristine space, the absolute space of phenomena, is there any benefit from virtue or harm from negative actions, and is there anyone who is helped by gods [86] or harmed by demons and other malevolent beings? Teacher, please explain!"

He replied, "O Lord of Appearances, where are all the virtues committed with the body, speech, and mind? Examine where they have been stored and the manner in which they are gathered. All accumulated virtuous karma has become nothing, empty, nonobjective, and intangible. As not even one action is established as being real, virtuous action consists of nothing but appearances of wholesome conduct."

Lord of Appearances then asked, "Are such deeds of no benefit to the mind?"

He replied, "Examine where in the mind they might be of benefit, in terms of its outside, inside, front, back, and so forth. If neither that which benefits nor that which is benefited is established as being real, there is certainly no benefit. Also, examine the direction and location in which all accumulated negative actions have been assembled, and observe how they exist. They have always been unestablished and nonabiding, so if you think they have afflicted your mind, investigate and analyze the mind's exterior, interior, top, bottom, front, back, and so on. By doing so, you will see that negative actions are mere empty appearances; consequently there is not the slightest bit of harm inflicted by them." [87]

Lord of Appearances responded, "Although there seems to be no benefit or harm, I still think they exist. Please clarify!"

He replied, "O Lord of Appearances, if you inspect the mindstream of an old man who has devoted his whole life to physical and verbal virtues and that of an old man who has applied his whole life to negative actions and nonvirtue, you will find they both want happiness and don't want suffering. They see themselves as gods and regard others as demons. They have such thoughts as hoping for good things and fearing bad things, and all their desires are alike, with neither one better than the other. In the past as well, with these thoughts, their behavior, and the orientation of their desires, they have been endlessly deluded in saṃsāra; therefore, in the future they are bound to be deluded in the same way. So there appears to be no difference between them."

Lord of Appearances asked, "Is there no ripening of karma from positive and negative conduct? Teacher, please explain!"

He replied, "O great being, whatever positive or negative actions [88] have been committed, until the ripening of each of them has run its course, the appearances of pleasure and suffering will continue to occur. Then, with the exhaustion of that karma, one becomes involved in other actions and their consequences. Through physical and verbal virtues, one merely accumulates temporary merit, which perpetuates saṃsāra. But know that this will definitely not lead to the attainment of eternal bliss.

"O Lord of Appearances, in emptiness free of conceptual elaboration there is no benefit bestowed by altruistic gods. Look and you will see there is no father, mother, cause, contributing condition, arising, abiding, going, form, shape, or color of a so-called god. There is no region or direction in which gods dwell in the east, south, west, or north, above, below, or in any of the intermediate directions. Since there is no place where they dwell and no region where they are based, they have no forms seen with the eyes, no sounds heard with the ears, no odors smelled with the nose, no tastes experienced with the tongue, and no tactile sensations felt with the body. So how can they be of benefit?

"If you investigate and analyze everywhere in your own home—outside, inside, and in between—and in the front, back, top, bottom, exterior, and interior of your body, you will see that they are not present and are not established as being anywhere. Look for gods anywhere in the mountains, orchards, and forests, [89] right down to the level of particles. Investigate the abodes of gods and their inhabitants from the level of minute particles and partless particles on up. If gods were to exist, how could insubstantial gods be of benefit to those who are substantial? Examine how that which is empty has no ability to benefit that which is empty, and you will certainly see that they are both nonobjective.

"Furthermore, investigate malevolent demons like this: Enemies are called demons, fearful beings whom everyone takes to be malevolent. From where do they first arise? Are they born from earth or from water, or do they arise from the air or space? Upon investigation, if you think they emerge from some origin, reduce those substances to their constituent particles. Examine them after reducing them to minute particles and partless particles. No origin is found by means of such inquiry. If you think they arise from living beings, inspect and analyze them down to their elements, sense bases, flesh, blood, bone, and marrow, and you will see that they have no objective existence.

"If you still think the consciousnesses of deluded sentient beings turn into demons, seek out their location. By inspecting where they might dwell among the elements of earth, water, fire, and air, [90] you will not find them to exist anywhere. If you still think they exist, what kind of form, shape, color, and sense bases do these beings have? Examine whether or not they have any forms that appear in your field of vision, any sounds that appear to your ears, any odors that appear as olfactory objects, any tastes that appear as gustatory objects, or any tactile sensations that appear as tactile objects. By doing so, you will see that they have no objective existence. In the end, the investigation of a place of movement and an agent who moves reveals that neither the object nor agent of moving is established as real.

"Furthermore, if so-called demons were immaterial entities not belonging to the realm of form, sound, smell, taste, and touch, how could they harm someone who is physically existent? Since the aggressors are empty and nonobjective, and the objects of aggression are also empty and not established as being real, there is no way for harm to be inflicted upon that which is empty. If it were possible for empty consciousness to harm something else, then the consciousnesses of all sentient beings would be devouring and destroying each other. Thus, understand that demons do not exist by their own characteristics.

"Hence, even though so-called demons are neither seen nor felt, if you still think that gods and demons are responsible for the various appearances of pleasure and suffering that beset your body, speech, and mind, [91] then when you experience illness and suffering, you should see the wounds from being struck with weapons by those demons, and you should see the swelling and bruises from being beaten by them with sticks and stones. And if you are afflicted with an internal disease, you should be able to feel it when they reach inside you with their hands. Check carefully to see if that is so.

"Happiness arises and is experienced in your mindstream as a result of different sorts of food, clothing, and sensory objects, and not because of divine protection. Being pierced by a thorn in your upper or lower body, the pain of being struck by a spark, the suffering of experiencing sunburn, and the suffering of experiencing cold from frigid conditions are not due to attacks by demons. Likewise, when the fruits of bad karma ripen, all illness, poverty, assaults by enemies, separation from friends, difficulties, hunger, and thirst arise as the miserable experiences of the ripening of previous karma. It is crucial that you know with certainty that there is no objective existence of afflictions or objects of affliction by malevolent beings or other demons.

"In general, living creatures experience what they have brought upon themselves, like a spider caught in its own web. Fear of demons fabricated by old superstitions [92] is like a bird frightened by the sound of its own wings, and like a deer terrified at the sound of its own footsteps. Know that there are no demons other than those you create.

"Generally speaking, your own appearances arise as demons: By regarding the appearance of the head as divine, hats and so on are regarded as clean; by regarding the appearance of the lower part of the body as demonic, lower garments are regarded as unclean.[57] In particular, since the feet are taken to be especially demonic, if anything touches your shoes, people mistakenly believe that the pollution from this brings great harm to your body, speech, and mind. When any foul substance such as mucus or spittle that flows from inside the body hits the ground, people regard it as if it were demonic or poisonous. Observe how people with these attitudes take their own appearances to be demonic and regard them as their enemies!

"See how people who wish to make offerings to the gods ensure that all the offerings are undisturbed for a long time, without anyone eating them or making use of them. Observe that when people wish to exorcise a demon, although they bring many possessions as offerings, those things stay right where they are, without anyone taking them. If people think demons are present in anything, from a needle and thread up to a house or a weapon, [93] and if they engage in such acts as killing, beating, or pulverizing, why aren't the demons killed and destroyed? There are many people who discard clothing, ornaments, tents, and houses that they have made, built, or erected because they think demons inhabit them. If you examine and analyze this situation, you will see that it is like a skunk smelling its own odor in its den and then abandoning its home. Know for yourself the fallacy of people fabricating demons out of their own superstitions."

Lord of Appearances asked, "Why should we dismiss the benefit and harm brought about by virtue and vice and by gods and demons in that way? Bhagavān, please explain!"

He replied, "O Lord of Appearances, here are the reasons for so determining the absence of benefit or harm due to virtue and vice. Emptiness is

57. Tibetan custom regards the upper part of the body as clean and the lower part, especially the feet, as filthy.

the path for achieving the states of liberation and omniscience. But when foolish people who are attracted to exotic experiences meditate on profound emptiness, [94] no fascinating experiences come to mind, so they lose their belief and trust. Then, worrying that they may be in danger of wasting their lives by not striving or creating anything in their minds, they apply themselves ardently to such practices as prostrations, circumambulations, offerings, and chanting. Then, when the exceptional benefits of this meditation are explained to them, they think they'd like to try it again. Although they meditate a little bit, they understand and experience nothing, so they once again apply themselves to methods for purifying obscurations and accumulating merit.

"You will not accomplish your goal with a vacillating mind, so even if you strive sporadically like that for a long time, in the end you will not escape dying an ordinary death. Therefore, if you do not know how to distinguish between what is and what is not Dharma, even if you say you have been introduced to meditation, the view will remain hidden from you, and you will have no belief in the ultimate Dharma. With the power of mental activity, all virtues and vices produce merely the experiential appearances of various joys and sorrows. But all positive and negative karmas have no form and no substance, and they are totally unestablished and nonexistent. Knowledge of this brings about confidence in meditation, and it leads to the conviction that the [95] ground of all virtue and vice is emptiness.

"You are obscured by your ignorance of your own essential nature. By not knowing or realizing the ground of great emptiness as displays of all of saṃsāra and nirvāṇa, you wander in saṃsāra. Know that engaging in mere physical and verbal virtue does not purify this obscuration. Believe and trust in your own awareness—then the dust will be removed from your eye of wisdom.

"Examine and recognize whether those gods and demons and all virtue and vice actually do any good. Otherwise, from the moment that the aggregates grasped as the 'I' come into existence, there will arise a constant stream of appearances of the six classes of sentient beings. So for as long as you are involved in mental grasping at activities such as meditations, views, goals, merging, and inner withdrawal,[58] you will constantly have various experiences of outer upheavals of apparitions of gods and demons, inner upheavals

58. *Merging* refers to the meditative practice of imagining your spiritual mentor and personal deity merging with yourself, and *inner withdrawal* refers to the practice of imagining the entire phenomenal world dissolving into emptiness. If such practices are done with conceptual grasping, they will only perpetuate your existence in saṃsāra.

of physical illnesses, and secret upheavals of experiences of joys and sorrows. Succumbing to the superstition that these are demons, and clinging to this, people turn away from the true path and go astray. Therefore, it is crucial to comprehend this.

"Moreover, once you [96] have ventured into the teachings on severance[59] and practice it, you will recognize that gods and demons are none other than your own appearances. The knowledge that there are no gods and no demons is the teaching and the main practice of severance, so this is of the utmost importance. Likewise in the meditation on deities in the stage of generation, if you take gods and demons to be autonomous, you will veer off to a path of delusion. So in that context, too, this point is extremely important. Furthermore, whatever yāna you enter, if you fail to recognize this point and mistakenly take gods and demons and virtue and vice to exist objectively, by their own characteristics, you will certainly fall into delusion. So ascertain this as the quintessence of the practical instructions and the essential nature of the path.

"If you do not recognize how gods and demons are nonexistent, when you dream of a monk, you may take him to be a demon. When you dream of a woman, you may take her to be a demoness; when you dream of a child, you may take him to be a spirit; and when you dream of a tadpole, you may take it to be a *nāga*[60] or an earth spirit. All these are just delusive appearances that are not established as real. When you dream of acquiring such things as food, livestock, and lodging, by the next morning they have vanished from sight, so they are unreal and empty of inherent existence.

"When people go from village to village hoping to acquire material gain and devoting themselves to religious rituals and subjugating demons, [97] even though they try to trick others with various techniques for slaying and subjugating demons, people constantly feel anxiety and a terror of demons. Hope in gods arises in the same way, and people's own superstitions manifest as their enemies. As a result, illnesses and various joys and sorrows may occur continuously. Therefore, if you know in this way how gods and demons

59. Tib. *gcod.* A meditative practice of imaginatively offering up your entire being as a means to realizing the empty nature of all phenomena, severing all clinging to the appearances of the three realms, and realizing that all gods and demons are none other than your own appearances.

60. Tib. *klu.* A serpent-like creature whose actual nature is that of delusions produced by the causes and conditions of ignorance. Such beings may be called into the service of the Dharma.

are nonexistent, you will have fathomed the exceptionally deep teachings on severance.

"If you don't recognize the importance of this, you may think that even finding a needle and thread is due to divine intervention and then worship the gods for it. If your hand or foot is pricked by a thorn, you may attribute it to a demon. Then, with the arousal of your superstitions, any misfortune that occurs will seem to have been brought about by demons, and your mind will be filled with anxiety. Demons are conjured up by ideas about demons, which result in a lifetime of devils. So the teachings on severance are extraordinarily profound for turning away from this false path."

Collapsing the False Cave of Hopes and Fears

Lord of Appearances then asked, "O Teacher, Bhagavān, are the objects of hope and fear within all of saṃsāra and nirvāṇa established in reality by their own characteristics or not? Teacher, please explain!" [98]

He replied, "O Lord of Appearances, the objects of hope called *buddhas* are neither primordially established nor are they present in reality. If a buddha had a body, wouldn't it have been produced by the causes and contributing conditions of parents? If so, a buddha would fall to the extreme of birth. If a buddha had a buddhafield, sensory objects, and a retinue, wouldn't they appear because of grasping at the phenomenal identities of apprehended objects? If a buddha appeared to have a body, wouldn't that occur because of grasping at a personal identity? If you believe buddhas finally pass away into nirvāṇa, wouldn't that imply that they fall to the extreme of death and annihilation? If you believe buddhas remain in the meantime, you are falling to the extreme of eternalism.

"If you think buddhas reveal the Dharma to many beings, then those things that are apprehended, appear, and arise as the individuals who reveal the Dharma, as the Dharma that is revealed, and as the disciples who are taught are all astonishing delusions of dualistic grasping. If you believe buddhas exist like that, you are deluded by the foggy misconception of regarding buddhas as sentient beings.

"Moreover, don't think a buddha has eyes. [99] If you thought that, a buddha would have to have visual consciousness, inevitably implying the presence of appearances as form. If that were so, there would have to be objects apprehended by the eyes, and subtle thoughts that take their configurations to be good, bad, or neutral. That visual apprehension would be called the *mind*.

"Don't think a buddha has ears. If you thought that, apprehended objects and the subtle conceptualization that grasps at sounds would appear simultaneously with the auditory consciousness and appearance of sound, and that would be *grasping*.

"Don't think a buddha has a nose. If you thought that, there would be olfactory consciousness and the appearance of smells as apprehended objects, and the subtle conceptualization that grasps at odors would be *grasping*.

"Don't think a buddha has a tongue. If you thought that, there would be gustatory consciousness and the appearance of tastes as apprehended objects, and conceptual fixation on them would be called the *grasping mind*.

"Don't think a buddha has a body. If you thought that, [100] he would have to have bodily consciousness and tactile sensations. Just as the presence of water naturally implies moisture and the presence of fire implies heat, the five doors of the senses are avenues of delusion. So all kinds of consciousness, appearances, and grasping minds occur of their own accord as dependently related events.

"The subtle thoughts that hold fast to tactile objects entail tactile grasping, and the three realms of saṃsāra are brought into existence by dualistic minds. As for the five senses, the aspects of radiance and clarity of the mind unimpededly emerge as mental states and appearances, and they are given various names. The six aggregates of consciousness are called the *mind*. Those who have minds are called *sentient beings*, just as creatures having horns are called *horned creatures*. Recognize how important it is not to confuse buddhas with sentient beings in that way.

"If you still think buddhas are autonomous like sentient beings, seek out those buddhas' source of arising and examine where they dwell in the meantime: in the east, south, west, north, or some intermediate direction? If you think they dwell above, [101] and if a world called a *buddhafield* were to exist in the sky without anything to support it, it should fall to the ground. If it were present on earth, there would be no reason why you couldn't travel there now and reach it. If it were underground, you should be able to dig it up and see it. And when you die, why would you be able to go to places that can't be seen or felt now?

"If you suggest that it is not a place that can be reached by corporeal beings, do you believe that the consciousnesses of all beings who have died must have arrived at this place? Isn't it a place that can be experienced by beings with bad karma? If all those who go from one place to another and all the places they go arise due to dualistic deluded minds, then there is no bad karma other than dualistic grasping. Nevertheless, these places are certainly experienced by everyone.

"Moreover, if such places were to exist, beings bound by the two types of self-grasping and endowed with the five senses and six aggregates of consciousness might go there. But because of the impurity of their mindstreams, they could experience only the fruition of temporary pleasure, without reaching a state of eternal bliss. This becomes obvious by observing the unstable, transitory nature of dualistic appearances. The characteristics of the appearances of the dualistic mind [102] as emergence and cessation are originally unestablished, which reveals their own lack of true existence.

"Some people say that the physical worlds and their sentient inhabitants exist in the buddhafields with a bounty of joy and prosperity naturally present there, and that the physical world, its sentient inhabitants, the teacher, and retinue all have the extraordinarily fine qualities of serenity, coolness, radiance, and freedom from impurity. If so, they are no better than the gods of the form realm, so these are mental appearances to sentient beings. The various appearances of this world are apparitions of ignorance, which shows that this is a limitation of sentient beings."[61]

The Ground for the Arising of the Appearances of All Phenomena

Lord of Appearances then asked, "There appear to be many deeds, writings, temples, and reliquaries of numerous yogins and *siddha*s of the past. How is that? Teacher, please explain!"

He replied, "O Lord of Appearances, when someone falls asleep and dreams, he may hear many accounts of the early formation of the cosmos and the evolution of human and nonhuman life forms. He may witness many teachers and masters propounding the Dharma, see many images of numerous temples and reliquaries, and observe many writings. [103] Many people will seem to tell him that the images of those temples and reliquaries were constructed by certain patrons, artists, and smiths, and that those writings were composed by specific teachers. However, when that person wakes up the next morning, it turns out that all those perceived appearances and reports were nothing but his own appearances emerging from and disappearing back into his own nature.

"Likewise, all the representations of the body, speech, and mind of the buddhas that appear in this way emerge as appearances of this morning and this present moment. But they did not exist earlier, nor do they depend upon anything earlier. Ascertain that they are all your own delusive appearances.

61. The above discussion of the buddhas and buddhafields is not meant to suggest that they are utterly nonexistent. Rather, those phenomena as sentient beings conceive of them do not exist objectively, independently of conceptual designation.

Buddhahood is just this ground of all sentient beings—emptiness free of conceptual elaboration.

"That which is called a *vision of the buddha* is the buddha gazing upon sentient beings, and it is simply a delusive, muddled visionary experience, for the observer and the object observed do not exist—they are nothing more than intangible displays of emptiness. The buddha is no more than your own appearances; so without placing your hopes in any other object, empty out the object of your hopes!

"Now, by examining and analyzing the fundamental ground of the domains of impure saṃsāra, you must realize that frightening regions do not exist apart from yourself. [104] Here is the situation: First of all, once you have cast off this body, if you were to wander to a realm called the *intermediate period*, does it exist to the east, south, west, or north of this spot? Or is it right here, or in some intermediate direction or another one? By examining this, you see that such a region is not established as real. When your previous body has been discarded, as you examine the parents, source, dwelling place, and demise of your body in the intermediate period, you should find that they have truly existent, real characteristics. But instead you see that the visions of the intermediate period arise as mere appearances of a dream body and a dream environment. And you see that the body, environment, and all sensory objects that appear in this life are mere transitory appearances that lack real characteristics and true existence.

"Do all the hell realms, together with their inhabitants, exist underground or above ground? Examine whether these worlds exist where you are, or to the east, south, west, or north. Who built the floors of molten iron? Where was the firewood gathered? Who forged the weapons of hell? From which parents, causes, and conditions did the workers in hell originate? If their torsos, legs, and arms are not burned by fire, why are other sentient beings burned? [105] Since these workers inflict such horrible suffering on beings, where do they experience the karmic consequences of their deeds?

"If you investigate this, you will recognize everything to be like a dream world of delusive appearances. If merely wounding and beating sentient beings in the present results in their death, why doesn't such suffering in hell kill them as well? If they go from one place to another, we should be able to experientially confirm the existence of these places now. But why is it that they are not seen except by the dead? If you investigate this, you will know that they do not exist apart from your own appearances.

"Likewise, does the world of pretas with their unendurable suffering really exist or not? If this realm exists autonomously, examine its location in the cardinal and intermediate directions, above, below, and so on. If people of the present can die as a result of starvation over a period of days or a few months, why don't pretas die as a result of their eons of suffering from hunger and thirst? If you consider this carefully, [106] you will see that even if they have nothing to eat for beginningless and endless lifetimes, they are happy at the sight of food because of their craving in anticipation of it. But instead they starve, which they experience as suffering.

"Likewise, by meticulously investigating all the origins, locations, and destinations of all the worlds of the six types of sentient beings, you will come to a deep certainty that the appearances of these kinds of beings emerge like dream appearances that occur when waking appearances subside, and that these realms do not exist autonomously.

"Therefore, once this delusion of your own appearances has dissolved into absolute space, then the realm of ultimate reality, or suchness, manifests. Be certain that effectively striving to realize this from the depths of your own being is the very nature of the simultaneous perfection of the path, the fruition, and the essence of omniscient, perfect buddhahood.

"Now ultimate reality, the sugatagarbha, is the ground for the arising of the appearances of all phenomena; it is their essential nature, and this is the decisive point of emptiness. If form had no essential nature, it would not appear; if sounds, smells, tastes, tactile sensations, and mental objects had no essential nature, [107] none of them would appear. If space had no essential nature, no appearances would arise in space. If earth, water, fire, air, and all sentient beings had no essential nature, ground, or root, they would not appear. Thus, the essential nature of space is emptiness, and the essential nature of earth, water, fire, air, form, sound, smell, taste, touch, and all mental objects is emptiness. In the same way, recognize that the ground of everything is nothing other than emptiness, and emptiness is its essential nature.

"The essential nature of all the reflections of planets and stars in the ocean is the ocean itself, and the essential nature of the entire universe is space. The essential nature of all of saṃsāra and nirvāṇa is none other than the ultimate nature of the mind,[62] the sugatagarbha. That which is called the sugatagarbha is nowhere else. By counteracting the reification of space itself as being something else, by determining with discerning wisdom that saṃsāra and nirvāṇa are of the nature of the space of emptiness, and by experiencing the wisdom of realizing identitylessness, [108] you will ascertain the ground of being as space itself. But if you suppose that this is an absence of matter, or that it is something ethically neutral, devoid of faults and virtues, you are wrong.

62. Tib. *sems nyid*; Skt. *cittatā*. The ultimate nature of the mind, which is awareness, is also known as the *sugatagarbha*.

"When sentient beings are deluded, space is the essential nature of all the elements, the physical worlds, their sentient inhabitants, and sensory objects—they are all displays of space. Although the essential nature of the ground is the nature of space, the ground is obscured by ignorance and is thus taken to be autonomous. Because the identityless nature of pervasive space is apprehended as the self, it appears as the self. When the ground is apprehended as something external, space then appears as an absence of matter.

"Due to the radiant, clear aspect of space, it can appear as earth, fire, water, air, form, sound, smell, taste, and tactile objects. This is like the appearance of various reflections of planets and stars due to the lucid, clear aspect of the ocean. All these reflections, planets, and stars are none other than the ocean itself, and they are of the same nature. Likewise, [109] all of saṃsāra and nirvāṇa is nothing other than space itself, and it is all of one taste. Thus, recognizing and ascertaining all of saṃsāra and nirvāṇa as displays of space is called the *wisdom of pristine space*. The manifestation of space is called the *primordial consciousness that is pristine awareness*."[63]

The Manifestation of Space as Primordial Consciousness That Is Pristine Awareness

Lord of Appearances then asked, "To what does the term *awareness* refer? Teacher, please explain!"

He replied, "O son of the family, because all beings of the three realms are unaware of the mode of existence of their own pristine space, it does not manifest. This is called *unawareness*. By comprehending with discerning wisdom all phenomena of saṃsāra and nirvāṇa, you recognize that they are the void, empty, intangible, nonobjective displays of space. This manifestation of space is the great, infinite ground awareness."

Lord of Appearances then asked, "Aren't things seen with the physical eyes? To say these things are awareness is not correct, so does an inner knower exist or not? Teacher, please explain!"

He replied, "Your eyeballs do not see waking appearances, dream appearances, or appearances following this life. [110] Even a trillion eyeballs would not experience form. The manifestation of all daytime appearances, nighttime appearances, and appearances during and following this life is due solely

63. This does not equate space with emptiness, but rather uses space as a metaphor for the ultimate ground of existence. Space itself is within the domain of the intellect and is relative, but its characteristics are analogous to those of emptiness, so this metaphor is used to bring disciples closer to a realization of the nature of ultimate reality.

to beings' minds, which are of the nature of clear light—which is primordially present, unimpeded, radiant, luminous consciousness, free of contamination. Such minds have the capacity to make anything appear.

"It's like this: The stream of consciousness that determines, ascertains, and perceives saṃsāra and nirvāṇa to be great emptiness is called the *wisdom of realizing identitylessness*. This is the nature of the primordial consciousness that comprehends the essence of the great, infinite ground awareness,[64] the most sublime of all phenomena.

"Here are its qualities: Son of the family, just as the rising sun utterly dispels all darkness, the wisdom of realizing identitylessness utterly dispels all the dark ignorance of self-concepts simply by establishing their nature; and the mode of existence of ultimate reality, or suchness, is made manifest. Just as the explosion of the great conflagration at the end of the eon disintegrates all gross substances and utterly annihilates even the tiniest organisms, [111] leaving not even a trace of ash, so does the wisdom of realizing identitylessness overwhelm all known vices and utterly extinguish all unknown vices and obscurations.

"Great wisdom is like an eye that sees, for it experiences all the phenomena of the path and fruition. Great wisdom is like the water of a great ocean, for just as all rivers and streams originate from the ocean and return to it, so do all the phenomena of the path and fruition originate from great wisdom and return to it. Great wisdom is like space, for just as there is nothing in the world that is not within its domain, in the very instant that all the phenomena in saṃsāra and nirvāṇa are perceived with great wisdom, they are encompassed within it.

"In one moment, beings may be like slaves of Māra, heaps of mental afflictions, and sacks of poison, and such blind, wicked beings are not revered by anyone. But if in the next moment they identify great wisdom and actualize it, they are immediately worthy of homage, devotion, and worship [112] by multitudes of beings, including the gods, and they become fields for accumulating merit.

"Great wisdom is free of all the harshness of mental afflictions, so it is *gentle*. Its precious, spontaneous, melodious speech is known to bear the sixty attributes of the voice of Brahmā, so it is *melodious*.[65] It sees the equality of saṃsāra and nirvāṇa, so it is an *eye*. It is none other than the absolute space

64. When one realizes the essential nature of the ground consciousness, one ascertains it to be the ground awareness referred to here.

65. This etymologizes "Mañjughoṣa" (Tib. *'jam dbyangs*): gentle (*'jam*), melodious (*dbyangs*).

that pervades the essence of everything, so it is *constant*. It uniquely perceives all phenomena of the ground, path, and fruition as primordial consciousness, so it *sees*.[66] It releases self-concepts into absolute space, so it is *powerful*. It is the source of all might and strength, so it is *great*. It accomplishes the great confidence of fearlessness, so it is *accomplished*.[67]

"As soon as great wisdom manifests, one radically *surpasses* mundane existence. It synthesizes all the types of inexhaustible ornamental wheels of the three secrets,[68] so it is of the *three types*. It is the protector of all beings of the three realms, so it is a *protector*.[69] All of these are none other than great wisdom.

"With great wisdom, all appearances of phenomena and dualistic grasping are naturally pacified in the suchness of ultimate reality. [113] This is the array of peaceful forms. Those who sever the life force of saṃsāra and reach the state of nirvāṇa with manifestations lacking compassion are merely referred to as emanations of wrathful forms. As soon as this great wisdom of realizing identitylessness is actualized, mental afflictions transform into displays of primordial consciousness.

"The enduring, tenacious fallacy of not being aware of your own essential nature is called *delusion*. With the actualization of the wisdom of realizing identitylessness, all of saṃsāra and nirvāṇa naturally dissolves into displays of the clear light of ultimate reality, so this wisdom is the *vajra of delusion*. In the realm of the radiant, clear space of awareness of the ground, free of contamination, hatred in relation to dualistic appearances is naturally vanquished, so this wisdom is the *vajra of hatred*. In the realm of the great purity and equality of saṃsāra and nirvāṇa, the pride of self-concepts is naturally vanquished, so this wisdom is the *vajra of pride*. Once the energy-mind has dissolved into empty absolute space, the attachment and craving that arouse thoughts are naturally vanquished, so this wisdom is the *vajra of attachment*. With the sense of the self dissolving into unreality, envy entailing grasping at signs is naturally vanquished, so this wisdom is the *vajra of envy*.

66. This etymologizes "Avalokiteśvara" (Tib. *spyan ras gzigs*): eye (*spyan*), constant (*ras*), sees (*gzigs*).

67. This etymologizes an epithet of Vajrapāṇi, "Mahāsthāmaprāpta" (Tib. *mthu chen thob*): powerful (*mthu*), great (*chen*), accomplished (*thob*).

68. The three secrets are the body, speech, and mind of the buddhas.

69. This etymologizes "nobles of the three types," referring to Mañjuśrī, Avalokiteśvara, and Vajrapāṇi (Tib. *'phags pa rigs gsum mgon po*): surpasses (*'phags pa*), three types (*rigs gsum*), protector (*mgon po*).

"Since the mental afflictions conquer themselves, they manifest as wrathful forms. This great wisdom that is replete with all such enlightened qualities [114] makes manifest the primordial consciousness of the dharmakāya, which is present in the ground."

Lord of Appearances then said, "O Teacher, Bhagavān, if there were present in oneself a buddha who has fundamentally never known or experienced delusion—whether one recognizes it or not—since this is a buddha, there should be no need to display wisdom or primordial consciousness to this being. Moreover, there would be no reason why sentient beings should wander in saṃsāra, having to experience joys and sorrows. Teacher, please explain!"

He replied, "O son of the family, by reducing the ground of being to something ethically neutral, it can then be of no benefit or harm. Here is an analogy to illustrate the reduction of fundamental, eternal ultimate reality to an ethically neutral state: Even if you possess a wish-fulfilling gem for your whole life, by failing to recognize it and mistaking it for an ordinary stone, you may be tormented by the miseries of poverty. The gem has not become powerless, but by failing to recognize it, you don't pay attention to it, and consequently you gain no siddhis.

"Never, even for an instant, have you been separated from the originally pure ground, free of conceptual elaboration; but by failing to recognize it, [115] you have not apprehended your own nature for yourself. As a consequence, you have been deluded by grasping at the true existence of a constant stream of joyful and painful appearances. Now with great wisdom you recognize manifest primordial consciousness, and by apprehending the profundity of your own state, you are self-liberated. This is like recognizing the wish-fulfilling gem and honoring it, which then frees you from poverty.

"The presence of the ground as an ethically neutral state is like a field without an owner; the freedom that ensues from identifying your own essence for yourself is like sowing a crop in the field and enjoying the harvest. The ethically neutral ground is like an ownerless, empty castle, which is therefore of no benefit or harm; the manifestation of the ground is like the owner making use of the castle. The ethically neutral ground is like the sky obscured by darkness; the manifestation of the ground is like the sun rising in the sky. The ethically neutral ground is an object of delusion for sentient beings, so it is of no benefit or harm; the actualization of the ground provides mastery over the grounds and paths to liberation. In this way, the actualization of all the great qualities of the ground is due to the power of great wisdom." [116]

Lord of Appearances asked, "Bhagavān, is there or is there not a difference between the dharmakāya, or pristine awareness that is present in the ground, and the path pristine awareness? If there is, Teacher, please explain their essential natures and distinctions, the manner in which enlightened qualities are perfected, the way sentient beings become deluded, and the nature of sentient beings' existence."

He replied, "O great being, there are both path pristine awareness and ground pristine awareness. As for path pristine awareness, once you have identified in yourself primordially present, unimpeded consciousness, you transcend all modes of grasping involving analytical constructs, and you disappear into your own natural state. By settling in meditative equipoise in this state, without the three types of modification,[70] even though this is not actual wisdom or primordial consciousness, it is their radiance. Therefore, by remaining in such meditative equipoise, eventually you will see the truth of ultimate reality and actualize the ground pristine awareness.

"As for the pristine awareness that is present in the ground, in terms of the names, substances, origin, location, and destination of yourself and all appearances, they are determined to be of the nature of the ten types of objects of knowledge.[71] Once you have recognized all phenomena included within saṃsāra and nirvāṇa as displays of your own appearances alone, you will actualize the great, all-pervasive realm of pristine space, which is self-emergent, spontaneous primordial consciousness. [117]

"Here are its qualities:

- Pristine ethical discipline comes from not confusing pristine awareness for the mind.
- Pristine generosity comes by mastering pristine awareness—leaving it as it is, without activity.
- Pristine patience comes by pristine awareness apprehending its own nature for itself.
- Pristine enthusiasm comes from not transgressing the three types of nonmodification in meditative equipoise or the three relinquishments during the postmeditative state.[72]
- Pristine meditation comes by transforming thoughts into primordial consciousness.

70. The three types of modification are of the body, speech, and mind.

71. The ten types of objects of knowledge are the ten analogies indicating the illusory nature of all phenomena. See GD 71–86.

72. In meditative equipoise the body, speech, and mind are not to be structured or modified in any way, nor is the natural state of these three to be relinquished during the postmeditative state.

- Pristine wisdom comes out of the displays of the equality of saṃsāra and nirvāṇa.

"This is the spontaneous actualization of the essential nature of the six perfections.

"From the great, original resting place, free of activity and grasping, comes pristine meditative equipoise by abiding in the equilibrium of great, naturally settled ultimate reality. The pristine postmeditative state comes by not letting your view, meditation, or conduct revert to the ordinary state. This is the simultaneous perfection of the essential nature of nondual meditative equipoise and the postmeditative state.

"The contamination of ignorance is *purified* in absolute space, and all the qualities of primordial consciousness naturally arise within great primordial consciousness, pristine awareness, where they *expand* as great spontaneous actualization.[73] *Ultimate reality* is so designated because all the *phenomena* included within saṃsāra and nirvāṇa are naturally present, [118] without modification, in the nature of awareness itself.[74] The *Saṅgha* is so designated because all *virtuous* qualities are *desired*, without differentiation, in self-emergent, great primordial consciousness, pristine awareness.[75]

"The outer Three Jewels are of one taste in the nature of pristine awareness, ultimate reality; and because they are of the essential nature of all of saṃsāra and nirvāṇa, they are *supreme*. Bringing all beings to a state of eternal bliss is the *mother*.[76] *Binding the mind* without allowing it to depart from the state of your own pristine awareness is the personal deity.[77] Because of being like a mother who is pregnant with saṃsāra and nirvāṇa in the expanse of space, one speaks of *space*; and because of moving through the many gateways of skillful means and dependent origination, one speaks of *going*.[78] These are present in the essential nature of all the inner objects of refuge of the secret mantra.

"The essential nature, great primordial emptiness, is unborn primordial

73. This etymologizes "Buddha" (Tib. *sangs rgyas*): purified (*sangs*), expand (*rgyas*).

74. This etymologizes "ultimate reality" (Tib. *chos nyid*; Skt. *dharmatā*), which in this context refers to the refuge of the Dharma (Tib. *chos*): phenomena (*chos nyid*).

75. This etymologizes "Saṅgha" (Tib. *dge 'dun*): virtuous (*dge*), desired (*'dun*).

76. This etymologizes "guru" (Tib. *bla ma*): supreme (*bla*) mother (*ma*).

77. This etymologizes "personal deity" (Tib. *yi dam*): mind (*yid*) binding (*dam*).

78. This etymologizes "ḍākinī" (Tib. *mkha' 'gro*): space (*mkha'*) going (*'gro*).

consciousness, the *dharmakāya*. Since unimpeded primordial consciousness is the natural spontaneous actualization of the kāyas and the natural perfection of enjoyment of the displays of the facets of primordial consciousness, it is the *saṃbhogakāya*. Because the great primordial consciousness of all-pervasive compassion arises for the sake of sentient beings, it is the *nirmāṇakāya*. These secret, unsurpassed Three Jewels are also completely present in great primordial consciousness, pristine awareness. Properly recognize the spontaneous actualization in the essential nature of the synthesis of these Jewels. Recognize this as the sublime protector of disciples, and devote yourself to it. [119] Not being divorced from this state is the real taking of refuge in the nature of being. It is the supreme and foremost of all the ways of taking refuge.

"As a means for cultivating bodhicitta, this is far superior to other paths: To recognize that the essential nature of the all-pervasive equality of saṃsāra and nirvāṇa is your own essential nature is to actualize the most sublime of all ways of cultivating bodhicitta. In the expanse of pristine awareness—ultimate reality, free of conceptual elaboration—the effortless, self-emergent nature of all the ornamental wheels of the inexhaustible enlightened body, speech, mind, qualities, and activities of all the jinas and jinaputras of the three times is established. Ascertaining this and practicing it is the essential nature of all sādhanas and maṇḍalas combined, and this alone is the immutable accomplishment, so recognize it!

"If pristine awareness is committed to its own state, and if you achieve the confidence of not departing from it, you will effortlessly achieve the supreme siddhi in this lifetime. If you do slip away from it and fall into a state of ignorance, the sufferings of saṃsāra and the miserable states of existence will scorch you like fire. So this is the great samaya: the essential nature of all vows consists of binding yourself to the space of pristine awareness, unconfused with respect to the deluded ways of grasping at substantiality. [120]

"For beginningless lifetimes, the veil of ignorance has obscured the displays of the originally pure ground, absolute space. The realization of the face of infinite, sovereign pristine awareness, ultimate reality, which transcends causality, dissolves that obscuration into nonobjective, great openness. So this is the purification of obscurations. However much you strive in tainted virtue to benefit the mind with the body and speech, you are merely accumulating merit within saṃsāra, but you will not reach the state of liberation. Why not? Fundamental ignorance is the ground of saṃsāra and of all delusive appearances and mindsets. Thus, none of the virtuous and nonvirtuous deeds based upon this foundation transcend saṃsāra."

The Ground of Saṃsāra and of All Delusive Appearances and Mindsets

Lord of Appearances then asked, "O Teacher, Bhagavān, in that case, if the ultimate nature of the mind has always been enlightened and untainted by faults or stains, please explain the whole of this delusive ground, path, and fruition."

He replied, "O Lord of Appearances, the pure ground is enlightened as the originally pure primordial protector. Its actualization is the buddha of self-emergent awareness. In terms of its characteristics, since its essential nature is [121] primordial great emptiness, the absolute space of all of saṃsāra and nirvāṇa, it is the *primordial consciousness of the absolute space of phenomena*. Being of a lucid, clear nature, free of contamination, which allows for the unimpeded appearances of all kinds of objects, it is *mirror-like primordial consciousness*. Because it equally pervades the objectless emptiness of all of saṃsāra and nirvāṇa, it is the *primordial consciousness of equality*. Because it is an unimpeded avenue that illuminates the qualities of primordial consciousness, it is *discerning primordial consciousness*. Because all pure, free, simultaneously perfected deeds and activities are accomplished naturally, of their own accord, it is the *primordial consciousness of accomplishment*. When the natural glow of pristine awareness that is present in the ground—the dharmakāya, in which the five facets of primordial consciousness are simultaneously perfected—dissolves into its inner luminosity, it is called *unobscured primordial consciousness*.

"Ignorance of this nature is determined as the cause of delusion. How? Mere ignorance of the nature of the displays of the all-pervasive ground acts as the cause. As this becomes somewhat fortified, it dwells as the actual substrate, which is immaterial like space—a blank, unthinking void. Entering this state corresponds to states such as fainting; abiding in the meditative absorptions,[79] meditative experiences induced by the dhyānas; becoming engulfed by deep sleep in the substrate, [122] in which appearances have dissolved into the space of awareness; and reaching the point of death, in which appearances have vanished. This is called the *actual substrate*. Free of clinging to the experiences of the intellect and mentation, one is absorbed in an immaterial ground.

"From that state arises radiant, clear consciousness itself as the basis of the emergence of appearances, and this is the substrate consciousness. Moreover,

79. Tib. *snyoms 'jug*; Skt. *samāpatti*. One of eight attainments corresponding to the dhyānas of the form and formless realms.

no objects are established that are not expressions of its own luminosity, and while it can give rise to all kinds of appearances, it does not enter into anything. This is like planets and stars appearing in lucid, clear water; like reflections appearing in a lucid, clear mirror; and like the physical worlds and their sentient inhabitants appearing in lucid, clear space. In the same way, appearances emerge in the empty, clear substrate consciousness.

"From that state, due to the mere appearance of the 'I' that appears as the self, consciousness arises; and by apprehending the self as being here, the ground appears to be over there, thus establishing the appearance of immaterial space. As this becomes entrenched, it is made manifest, and so-called mentation arises—which is the basis for the emergence of appearances—revealing the aspect of luminosity. From this the five types of appearing objects arise, and with the reification of them, there is clinging and delusion.

"Thus, obscuring ignorance veils the natural glow of the ground: self-emergent, innate primordial consciousness. [123] As a result, its radiance transforms into an external display. Here is how this occurs: When the primordial consciousness of accomplishment is obscured, its radiance is transformed into subtle grasping. When the primordial consciousness of equality is obscured, its radiance is transformed into afflictive mentation. And when discerning primordial consciousness is obscured, its radiance is transformed into so-called mentation.

"Here is how this radiance is transformed from the five facets of absolute space into the five great elements and the five derivative elements: In the all-pervasive space of the dharmakāya, the inner glow of the primordial consciousness of accomplishment is obscured. Consequently, due to the contributing condition of the movement of karmic energies, a great element arises inwardly in the nature of the quintessence of air, and this primary cause is transformed into radiant green light. As a consequence of grasping at this as being real and clinging to it as truly existent, it is reified and fully developed, and it arises externally as the derivative element of air, which is of the nature of a residue.

"Likewise, when the primordial consciousness of the absolute space of phenomena is obscured by ignorance, its radiance appears as the great element of indigo light. From grasping at this as being real and clinging to it as truly existent, the derivative element of space appears. When mirror-like primordial consciousness is obscured by ignorance, [124] its radiance appears as the great element of white light. From grasping at this as being real and clinging to it as truly existent, it appears as the derivative element of water. When the primordial consciousness of equality is obscured by ignorance, its radiance appears as the great element of yellow light. From grasping at this as being real and clinging to it as truly existent, it appears as the derivative element of earth. When discerning primordial consciousness is obscured by ignorance, its radiance appears as the great element of red light. From grasping at this as being real and clinging to it as truly existent, it appears as the derivative element of fire. This is the way in which all the elements emerge from the five facets of absolute space and solidify. So know this.

"The appearance of the formation of the cosmos from the five facets of absolute space is as follows: Relatively speaking, in the realm of baseless space the maṇḍala of air is formed as the underlying ground. Upon it forms a serene, clear, pure ocean, and upon this is the mighty, golden earth. The maṇḍala of fire is said to be established in their midst, and it is said that all beings come into being as something like their essence and vapor.

"Although this explanation serves the function of guiding disciples, in ultimate terms, because the subtle grasping that initially obscures the primordial consciousness of the absolute space of phenomena is of the nature of air, [125] as soon as it enters into the ground space of awareness, the ground appears as baseless emptiness, and this is space. From it, appearances of space emerge unimpededly. Subtle grasping sustains the basis of ignorance and obscures the primordial consciousness of accomplishment. Consequently, appearances of its radiance emerge unimpededly as air. When mirror-like primordial consciousness is obscured by ignorance, appearances of its radiance emerge unimpededly as water. By grasping at the primordial consciousness of equality as being real, its appearances as earth emerge unimpededly. When discerning primordial consciousness is obscured by ignorance, its appearances as fire emerge unimpededly.

"From the obscuration of their essential nature, thoughts emerge. From the obscuration of the primordial consciousness of the absolute space of phenomena, thoughts of delusion emerge. From the obscuration of mirror-like primordial consciousness, thoughts of hatred emerge. From the obscuration of the primordial consciousness of equality, thoughts of pride emerge. From the obscuration of discerning primordial consciousness, thoughts of attachment emerge. From the obscuration of the primordial consciousness of accomplishment, thoughts of envy constantly arise. All mental afflictions and facets of primordial consciousness are of the same essential nature, but they appear as different radiances.

"Here are indications that for all phenomena, [126] all five elements appear from each of them:

"From fire there are—

- Water, because water arises from fire

- Air, because there is the motility of air in fire
- Fire, because heat emerges from fire
- Earth, because minute and partless particles emerge from fire

"Likewise, from earth there are—
- Water, because moisture arises from earth
- The nature of air, because earth emerges from partless particles
- Fire, because warmth arises from earth
- The nature of earth, due to its heaviness and solidity

"As for water, there are—
- Earth, because minute particles are created from the midst of partless particles of water
- Air, due to the power and agitation of water in the form of great waves
- Fire, due to warmth preventing the lower regions of water from freezing and the rising of warmth causing the warmth of fire to emerge
- Moisture, as the defining characteristic of water

"Likewise, regarding air there are—
- Air, which is defined by lightness and motility
- Earth, in that air is present in the midst of partless particles
- Fire, in that heat evaporates the moisture of water
- Water, in that air is cold to the touch

"The essential nature of all of them is space, so all five elements are present in each one.

"In the one ultimate reality all five kinds of inner glow are present. Moreover, in each of the five transformations of inner glow into radiance, this set of five is complete, which indicates that the nature of one primordial consciousness appears in different aspects. Space appears as earth, [127] fire, water, air, and space. They all originate from space, so they are known as *elements*.

"Saṃsāra appears from the five aggregates in this way: With the entry of dualistic appearances into the domain of the primordial consciousness of the absolute space of phenomena, it appears as the aggregate of form. With the entrenchment of grasping and craving in mirror-like primordial consciousness, there is the aggregate of consciousness. With the entry of dualistic grasping into the primordial consciousness of equality, there is the aggregate of feeling. With the arising of clinging to reality in discerning primordial consciousness, there is the aggregate of recognition. With the entrenchment of clinging to reality in the primordial consciousness of accomplishment, it arises as the aggregate of compositional factors.

"In this way, the five aggregates result from the obscuration of the five essential natures. The five colors result from the obscuration of the five kinds of inner glow. The five elements result from the obscuration of the five facets of absolute space, and the five mental afflictions result from the obscuration of the five facets of primordial consciousness. In short, the formless realm is a result of the bondage imposed by grasping at the domain of the substrate; the form realm is a result of the entrenchment of grasping at the domain of the substrate consciousness. By achieving stability in the domain of mentation, you transmigrate as a deva of the desire realm. [128]

"Through the emergence of appearances by way of hatred, the phenomena of hell manifest; through the emergence of appearances by way of attachment, the phenomena of the preta realm arise; and through the emergence of appearances by way of delusion, phenomena of the animal realm appear. When even a little virtuous karma is mixed with dominant thoughts of envy, at the time of death, that karma is catalyzed by a similar kind of craving and grasping, and this creates the phenomena of the asura realm. Even though you have strived in the virtues by which merit is accumulated, under the causal influence of the mental afflictions known as the five poisons and the catalytic influence of a virtuous mind at the time of death, the phenomena of the human realm emerge. By the power of achieving stability in the virtue of a contaminated yet highly virtuous mind activated by the ignorance that is the basis of grasping at the 'I,' you transmigrate as a deva of the three realms, and those phenomena emerge. This is like the emergence of dream appearances.

"As for all the daytime and nighttime phenomena among such delusive appearances, in the expanse of phenomena of the physical worlds, there are diverse appearances of the sentient beings inhabiting them. Such beings are like their essence and vapor, with all their various forms, shapes, colors, sensory faculties, languages, species, and so forth. Three modes of appearances[80] manifest according to the degree of your virtue; [129] and in terms of residues, there are appearances of quintessences, residues, and that which is between.[81] By the activation of your motivation, the consequences of heavy,

80. The three modes of appearances are of one's environment (Tib. *gnas su snang ba*), sense objects (Tib. *don du snang ba*), and body (Tib. *lus su snang ba*) in any of the six states of existence.

81. The terms *quintessence* and *residue* appear in Tibetan medical texts describing the digestive process. Each stage of digestion divides the ingested food and drink into two parts, in

light, and intermediate nonvirtuous actions emerge and are experienced as all the miseries of the physical worlds and their sentient inhabitants.

"In the vast, immense expanse of radiant, clear mentation, free of contamination, like space, the six appearing objects of the sense fields emerge naturally. Apart from their demarcations by naming, there are no separate apertures of the senses that exist by their own characteristics. The continuous objects that present forms to radiant, clear mentation, together with the forms themselves, are called *visually perceived objects*. They are taken to be good, bad, and neutral; they are named, apprehended as objects of reference, and with subtle conceptualization they are viewed as truly existent things. In your mind, this is called *visual perception*. In reality, subtle and coarse types of mentation are called *visual perception* and *visually perceived objects*. These appearances are not objects. The planets and stars in the ocean are not the ocean. For just as there are no stars in the water, appearances are not the mind.[82] Just as no stars appear in the ocean apart from the ocean, there are no appearances apart from the mind. [130] As soon as an appearance arises as a dependently related event, it is not established as being real. Certainty about this is a key point.

"Therefore, if visual consciousness were form, form would not be other than visual consciousness; form and consciousness would be inseparable, such that no more than one form could ever arise. So form has no enduring presence, and from the very moment it appears, it vanishes into the space of awareness and then reappears in other indeterminate ways. When it transforms, this indicates no change apart from a period of unconsciousness with regard to the appearing object.

"For example, by means of coarse conceptualization, you know that you are walking. By means of subtle conceptualization, while you appear to be taking steps, with each step, the appearing earth, stones, mountains, caves, fruit trees, animals, and so on vanish into emptiness as soon as they appear. As these appearances successively arise and then vanish into emptiness, this subtle mental consciousness is called *grasping*.

- Such grasping is vital energy, so this is called *emanating vital energy*.
- Subtle vital energy transforms things, so this is called *transforming vital energy*.
- The body appears due to grasping at the self, called 'I,' and with the

---

an increasingly subtle progression. The subtler part is called the *nutritive aspect*, or *quintessence*, whereas the grosser part is called the *residue*.

82. The essential nature of appearances is the mind, the essential nature of the mind is awareness, and the essential nature of awareness is ultimate reality.

entrenched pride of ongoing appearances and consciousness, a kind of energy reifies the basis of appearances and the mind, so this is called *reifying vital energy*. [131]

- One kind of energy differentiates everything within the all-pervasive ground—as objects far and near and so forth—so this is called *differentiating vital energy*.
- One kind of energy dissolves all such mental states and appearances into the realm of the vacuous substrate, so this is called *destructive vital energy*.

"These five impure, saṃsāric vital energies are not different from mental consciousness and subtle ideation.

"Likewise, all objects that emerge as appearances of sounds in the realm of radiant, clear mentation are called *auditory consciousness*.[83] Coarse mental perceptions of objects variously emerging as appearances of sounds are called *perceived auditory objects*, and the subtle, conceptual mental consciousness that holds on to sounds is called *auditory perception*.

"Similarly, those objects that emerge as appearances of smells in the field of radiant, clear mentation are *olfactory consciousness*. Coarse mental perceptions of objects variously emerging as appearances of smells are called *objects perceived by olfactory consciousness*, and the subtle, conceptual mental consciousness that holds on to smells is called the *mind of olfactory perception*.

"Likewise, coarse mental perceptions emerging as gustatory objects, appearing as tastes and constituting the objects of emerging tastes, are called *objects perceived by gustatory consciousness*, [132] and the subtle, conceptual mental consciousness that holds on to good, bad, and neutral tastes is called the *mind of gustatory perception*.

"Similarly, coarse mental perceptions emerging as tactile objects are called *objects perceived by tactile consciousness*, and the subtle, conceptual mental consciousness that holds on to good, bad, and neutral tactile sensations is merely named the *mind of tactile perception*.

"You must know that there are no appearances other than these types of consciousness, and consciousness itself is not appearances. If consciousness were appearances, the mind would be dominated by the arising and passing of appearances; and when they vanished, the mind would also have to vanish. So appearances are not asserted to be the mind.

"If you think that they are other than the mind, then during the daytime,

83. The meaning here is not that objects themselves are consciousness, but rather that the potency that allows them to appear and be apprehended is consciousness.

nighttime, and the intermediate period, why do appearances continuously occur to the mind? There would be no reason why earlier appearances should cease and later appearances should arise. Therefore, appearances are not the mind, yet there are no appearances other than the mind. By ascertaining that no philosophical stance can be established for actual appearances, you are freed of all philosophical assertions. This is the meaning of appearances not being other than the mind.

"In this way, when all appearances and mindsets arise in their natural order, the whole of saṃsāra appears. [133] By reversing their natural order, they withdraw into the womb of the substrate, suddenly vanishing without the slightest trace. As for the individual names of the *doors of the senses*, they are so designated because even though there are no such doors, they appear to exist. Because the 'I' appears to have a body, six types of coarse appearing objects and mental consciousness are described. Beings are deceived because they appear to have sight, hearing, feeling, and experiencing through their individual sense apertures. So recognize the importance of knowing how this takes place.

"Appearances in dreams and in the intermediate period indicate that these appearances are not due to sense apertures. Even if your eyes are closed or you are blind, forms appear to mentation. Induced by conceptualization, sounds appear to mentation. Likewise, the mere appearances of all smells, tastes, and tactile sensations to the doors of sensory perception actually arise in mentation. The very nature of the sense doors reveals that they are none other than mentation.

"In general, outwardly, the object of ego-grasping is your personal identity. External appearances of the physical worlds, their sentient inhabitants, and the intervening appearances of the five sensory objects are all said to be *apprehended objects*. Inwardly, afflictive mentations are also called *apprehended objects*, and the mentation that holds on to objects is called the *apprehending mind*. [134] Secretly, mental consciousness is known as the *initial consciousness*. Due to contributing circumstances, it transforms into the nature of objects known as *apprehended objects*. That which names, grasps the referents of names, differentiates, and holds on to all good, bad, and indifferent things is known as the *apprehending mind*.[84] In reality, you must ascertain all the phenomena of saṃsāra and nirvāṇa as great emptiness. As a result of knowing this through investigation and analysis, great wisdom manifests. This is called *realization*.

"O Lord of Appearances, recognize that all phenomena are self-appearing! There is no wisdom other than this. Know that all of saṃsāra and nirvāṇa is

84. A single Tibetan term, *'dzin pa*, is here translated both as "grasp" and as "apprehend."

great emptiness! There is no realization apart from this knowledge. This is the direct vision of emptiness, and there is no meditation apart from this vision. This very luminosity that makes appearing objects manifest is said to be the *mind*, which by nature is *clear light*. Identifying this is called the *clear light of your own awareness*, and there is no unprecedented clear light apart from this. Apart from the realization of the great emptiness of saṃsāra and nirvāṇa, there is no so-called Madhyamaka.[85] Apart from the dissolution of the energy-mind into primordial consciousness in the great center, [135] in which the absolute space of the ground is actualized, there is no insertion of the energy-mind into the central channel.

"In the past, you have reified all of saṃsāra and nirvāṇa, the physical worlds, their sentient inhabitants, and sensory objects, for you were ignorant of how they are not established as being real. Now, apart from coming to rest in this reality through such knowledge, there is nothing else called *pristine awareness*. There is no so-called severance apart from severing your clinging to the appearances of the three realms [and releasing them] into identityless absolute space.

"This very ground of the three realms, which is ethically neutral, lucid, and clear, is called Īśvara Mahādeva. His body appears as the desire realm, his speech appears as the form realm, and his mind appears as the formless realm. The five sensory faculties emerge from the essential nature of his six types of consciousness. The eight classes of haughty gods and demons[86] emerge from the radiance of his eight types of consciousness. The higher classes of gods and demons emerge from the coarse arrays of his thoughts included among the 84,000 mental afflictions. *Vighnas*,[87] *grahas*,[88] demons, *rākṣasas*,[89] and *bhūtas*[90] emerge from the arrays of his subtle thoughts.

"The body, composed of the four elements, is maintained by flesh as earth,

85. Tib. *dbu ma*; Skt. *Madhyamaka*. The Middle Way, the higher of the two Mahāyāna schools in the sūtra system.

86. Tib. *dregs pa'i lha srin sde brgyad*; Skt. *aṣṭasenā*. These include devas, nāgas, yakṣas, asuras, gandharvas, garuḍas, kiṃnaras, and mahorāgas. The Tibetan has been corrected from *lha ma srin sde brgyad*.

87. Tib. *bgegs*. Lit. "obstructer," a being among the eighty thousand types of demons that obstruct the path to liberation; they are actually mere projections of thoughts of ego-grasping, craving, and attachment.

88. Tib. *gdon*. A malevolent, demonic being that torments one in lifetime after lifetime.

89. Tib. *srin po*. A wrathful emanation of good thoughts induced by ego-grasping.

90. Tib. *'byung po*. An "elemental" demonic force or being.

blood as water, warmth as fire, and breath as air. Empty space manifests as the mind, and embodiments of subtle arrays of thoughts emanate as various forms of sentient beings. [136] Therefore, the cause of this god is located in the substrates of sentient beings. Emptiness is apprehended as form, and form is brought to mind. By constantly invoking forms by name, in order to refresh your memory of them and not forget them, and by repeatedly imagining many such forms dissolving from the realm of the five elements, you achieve a little stability in these imagined objects. In doing so, mental forms are actually brought into being, just as you imagined them. As a consequence of grasping at empty space as real, the entire phenomenal universe is established in actuality. These are undoubtedly apparitions of one type of grasping.

"Actualizing a deity from a realm in which the deity is not established as being real is a result of the ignorance of your own ground acting as the cause of the entire realm of the deity. So with this very cause, the mind presents and imagines the deity as a form. As a result, it is really actualized in no more than two or three months. If there were some autonomous deity apart from this, it would be realized by anyone who invoked it. It is easy to determine that no one actualizes the deity other than the individual who has realized it. If there were no cause of a deity, it would not be actualized even if you tried. This can certainly be understood by taking a close look at mundane activities. Son of the family, the quintessence of the *Tantra of the Black Apparitions of Īśvara* [137] is none other than this. If this is not realized, even if you try to actualize a deity, it will be difficult to succeed. Know that your lack of success would be like that of a person shouting into an empty valley and counting the times he does so.

"Because the Black Protector Mahākāla is in control of the three realms, he is their basis. He is rich in his enjoyment of emanating the three realms of existence. The aspect of clarity of his nature is the great differentiation of saṃsāra and nirvāṇa. With innate, originally present primordial consciousness as the cause, the bodily aspect of the apparitional Black Protector Mahākāla appears and comes into existence. The realm of his speech consists of spontaneous displays. The realm of his mind is empty and clear. All the phenomena of the path and fruition emanate from the aspects of his virtuous qualities. The emanating appearances of all the Protector Father Tantras from the aspect of his enlightened activities are of the nature of skillful means. All the Goddess Mother Tantras emanate from the aspect of the wisdom of emptiness.

"Radiant, clear space itself is the Space Protector. The quintessence of earth is the Earth Protector. The quintessence of water is the Water Protector. The quintessence of fire is the Fire Protector. The quintessence of air is the Air Protector. The quintessence of the vital essence is the Vital Essence Protector. [138]

"All of these are emanated from the aspects of radiance and luminosity. The substrate consciousness, with its vacuous and clear nature, abides as the cause of everything that is emanated. The mind that emanates from this substrate consciousness presents forms, which are stabilized by a continuous stream of consciousness. Then you conceptually regard all the quintessences and vital essences of the physical worlds and their sentient inhabitants as *rūpakāyas*.[91] By meditating on them, their splendor and power grow. By invoking them by name, with unwavering mindfulness, signs of accomplishment will occur at least monthly. After only a year has passed, they will unquestionably be actualized in the fields of your sensory perception. Whatever deeds you perform, you are a *jñānasattva*,[92] and your actions will disband the foes of ignorance and grasping at the reality of appearances—so that they will vanish altogether.

"Because your essential nature is primordial consciousness, you are a jñānasattva, and because your form manifests as the aggregate of consciousness, you are a mundane being. So one half dwells in the essential nature of a jñānasattva, while the other half, in the nature of a mundane being, is presented as a glorious tantric protector who is actualized by the mind.[93] The *Tantra of the Enlightened Activity of the Black Protector* is none other than this. [139]

"The emanated apparition of the Black Protector—the great lord of the outer and inner elements, the embodiment of afflictive mentation—grasps at the reality of the elements in which the five poisons are equalized. By grasping at that which is nondual as being dual, it is he who differentiates the states of self and other.

"This is the way he abides: The faculty of pride that ultimately sees space as autonomous is the Space Rāhula. The faculty of delusion that sees earth as autonomous is the Earth Rāhula. The faculty of attachment that sees water as autonomous is the Water Rāhula. The faculty of hatred that sees fire as

91. Tib. *gzugs kyi sku*. A form embodiment of an enlightened being, including nirmāṇakāyas and saṃbhogakāyas.

92. Tib. *ye shes sems dpa'*. A "primordial-consciousness being" whom one invites and with whom one merges inseparably in the practice of the stage of generation.

93. When we are still involved in grasping, we are sentient beings; but when we are free of grasping, we are jñānasattvas.

autonomous is the Fire Rāhula. The faculty of envy that sees air as autonomous is the Air Rāhula.

"Their quintessences and vital essences are the cause of the movement and preservation of the flesh, blood, warmth, and breath of living beings; they are imagined as the embodiments of the five poisons. By bringing them to mind and repeatedly imagining countless numbers of them arising from their own respective elements and dissolving, their power increases; and while imagining yourself as a deity, they are actualized with unwavering consciousness. To stabilize this, you apply yourself to the mantra of invocation, focusing on your object of meditation without being distracted elsewhere. By doing so, before long you will experience them in actuality. [140] Then, by conceptually performing actions and consciously making them concrete, the great Rāhula—who is actualized from the apparitional thoughts of the deity, which are apprehended as a deity—will annihilate on the spot the enemies that arise from these apparitional thoughts. The *Tantra of the Aggregate of Contact of the Black Planetary Māra* is none other than this.

"Consciousness, which consumes the objects that appear and creates various apparitions, and appearances, which are of the nature of lucid, conscious awareness, exist by the power of profound skillful means and dependent relationships. They provide a bounty of enjoyments for the samaya-bound people who assault the enemies of the ten fields[94] and gain accomplishment. They gain mastery over all the elements, the physical worlds, and their sentient inhabitants of the three realms, and they are executioners who withdraw into absolute space the life and breath of the enemies of the teachings of secret mantra.

"They are red in color, for they have the quality of power. As a sign that they are involved in wrathful, violent activity, they have a black glow. The ten directional guardians appear from self-emergent consciousness that apprehends all the cardinal and intermediate directions and above and below. From the vital essence of consciousness appear the apparitions of the eight classes of violent *matta*s. The self-illuminating faculty of radiant, clear mentation [141] manifests everything. By accomplishing the assembly of dependent relationships through clear visualization of the meditative object, with

94. According to the tantras, enemies of the Dharma who are to be vanquished must have ten qualities, namely, that they: (1) destroy the Dharma, (2) disparage the Three Jewels, (3) rob the Saṅgha of its possessions, (4) revile the Mahāyāna, (5) harm the body of the guru, (6) denigrate their vajra siblings and so on, (7) obstruct others' Dharma practice, (8) are utterly devoid of love and compassion, (9) break their vows and samayas, and (10) hold false views regarding the laws of karma.

the power of stable apprehension as the cause, and with aggressive concentration as the contributing condition, you swiftly succeed in such practice. The *Tantra of the Butcher Marlen Yakṣa* is none other than this.

"The basis of emanation of all the eight classes of matta guardians of the teachings is the Black Planetary Māra, imbued with afflictive mentation. From his inner five elements, and with the power of the outer elements, the powerful red assembly is created and dwells in the warmth of the fire element. There are savage *tsens*[95] of the flesh who move in the warmth of the flesh. There are savage tsens of the blood who move in the warmth of the blood. There are savage tsens of the air who move in the warmth of the breath, and there are savage tsens who appear as the warmth of appearances. The domain of hatred in the mind consists of the savage tsens of the mind. The heat of fire appears from its radiance, and they are the red tsens of fire. Yellow tsens of earth move in the warmth of earth. White tsens of water move in the warmth of water. Green tsens of air move in the warmth of air. Indigo tsens of space move in the warmth of the sky.

"All these are apparitions of hatred that blaze like fire. They are all under the power of great emptiness, [142] which is the ground of the mind. Thus, absolute space is apprehended as form. Such form is created and meditated upon with continuous apprehending consciousness, and when stability is achieved, empty form is experientially actualized. As for the method to make the enemies and demonic forces that arise from the elements and derivative elements destroy themselves, the fire element is the cause, and the achievement of stability in the clear visualization of this is the contributing condition. From their dependent relationship, the classes of savage tsens arise, so that action will unquestionably be accomplished. The *Tantra of the Savage Tsen Blazing Like Fire* is none other than this.

"The apparitional Yamarāja, the Lord of Death, the embodiment of pride, is a being imbued with afflictive mentation who presents delusive appearances. As a wrathful apparition who pervades and enters the whole universe, he displays himself in phenomena. This is how he thoroughly enters the elements: The Fire Yama is present in earth in the midst of partless particles of fire. Earth is the Earth Yama in the aggregates of particles of earth. Water is the Water Yama, of the nature of earth, in the midst of partless particles. Air is the Air Yama, present as earth in the midst of partless particles. Space is called the Space Yama, for it appears as earth from the empty space of awareness. In the domain of the inner elements as well, all flesh, blood, warmth, and breath appear from the assembly of the nature of minute and partless particles, [143]

95. Tib. *btsan*. A type of evil demon.

so they are Yama. So grasping at the reality of appearances is called the Mind Yama. It is the Lord of Death who assembles the causes and conditions that dissolve appearances into absolute space.

"Like this, with pride as the cause and the mind as the contributing condition, you create these and meditate upon them. As a result of continuous consciousness, an unprecedented, sudden dependent relationship is brought about. The *Tantra of Wrathful Yama, Lord of Death* is none other than this.

"The emanation of Mahāviṣṇu, an apparition of the mental affliction of self-grasping, the embodiment of the violent vortex of envy, appears as the *yakṣa*[96] called Kālayakṣa. The Fire Yakṣa is the movement of the motile vital energy in the nature of fire. The Earth Yakṣa is the movement of the basic vital energy of grasping in the element of earth. The Water Yakṣa is the movement of the powerful, sucking vital energy in the element of water. The Air Yakṣa is the presence of the vital energy that moves and pulses in the air element. The Space Yakṣa is the movement of the obscuring vital energy in the element of space. These are the causes and conditions for accomplishing the yakṣas with practice.

"Likewise, all the inner yakṣas are the basic root of the appearances of outer elements that also appear internally as the five impure vital energies of saṃsāra. [144] They are the basis by which those who greatly desire wealth and prosperity accomplish this in the three realms. Since grasping is vital energy, if you call the vital energies yakṣas and increase them and generate them, this is thought to be especially effective in performing enriching activity. If you don't practice, you won't succeed, but if you do generate them and practice with clarity and stability, it will bring success. The *Tantra of the Treasury of the Black Yakṣa* is none other than this.

"Likewise, emanations who present all manner of appearances, the embodiments of attachment, who, like water, create upheavals, are the *mātṛkās*;[97] and these lords of attachment who totally pervade the psycho-physical aggregates, elements, and sense bases are the inner mātṛkās. The moisture present in the earth element is the great Earth Mātṛkā. The water present in the fire element is the great Fire Mātṛkā. The moisture present in the water element is the great Water Mātṛkā. The coolness present in the air element is the water of air, and this is the great Air Mātṛkā. The appearance of space as water is the great Space Mātṛkā. By the practice of creating and meditating on the causal

96. Tib. *gnod sbyin*. A type of malevolent nonhuman being belonging to the eight classes of gods and demons.

97. Tib. *ma mo*. A being who takes on all kinds of forms and is an embodiment of disturbing attachments.

appearances of all the faculties and sense bases existing by their own characteristics, the mātṛkās appear even though they do not exist. By conceptually creating and meditating on them, you will succeed in the activity of annihilating all appearing enemies and malevolent beings. The *Tantra of the Display of the Ocean of Blood of the Black Mātṛkā* is none other than this.[98] [145]

"The emanation of the wrathful, untamed Viṣṇu, imbued with afflictive mentation, the natural glow of the darkness of ignorance and delusion, is called the Nine-Headed Nāgamāra Lord of Death. The apparition created from the power of generating and meditating on this being brings forth ignorance that pervades and enters everything. This is how it is done: Ignorance of the state of emptiness of all the inner elements is the Inner Nāga. Ignorance of the identitylessness of fire is the Fire Nāgamāra. Ignorance of the empty nature of earth is the Earth Nāgamāra. Ignorance of the state of emptiness of water is the Water Nāgamāra. Ignorance of the state of emptiness of air is the Air Nāgamāra. Ignorance of the empty state of space is called the Space Nāgamāra. They are all causal ignorance, and by the contributing power of focusing on them and creating them, they are actualized. Apart from this, there is nothing whatsoever called a *nāga*. The *Tantra of the Black Darkness of Nāgas* is none other than this.

"*Pārthivas*[99] emerge from the aggregates of grasping at the 'I.' They are the conceptual mental factors that grasp at the reality of appearances. There are pārthivas who maintain the five elements as flesh, pārthivas who maintain the five elements as blood, pārthivas who maintain the five elements as warmth, pārthivas who maintain the five elements as the breath, pārthivas who maintain the five elements as earth, [146] pārthivas who maintain the five elements as water, pārthivas who maintain the five elements as fire, pārthivas who maintain the five elements as air, and pārthivas who maintain the five elements as space. Thus, all the outer and inner pārthivas are included in each of the five elements, and the appearance of them as a single entity is the cause of all the classes of pārthivas. The pārthivas and *vigrahas*[100] are created by conceptually focusing on them. By meditating on them, the

98. The tantras cited here are found in the *Canon of Nyingma Tantras* (Tib. *Rnying ma'i rgyud 'bum*). This discussion simply explains how all these entities are created by the mind, without detailing the practices for accomplishing mundane siddhis by sublimating these beings.

99. Tib. *rgyal po.* A demonic force or being that emerges from the aggregates of grasping at the "I" and consists of the conceptual mental factors that reify appearances, which arise as apparitions of ignorance.

100. Tib. *'gong po.* A demonic force or being that arises as a projection of hatred.

contributing conditions appear for this cause.[101] The *Tantra of the Pārthivas' Assemblage of the Elements* is none other than this.

"The white Devamāra, the Lord of Pleasure, draws you to beautifully appearing objects such as form, sound, smell, taste, and tactile sensations. As Mahāviṣṇu he is the cause of a vicious great māra, who is an emanation of afflictive mentation. Surrounded by the assembly of subtle and coarse afflictive thoughts, this Māra of the Afflictions with unimpeded power leads beings astray to the miserable states of existence. The great Māra of the Aggregates, as the limited sense faculties, leads beings to the good, bad, and neutral objects that manifestly appear.

"The black, arrogant Māra of Death brings about clinging to appearances with various sorts of delusion in the darkness of ignorance, and he steals away the vitality of liberation and omniscience. [147] Moving among and pervading the five elements, the self-destroying Lord of Māras known as the Long Arm of Grasping arises as wild, vicious objects. In order to preserve the cause of all such māras and to actualize those that have not been actualized, these objects are clearly brought to mind. Imputing them with the intellect, you accomplish vividness and stability with a continuous stream of consciousness. You seal this with mindfulness, without letting the mind become distracted elsewhere. By invoking them by name, the simultaneous assembly of dependent events of the catalyst of immutable mindfulness empirically actualizes the mattas. The *Tantra of the Black Māra Who Obscures Like Darkness* is none other than this.

"Apparitions of the faculties of emanations of afflictive mentation and so on attract you to enjoyments and desirable objects, and by clinging to appearances, the Mahādeva Hṛiṣīkeśa is manifested in your thoughts. As he roves in the domain of the inner elements, he creates the taste of pleasure and causes it to be experienced. Roving in the domain of the five outer elements, he creates desirable objects. With the cause of the deva, the contributing condition of the diligent practice of generating him by visualizing him [148] experientially actualizes this dependently related event. The *Tantra of the Illusory Creations of Enjoyments of the Mahādeva Hṛiṣīkeśa* is none other than this.

"If you do not know how to actualize the proud guardians of the doctrine by the power of the dependent relationship of their causes and contributing conditions, and if you do not know this tantra for their creation, even if mattas were substantiated, you would not be able to set them to tasks. Even if you actualized them, they would not obey you. Regardless of how much you made offerings and supplications to them, the flow of their malice would not

101. This phrase means that the contributing conditions interact with the primary cause.

stop. Even if you set them on your enemies, your own life would be at risk, and your path to liberation would be blocked. At the beginning, middle, and end, there would be no constancy, and various good and bad things would happen. Therefore, this most sublime of all tantras of generation, exceptionally profound for transforming all practices into primordial consciousness, is the unsurpassed essence of all practices. Why? By recognizing everything as being none other than your own appearances, you achieve great mastery over the vitality of saṃsāra and nirvāṇa.

"For example, when the one moon in the sky is eclipsed by Rāhula, every single reflection of the moon in every body of water is eclipsed. Likewise, from the jinas, the perfected buddhas, down to māras, rākṣasas, and *rūdras*,[102] all of saṃsāra and nirvāṇa is of the same taste in the absolute space of Samantabhadra, the original ground dharmakāya. [149] For people who know this and ascertain it, all beings from the five families of buddhas down to subtle demons and rākṣasas are ascertained solely as jñānasattvas who are none other than displays of Samantabhadra. Individuals who establish devas by making them autonomous—by grasping at objects as existing by their own characteristics—will actually realize only mundane beings; it is certain that not even one will be a jñānasattva.

"Therefore, knowing this tantra for the generation of mattas in general is the cause for establishing them as jñānasattvas—regardless of the deva you actualize—and the means of swift success will be within you. Moreover, the deva who is your own creation will be under the mastery of your own ground; and the devas, who are established as apparitions imputed by conceptualization upon appearing objects, will unquestionably accomplish enlightened activities in an instant. Within these displays, they cannot inflict harm. Devas, who are actualized with vivid, stable, manifest consciousness, kill enemies and demons that arise from the potency of thoughts. No karma or karmic consequences arise from such deeds.

"All the devas and guardians who are worshiped and actualized in these ways were not established as being real from the beginning; they have never existed, and they have none of the fundamental roots of arising, abiding, or departing. The cause that makes what does not exist appear to exist is present in your own mindstream. [150] By the power of generating them and

102. The text uses the Sanskrit term *rūdra*. A meditator takes birth as a rūdra, a type of demon, by firmly and clearly visualizing himself or herself as a wrathful deity—while having no realization of emptiness and no motivation of compassion. It can also mean the conceptual grasping by which one reifies the distinctions of outer, inner, and secret phenomena.

meditating on them as forms and as entities with signs, they are experientially actualized. While all physical worlds, their sentient inhabitants, and all sensory objects are originally free of any fundamental basis and not established as being real, the entire phenomenal world with all its sensory objects is made to appear directly and is illuminated by mentation. It is imputed by the intellect and tenaciously grasped by conceptualization as being real. In this way it is brought forth and actualized as if it were truly existent. Know this to be so.[103]

"Owing to the obscuration by ignorance of the original, primordial ground, all the qualities of the appearances of the ground are hidden within. Appearances of its radiance that arise as truly existent from the side of the appearances are skillful means. The nothingness from the side of emptiness is wisdom. The union of the divine father and mother is the ultimate path, ultimate reality, which is none other than nonconceptual primordial consciousness, and it arises from the dependently related assemblage of causes and contributing conditions.

"In this way, generate the power of meditation; lay out the collection of offerings, which are like illusory substances; recite the increasing mantra, which is like an illusory mantra; and display and visualize these offerings as objects to the six senses, like illusory apparitions. [151] Until these sensory objects are dissolved back into absolute space, visualize inexhaustible sensory objects as a treasury of space. This is called the *illusory apparition of samādhi*, and it is unsurpassed, the greatest of all offerings and gifts. Symbolically, this is like the displays of enjoyments of Nirmāṇarati.[104]

"Take the analogy of a person caught up in a dream in which he experiences only misery, with no enjoyment whatsoever. While in that state, someone forcefully awakens him, transforming his appearances and revealing all manner of wonderful things, bringing him to a state of happiness. Like this, you transform the appearances of the offerings and gifts, emanating these sensory objects as a treasury of space. In the expanse of the six lucid, clear, uncontaminated faculties of all the recipients of offerings and gifts, which are like a body of water, the power of the dependently related causes and contributing conditions of the sensory objects, mantras, and samādhi emanates

103. Realize the nature of all guardians, demons, and gods as projections of your own mind. Then realize the nature of your own mind to be awareness, and the nature of awareness to be the sugatagarbha. By thus realizing all of saṃsāra and nirvāṇa to be of the same nature, it is easy to accomplish all mundane and supermundane siddhis.

104. Tib. *'phrul dga'.* The penultimate heaven in the desire realm, where devas enjoy their own manifestations unthreatened by asuras.

them. Recognize them as being like the sudden appearance of reflections of the planets and stars.

"These crucial points are the unsurpassed realm of experience of people who directly see the nature of existence of ultimate reality. [152] Those who do not know this are merely playing children's games with all their acts of offering and giving, and they will not succeed in their true aims. So be like an illusionist and project an illusion-like feast of sensory objects and enjoyments to the recipients of these offerings and gifts, who are like the illusionist's audience, pleasing the recipients of the offerings and gifts. Finally, as the illusory creation dissolves into absolute space, likewise, the agent, act, and object of the act are left in the expanse of nonobjective absolute space. This is the samādhi of ultimate reality manifesting as illusions.

"The causes of the collection of merit are accumulated by the mind, and the resultant great collection of knowledge perfectly manifests as awareness. So without mental projection, the collection of merit is not perfected, which is not pleasing to the recipients of the offerings. Even if you dedicate something as a ransom to demons or to help the deceased, the debt is not paid off, for it is impossible to dispel the various torments of suffering. When the demons that are brought into existence from conceptual grasping at demons appear as your enemies, it is as if you kill yourself with your own weapons. Therefore, observe how all ritual activities of subjugating demons, protecting the living, and guiding the deceased are impotent, and recognize the importance of abandoning activities that fail, in this and future lives. [153]

"Yogins who realize the nature of ultimate reality, suchness, strive to accomplish the welfare of themselves and others, but it is definitely through the strength of the blessings of the samādhi of the illusory displays of ultimate reality that they succeed without difficulty."

The Profound Practice of the Severance of Māras

Lord of Appearances then asked, "O Bhagavān, what kind of things need to be known by people who engage in the profound practice of the severance of māras? May the Teacher explain!"

He replied, "O Lord of Appearances, the profound wisdom of realizing identitylessness is called the *object of the severance of māras*. Here is what needs to be known in this regard: First of all, it is the causal ignorance of yourself alone that obscures your own face as the dharmakāya. Once the consciousness of grasping at the 'I' has arisen, that which is not a body appears as a body. The very firm, dense consciousness of obsessive grasping apprehends this body as yourself, and it devotedly guards the body and holds on to all manner of hopes, fears, pleasures, and pains. Delusion in saṃsāra is such that even when you are merely dreaming, you obsessively grasp at this body, [154] and for the sake of its sustenance, pleasure, and beauty, you are tightly bound and totally ensnared by various emotions of attachment and hatred. As a result, you are deluded endlessly in saṃsāra, and [such objects of attachment and hatred] become māras, vighnas, demons, and grahas.

"Thinking that they are threatening your physical survival, they are feared as enemies. When they appear to be robbing you of possessions and enjoyments, hatred arises toward them. With the appearance of physical illness and discomfort, fear of demons arises. With the desire for bodily well-being, hopeful thoughts arise for all good things; and fearing harm to your body, fear arises toward all bad things. When illness strikes the body, the mind is distressed by the body. When appearances of hunger and thirst arise in the body, the mind is distressed by them. When heat and cold arise in the body, the mind is distressed by them. When pleasurable or painful conditions emerge regarding the body, the mind is drawn to disagreeable objects and is tormented with suffering. In all your lifetimes, apart from rare occasions of unconsciousness, the mind accompanies this defiled, closely held body as if it were its shadow, so the body is the basis for various types of suffering. [155]

"All objects that are sources of hope are called the *higher māras* of hope for the positive, and all fears are called the *lower māras* of fear of the negative. Therefore, the foundation of saṃsāra and the miserable states of existence is obsessive grasping at your body. A way to sever such obsessive grasping is to regard this body as being like a corpse, consciousness as the corpse-bearer, craving as the rope, haunted places as charnel grounds, and gods and demons as birds and carnivores. In these five ways you practice generosity.

"This is to be known at all times and in every situation: You spend your life clothing this body with beautiful, warm garments and supplying it with tasty, nutritious food. Toward this end, you take on hardships, think nothing of fatigue, and shoulder a great burden of suffering. While ignoring the causes of lasting joy and their consequences, you strive diligently and without satisfaction. In the end, the flesh between your skin and bones withers away, and your skin becomes covered with wrinkles. Your legs and arms become like sticks, your complexion deteriorates, and you take on the color of a rotten, moldy corpse. [156] Your chest and spine become crooked like stairsteps. Your dark hair becomes white. Your teeth fall out and your mouth caves in. Your eyes grow dim and you cannot see your way. It becomes difficult to get up, as if you were hoisting a corpse; and it becomes difficult to sit still, as if you were carrying a burden. Your intestines rumble from indigestion. Unable to quench your thirst, you need to urinate frequently.

Disturbed by a blizzard-like barrage of all such pains and miseries, there will come a time when not a trace of joy remains. Then this body cannot be sustained even with care, nor can it be protected. Repeatedly ponder the pointlessness of striving for the sake of this body.

"In general, demons are devourers, for they consume the fruits of omniscience; *vadhakas*[105] are murderers, for they display birth and death within saṃsāra. They cut off your vitality, for they sever the artery of liberation; they take away your breath, for they steal the breath of happiness. The myriad demons of mundane existence are so designated because they cause the coming into being of saṃsāra that has not yet come into being. The ten grahas are so designated because they torment you in lifetime after lifetime. The *hāriṇīs*[106] are so designated because they steal your collections of merit and knowledge.

"Nāgas, grahas, and *kṣamāpatis*[107] are the delusions produced by the causes and conditions of ignorance. Male grahas, pārthivas, and vigrahas are apparitions of hatred toward other objects. [157] Female grahas and demonesses are apparitions of attachment toward sensually pleasing phenomena. The eighty thousand types of vighnas are so designated because they obstruct the path to liberation. Village demons and village *gyuks*[108] are so designated because they dwell in the village of the five aggregates. *Seraks*[109] are so designated for they have no contentment or satisfaction. *Damsis*[110] are so designated for they cause you to transgress your samayas. All grahas, vighnas, *vināyakas*,[111] and bhūtas are assembled in this very body—they do not exist anywhere else. Upon examining this condition, sever obsessive grasping. To counteract such craving, recognize the importance of dedicating yourself to giving away your body.

"Then, with regard to recognizing the body, inwardly it is an illusory body that is defiled and closely held. Between the internal and external, it is an

105. Tib. *gshed.* Lit. "executioner," a demonic being that displays the appearances of birth and death within saṃsāra.

106. Tib. *'phrog ma.* A malevolent demonic being.

107. Tib. *sa bdag.* An earth spirit whose actual nature is that of delusions produced by the causes and conditions of ignorance.

108. Tib. *rgyug.* A village spirit.

109. Tib. *bse rag.* A type of preta that consumes the vital essence of food and wealth.

110. Tib. *dam sri.* A "samaya demon," which has taken on such rebirth due to transgressing the samayas of secret mantra.

111. Tib. *log 'dren.* A malevolent demon that arises from negative thoughts.

illusory body of delusive appearances of sensory objects. Externally it is an illusory body of tangible appearances of the elements. The essential nature of all these is emptiness. Since the conscious awareness that reifies that which is empty is the mind, the mind is transferred to absolute space.[112] Once your body has turned into a corpse, then you recognize that the self, who does this, is like an illusionist.

"Having recognized that objects of generosity are like an emanated, illusory gathering, for the white feast, the corpse transforms into the three white and the three sweet offerings. [158] For the mixed feast, the corpse is imagined as a splendid array of various desirable things and is then offered. As for the red feast, imagine the corpse as an offering of flesh, blood, bones, marrow, and fat. For the black offerings, imagine it as black fluid to purify illnesses, grahas, vices, and obscurations. Perform these offerings at the four times.

"At all times and in all situations, use all anxieties and doubts as the cutting edge of your practice. Directly embrace all undesirable circumstances, such as illness and suffering, and rejoice. It is a crucial point to be able to train earnestly in the attitude of taking the sufferings of others upon yourself and giving them your happiness.[113] Then, by going to all the places that are inhabited by demons, directly embrace all discursive thoughts and diligently train in the key points of practice.

"The outer upheavals of gods and demons are originally nonexistent. However, rejoice if the gods and demons conjured up by thoughts or illusory apparitions appear like a vulture dismembering a corpse. When the inner upheavals of physical pain and discomfort occur, rejoice as if you were a beggar who has obtained food and wealth, [159] thinking and saying, 'May many more such things continue to happen!' Moreover, when the secret upheavals of mental joy and happiness occur, immediately cut through attachment and craving. As soon as any sort of suffering or unhappiness occurs, by directly severing hope and fear, rejoice. The most essential point is to dismiss such attitudes by thinking, 'I cannot bear it any longer if this body is not taken away.' Recognize that these three are the outer, inner, and secret upheavals.

"Think that 'When this body turns into a corpse, whether it is incinerated, thrown into a river, or buried underground, all my efforts and all the difficulties I have undergone on its behalf will be in vain. What a great waste! It is

112. That is, the mind is separated from the body and departs in the form of a primordial consciousness ḍākinī.

113. Tib. *gtong len*. Lit. "giving and taking," this refers to the exchange of self and others in order to reduce self-cherishing and cultivate bodhicitta, practiced by giving others your happiness with the out breath and taking on their sufferings with the in breath.

best to give away this body, which is my most prized possession in the world. Now, why couldn't I disengage from this basis of saṃsāra and the miserable states of existence and proceed onward to the citadel of great liberation!' In this way apply yourself to the profound practice of the severance of māras. If you do not properly comprehend this critical point, the practice called severance will be nothing more than oral recitation and noisemaking with a drum and bell.

"First of all, correctly establish and realize the nature of profound emptiness, [160] which is the basis of severance. This is something you must know. Arriving at the realization of the meaning of the consummation of all of saṃsāra and nirvāṇa as the perfectly pure space of reality is the ultimate, supreme goal. The *Tantra of the Profound Practice of the Severance of Māras* is none other than this."

Phase 4: Determining the Characteristics and Qualities of the Ground

Emptiness as the Universal Foundation of All Yānas

THEN Bodhisattva Vajra of Pristine Awareness rose from his seat and said to the Bhagavān, "O Teacher, Bhagavān, how excellent! Is it true or not that simply by knowing one's own nature, called the *Great Perfection of empty awareness*, and knowing that all the phenomena in the universe are by nature not established as real, as well as knowing their empty status and origination, one has certainty regarding this yāna? Teacher, please explain!"

He replied, "O Vajra of Pristine Awareness, knowing the way of emptiness in which all phenomena are by nature not established as real is the great, universal foundation of all the yānas, and not of just one yāna alone. All meditations performed by those who do not know this may constitute mental virtue, but such meditations do not bring them even a hair's breadth closer to the path of liberation. Therefore, the sublime quintessence of the teachings of all the buddhas is the revelation that all phenomena—from form up to the omniscient mind—are emptiness, [161] and this is called the *universal foundation of all the yānas.*

"This view is the indispensable, great, fundamental ground of all paths. Due to the specific paths that accord with individuals of superior, middling, and lesser faculties—which, in turn, are due to their constitutions and the functioning of their senses—many sorts of yānas are revealed. By knowing, just as it is, the way in which the Great Perfection abides as the ground and fruition of all the yānas, you will arrive at the nature of the absolute ground.

"The essential nature of existence is like this: It is the great nature that is baseless from the root, the uniform pervasiveness of the sphere of space, a nonobjective, unimpeded display. This is the great, original nature, free from all faults, stains, and habitual propensities. In terms of external objects, there is no buddha other than this. Taking into account the many vast, inconceivable buddhas throughout the full extent of space, if all their facets of primordial consciousness and sublime qualities were to be applied to improve this ground, they would not enhance it in the slightest. [162] Why not? Because there is no object to be enhanced.

"See that in the unimpeded space of the dharmakāya, no buddha in the past has wandered in saṃsāra. Except for the delusion that what does not exist appears to exist, there is not a single sentient being. Even if all the vices, obscurations, and miseries of the infinite, limitless sentient beings throughout the whole of space were assembled and used in an attempt to harm the unimpeded primordial ground of space, know that not even the slightest bit of harm could be inflicted, for this ground is not established as being objectively real. Saṃsāra merely appears from the grasping of consciousness, but it is not established as real, while the ground of original purity is unwaveringly flawless.

"First of all, by examining the location of birth and the one who is born, you ascertain that they do not exist in the past or the future, nor is there birth in the present. The one who is born and this person's location do not exist anywhere, so the ground is free from the extreme of birth. Likewise, cessation does not exist in the past or the future, nor does it exist in the present. Seeing that the one who has ceased is also nonobjective, the ground is free from the extreme of cessation.

"Either annihilation is nothing or, [163] if it is examined, it is the ground of both the appearances of impure saṃsāra and all the pure facets of primordial consciousness and qualities of the buddhas. Since these are not baseless, the ground is free from the extreme of nihilism. Under analysis, if existent phenomena were found to be permanent, they should be directly visible to the eyes and ultimately graspable with the hands. But since even the eyes of the buddhas do not see them, the ground is free from the extreme of permanence.

"If you examine where you come from and the one who is coming, you see that they are neither in the past nor the future. They should be determined by direct valid perception in the present, but the agent who comes and the entire environment are nonobjective. So the ground is free from the extreme of coming. When examining where you go and the one who is going, they, too, are not observed in the past or in the future. In the present, this directly verifiable entity is seen to be nonobjective. So the ground is free from the extreme of going.

"To examine the ground in terms of diversity, since all phenomena are of one taste, without differentiation, in the absolute space of the ground sugatagarbha, the ground is free from the extreme of diversity. To examine the ground in terms of unity, all the phenomena included within saṃsāra and nirvāṇa appear individually, with their own unique features, so the ground is free from the extreme of unity. [164]

"As an analogy for those two, if you check to see whether the unimaginable planets and stars that appear in the ocean are different from it, you find that not even a single particle of these stars exists apart from the ocean. If you consider them to be identical, you find that they appear individually without merging together. Accordingly, come to the conclusion of disengaging from all philosophical assertions.

"Due to the fact that all phenomena arising as dependently related events are nonexistent and not established as real, they are totally free of the eight extremes of conceptual elaboration.[114] If you adopt a position that falls to an extreme, with factional, errant views, you have strayed an immeasurable distance from the state of buddhahood. Such a person wanders around dazed in the midst of a dark jungle, far from the path to liberation.

"The originally pure primordial protector, the Omnipresent Lord and Immutable Sovereign, the sugatagarbha, Samantabhadra, is of the nature of perfect liberation. Examining and analyzing all external appearances, they are found to be the emptiness of not being established as substances, the emptiness of not being established as signs, and the emptiness of not being established as real. Examining and analyzing your own mind internally, it is found to be a nonobjective openness without any ground, pervasive ultimate reality without any root, [165] and free of all extremes of conceptual elaboration: this is inner emptiness. Examining the intermediate mode of existence of both appearances and the mind, they are found to be undifferentiated from the great, nondual single taste. Appearing from yourself and dissolving into yourself, the mind and appearances are neither conjoined nor separated. This nature of emptiness, which cannot be eliminated, is called *emptiness as the door of liberation*.

"Ground awareness, the great liberation from extremes, cannot be revealed with words, for it transcends anything that can be articulated. It is incomparable and transcends all partial extremes, so it cannot be indicated with any analogy. It transcends all conceptual objects of the intellect, so it cannot be pointed to with any referent. In this way you come upon ultimate reality, the self-emergent nature, primordially at rest and free of clinging to experience. This is *the absence of signs as the door of liberation*.

"The ground, the ultimate nature of mind, the primordial Buddha Samantabhadra, the great, pervasive lord of all of saṃsāra and nirvāṇa, knows its own essential nature and is naturally liberated within itself. Thus, no matter what you do to enhance this ground by way of physical, verbal, and mental striving stemming from the natural perfection of the displays of the kāyas

114. Tib. *spros pa'i mtha'a brgyad.* The philosophical assertions of origination, cessation, existence, nonexistence, coming, going, diversity, and unity.

and facets of primordial consciousness, this does not benefit it in the slightest. Even if this ground wished to go from this location to some other realm, [166] when you perceive the fact that the great realm of pervasive space is free of all going and coming in the three times, you certainly do not yearn for that situation. This is *the absence of desire as the door of liberation*. These are the characteristics of the nature of the ground, the original Great Perfection."

Then Bodhisattva Vajra of Pristine Awareness asked, "O Teacher, Bhagavān, if the facets of primordial consciousness and enlightened qualities eventually arise from this ground, which is the original dharmakāya and the nature of Samantabhadra, and if origination and accomplishment do not exist, since all sentient beings are none other than buddhas—how does one distinguish between buddhas and sentient beings? Teacher, please explain!"

He replied, "O Vajra of Pristine Awareness, in a state of ignorance, the ground becomes ethically neutral, not helped or impaired by positive qualities—like a drawing of a lamp. Here are examples of the way sentient beings are deluded: mistaking a boulder for a deer, a pile of stones for a human, or a striped rope for a snake, and mistaking silver for zinc, gold for pyrite, or a gem for an ordinary rock. When you know the nature of the ground, the primordial Great Perfection of enlightened qualities, [167] you realize that appearances have no true existence. This is like ascertaining that the boulder is not a deer, like rejecting the perception of a mirage as water or of a pile of stones as a human, and like rejecting the perception of a striped rope as a snake. Just as you recognize these as mistakes, you reject the delusive clinging of grasping at reality and realize that things are identityless. Then the ascertainment of the ground as nonobjective great openness is the essential nature of meditation.

"The superiority of this realization over the mundane view of sentient beings is like recognizing gold and silver, so that they manifest as a treasure, and like recognizing a gem for what it is, after mistaking it for an ordinary rock. This recognition is called the *wisdom of realization*. Far surpassing that of sentient beings, this wisdom rots the seeds of mundane existence. Other analogies for the destruction of mundane existence by wisdom include water saturated by salt, camphor dispersed by wind, and ice melted by warmth. Like these analogies, you should know the way mundane existence is shredded."

Bodhisattva Vajra of Pristine Awareness asked, "O Teacher, Bhagavān, can one become a buddha simply by knowing the essential nature of the ground, [168] without needing to meditate? Teacher, please explain!"

He replied, "O Vajra of Pristine Awareness, if you do not know the essential nature of the ground, you will not become enlightened. Therefore, the body of knowledge of the intermediate teachings,[115] namely, the *Dharma without characteristics*, reveals that all phenomena—ranging from form up to the omniscient mind—are of the nature of emptiness. Without knowing this, you will not be liberated, which is why the 6,400,000 sets of tantras of the Great Perfection were revealed. Be aware that if you could become enlightened without needing to know this, there would be no need for these teachings.

"Even if you know the emptiness of your own mind but do not know the emptiness of all three realms of the physical worlds and their sentient inhabitants, you have not realized anything more than personal identitylessness—so you have not surpassed the Śrāvakayāna. Even though you know that all physical worlds and their sentient inhabitants are empty from their own side, if you do not deduce their essential nature as emptiness and know the ground to be emptiness, then emptiness is reduced to an ethically neutral state—and no benefit is derived.

"Even if you know emptiness, you might think that it has no good or bad qualities and that enlightened qualities and activities must stem from somewhere else. [169] Understanding emptiness to be the emptiness of a vessel and enlightened qualities and activities to be its contents, you might assert that enlightened activities enter into it from somewhere else. In that case, some other wealthy benefactor of enlightened activities, a donor who fills up that vessel, would have to exist somewhere else. So if it were possible for the buddha of that place to exist as someone permanent, stable, and immutable, he would not be empty. If emptiness were an absence of matter, with no good or bad qualities, this would falsely imply that all the phenomena and sensory objects of the physical worlds and their sentient inhabitants appearing throughout this life, in the dream state, and following this life are self-emergent and self-sufficient; and the appearances and mind of saṃsāra would be established as real. When you know the nature of this and achieve penetration, appearances manifest as displays of the kāyas and facets of primordial consciousness. Due to this transmutation, the state of buddhahood becomes manifest and the aspects of its enlightened qualities are naturally perfected.

"Many people may apprehend space as an absence of materiality without any good or bad qualities. Nevertheless, since space is the ground and essential nature of the five elements and the various sensory objects, why should you believe it to be an absence of materiality with no good or bad qualities? There are no appearing objects other than space, [170] and if you grasp at space as something autonomous, there is no point in asserting saṃsāra and

115. This refers to the second of the three turnings of the Wheel of Dharma.

nirvāṇa to be great emptiness. If there were something on which to meditate other than the manifestations of the realm of pervasive space, what would be the point of speaking of *no meditation*, *no reference*, and *no grasping*? The essential nature of the subject of meditation is emptiness, and if this is not recognized, your meditation with no view is reduced to something ethically neutral. So how could that possibly be genuine meditation?

"If you fail to recognize and understand saṃsāra and nirvāṇa as self-appearing displays, what is the point of identifying pristine awareness? Realization is establishing that ultimately saṃsāra and nirvāṇa are of the nature of great emptiness, and then recognizing and ascertaining everything to be of the nature of one space. Just this is the view.

"O Vajra of Pristine Awareness, by knowing this, thoroughly fathoming it, gaining conviction, and then earnestly applying yourself to the practice of meditation, you finally reach the state of liberation. This is the sublime key to practice. By comparison, if having mere intellectual knowledge were enough, without any need to meditate, then all the yogins, vidyādharas, and *mahāsiddhas*[116] [171] of the past who practiced meditation on the basis of realization, while courageously taking on hardships, would have been wasting their time. On the contrary, know that it is necessary to apply yourself to the essential practice of meditating on the basis of realization.

"The reduction of the inwardly present ground to an ethically neutral state is like the sky covered with darkness, while manifest ground pristine awareness is like the dawn breaking and the sun rising. Being ignorant of the ground is like having no master for an entire kingdom. Identifying manifest pristine awareness for yourself is like a poor person without any status or possessions being enthroned as a king and enjoying royal privileges. Being obscured by dualistic grasping and ignorance of the ground, the primordial Great Perfection, you experience endless suffering in saṃsāra because of this obscuration. This is like being a wealthy person who is imprisoned by a king or an enemy and suffers from starvation, thirst, torture, and a terrible environment for a long time. Finally, identifying pristine awareness so that it becomes manifest is like that person being freed from prison, dwelling in his own home, [172] and experiencing joy and happiness. Pristine awareness is far, far superior to the ethically neutral ground.

"As an analogy for the presence of the ground as ethically neutral, imagine that a person is afflicted with a disease, and right under his bed is a

116. Tib. *sgrub chen*. A "great adept," who has accomplished mundane and supermundane abilities and realizations.

medicine endowed with eight excellent qualities.[117] But since he does not recognize it, he is tormented for a long time by his terrible illness. Then, after some time he recognizes it as a healing medicine and ingests it, and consequently his disease is cured and he is restored to good health. Similarly, once you have truly realized the essential nature of the ground, manifest pristine awareness apprehends its own state for itself. Consequently, the great, chronic disease of saṃsāra is cleared out altogether, and you are brought to a state of eternal bliss.

"Even if you have identified pristine awareness that is present in the ground, there is no benefit if you do not sustain it. Even though you may have gold in hand, if you do not trade it for food and clothing, but instead use it as a pillow, you will die of starvation and exposure to the elements. Reducing pristine awareness that has been identified to an ethically neutral state is just like that. Even if you recognize a wish-fulfilling jewel for what it is, no siddhis are granted if you do not treat it with respect. Reducing pristine awareness that has been identified to an ethically neutral state is just like that. Even though you have beautiful, warm clothing, if you do not wear it, [173] you will die from the cold and wind. Reducing pristine awareness that has been identified to an ethically neutral state is just like that. Even though you live in a house with plenty of food, you will die of starvation if you do not eat it. Reducing pristine awareness that has been identified to an ethically neutral state is just like that. Recognize that the crucial point is to practice after acquiring knowledge and realization."

Bodhisattva Vajra of Pristine Awareness then asked, "O Teacher, Bhagavān, so it is. Is there any difference between a deluded individual who has identified pristine awareness and one who has not?"

He replied, "O son of the family, there is no difference between a person who knows the route taking the wrong trail and another person who does not know the route taking the wrong trail. There is no difference between being robbed by an enemy who is an acquaintance and being robbed by an enemy who is a stranger. There is no difference between a person knowing about a cliff and still falling over it, and another person not knowing about it and falling over it. Similarly, [174] there is not even the slightest difference between those two."

Vajra of Pristine Awareness then asked, "Bhagavān, so it is. What is the

117. See page 7, note 24.

name of the yāna for the knowledge of this reality endowed with all these enlightened qualities? Teacher, please explain!"

He replied, "O Vajra of Pristine Awareness, the ground sugatagarbha cannot be improved, nor can it be impaired by wicked sentient beings. It is free of the eight extremes of conceptual elaboration, it is imbued with the three doors of liberation, and it is the natural perfection of all displays of the kāyas and facets of primordial consciousness. Knowledge of this truth and the reasons for it constitutes realization, and this is what determines its superiority over other yānas. Understanding through the other yānas that the ground is empty is a commonly shared field of experience, but this perfect bodhicitta is a supreme distinction of this swift path. It is called *ultimate bodhicitta* or the supreme yāna of the profound, mysterious fruitional Great Perfection."

The Nature of the Kāyas and Facets of Primordial Consciousness

Vajra of Pristine Awareness then asked, "What is the nature of the kāyas and facets of primordial consciousness? Teacher, please explain!" [175]

He replied, "O Vajra of Pristine Awareness, the kāyas are like this: Many avenues of accumulating merit arise in the aspect of beings' delusive appearances. For example, when making prostrations, getting up and lying down do not accumulate merit. Rather, the faith and reverence in knowing that you are prostrating and the virtuous thought of doing so generate a great deal of merit. Knowing this fact is an aspect of the sugatagarbha, so it is an avenue for accumulating merit. Taking steps in performing a circumambulation does not accumulate merit. Rather, the very consciousness of circumambulating is an aspect of the sugatagarbha, which makes it the avenue for the generation of masses of merit.

"As for making *tsatsa*[118] images and constructing *stūpa*s,[119] to make forms of clay and stone is not to accumulate merit. Rather, the very discernment of performing virtue is an aspect of the sugatagarbha, which makes it the avenue for the generation of masses of merit. In offering butter lamps, burning butter does not accumulate merit. [176] Rather, the very discernment of making an offering is a facet of the sugatagarbha, which makes it the avenue for the generation of masses of merit. In making water offerings, filling a bowl with

118. Tib. *tsha tsha*. A small image of an enlightened being, usually molded of clay and produced in large quantities.

119. Tib. *mchod rten*. A reliquary that holds sacred objects, such as the remains of an enlightened being; its form symbolizes the mind of a buddha.

water is not accumulating merit. Rather, the very discernment of offering the bowls of water generates merit, which makes it the avenue for generating merit.

"Whatever offerings are made, there is no real being who partakes of them, so if there were a direct valid perception of someone present there, this would not constitute the accumulation of merit. But the discernment that generates virtuous merit acts as a cause for agreeable conditions and an occasional sense of happiness to arise in your mind, only temporarily, in the future. As for verbal recitations, merely uttering syllables is not a cause of merit. Rather, the virtuous consciousness of your intention is an aspect of the ground, so this also produces the result. The avenue to these virtues is ultimate reality, your own primordial consciousness. For example, if you scoop up some water from a great ocean and say, 'This is the ocean,' it is not in fact the ocean itself but a portion of the ocean. Yet it is also not water from anything other than the ocean.

"Likewise, practices of generosity constitute the entrance to the path for beings to generate a little temporary happiness, [177] and these are creative expressions of ultimate reality. For example, you may dream of seeing a beautiful temple with a fine array of images representing the body of the Buddha, various syllables representing the speech of the Buddha, and stūpas, vajras, *kīlas*,[120] and so forth representing the mind of the Buddha. And you may then dream of prostrating to them, making offerings to them, circumambulating them, and so on. When you awake, if you think, 'That was definitely done,' you generate an immeasurable mass of merit."

Then Bodhisattva Vajra of Pristine Awareness asked, "O Teacher, Bhagavān, if the activation of such an intention makes an action virtuous and as a virtue it is transformed into the path, then even if one engages in actions involving the ten nonvirtues and so on, do they also turn into virtue, or not? Bhagavān, please explain!"

He replied, "O Vajra of Pristine Awareness, with the basis of recognizing someone as a sentient being, the intention of taking that person's life, the deed of making a deadly attack, and the culmination of taking that being's life, there is your own intentional consciousness and the subliminal consciousness[121] of the appearance of someone else. The same is true for all nonvirtuous actions.

120. Tib. *phur ba*. A sacred, three-edged, ritual dagger that may be used as an object of devotions such as prostrations, offerings, and circumambulations.

121. Tib. *shes pa bag nyal*. This presumably means that even in very primitive creatures that prey on one another, there is at least a subliminal awareness that the being they are attacking is other than themselves.

[178] This produces nonvirtuous karma, and this nonvirtue does not become virtue simply by imagining it to be so. All virtuous and nonvirtuous actions are not merely due to conceptualization. Know that the basis is knowledge: it is only this function that produces joy and sorrow."[122]

Bodhisattva Vajra of Pristine Awareness then asked, "O Teacher, Bhagavān, since every single thought is thus an aspect of the sugatagarbha,[123] I understand that thoughts are the cause of merit, which produces happiness, and that they are also the cause of suffering. Therefore, please explain what distinguishes them."

He replied, "O Vajra of Pristine Awareness, even though every single thought is a facet of the sugatagarbha, your subliminal ground consciousness is aroused by your motivation, and consequences ripen into fruition according to your actions. Thus, the occurrences of pleasant, unpleasant, and indifferent appearances and so forth are determined solely by your good and bad motivations. The fact that pungent fruit ripens from pungent seeds, bitter fruit from bitter seeds, [179] and sweet fruit from sweet seeds is because these seeds causally produce their fruits. If thoughts were not aspects of the sugatagarbha, there would be no way consequences could ripen from actions.

"Even though pleasant appearances arise, they do not last, but are merely temporary, so they have no essence. Experiences of suffering, too, do not last, but are experienced only for a while, and the appearances of such experiences are like dreams. For those who accumulate bad karma, the accumulation of the causal bad karma, which is the route they follow, may yield temporary pleasure, but in the end, suffering arises. With respect to those who accumulate good karma, by following that route, they may willingly take on the temporary suffering of hardships and so on, but the fruition of this is the emergence of the pleasant appearances of the fortunate realms of existence. And when these experiences come to an end, such beings proceed from one round of saṃsāra to another, and they continue to experience suffering. Due to the very ignorance that obscures your own nature as the ground of being, all joys and sorrows and good and bad karma are accumulated as causes of saṃsāra, so the grounds and paths to liberation are obscured. Therefore, by diligently applying themselves to sustaining their attention, people who practice meditation [180] experience all manner of pleasurable and painful sensations with a single grasping consciousness."

122. The point here is that knowledge of the nature and object of one's act is crucial in determining whether one's action bears the karmic consequences of joy or sorrow.

123. Every thought is an aspect of the sugatagarbha if one recognizes its essential nature; otherwise it is simply an aspect of saṃsāra.

Then Bodhisattva Vajra of Pristine Awareness asked, "O Teacher, Bhagavān, in terms of causal good and bad deeds and their consequences, is there any difference in the way they obscure one's own nature as the ground? Teacher, please explain!"

He replied, "O Vajra of Pristine Awareness, to accumulate good karma is to accumulate merit in saṃsāra. To accumulate bad karma is to store causes of saṃsāra. Both of them contribute to saṃsāra, so there is no difference in terms of their obscuring the nature of ultimate reality. For example, a white cloud and a black cloud both obscure the rising of the sun in the sky. There is no difference in that regard, for in both cases the face of the sun is hidden. Likewise, there is no difference in the obscuration of the natural glow of the ground by virtue or vice. They both conceal the grounds and paths to omniscience.

"Whatever joy or sorrow you experience, it has never existed in an ultimate sense, so it certainly does not help or harm you in the slightest. Upon careful examination, [181] if you ascertain that joy and sorrow are not established as real, you may wonder, 'What harm is there in something that is nonexistent and that merely appears to exist?' There is no difference between this and the experience of suffering that arises in a dream, which in fact is not established in reality at all. So, likewise, there is no difference between satisfying pleasure and unbearable pain."

The Purpose and Nature of the Teachings

Then Bodhisattva Vajra of Pristine Awareness asked, "O Teacher, Bhagavān, if buddhas and sentient beings and all qualities of the path and fruition are none other than the ground dharmakāya, the sugatagarbha, what is the purpose and the nature of the teachings on the many sādhanas, maṇḍalas, buddhafields, teachers and their retinues, and so forth? Please explain!"

He replied, "O Vajra of Pristine Awareness, for the nature of the ground sugatagarbha to be made manifest, you may strive in various ways to create and transform things with your intellect. Consequently, all contrived experiences of bliss, luminosity, and nonconceptuality; of attentional dispersion, excitation, and scattering; of laxity, dullness, and torpor; and of pains, joys, and sorrows are forcefully aroused, until finally all thoughts are calmed in the nature of the ground, and primordially present consciousness is identified. Such meditation entails transforming the nirmāṇakāya into the path, in which the state of naturally settled mindfulness is sustained. [182] Nowadays, everyone regards this as their standard practice, but the problem is that they do not attain the fruition of liberation. So once you have ascertained the view, you must reveal the nature of the ground, Samantabhadra. For this there are two possibilities: directly identifying it in your own being, and identifying it in dependence upon the expedient path of the stage of generation.

"O Vajra of Pristine Awareness, for the direct identification within your own being, you first establish all the phenomena included in saṃsāra and nirvāṇa as emptiness. Once you have ascertained them as displays of the space of ultimate reality, you identify this state as the great revelation and apprehend your own nature. As a result, you naturally settle in ground pristine awareness as the great freedom from extremes. This is the swift path, the yāna of the Great Perfection. If you practice by resting naturally and effortlessly until the culmination of the dying process, you will unquestionably become a buddha. On the other hand, if, through the power of previous bad karma, you fall under the influence of distractions and spiritual sloth, at the point of death you will die as an ordinary being.

"Some people, deceived by māras, seem to acquire a taste for conversation and human words. Clinging to them with attachment, [183] they become addicted to amusements and waste their lives in futile chatter. Unable to meditate, at the time of death they die as ordinary beings. With self-praise, some people fill their minds with desires for greatness in this life—for fame, high self-esteem, and high visibility. Wasting their lives in performing magic rituals, they, too, die as ordinary beings. Some continue to burden their minds with desires for personal greatness, fame, and so on, even when their health is failing, and on the verge of death they are struck by compounding illnesses. Having dismissed meditative practice as if it were a clot of spittle, at the time of death they are more pathetic than ordinary beings, and they are compelled to die in misery.

"Others who crave experiences apply themselves solely to intellectual matters. Since they are not satisfied with and do not trust the view and meditation that are effortless and disengaged from activity, they do not engage in such practice. Some people identify awareness, but since they have no confidence in it, they do not practice. Some are satisfied with merely identifying awareness, but they do not progress beyond this understanding. Some people maintain a false understanding of the meaning, and they remain deluded due to negligence.

"Such people who lack fortunate karma are very difficult to lead onto the ultimate, [184] effortless path. Therefore, in reliance upon the relative, effortful path—as a means for leading beings to ultimate, effortless absolute space—the kāyas and facets of primordial consciousness of the ground sugatagarbha are generated as signs. And many sādhanas involving visualizations and recitations are taught in accordance with the many accounts of the names and meanings of deities to be revealed, buddhafields, palaces, teachers, and retinues. All accounts asserting that by striving in meditative practice you will reach some vast region somewhere else, called a *buddhafield*, are called *paths of expedient means*.

"All the jinas and jinaputras of the three times are said to be included among the displays of the five kāyas, the five families of buddhas, and the five facets of primordial consciousness. Moreover, they are not established as existing objectively by their own characteristics. Rather, taking all kinds of primordial consciousness and qualities of the realm of the ground sugatagarbha as the basis, the teachings for the sake of disciples consist of (1) the signless dharmakāya, which is the ultimate or definitive meaning, and (2) discussions of names and objects as if they existed by their own characteristics, by which you are trapped in the cage of signs, and which pertain to relative, or provisional, meanings.

"First, the explanation of the five kāyas is as follows: All kinds of phenomena that appear [185] as various subjects are of one taste in ultimate reality, emptiness, so ultimate reality is called *dharma*. It is called *kāya* for it is like an accumulation or aggregation of inconceivable entrances to the path, inconceivable experiences, and inconceivable fruitional accomplishments, stemming from the inconceivable array of specific constitutions and faculties.[124]

"With respect to beings' obscurations due to ignorance, karma, and mental afflictions, from the very moment that the ego-grasping consciousness arises, all the appearances of the dream state, the waking state, and the hereafter, as well as all physical worlds, their sentient inhabitants, and all sensory objects, are not created by activities or brought about by effort, but are naturally *wholly present* as one's domain of experience (saṃbhoga). Likewise, at the time of buddhahood as well, purification, liberation, and all displays of the kāyas and facets of primordial consciousness are not created by activities or accomplished by effort. Rather, they are naturally perfected as one's *enjoyments*. For that reason they are called *saṃbhoga*.[125]

"The mind has never been moved and does not move by thinking 'I shall send forth emanations from the state of the ground sugatagarbha.' Emanations have never been intentionally emanated, so they are not emanated. Just as the planets and stars in the ocean do not exist as anything other than the

124. This etymologizes "dharmakāya" (Tib. *chos kyi sku*): dharma (*chos*) kāya (*sku*).

125. This etymologizes "saṃbhoga [kāya]" (Tib. *longs spyod rdzogs pa*): wholly present (*rdzogs pa*) enjoyments (*longs spyod*).

ocean, so do all appearances of saṃsāra and nirvāṇa naturally arise as various emanations [186] that are not other than the sugatagarbha itself. For that reason they are called *nirmāṇakāyas.*

"As soon as there is the conscious sense of ego-grasping, one's body must appear. Thus, in all dream appearances, waking appearances, and appearances following this life, the self arises from thoughts of ego-grasping. Accompanying this are various types of living beings constantly being experienced as objects, going through the processes of birth and death, and moving to and fro. All these appearances are called *living-being nirmāṇakāyas.*

"For disciples who have the karma of being suitable vessels, the various avenues of accumulating merit in accordance with their own constitutions and faculties, the various stages of the path, and the various kinds of rūpakāyas that accord with their own forms, languages, conducts, gurus, teachers, writings, and so forth for training disciples are all emanations of their own sugatagarbha. So the teachers who reveal the path to themselves are called *teacher nirmāṇakāyas.*

"Representations of the bodies of enlightened beings, including paintings and statues that were created by artists and commissioned by patrons, as well as self-appearing images formed from colored sand; representations of the speech of enlightened beings such as various letters, manuscripts, and books; and representations of the mind of enlightened beings such as stūpas, kīlas, and meteorite vajras [187] are all objects of worship such as prostrations, offerings, and circumambulations. These appearances as fields for accumulating merit are not due to the patrons or artisans. Rather, emanations of your own sugatagarbha appear to yourself, and they are called *created nirmāṇakāyas.*

"Objects for the use of the mere appearance of the self include an inconceivable array of both individual requisites of life and nonessential substances, such as clothing, ornaments, household goods, bedding, food, drink, earth, water, fire, air, houses, grass, trees, stones, iron, copper, silver, gold, and brass. Phenomena that appear like this, without mind or consciousness, are *material nirmāṇakāyas.*

"These four types of nirmāṇakāyas are *emanations* of the sugatagarbha that arise naturally in the objective field of ego-grasping consciousness. As an analogy, they are like the appearances in a vessel of water of the planets and stars in the sky, such that these reflections in the water arise in dependence upon the simultaneous configuration of causes and contributing conditions. Thus, until self-grasping on the part of disciples disappears into absolute space, a continuous stream of nirmāṇakāya emanations appears. When self-grasping dissolves into absolute space, [188] the purpose of the nirmāṇakāyas is fulfilled, just as the images of planets and stars disappear back into the planets and stars in the sky when the pools in which they are reflected dry up. The unbroken stream of nirmāṇakāya appearances that take place until self-grasping has dissolved into absolute space is like continuous reflections in lucid, clear water until the water dries up. The various kinds of emanations are accumulated like aggregations, so they are called *kāyas*.[126]

"The nonconceptual primordial consciousness of ultimate reality is the great reality in which the essence of all sugatagarbha emanations is unified, and it is the absolute space of one taste, which is the essential nature of all of saṃsāra and nirvāṇa. Thus, it is called the *svabhāva*, and because it is like an accumulated aggregation of all the facets of primordial consciousness and enlightened qualities, it is called *kāya*.[127]

"The ground is unmoving throughout the three times, and it does not change for the better or the worse, so it is called *immutable*. Because it is endowed with the seven indestructible vajra qualities, it is called *vajra*. Here are its seven qualities. It is:

1. Invulnerable to all karmas, mental afflictions, and habitual propensities
2. Indestructible by all objects and contributing conditions
3. Real, for it abides as the originally pure intrinsic nature of the great primordial ground of all of saṃsāra and nirvāṇa
4. Incorruptible, for it cannot be contaminated by any good or bad qualities
5. Stable, for it is unfluctuating and unmoving throughout the three times [189]
6. Totally unobstructable, for it can pierce even the subtlest cognitive obscurations in the absolute space of ultimate reality, which transcends causality
7. Invincible, for it cannot be transformed by either saṃsāra or nirvāṇa

"Thus, beings who lack the necessary karmic propensities cannot possibly realize the entire mode of existence and nature of being of the sugatagarbha, the dharmakāya that is present in the ground, so they remain deluded endlessly in saṃsāra. For all those who realize it, it is impossible for them not to acquire confidence in it. If they achieve such penetration, it is impossible that they will not become liberated; and if they are liberated, it is impossible for them not to

126. This etymologizes "nirmāṇakāya" (Tib. *sprul pa'i sku*): emanation (*sprul pa*) kāya (*sku*).

127. This etymologizes "svabhāvikakāya" (Tib. *ngo bo nyid kyi sku*): svabhāva (*ngo bo nyid*) kāya (*sku*).

become enlightened. So it is endowed with these four vajra pledges,[128] and it is called the *ultimate, indestructible vajra*. Within this authentic vajra, all paths and fruitions and all the enlightened qualities of the wonderful displays of the kāyas and facets of primordial consciousness are gathered together, or assembled, as it were. Because of this aggregation and completion, it is called *kāya*.[129]

"All the jinas and jinaputras of the three times are included and revealed in the five kāyas. All of them are naturally perfected in the ground itself, and this is the characteristic of the ultimate ground. It does not exist as a separate reality, it has no real characteristics that exist individually, and it has no basis [190] for verbal articulation. All teachings concerning names and individual, real characteristics are called *relative*.

"Moreover, the ground from which all the deities emerge is revealed as Samantabhadra. As its creative expressions, the five families of buddhas are said to come into existence from the five facets of primordial consciousness. The buddha of the center, his physical world, and its sentient inhabitants arise from the primordial consciousness of the absolute space of phenomena. The buddha of the east and his world arise from mirror-like primordial consciousness. The buddha of the south, his physical world, and its sentient inhabitants arise from the primordial consciousness of equality. The buddha of the west, his physical world, and its sentient inhabitants arise from discerning primordial consciousness. The buddha of the north, his physical world, and its sentient inhabitants arise from the primordial consciousness of accomplishment. These assertions, however, are not of a definitive nature.

"Ultimately, emptiness, the essential nature of the ground, is the universal ground of all of saṃsāra and nirvāṇa. As such, it is called the *absolute space of phenomena*, and because it is primordially self-emergent, it is called *primordial consciousness*.[130] It is not located in the center—placing it in the center is a mere convention.

"Because the radiant, clear ground, free of contamination, gives rise to all manner of appearances of saṃsāra and nirvāṇa, it is called a *mirror*, and this very consciousness, which is self-emergent and primordially present, is

128. Tib. *dam bca' bzhi*. See also GD 221.

129. This etymologizes "immutable vajrakāya" (Tib. *mi 'gyur rdo rje'i sku*): immutable (*mi 'gyur*) vajra (*rdo rje*) kāya (*sku*).

130. This etymologizes "primordial consciousness of the absolute space of phenomena" (Tib. *chos kyi dbyings kyi ye shes*): absolute space of phenomena (*chos kyi dbyings*), primordial consciousness (*ye shes*).

called *primordial consciousness*.[131] Speaking of it as being in the east is a mere convention. [191]

"Since all of saṃsāra, nirvāṇa, and the path abides in the purity and equality of the absolute space of the sugatagarbha, this is called *equality*. Transcending consciousness and objects of consciousness, that which reveals the nature of suchness without concealment is called *primordial consciousness*.[132] Placing it in the south is a mere convention.

"Primordial consciousness that knows reality as it is and perceives the full range of phenomena forms an unimpeded avenue for the unmingled arising of individual phenomena, which is called *discernment*, and because it realizes this nature as it is, it is called *primordial consciousness*.[133] Placing it in the west is a mere convention.

"All purification and liberation and all displays of the kāyas and facets of primordial consciousness are not created by *actions*, nor accomplished with effort, but are spontaneously actualized, so this is called *accomplishment*. The actualization of such a mode of existence is called *primordial consciousness*.[134] Placing it in the north is a mere convention.

"These five facets of primordial consciousness are not separate or distinct. All the individual names designated upon the essential nature of the ground sugatagarbha consist of relative, provisional meanings. Know that ultimately, names and things do not exist as signs, and the dharmakāya, which is unassociated with any direction, is free of signs.

"For individuals who cling to objects, objective buddhafields are taught in accordance with their own mindstreams. [192] In terms of relative, provisional meanings, the buddhafield of Ghanavyūha is said to be in the central region. But ultimately, the infinite and boundless aspect of the compact displays of primordial consciousness and the magnificent qualities of the primordial ground, the sugatagarbha, is called *Ghanavyūha*. Because it is like a field, a great domain in which the appearances of all of saṃsāra and nirvāṇa

131. This etymologizes "mirror-like primordial consciousness" (Tib. *me long lta bu'i ye shes*): mirror (*me long*) primordial consciousness (*ye shes*).

132. This etymologizes "primordial consciousness of equality" (Tib. *mnyam pa nyid kyi ye shes*): equality (*mnyam pa nyid*) primordial consciousness (*ye shes*).

133. This etymologizes "discerning primordial consciousness" (Tib. *so sor rtog pa'i ye shes*): discernment (*so sor rtog pa*) primordial consciousness (*ye shes*).

134. This etymologizes "primordial consciousness of accomplishment" (Tib. *bya ba sgrub pa'i ye shes*): actions (*bya ba*), accomplishment (*sgrub pa*), primordial consciousness (*ye shes*).

emerge, it is called a *field*. And since everything that arises in saṃsāra and nirvāṇa is of one taste in the sugatagarbha itself, it is called a *realm*.[135]

"As for that which is called the buddhafield of Abhirati, in the nature of the absolute space of the ground, lucid, clear, and uncontaminated, the aspect of great bliss, which is not created by objective conditions or agents, is the buddhafield of *Abhirati*. All facets of primordial consciousness and enlightened qualities and all the phenomena of the paths and fruition are naturally perfected in the ground, so it is a glorious *buddhafield*.[136]

"The nature of great bliss of the absolute space of the ground, ultimate reality, is called the *buddhafield of Sukhāvatī*.[137]

"In the ground itself, all deeds of purificatory and liberating primordial consciousness and all enlightened qualities are naturally, effortlessly perfected, so it is called the *buddhafield of Karmaprasiddhi*.[138]

"Teachings concerning their existence in the east, south, west, and north [193] are not to be taken literally. Rather, they are taught for the sake of leading disciples who grasp at directions. So the nonexistence of a buddhafield is called a *field*. While they are presented by the intellect and mentation as regions, the great, primordial perfection of the qualities of the ground sugatagarbha cannot be measured or fathomed by the intellect, mentation, or thought, so they are called *immeasurable*. They suffuse all of saṃsāra and nirvāṇa, just as the abodes of the planets, stars, and other reflections in the ocean are seen in the great ocean. And just as space is like the domain of all physical worlds and their sentient inhabitants, the expanse of space is like the *domain* in which saṃsāra and nirvāṇa appear. The perfection of all of these as displays of absolute space is ultimate, and discussions of their forms, shapes, and colors are relative.[139]

135. This etymologizes "buddhafield of Ghanavyūha" (Tib. *stug po bkod pa'i zhing khams*), that of Vairocana in the central direction: Compact Display (*stug po bkod*) buddhafield (*zhing khams*).

136. This etymologizes "buddhafield of Abhirati" (Tib. *mngon par dga' ba'i zhing khams*), that of Akṣobhya in the eastern direction: Manifest Joy (*mngon par dga' ba*) buddhafield (*zhing khams*).

137. This etymologizes "buddhafield of Sukhāvatī" (Tib. *bde ba can gyi zhing khams*), that of Amitābha in the western direction: Blissful (*bde ba can*) buddhafield (*zhing khams*).

138. This etymologizes "buddhafield of Karmaprasiddhi" (Tib. *las rab rdzogs pa'i zhing khams*), that of Amoghasiddhi in the northern direction: Perfection of Excellent Deeds (*las rab rdzogs pa*) buddhafield (*zhing khams*).

139. This etymologizes the term translated as "celestial palace" (Tib. *gzhal yas khang*): immeasurable (*gzhal yas*) domain (*khang*).

"For people who cling to castes, the leader of two thousand, three thousand, or more cities is a king, and those who belong to this caste are called *kṣatriyas*.[140] Leaders of one hundred or fewer cities are *vaiśyas*; those belonging to that caste are also regarded as vaiśyas.[141] Those belonging to the servant caste are *śūdras*.[142] [194] Those who participate in pure conduct, partake of pure food, and are seen to have virtuous attitudes are brāhmins.[143] Those having no regard for hygiene, who partake of blood and flesh, and who constantly delight in evil thoughts and deeds are regarded as *caṇḍālas*.[144]

"The meaning of the teachings on the buddha families is in accordance with this custom. The defilements of karma, mental afflictions, and ignorance of the great absolute space of one taste—in which the essential nature of the ground is nondual with all the jinas of the three times—are purified in absolute space, so it is said to be *pure*. Because the nature of primordial consciousness and enlightened qualities is expansive, it is called *expansive*. Emanations from the aspect of its essential nature are called the *buddha family*.[145]

"The indestructible ground is endowed with the seven vajra attributes, so it is called *vajra*, and emanations from the indestructible, vajra-like ground are called the *vajra family*.[146]

"A wish-fulfilling *jewel* grants all the wishes of its owner. Likewise, inconceivable entrances to the path, inconceivable meditative experiences, and inconceivable fruitional attainments [195] arise from the ground sugatagarbha in accordance with the mindstreams of all disciples, all with their own inconceivable constitutions and faculties. So they are said to be of the *jewel family*.[147]

"Although a *lotus* flower is born from mire, it has none of the faults of mire. Likewise, the ground sugatagarbha itself is uncontaminated by the taints of the three worlds, so such emanations are said to be of the *lotus family*.[148]

140. Tib. *rgyal rigs*.

141. Tib. *rje rigs*.

142. Tib. *dmangs rigs*.

143. Tib. *bram ze*.

144. Tib. *gdol pa'i rigs*.

145. This etymologizes "buddha family," which is also translated as "buddha nature" (Tib. *sangs rgyas kyi rigs*): pure (*sangs*) expansive (*rgyas*) family (*rigs*).

146. This etymologizes "vajra family" (Tib. *rdo rje'i rigs*): vajra (*rdo rje*) family (*rigs*).

147. This etymologizes "jewel family" (Tib. *rin chen rigs*): jewel (*rin chen*) family (*rigs*).

148. This etymologizes "lotus family" (Tib. *padma rigs*): lotus (*padma*) family (*rigs*).

"In the domain of the ground sugatagarbha all deeds are self-emergent and complete, without acting or striving, so such emanations are said to be of the *karma family*.[149]

"These are merely verbal designations. In this way, the nondifferentiation and natural perfection of the families is taught as the ultimate meaning, and the contrived differentiation of the families is taught as the relative, provisional meaning.

"Vairocana, referred to as the lord of the central region, as the basis of emanation of all the buddhas belonging to the buddha family, is not ultimately established as real. The radiant, clear aspect of the natural glow of the ground, empty absolute space, is made manifest by pervasive, all-seeing great wisdom. Simply by actualizing this all the facets of primordial consciousness and enlightened qualities of the domain of the ground sugatagarbha are fully *illuminated*, so he is called Vairocana.[150] Without actualizing this, there is no buddhahood, while by actualizing this alone, there is no difficulty in becoming a buddha; [196] therefore, such beings are said to belong to the buddha family.

"Vibhūvajra is so designated because he is the *indestructible great being* endowed with the seven *vajra* attributes—the absolute space of the ground.[151] The great Akṣobhya is so designated because he is *immovable* in the three times.[152] Ratnasaṃbhava is so designated because all supreme and common siddhis arise from the great displays of the kāyas and facets of primordial consciousness of the precious, spontaneously actualized absolute space of the ground, and he is absolute space endowed with all authentic realities.[153] Amitābha is so designated because he *illuminates* the inconceivable displays of appearances from the ground, and because he is *boundless*.[154] Amoghasiddhi is so designated because in the ground absolute space itself, the *meaning*

149. This etymologizes "karma family" (Tib. *las kyi rigs*): karma (*las*) family (*rigs*).

150. This etymologizes "Vairocana" (Tib. *rnam par snang mdzad*), lit. "Illuminator."

151. This etymologizes "Vibhūvajra" (Tib. *khyab bdag rdo rje*), lit. "Vajra Omnipresent Lord."

152. This etymologizes "Akṣobhya" (Tib. *mi bskyod pa*), lit. "Immovable."

153. This etymologizes "Ratnasaṃbhava" (Tib. *rin chen 'byung ldan*), lit. "Source of Great Value."

154. This etymologizes "Amitābha" (Tib. *snang ba mtha' yas*), lit. "Boundless Light."

of all sublime Dharmas is naturally present, so he is called *amogha*; and since all enlightened activities are completely *accomplished*, he is called *siddhi*.[155]

"Māmānyaśrī-Dhātviśvarī is so designated because emptiness, the vajra of space, the great absolute space of all of saṃsāra and nirvāṇa, replete with all the facets of primordial consciousness and enlightened qualities, is the creator of saṃsāra and nirvāṇa. Because she is the Great Mother of all of saṃsāra and nirvāṇa, free of movement throughout the three times, she is called *queen*.[156] Great emptiness, the great pervasive mother, is endowed with the seven indestructible vajra attributes, so Vajraḍākinī is called *vajra*. Since all the phenomena in the universe appear in the aspect of objects coming and going in the absolute domain of space, the great pervasive emptiness vajra, she is called *ḍākinī*.[157] [197] All manner of desirable objects arise from the primordial ground—originally pure, spontaneously actualized, absolute space—so Ratnaḍākinī is called *ratna*. Because all appearances of the path and all qualities of the fruition emerge from the power of compassion in the immutable space of ultimate reality, she is called *ḍākinī*.[158] Just as a lotus flower is unstained by mud, so is the sugatagarbha unstained by the fault of attachment, so Padmaḍākinī is called *padma*. Because many avenues of skillful means arise from the power of compassion in the space of ultimate reality, she is called *ḍākinī*.[159] Within the great, original perfection of the ground of all enlightened qualities, everything is accomplished free from activity, so Karmaḍākinī is called *karma*. The appearances of coming and going of all the phenomena of saṃsāra and nirvāṇa in the expanse of the space of emptiness of Karmaḍākinī is called *going*.[160] These, too, are merely verbal designations.

"Space appearing as the nature of space is skillful means and is relative, while the manifestation of the noninherent nature of space is wisdom and is

155. This etymologizes "Amoghasiddhi" (Tib. *don yod grub pa*), lit. "Accomplisher of Meaning."

156. This etymologizes "Māmānyaśrī-Dhātviśvarī" (Tib. *spyi dpal dbyings phyug*), lit. "Queen of the Expanse," another name for Ākāśadhātvīśvarī, the consort of Vairocana.

157. This etymologizes "Vajraḍākinī" (Tib. *rdo rje mkha' 'gro ma*), another name for Buddhalocanā, the consort of Akṣobhya.

158. This etymologizes "Ratnaḍākinī" (Tib. *rin po che mkha' 'gro*), another name for Māmakī, the consort of Ratnasaṃbhava.

159. This etymologizes "Padmaḍākinī" (Tib. *padma mkha' 'gro*), another name for Pāṇḍaravāsinī, the consort of Amitābha.

160. This etymologizes "Karmaḍākinī" (Tib. *las kyi mkha' 'gro*), another name for Samayatārā, the consort of Amoghasiddhi.

ultimate. The explanation of this as the ḍākinīs of the buddha family is a provisional meaning. The appearance of earth as earth is skillful means and is relative, while the manifestation of the noninherent nature of earth is wisdom and is ultimate. The designation of Ratnaḍākinī is a provisional meaning. [198] The nature of water appearing as water is skillful means and is relative, while the manifestation of the noninherent nature of water is wisdom and is ultimate. References to Vajraḍākinī consist of provisional meanings. The appearance of fire as fire is skillful means and is relative, while the manifestation of the noninherent nature of fire is wisdom and is ultimate. The designation of Padmaḍākinī is a provisional meaning. The appearance of air as air is skillful means and is relative, while the manifestation of the noninherent nature of air is ultimate and is wisdom. References to Karmaḍākinī consist of provisional meanings.

"All the jinas and jinaputras, including the thousand buddhas of this fortunate eon, who teach in order to guide disciples, are none other than the five kāyas and the five facets of primordial consciousness. So all the buddhas without exception are none other than their displays. People within saṃsāra perceive, cling to, and are deluded by such things as class, genealogy, regions, homes, and gender. So if they were not taught accordingly, disciples who cling to these things, fixating on their permanence, would not be satisfied, and they would not follow the path of liberation. [199] With this realization, and taking the kāyas and facets of primordial consciousness of the signless dharmakāya as the basis, they are described as having signs. But in reality, it is certain that of all the deities and buddhafields, not even a single one is established as real."

How to Practice the Teachings

Then Bodhisattva Vajra of Pristine Awareness asked, "O Teacher, Bhagavān, taking the signless dharmakāya—devoid of all extremes of conceptual elaboration—as the basis, for the sake of disciples who grasp at eternalism, the path is taught as having signs and objectivity. How does one practice these teachings? Teacher, please explain!"

He replied, "O Vajra of Pristine Awareness, although the referential path[161] of the stage of generation has many classifications, our path of secret mantra, Vajrayāna, has two, called the *path of definite perfection* and the *path of the power of the view*. The former teaches the deities and buddhafields as objects

161. The referential path (Tib. *dmigs bcas kyi lam*) is so designated because it entails objects that are grasped with the mind as if they existed by their own characteristics.

definitely existing by their own characteristics, and it emphasizes only the avenue of relative skillful means. The ultimate view is merely implied, but not explicitly emphasized.

"As for our path of the power of the view, you first establish the view [200] and thereby correctly realize that the deities and maṇḍala do not exist as anything other than the illusory displays of the original, primordial ground alone. Then, in order to transfer and merge your own body, speech, and mind into the domain of the three vajras, you take the illusion-like samādhi as your basis and recognize the manner in which the appearances of deities are created like illusions. Thus, by becoming accustomed to the visualized appearances of the stage of generation, you achieve stability in your own awareness. Ordinary appearances and clinging are *transferred* to the nature of buddhafields, and your body, speech, and mind are transferred to the *dwelling* of the three vajras. Hence, this is called *transference by entering the dwelling*.[162]

"First, you establish that all phenomena in all of saṃsāra and nirvāṇa are of an empty, identityless nature. In the end, you confirm firsthand that your own pristine awareness has never been anything but displays of the kāyas and facets of primordial consciousness. This is what is called the *ultimate taking of refuge in the essential nature*. The essential nature of taking refuge consists of remaining without veering from the state in which all the jinas and jinaputras of the three times are united and in which their vital essence is unified.

"Yearning for a result and then devoting yourself to its cause is an approach that corresponds to the ways of the world. For example, if a man went to a foreign kingdom, casually occupied some land, and set about farming it, [201] he would inevitably be punished by the reigning king. But if he were to seek the protection of the king and submit a petition to him, then he would have the authority to farm or do whatever he wanted with his land in that kingdom.

"Likewise, if you do not take refuge by mentally taking the natural radiance of pristine awareness that is present in the ground dharmakāya as your outer, inner, and secret object of refuge, you are not authorized to engage in the deeds of the Three Jewels. Consequently, the result would not be granted, you would succumb to obstacles, and you would be an unsuitable vessel for empowerments and spiritual counseling. Therefore, the foundation for all the samayas and vows and the root of all empowerments and siddhis is taking refuge by way of the threefold faith in the Three Jewels; offering them your body, speech, and mind and all your enjoyments and possessions without attachment, clinging, or grasping; and at all times and situations never for

162. Tib. *'pho ba grong 'jug*. The culminating phase of the stage of generation.

even an instant failing to entrust yourself to the sublime objects of refuge. So maintain this as your very life essence itself.

"Whether you are lifted up or cast down, whether you are elated with happiness or tormented with pain, and when you engage in any type of activity, reflect that 'The Three Jewels know!' This is the sublime, fundamental ground of all practice. [202] In particular, know that the self-appearing, supreme teacher of disciples is the holy guru, whose body is the Saṅgha, whose speech is the holy Dharma, and whose mind is the Buddha. Know that the guru is the synthesis of all the sublime objects of refuge. Know that the secret body appearing as the spiritual mentor of living beings is the root of all blessings. The secret mind, the treasury of primordial consciousness, which is the unified display of all the personal deities, is the root of all siddhis. And know that the illusory displays of compassion that appear as myriad guardians of the doctrine and *dharmapālas* are the root of all enlightened activities.

"Their essential nature is the dharmakāya, devoid of signs. Their characteristic is the saṃbhogakāya, which consists of displays of the kāyas and facets of primordial consciousness. The natural creative expression of their compassion is the supreme nirmāṇakāya, consisting of the entrances to the path and fruition. Recognize these as the omnipresent lords of all the maṇḍalas, and take refuge in them without being separated from them for even an instant. Remain under their protection. Utterly entrust your mind, heart, and body to them. Practice without abandoning them even at the cost of your life, and rely upon the principal deity of all the maṇḍalas without displeasing this being in the slightest way.

"If you indulge in false views or displease the deity, even in a dream, it is crucial that you generate remorse and confess this. If you abandon the vajra guru, [203] this is tantamount to abandoning the Three Jewels, Three Roots, three kāyas, buddhas, and bodhisattvas. Primordial consciousness, enlightened qualities, and all the meditative experiences and realizations will not mature in the mindstream of one who does so. And however much such a person strives physically, verbally, and mentally, the accumulations of merit and knowledge will not be perfected, and the fruition will not come to maturation. Even if one devotes oneself to another guru, blessings and siddhis will not occur. Possessed by the evil spirit of degenerated samayas, one will transgress them.

"For example, seedlings and fruit do not mature from a rotten seed, and branches and leaves do not grow from a trunk with a rotten root. Likewise, the vajra guru is like the root of the tree of the secret mantra; the vajra guru is like the seed and the field of the harvest of omniscience. Thus, recognize this fact, and devote yourself to the vajra guru without abandoning this being for even an instant. Know that if you recognize the guru in this way as the synthesis of all the buddhas, and take refuge while meditating on your guru in the nature of your personal deity in the space in front of you, there is certainly no need to seek any object of refuge elsewhere.

"As for cultivating bodhicitta, cultivate *ultimate bodhicitta* as follows: [204] What we call *mind* is the narrow-minded, confining grasping at self alone that causes you to cling to pleasure, pain, and indifference and to regard all objects as existing by their own characteristics. Desires and cravings arise in an unbroken stream from such a mind. So all appearances and mindsets involving grasping at appearances as real things are to be understood with discerning wisdom, and self-concepts and the reification of dualistic appearances are to be subjugated until they disappear. Then the actualization of identitylessness as displays of the consummation of saṃsāra and nirvāṇa, free of activity and conceptual elaboration, is called the *cultivation of bodhicitta*, by which you enter the womb of the essential nature. This is the fruition of all ways of cultivating bodhicitta and is the most sublime of all dharmas.

"First, to realize bodhicitta, the ascertainment with discerning wisdom of the essential nature of all of saṃsāra and nirvāṇa is called *aspirational bodhicitta*. In the end, realizing the displays of the consummation of saṃsāra and nirvāṇa is called *engaged bodhicitta*. When some people speak of generating bodhicitta, they do not realize this key point and claim to accomplish its cause by aspiring for the fruitional bodhicitta. They speak of cultivating a mere aspiration—which is not bodhicitta—as an object of conceptualization. [205] Such talk is like giving a boy's name to a mere fetus in a pregnant woman's womb;[163] they do not have even the faintest realization of engaged bodhicitta.

"Therefore, for those who lack the fortune to sustain the direct perception of authentic bodhicitta but who cultivate good thoughts, here are just a few words to reveal aspirational and engaged bodhicitta. Visualizing the objects of refuge in the space in front of you, think that 'I shall lift up and free all sentient beings of the three worlds from the ocean of suffering of mundane existence and bring them to the state of omniscience.' With this thought, commit yourself to accomplishing the great welfare of sentient beings by way of the four immeasurables: compassion, loving-kindness, empathetic joy, and equanimity. In particular, the thought 'I shall practice the meditation and recitation of the supreme personal deity!' is called *aspirational bodhicitta*. Steadfastly engaging in the meditation and recitation of the deity as profound means for simultaneously accomplishing the six perfections for the sake of all beings is called *engaged bodhicitta*. Know this to be the means by

163. That is, such talk is like giving a boy's name to a fetus of unknown gender.

which your entire practice of Dharma will serve as a cause of perfect, great buddhahood. [206]

"That which obscures the face of suchness, ultimate reality, and creates the three realms of saṃsāra—the grahas, vighnas, bhūtas, and the great demons—is ego-grasping. Good, positive thoughts that emerge from this are devas and rākṣasas; all bad, negative thoughts are great, evil demons; and the subtle configurations of thoughts of craving and attachment are the class of vighnas, who are the masters and mistresses of adversity. Thus, since not even a trace of any other demon or graha exists, even if you do things to expel and liberate them, you will not attain the fruition of liberation. Therefore, the unconquerable wrathful being who severs the vital root of self-concepts and saṃsāra is empty awareness, which appears in the form of the vajra of hatred, Heruka, with his messengers and servants. Through this, the rūdra of the view of the self is expelled into absolute space, and the root of mundane existence is utterly expunged.

"As the great wisdom that realizes identitylessness arises as the underlying splendor of saṃsāra and nirvāṇa, appearances arise as ornaments of awareness. Apart from the manifestation of kāyas of the original ground, there is no other expulsion of vighnas. So take this fact as the basis.

"According to the ways of saṃsāra, before you move to a region, [207] you first make it safe by expelling harmful beings such as enemies, thieves, and dangerous carnivores; only thereafter do you settle on the land. Similarly, with yourself in the role of an illusionist, you create the illusory recipients of your generosity, as if they were observing the embodiments of your thoughts. Over the white offerings, red offerings, and ransom *tormas*,[164] which are like illusory substances, you recite the purifying mantras and increasing mantras, which are illusory mantras for substances. Then with illusion-like samādhi you dedicate these projected appearances of sensory objects, like reflections of planets and stars, to the domains of the six faculties of those beings, like a vessel of water. This visualization for dealing with all adversities, settling all your debts, and becoming reconciled with those who are hostile is praised as the best means of overcoming all adversities and obstacles.

"Then you instantaneously imagine yourself as a ferocious, majestic, terrifying, wrathful primordial-consciousness being. From your body, speech, and mind, billowing flames, foul odors, assemblies of wrathful beings, iron scorpions, weapons, and various sorcerer's substances are emanated like hail. As a result, all the malevolent grahas, vighnas, and vināyakas, dazed and confused, [208] are totally and helplessly cast out into the darkness behind the

164. Tib. [*ba ling*] *gtor ma*; Skt. *bali*. A ritual offering cake.

outermost black iron fence, like paper blown away by the wind. Imagining this is called the *visualization for expelling vighnas*. It is taught as a method for preventing the occurrence of obstacles in your meditation on the deities and maṇḍala that you are actualizing. Regarding discursive thoughts as demons is a profound technique for getting rid of hindrances that might destroy emerging siddhis.

"As for the wheel of protection, the ultimate wheel of protection is ascertaining that all violent beings and objects of their violence are originally not established as being real, by knowing that all of saṃsāra and nirvāṇa is the display of bodhicitta. This liberates all the vighnas and malevolent beings right where they are, making them disappear. This is called the *ultimate wheel of protection* or the *self-emergent, pristine wheel of protection*.

"Here is a method for those who know this but do not have confidence when it comes to their sensory activities: Withdraw the minor wrathful beings and sorcerer's substances that set the boundaries for the emanated apparitions of enlightened activity. In this way, all regions above, below, and in between are sealed closed with no gaps, and they appear in the aspect of a celestial palace formed as a blazing wheel, having the essential nature of the primordial consciousness of the absolute space of phenomena. [209]

"On its outer periphery, the essential nature of mirror-like primordial consciousness appears in the aspect of a celestial palace of blazing vajras. Outside of that, the essential nature of the primordial consciousness of equality appears in the aspect of a celestial palace of blazing jewels. Outside of that, the essential nature of discerning primordial consciousness appears in the aspect of a celestial palace of blazing lotuses. Outside of that, the essential nature of the primordial consciousness of accomplishment appears in the aspect of a celestial palace of blazing swastikas. Outside of that are a blazing mountain of primordial consciousness and a fence of a mass of fire. Outside of that are a great celestial palace of a dark vajra wind and razor-sharp blades. And outside of that is a fence of crashing waves of a vajra river.

"Visualizing this definitely puts an end to all the grahas and vighnas that arise from the projections of thoughts. This is like constructing a fence as protection from your enemies. Determining the nature of all impure, deluded mental states and appearances, and then accurately recognizing the essential nature, or mode of being, of the ground puts a stop to misleading confusion. All nonrealizations and misconceptions are great flaws in the practice of meditation, so there is a real blessing in first gaining knowledge and realization.

"For this purpose, according to the ways of saṃsāra, [210] before you move into a new house, you eliminate all its defects and then clean it so that it is comfortable, beautiful, well decorated, and attractive. Similarly, with the force of your great faith, admiration, and reverence, emanate rays of light from your heart, invoking the minds of the jinas and jinaputras. Consequently, the rūpakāyas arise from the absolute space of phenomena, and empowerments, blessings, and siddhis all dissolve into you, your environment, your place of practice, and your practice substances in the aspect of mounds of five-colored lights and masses of rainbow clouds, together with kāyas in the form of subtle mudrās, enlightened speech in the form of various seed syllables, and enlightened mind in the form of various hand emblems.

"Repeatedly imagine, as a result, that your environment is blessed as the self-appearing, actual Akaniṣṭha, your house is blessed as a palace created from primordial consciousness, your practice substances are blessed as ambrosia, and your body, speech, and mind are blessed as the nature of the three vajras. This is the correct way to establish your place of practice, your house, your practice substances, and yourself as deities and the maṇḍala.

"The ultimate blessing of the offerings is the actualization of the dharmakāya, absolute space free of the extremes of conceptual elaboration, which is the spontaneously actualized, self-emergent display of the kāyas and facets of primordial consciousness. [211] In terms of relative truth, the self-appearing displays of sensory objects delusively appearing to the senses of sentient beings are sealed with the kāyas and facets of great primordial consciousness. Imagine that infinite clouds of offerings, including the seven outer enjoyments and the five inner sensory objects, appear in the nature of unimpeded streams of displays of the ornamental wheels in all the self-appearing maṇḍalas of primordial consciousness.

"In particular, visualize the five poisons melting into the essential nature of the five facets of primordial consciousness, the medicine swirling about as an ambrosial ocean of the primordial consciousness of bliss and emptiness, and the cosmos as a red baling torma in which the nutritive essence is synthesized, acting as a source of all desirable things. Imagine the attachment of the three realms of saṃsāra melting into the essential nature of the bliss of detachment, appearing as a boiling ocean of great, wish-fulfilling red *rakta*[165] and so forth. This is offered to each of the deities and blessed with the essence of the three vajras. And imagine that each of the illusion-like arranged objects expresses its own illusion-like mantra, such that they are of the nature of these appearances.

"The projection of the offering substances is called [212] the *treasury of space samādhi*. Until ego-grasping consciousness ceases, these unbroken

165. Skt. *rakta*. The element of blood, which symbolizes the wisdom of great emptiness.

streams of appearances of sensory objects are transformed into clouds of offerings. For example, by imprinting mantras of conjuring substances upon the realm of lucid, clear sky, various appearances of sensory objects arise for the spectators. Likewise, the sensory faculties of the recipients of the offerings and gifts are like the lucid, clear sky. The substances that have been set out are like conjuring substances. Your thoughts are like conjuring concepts. The recipients of the offerings and gifts are like a crowd of spectators, and all the enjoyments are visualized as if they were illusory, wish-fulfilling appearances. This is *illusion-like samādhi*.

"Illusion-like samādhi does not arise simply by visualizing and knowing in that way. Rather, it is experienced by people who have determined the self-appearing nature of saṃsāra and nirvāṇa. Know that those who do not understand this are visualizing the objects they bring to mind by means of discursive thinking. Ultimately, the way to actualize the pristine awareness that is present in the ground is taken as the basis of all this; while relatively speaking, there are the teachings of the preliminary practices of the stage of generation in accordance with the ways of saṃsāra. Moreover, [213] know that the methods for proceeding along the path are taught with respect to the characteristics of the ground itself, and they do not exist as objects other than this.

"Now for the main practice, before meditating on the supporting buddhafield and palace and on the deities who reside there, the impure karmic eon must be dissolved into absolute space and brought forth as pure appearances of primordial consciousness deities. For example, dream appearances and waking appearances do not both appear simultaneously, nor can the human realm and hell realm possibly manifest at the same time. Likewise, the impure appearances of saṃsāra and the buddhafields of primordial consciousness deities cannot possibly exist simultaneously.

"So first, imagine that the phenomenal physical worlds, the animate sentient beings who inhabit them, and the appearances of the five sensory objects all dissolve into absolute space as illusory apparitions dissolving into the nature of emptiness. The manifestation of this mode of existence of suchness, ultimate reality, is called the *samādhi of suchness*. Those who do not know the nature and mode of being of emptiness merely impose some kind of emptiness upon that which is not empty, and they do not directly experience the samādhi of suchness. [214] The actual samādhi of suchness is experienced only by yogins who have realized the view of emptiness.

"Once again, with the manifestation of the mode of being of the ground—great, all-pervasive primordial consciousness—all the phenomena of saṃsāra and nirvāṇa manifest as displays of great spontaneous actualization, like planets and stars in the ocean. This manifestation of everything is called the *all-illuminating samādhi*. This is in the realm of experience only of those yogins who have identified the dharmakāya, pristine awareness that is present in the ground. Others' cultivation of compassion for sentient beings by means of the intellect and mentation entails an object and cogitation, and the actual all-illuminating samādhi does not manifest. So recognize that one is merely a substitute for the other.

"Then in an instant, like rainbows suddenly appearing in the sky where none existed previously, and like planets and stars suddenly appearing in a pool of water where none existed before, from the absolute space of all-pervasive ultimate reality, free of conceptual elaboration, visualize your awareness as the causal syllable *Oṃ*, white and blazing with light and rays of light. This is the cause for the emergence of all foundational maṇḍalas and those who reside in them.

"The first two samādhis[166] are primordial consciousness that knows emptiness, transcending the objects of the intellect and mentation. [215] The latter [the causal samādhi] consists of apparitions involving objects and luminosity.[167]

"O Vajra of Pristine Awareness, like the explanation of the gradual formation of the elements due to the wind at the beginning of an eon, visualize a syllable *É* emerging from the *Oṃ* and transforming into the nature of empty, clear, all-pervasive space. *Yaṃ* emerges and transforms into an air maṇḍala, as the underlying ground, in the shape of a vajra swastika. *Baṃ* emerges and transforms into an ocean of the nature of lucid, clear, pure water in the shape of a swirling sphere. From the emanation of *Laṃ*, a vast, broad, square-shaped, golden ground appears. *Raṃ* emerges and transforms into the nature of fire in the composition of all the above, with the aspect of warmth, and in the form of a semicircle.

"All these appear but do not inherently exist, like the moon in water or a rainbow. Know them to be mere appearances, empty and unreal, like the expanse of space.

"Again, upon the golden ground of great power, *Suṃ* is emanated, such that the entire ground shines like lapis lazuli, blazing with radiant clear light. It is free of all rough things such as jagged mountains, pebbles, and thorn trees. Its vast surface is smooth and level like the face of a mirror, [216] such that when you step down it gives way four finger-widths, and when you lift up it rebounds four finger-widths.

"Aromatic fragrances waft from verdant hills covered with medicinal

166. Namely, the samādhi of suchness and the all-illuminating samādhi.

167. These five paragraphs compare with GD 240–42.

plants. The ground is completely covered with various beautiful, delightful lotus blossoms—blazing, clear, shimmering, and radiant, in colors of indigo, white, yellow, red, and green. The sky is crisscrossed with checkered patterns of rainbow lights, and the cardinal and intermediate directions are covered with masses of rainbow clouds.

"Within this expanse, all the assemblies of apparitional vīras and yoginīs of primordial consciousness perform beautiful dances, sing lovely melodies, and play various musical instruments. In the sky, various offering goddesses present bountiful clouds of offerings and make obeisance. Eight great oceans extend in the eight cardinal and intermediate directions of the ground. On their shores are jewel pebbles, golden sand, and lush turquoise meadows. Here dwells an inconceivable variety of innumerable, sweet-voiced birds, including the golden goose, the king of birds, [217] blue-headed wild ducks, *katika* birds, talking parrots, cuckoos, pheasants, hazel hens, and sparrows.

"These lovely birds also include ducks, eagles, hoopoes, celestial birds with voices like chiming bells, and *kritipa* birds appearing like golden vajras. They are white like the color of conch and silver, yellow like the color of gold and amber, red like the color of coral and ruby, green like the color of turquoise and emerald, indigo like the color of lapis lazuli and sapphire, and blue like the color of blue beryl.[168] These and other birds have pleasing colors and beautiful forms, sing lovely songs, engage in charming play, alight upon wish-fulfilling trees, and circle about over the ocean. In addition, various apparitional, beautifully formed deer frolic in enchanting, lovely play, and they listen to the Dharma.

"In the center, surrounded by a swirling moat and encircled by a metal fence composed of seven types of precious substances, is a pond of ambrosial water imbued with eight excellent qualities.[169] [218] By drinking it, thirst and hunger are dispelled, and simply by experiencing this water's aroma, all the pain of various illnesses is removed and replaced by untainted bliss.

"In the center of this display, in which there is nothing disagreeable, is a wonderful garden with a *Hūṃ* at its center, from which emerges a palace. Its eastern face is white and luminous like crystal, symbolizing mirror-like primordial consciousness. Its southern face is golden yellow, symbolizing the primordial consciousness of equality. Its western face is ruby red, symbolizing

168. Tib. *mu men*; Skt. *vairāṭa*. This is a dark blue gemstone that is astringent in taste. Its post-digestive effects are cooling, and in terms of its healing effects, it benefits illnesses from poisoning, leprosy, lymph disorders, and skin disorders. Blue beryl may match this description, but this requires further research.

169. See page 7, note 24.

discerning primordial consciousness. Its northern face is emerald green, symbolizing the primordial consciousness of accomplishment; and its center is the blue of lapis lazuli, symbolizing the primordial consciousness of the absolute space of phenomena.

"On its eastern side is a circular door of great compassion, symbolizing spontaneously actualized pacifying enlightened activity. On its southern side is a square door of great loving-kindness, symbolizing spontaneously actualized enriching enlightened activity. On its western side is a semicircular door of great empathetic joy, symbolizing spontaneously actualized powerful enlightened activity; and on its northern side is a triangular door of great equanimity, symbolizing spontaneously actualized wrathful enlightened activity. [219]

"It has four corners, symbolizing the four kāyas. On the outside it is surrounded by protective celestial palaces of the five facets of primordial consciousness and the five spontaneously actualized kāyas. On top of the palace are vase holders, vases, awnings, Dharma wheels, fine parasols, ornaments of the sun and moon with a jewel on top, lace curtains, and bells and little spherical bells producing the sounds of the Dharma. The jeweled doorframes, portals, steps, and so forth are adorned with immeasurable palatial qualities. On the four sides, the light from the sun and moon shines through the windows, striking the crystal windowpanes, producing rainbows and orbs of light during the day and clear light during the night. The mere sight of this is enchanting, and simply by entering the palace, the displays of the kāyas and facets of primordial consciousness become manifest.

"In the center of the palace is a jeweled throne of great height and beauty, symbolizing transcendence of mundane existence. It is supported by eight lions, symbolizing the purity of the eight aggregates of consciousness, and upon it descends a white causal seed syllable *Oṃ*, from which rays of light radiate upward. They make immeasurable offerings to all the jinas and jinaputras. Fully arousing the mindstreams of the personal deities, [220] all the empowerments, blessings, and siddhis of enlightened body, speech, mind, qualities, and activities, together with all the sublime qualities of primordial consciousness of knowledge, compassion, and power, are drawn in like a convergence of rainbow clouds, and they dissolve into the *Oṃ*. Rays of light radiating downward purify the mindstreams of all sentient beings of the three realms and free them from delusion, as if forcefully arousing them from sleep. As soon as the rays of light are reabsorbed, the vitality and merit of all sentient beings and all the splendor and vital essence of the physical worlds and their inhabitants are collected and dissolve into the *Oṃ*.

"The *Oṃ* transforms you into the great Bhagavān Vairocana, whose body is white in color like a snow mountain, symbolizing his freedom from the taints of habitual propensities. He has one face, symbolizing the sole bindu of the dharmakāya. His right eye symbolizes primordial consciousness that knows reality as it is, and his left eye symbolizes primordial consciousness that perceives the full range of phenomena. His right ear symbolizes ultimate truth, and his left ear symbolizes relative truth. His right nostril symbolizes the dharmakāya for his own sake, and his left nostril symbolizes the rūpakāya for the sake of others. His mouth symbolizes the great bliss of equality, [221] his teeth symbolize the perfection of the maṇḍala of pacification, and his tongue symbolizes the equal union of saṃsāra and nirvāṇa.

"His right arm symbolizes the skillful means of great bliss, and his left arm symbolizes the wisdom of great emptiness. The ten fingers of his hands symbolize the five kāyas and the five facets of primordial consciousness. His right leg symbolizes his not abiding in the extreme of mundane existence, and his left leg symbolizes his not abiding in the extreme of peace. His ten toes symbolize the perfection of the five buddha families and five consorts. His twelve joints, which are pliant and flexible like the tendrils of a vine, symbolize the purification of the twelve links of dependent origination.

"His entire body symbolizes his spontaneously actualized enlightened qualities. His body hair, blazing with the light of primordial consciousness, symbolizes the 84,000 collections of the Dharma. The hair on his head, tied in a bun, symbolizes his never having been subject to delusion. The dangling locks of hair flowing down his back symbolize his caring for sentient beings. His legs crossed in the vajra position symbolize that he is unmoved throughout the three times. His two hands in the mudrā of supreme enlightenment[170] symbolize that saṃsāra and nirvāṇa are displays of great buddhahood. [222] He holds a thousand-spoked golden wheel, which symbolizes the perfection of the wheel of primordial consciousness of the minds of all the jinas of the three times. He is adorned with all the saṃbhogakāya apparel, which symbolizes his love for beings. Surrounding him are light and rainbows that symbolize his perfection of all the kāyas and facets of primordial consciousness.

"In the eastern buddhafield of Abhirati, the entire ground appears like precious crystal. In the southern buddhafield of Śrīmat, the entire ground appears in the aspect of gold. In the western buddhafield of Sukhāvatī, the entire ground appears in the aspect of ruby. In the north, the buddhafield of Karmaprasiddhi appears with blazing light in the aspect of emerald.

"In the east, Tathāgata Akṣobhyavajra arises from *Hūṃ*, the blue-black

170. In the mudrā of supreme enlightenment, the hands touch at the fingertips, with the palms facing up.

color of his body symbolizing the unborn absolute space of phenomena. He presses one hand upon the ground, blocking the entrance to the three realms, and in the other he holds a vajra symbolizing indestructible ultimate reality.

"In the south, Ratnasaṃbhava arises from *Trāṃ*, the yellow color of his body symbolizing his perfection of enlightened qualities and enjoyments. [223] The mudrā of supreme generosity symbolizes his bestowal of supreme, eternal bliss to all beings, and he holds a precious jewel symbolizing his bestowal of the glory of service and bliss to all pitiable beings.

"In the west, Amitābha arises from *Hrīḥ*, the red color of his body symbolizing his mastery over all of saṃsāra and nirvāṇa. His two hands in the mudrā of meditative equipoise symbolize displays of saṃsāra and nirvāṇa as great purity and equality. Upon them, the lotus he holds symbolizes the complete unfurling of the mystery of the enlightened mind of great bliss.

"In the north, Amoghasiddhi arises from *Āḥ*, the green color of his body symbolizing his synthesis and perfection of all the ornamental wheels of the kāyas, facets of primordial consciousness, enlightened qualities, and inexhaustible enlightened activities. His mudrā of generosity is the great protection of fearlessness for beings, and he holds a variegated vajra symbolizing his training of disciples by means of the four kinds of enlightened activities.

"Whichever one of these deities you take as your main practice, imagine and practice all five for each one. Understand that this implicitly symbolizes the simultaneous perfection of the five kāyas and the five facets of primordial consciousness in the dharmakāya, the sugatagarbha. [224]

"Meditating on the deities in this way, they all appear but do not inherently exist, like rainbows in the sky, like images of the moon in water, like reflections in a mirror, and like transparent, clear water, free of contamination. In absolute space, all the kāyas and buddhafields of all the buddhas arise naturally, like bright heavenly bodies in the ocean, and they are visualized in the aspect of masses of light.

"Likewise, with respect to the wrathful maṇḍala—the physical worlds and their sentient inhabitants, together with your own body, aggregates, elements, and sense bases, disappear into the realm of space, the great emptiness of ultimate reality, like a dream vanishing into the space of awareness. Then rest in the mastery of the primordial consciousness of emptiness. Once again rest in meditative equipoise in which you experience clear primordial consciousness, and at the end, visualize your awareness as the blue-black flaming causal syllable *Hūṃ*, which is an apparition of the primordial consciousness of great, all-pervasive compassion.

"In your existence, when you encounter the dying process, which is to be purified, the outer appearances of the physical world, its inner animate sentient beings, and the intervening appearances of the five sensory objects all dissolve into clear emptiness. Openly resting in this for a while is the phase of the dissolution of mundane existence into the substrate. So by taking as the path the great expanse of the ground emptiness, which is the agent of purification [225] that will be recognized at the time of the fruition, you will gain mastery of ultimate reality, suchness. Therefore, it is of the utmost importance to become familiar with this.

"When the dying process, which is to be purified, is transferred to the clear light, this is like the autumn sky when it is not veiled in white by the contaminating condition of the sun, nor veiled in black by darkness, and when it is not contaminated by clouds, mist, or wind. Then the extent of your own awareness—lucid, clear, and free of contamination—is unlimited. Without veering in any direction, you attain uniform pervasiveness free of all extremes of conceptual elaboration. Then the purifying clear light of the time of the path, primordial consciousness, pristine awareness, identifies itself. By the power of this familiarization, at the time of fruition you acquire confidence within yourself, resulting in enlightenment as the dharmakāya.

"If you do not have the ability to be liberated in that way, the appearance of the ground clear light, which is grasped as the body to which you are experientially fixated, becomes the basis to be purified. By arousing purifying awareness as the causal syllable, gradually bring forth the appearance of a buddhafield. By doing so, the manifest presentation of the fruition will come to you. Therefore, you should know that it is of the utmost importance to familiarize yourself with the three samādhis[171] from now on. [226] The clear-light emptiness that is present in the ground does not become manifest merely through thinking and visualizing, so understand that this will only result in more thinking and visualizing.

"Again indigo light in the form of *É* radiates from the appearance of the causal syllable in the foundationless domain of the primordial ground, emptiness. This transforms into the nature of radiant, clear space, and green light in the form of *Yaṃ* radiates, manifesting as the maṇḍala of air. Red light in the form of *Ra* emanates, manifesting as a wave-tossed ocean of blood. *Keṃ* radiates, forming a triangular mountain of skeletons, equal in dimensions to the absolute space of phenomena. *Raṃ* radiates, becoming of the nature of a violently flaming, dark-red cosmic volcano billowing masses of fire. *Suṃ* emanates, appearing as indigo light from which a lapis-lazuli-colored ground emerges, clear as crystal. Beneath it a kīla-shaped mountain appears without obscuration.

"Outside is a blazing expanse of a roaring fire of primordial consciousness,

171. The three samādhis are the samādhi of suchness, the all-illuminating samādhi, and the causal samādhi.

resounding like the conflagration at the end of the eon. Within this expanse *Bhrūṃ* emerges, transforming into a wrathful palace with its exterior composed of various precious substances and its interior composed of three types of skulls: [227] dry skulls form the ceiling, old skulls with dry flesh and skin form the edges of the ceiling, and fresh skulls dripping with blood form the walls. They are all held in place with meteorite nails.

"The ceiling symbolizes the dharmakāya, the edges of the ceiling symbolize the saṃbhogakāya, and the walls symbolize the nirmāṇakāya. The meteorite nails are symbols of ultimate bodhicitta. The roof is made of human skin upon which victory banners of human corpses are hoisted. The bases of the pillars are the eight great nāgas, the pillars are the eight great devas, the tops of the pillars are the eight great planets, the directional guardians and terrifying ones[172] are the crisscrossing beams, and the constellations are displayed as the ceiling boards. Above, below, and in all directions, blood slowly drips from ornamental strings of heads of large and small rūdras. The entire environment is covered with corpses of humans and horses emerging from bubbles in a swirling ocean of blood.

"Everything outside roars with a violent, fiery wind like a hailstorm, with countless black-magic substances, weapons, and their wielders; and the naturally emitted sounds of wrathful mantras such as *Hūṃ Hūṃ Phaṭ Phaṭ* bellow forth like a thousand peals of thunder. Everywhere outside of this are many chaotic, spontaneously actualized maṇḍalas of wrathful male and female beings, including the eight great charnel grounds,[173] [228] the ten abodes of Heruka,[174] and the twenty-four pilgrimage spots.[175] There, all the

172. Tib. *'jigs byed*; Skt. *bhairava*. A class of protectors of the Dharma.

173. Tib. *dur khrod chen po brgyad*; Skt. *aṣṭamahāśmaśāna*. The eight great charnel grounds are Most Fierce (Tib. *gtum drag*, Skt. Caṇḍogrā), Dense Thicket (Tib. *tshang tshing 'khrigs pa*, Skt. Gahvara), Blazing Vajra (Tib. *rdo rje bar ba*, Skt. Vajrajvala), Endowed with Skeletons (Tib. *keng rus can*, Skt. Karaṇkin), Cool Grove (Tib. *bsil ba'i tshal*, Skt. Śītavana), Black Darkness (Tib. *mun pa nag po*, Skt. Ghorāndhakāra), Resonant with "Kilikili" (Tib. *ki li ki lir sgra sgrog pa*, Skt. Kilikilārava), and Wild Cries of "Ha Ha" (Tib. *ha ha rgod pa*, Skt. Aṭṭahāsa).

174. Tib. *He ru ka'i gnas bcu*. The ten abodes of Heruka are the (1) abodes (Tib. *gnas*, Skt. *pīṭha*), (2) outer abodes (Tib. *nye ba'i gnas*, Skt. *upapīṭha*), (3) fields (Tib. *zhing*; Skt. *kṣetra*), (4) outer fields (Tib. *nye ba'i zhing*, Skt. *upakṣetra*), (5) pleasing places (Tib. *tshan do*, Skt. *chandoha*), (6) outer pleasing places (Tib. *nye ba'i tshan do*, Skt. *upachandoha*), (7) meeting places (Tib. *'du ba*, Skt. *melāpaka*), (8) outer meeting places (Tib. *nye ba'i 'du ba*, Skt. *upamelāpaka*), (9) charnel grounds (Tib. *dur khrod*, Skt. *śmaśāna*), and (10) outer charnel grounds (Tib. *nye ba'i dur khrod*, Skt. *upaśmaśāna*).

175. Tib. *gnas nyi shu rtsa bzhi*. The twenty-four pilgrimage spots are the four abodes (1) Pullīramalaya, (2) Jālandhara, (3) Oḍḍiyāna, and (4) Arbuda; the four outer abodes (5)

guardians of the doctrine, dharmapālas, local guardians, and treasure keepers devour as their food the warm flesh and blood of the malevolent enemies of the doctrine. As for their tasks, they take away the life's breath of the enemies of the ten fields, and they guard the teachings of the Buddha. They proudly display terrifying forms and make sounds of killing and dismembering. Brandishing sharp weapons and rough instruments, they display beautiful apparitions and take wrathful delight in acts of killing. With their minds unmoved from the peaceful state of ultimate reality, they serve the needs of animate beings by subduing others with compassion. All of them are none other than emanations of the Great Glorious One [Heruka].

"In short, all these myriad haughty, terrifying beings surround the palace in the manner of kings, ministers, and the general populace, without any space between them. Imagine that they are encircled by nine concentric wheels of protection.

"In the center of this terrifying wrathful palace is an eight-spoked meteorite wheel, symbolizing the purification of the eight objects of consciousness. In its center are eight lions, symbolizing the purification of the eight aggregates of consciousness; [229] they support a vast, lofty throne of precious substances, symbolizing utter transcendence of mundane existence. Upon it is a lotus, symbolizing the great center, emptiness, and detachment from saṃsāra; a moon, symbolizing the skillful means of great bliss, the element of the white bindu, and the lack of contamination by the flaws of saṃsāra; a sun, symbolizing the wisdom of great emptiness, the element of red rakta, and the perfection of all enlightened qualities; and a seat of male and female corpses, symbolizing the dissolution of self-concepts into absolute space and the equality of nonconceptuality. From absolute space, a blue-black syllable *Hūṃ* descends upon this seat. Emanating rays of light upward, immeasurable pleasing offerings are made to all the jinas and jinaputras of the three times. Invoking their minds, all the empowerments and blessings of the ornamental wheels of the inexhaustible qualities and enlightened activities of their body, speech, and mind are drawn in like masses of light and rainbow clouds, and they dissolve into the *Hūṃ*.

Hūṃ

Godāvarī, (6) Rāmeśvara, (7) Devīkoṭa, and (8) Mālava; the two fields (9) Kāmarūpa and (10) Oḍra; the two outer fields (11) Triśakuni and (12) Kośala; the two pleasing places (13) Kaliṅga and (14) Lampāka; the two outer pleasing places (15) Kāñci and (16) Himālaya; the two meeting places (17) Pretapuri and (18) Gṛhadevatā; the two outer meeting places (19) Saurāṣṭra and (20) Suvarṇadvīpa; the two charnel grounds (21) Nagara and (22) Sindhu; and the two outer charnel grounds (23) Maru and (24) Kulatā.

"Then rays of light are emitted downward, utterly purifying all the vices, obscurations, habitual propensities, karma, mental afflictions, and miseries of all sentient beings in the three realms. [230] As if vigorously aroused from sleep, they are liberated into absolute space in which delusion is unknown. Then the rays of light are reabsorbed, whereupon imagine that all the life force, merit, radiance, and splendor of all beings, as well as the vital essence of the four elements and all sublime qualities, converge in the form of a five-colored mass of light and dissolve into the *Hūṃ*.

"The syllable *Hūṃ* transforms into pristine awareness as the causal Heruka, whose body is blue-black in color. He holds a vajra in his right hand and a blood-filled skull cup in his left. His naked body, devoid of clothing and ornaments, stands in an expanse of the blazing fire of primordial consciousness, with his two legs positioned in a wrathful posture. From the three places of his body, rays of light are emitted and then draw in every single one of the maṇḍalas of the three kāyas of the buddhas in the form of white, red, and indigo rays of light. Imagine that they dissolve into your own three places, generating great power and strength.

"Then in an instant you transform into the Great Glorious One, the supreme basis of emanation of all wrathful beings, Heruka. The blue-black color of your body symbolizes the immutable absolute space of phenomena, free of conceptual elaboration. Your central face—which symbolizes the dharmakāya, the empty, originally pure essential nature—is blue-black. Your right face—which symbolizes the saṃbhogakāya, [231] the clear, spontaneously actualized nature—is white. And your left face—which symbolizes the nirmāṇakāya, all-pervasive compassion—is flaming dark red.

"Your central eye is a symbol of the primordial consciousness of emptiness, your right eye is a symbol of the primordial consciousness of luminosity, and your left eye is a symbol of all-pervasive primordial consciousness. Your two ears symbolize the two truths. Your nose symbolizes the two goals. Your frown symbolizes all the paths and fruitions. Your mouth symbolizes the great bliss of equality. Your tongue symbolizes liberation in the equality of saṃsāra and nirvāṇa. The rows of your teeth, white like snowy mountains, symbolize the maṇḍala of absolute space of the blood-drinking vajra. Your four bared fangs symbolize the subjugation of beings by means of the four immeasurables. Your orange hair flaming upward symbolizes the primordial absence of delusion. Your eyebrows flashing like a thousand lightning bolts symbolize the elimination of the realm of darkness of ignorance and the manifestation of the illumination of primordial consciousness. Your flaming mustache and beard, emitting fiery sparks, symbolize the blazing majesty of the displays of the primordial consciousness of bliss and emptiness.

"Your six arms symbolize the six facets of primordial consciousness.[176] Your top right hand holds a nine-pointed vajra, symbolizing the sequence of nine yānas and the nine grounds. [232] Your middle right hand holds a five-pointed vajra, symbolizing the five kāyas and the five facets of primordial consciousness. And your bottom right hand holds a three-pointed vajra, symbolizing the three kāyas and the three facets of primordial consciousness.[177] Your top left hand holds a dry skull cup filled with blood, symbolizing saṃsāra of the formless realm displayed as blood. Your middle left hand holds a blood-filled skull cup covered with blood and skin, symbolizing saṃsāra of the form realm displayed as blood. And your bottom left hand holds a blood-filled skull cup covered with braided hair, symbolizing saṃsāra of the desire realm displayed as blood.

"Your four legs are wrathfully spread wide, symbolizing your possession of the four bases of miraculous power.[178] Your *garuḍa* wings, flaming with vajra jewels, are outstretched to your right and left, symbolizing your victory over the three realms and your venturing without impediment into the absolute space of ultimate reality. You are replete with the ornaments of the charnel ground and signs of glory, which symbolize the objects of consciousness arising as ornaments. You stand amid a blazing mass of fire like the cosmic conflagration at the end of the eon, symbolizing the incineration of the misconceptions of ignorance by great primordial consciousness. Above you hovers a black garuḍa, symbolizing delusion manifesting as wisdom. Samantabhadra and his consort reside on your crown as the lords of the buddha families, [233] symbolizing your unwavering presence in the peace of the dharmakāya.

"Arising as the display of Heruka in universal splendor, symbolizing the skillful means of great bliss, you embrace the pale blue body of your consort, Ākāśāmukhī, who symbolizes the wisdom of great emptiness. Her right hand holds a curved flaying knife[179] that cuts off the three poisons, and her left hand holds a blood-filled skull cup, which presents the three realms as blood.

176. These include the five well-known facets of primordial consciousness along with the primordial consciousness that knows reality as it is (Tib. *rnam pa thams cad mkhyen pa'i ye shes*).

177. Tib. *ye shes gsum*. Knowledge of all phenomena in the three times of the past, present, and future.

178. Tib. *rdzu 'phrul gyi rkang pa bzhi*; Skt. *catvāro ṛddhipādāḥ*. The samādhis of aspiration (Tib. *'dun pa*), enthusiasm (Tib. *brtson 'grus*), intention (Tib. *sems pa*), and analysis (Tib. *dpyod pa*).

179. Tib. *gri gug*; Skt. *karttṛkā*. A curved, hooked knife used for flaying hides.

Her left leg embraces the waist of her consort, symbolizing the union of bliss and emptiness, and her right leg presses on the heart of a corpse, symbolizing the closing of the door to the three realms of saṃsāra.

"As a sign of lust arising as an ornament, she wears an upper garment of human skin. As a sign of hatred arising as an ornament, she is adorned with garlands of snakes and human heads. As a sign of delusion arising as an ornament, she wears a moist leopard skin as a lower garment. As a sign of holding the three worlds with compassion, strands of her dark-red hair flow down her back. The penetration of the lotus of her womb by his vajra symbolizes the union of bliss and emptiness.

"The natural radiance of mirror-like primordial consciousness is hatred—the white vajra in the east. The natural radiance of the primordial consciousness of equality is pride—the yellow vajra in the south. [234] The natural radiance of discerning primordial consciousness is attachment—the red vajra in the west. The natural radiance of the primordial consciousness of accomplishment is envy—the dark-green vajra in the north.

"At the crowns of these majestic personal deities, imagine a thousand-spoked wheel of Dharma. At its center is a white *Oṃ*, pale and radiant like an autumnal moon. At their throats is an eight-petaled lotus, in the center of which is a red syllable *Āḥ*, more radiant than a hundred thousand suns. At their hearts is an erect, nine-pointed meteorite vajra, in the center of which is a sun seat. On it is a blue-black syllable *Hūṃ*, radiant like a lapis-lazuli mountain drenched in the light of a hundred thousand suns.

"White, red, and indigo rays of light radiate from these syllables, invoking the mindstreams of all the jinas and jinaputras of the ten directions and the four times. From the absolute space of phenomena, forms of rūpakāyas emerge as the five families of buddhas. They are invited into the space in front, and they empower you with the vase water, filling your body from the crown of your head. All the stains of afflictive and cognitive obscurations are totally purified, and the vajra essences enter your three places, sealing them with the three vajras. You are appointed as the regent of the buddhas and empowered to liberate the entirety of the three realms of saṃsāra. [235] The excess water spills over, crowning your head with the five families who abide as the principal lords of the buddha families.

"Again the essential nature of the nondual emptiness and bliss of the deities, in the form of a white and red mass of light, dissolves into you. Imagine that this brings forth the power and strength to dominate all of saṃsāra and nirvāṇa. White, red, and indigo rays of light radiate from your own three places, inviting from the domain of ultimate reality, the treasury of space, all the jinas and jinaputras of the four times and the ten directions, displayed as the foundational maṇḍala and the beings who reside in it. Repeatedly imagine that they converge upon you like a blizzard and then dissolve as one into you and your implements of practice, like snow falling into a great lake. Invite them in this way.

"Then, arriving in the sky above you and the maṇḍala, all the buddhas are offered seats according to their nature.[180] As soon as the seats are offered, the deities dissolve into the self- and front visualizations,[181] and you imagine that they each sit on their own seats. In this way request them to remain.

"From wherever you have visualized yourself as your personal deities, you emanate ordinary physical beings equal in number to the atoms of the earth, [236] who bow before the deities. Between their two pressed palms are precious jewels, from which emanate myriad clouds of immeasurable offerings to please the deities' enlightened body, speech, mind, qualities, and activities. The deities' mindstreams are pleased and satisfied, and immeasurable rays of light are emitted from their bodies, utterly purifying all negative actions and obscurations, and transforming everything into displays of the personal deities. Imagine that they dissolve into your heart as the imagined deity, bringing forth majestic power. This is the homage.

"Offerings of water cool their bodies, and water for bathing the feet cools their feet. Flowers are offered at their seats. Incense pervades the area with a fragrant aroma, lights remove the obscurations so that what appears to the mind is radiant and clear, and fragrantly scented water pervades all their bodies and accoutrements. Various foods satisfy their taste buds, and the sounds of various kinds of lovely music are offered, which satisfy their minds with the taste of bliss and emptiness. Beautiful, delightful goddesses of form make offerings pleasing to the eye, and they dissolve into the visual faculties. Goddesses of sound bearing lovely sounds [237] make offerings pleasing to the ear, and they dissolve into the auditory faculties. Goddesses of smell bearing delicious fragrances make offerings pleasing to the nose, and they dissolve into the olfactory faculties. Goddesses of taste bearing various foods make offerings pleasing to the tongue, and they dissolve into the gustatory faculties. Goddesses of touch bearing garments make offerings pleasing to the body, and they dissolve into the tactile faculties, satisfying the deities' minds with the taste of bliss and emptiness. These visualizations are the outer and inner offerings.

180. That is, seats symbolic of wrath are offered to wrathful deities, peaceful seats are offered to peaceful deities, and so on.

181. As you generate yourself as your personal deity, so do you imagine your personal deity in the space in front of you.

"The five poisons are transformed into the ambrosia of primordial consciousness and are offered, the physical world and its sentient inhabitants are transformed into displays of tormas and are offered, and saṃsāra is transformed into an ocean of blood and is offered. Appearances and emptiness—the union of the deity and consort—are offered as the uncontaminated great bliss of union. The vajra of skillful means—the primordial being of ultimate reality—liberates the rūdras of self-concepts of the three realms into the domain of the wisdom of identitylessness, and ordinary appearances of objects are transformed into mountains of flesh, oceans of blood, and piles of bones, and they are offered. Thus, all appearances of phenomena are extinguished in great, intellect-transcending ultimate reality. This is the liberation offering.[182]

"Again mentally visualize all the colors of the bodies, hand emblems, [238] ornaments, and garments of all the deities of the maṇḍala. As you recall their great qualities, imagine that you project from your body innumerable vīras and ḍākinīs who perform beautiful dances in the sky, play various musical instruments held in their hands, and make offerings of lovely songs of praise. This is the visualization of praise. Such meditation involving only visualized imagery is indispensable. Practicing without even this is no more meaningful than the chirping of birds, and no siddhis will arise, just as no butter emerges from churning water.

"In terms of ultimate reality, establishing the reality of emptiness transforms all appearances and mindsets of saṃsāra into the best, unsurpassed method of identifying the intrinsic nature of Samantabhadra, the supreme deity who dwells as the ground, the nature of emptiness. Relatively speaking, the method is to meditate on and visualize your body, speech, and mind as the three vajras.

"In the past, because of the obscuration of the habitual propensities of karma and mental afflictions, the deity who dwells as the ground has not manifested but has been reduced to an ethically neutral, immaterial vacuity. Now, by exercising the faculty of wisdom that realizes identitylessness, [239] primordial consciousness free of grasping at luminosity and vacuity manifests, and this is ultimate reality. Visualizing the *samayasattva*[183] deities as if they were tangible, inviting the jñānasattva deities from absolute space, and merging them indivisibly is relative. In reality, you do not invite them from one place to another; that is merely held by the intellect and mentation.

182. Tib. *bsgral mchod.*

183. Tib. *dam tshig sems dpa'.* The samaya being, your visualization of yourself as the deity.

"Identifying pristine awareness that is present in the ground dharmakāya and stabilizing this in your mindstream is ultimate. Imagining that the deities are there because you requested them to sit on their prepared seats is relative. Delight because of your belief in the manifestations of displays of self-appearing primordial consciousness is called the *homage of encountering the view*. In this, the person making homage and all the many objects of homage are of one taste; they are not different, and this is ultimate. In accordance with the ways of saṃsāra, you pay homage according to the custom of showing reverent obeisance to kings and so on, and this is relative. When you see the mode of existence of the Great Perfection, ultimate reality, you know that all sensory objects that appear in the world are not prepared, but are self-emergent offerings, and this is ultimate. Prepared substances like conjuring substances, enriching mantras like conjuring mantras, illusory visualizations like mental projections, [240] and illusory objects attractive to the senses of the appearing deities, who are like the audience, constitute relative offerings. The wondrous perception of the nature and qualities of the reality that is present in the ground dharmakāya is ultimate; praising the great qualities of the deities in the manner of praising and extolling great people such as kings is relative.

"Knowing that in reality the ground dharmakāya is totally present in yourself is the essence of the view of the Great Perfection, so recognize the utmost importance of attending single-pointedly to the manifest nature of pristine awareness.

"When you visualize the deity in this way, stabilize the pride of knowing that you are the deity. Previously, when you were wandering in saṃsāra, the subliminal consciousness that grasped at the appearance of a sentient being's body as yourself was pride. Since you are the agent of all appearances and mindsets, as such, visualize your own body as a deity. The unimpeded consciousness that grasps at the appearance of a sentient being's body as the 'I' is exchanged for the consciousness of the deity. Practicing with the unimpeded consciousness of yourself as the deity is called the *stabilization of divine pride* and *divine samādhi*. In performing this practice, if you disengage from this crucial point of transferring your own appearance to that of the deity, [241] no matter how you practice, the deity will not be actualized.

"If you achieve stability in divine pride in this way, finally, when you identify pristine awareness, you will have already achieved stability in pristine awareness for yourself, so this will propel you toward the state of liberation. Training in bringing forth clear appearances by vividly imagining the color of the deity's body, together with the hand emblems, ornaments, and garments, is to make them manifest, just as the appearances of your own aggregates, elements, and sense bases appear clearly and firmly due to your conceptual projections. By visualizing the divine field and the deities themselves again and again and nurturing this, the ground of firm pride is maintained. Know this to be of the utmost importance for actualizing the deity.

"From the primordial protector, the dharmakāya, down to all the māras and rūdras, not a single being exists as anything other than your own appearances. Fathoming this with certainty is the way to avoid the error of reifying the stage of generation, and it is a special, profound point for actualizing the deity as primordial consciousness. For yogins who realize that saṃsāra and nirvāṇa are none other than their own appearances, even if they practice meditating on demons, rākṣasas, and *theurangs*,[184] these are seen to be nothing other than emanations of Samantabhadra. [242] So they are all jñānasattvas, without a single mundane being among them—all are the enlightened displays of Samantabhadra.

"Without realizing this, those who grasp at themselves as themselves, at others as others, at deities as deities, and at demons as demons will stray into becoming gods of the form realm if they meditate on peaceful deities; and if they meditate on wrathful ones, they will become māras and rākṣasas. Even if they meditate on jñānasattvas, they will definitely remain as mundane beings. Why? By the power of ignorance they are deceptively led into dualistic grasping—unawareness—meaning they are unaware of the mode of being of the ground. Awareness means being aware of the mode of being of the ground. Because the power of ignorance establishes all the deities on whom you meditate as sentient beings, they are only mundane. By meditating on deities with the power of pristine awareness, they are all actualized as primordial consciousness. By realizing that all of saṃsāra and nirvāṇa consists of nothing other than displays of Samantabhadra, they all definitely arise as jñānasattvas, without even a trace of any mundane being.[185]

"Visualizing the deities in this way, imagine in your heart, on a lotus and sun seat, a jñānasattva, at whose heart is a nine-pointed meteorite vajra standing upright upon a sun. [243] At its center visualize a blue-black *Hūṃ*, the color of lapis lazuli, encircled by a mantra string and enclosed within a sun and moon like an amulet box. Directing your consciousness to the *Hūṃ* while reciting, and directing your consciousness to the bindu and *nāda* of the *Hūṃ* while reciting, is called *worshiping the deity*. Visualizing that the mantras rise from the seat and circle while reciting is called *close worship*.

184. Tib. *the'u rang*. A type of preta.

185. In this paragraph, the Tibetan term *rig pa* (Skt. *vidyā*) can be translated as "knowledge" or "awareness." The Tibetan *ma rig pa* (Skt. *avidyā*), translated here as "ignorance," might also be translated as "nonawareness."

"At this time vast rays of light are emitted, inviting forth the entire assembly of all the victorious buddhas, bodhisattvas, gurus, personal deities, vīras, and ḍākinīs of the ten directions without exception. Imagine again and again that they dissolve into the self- and front generations and recite. Direct your consciousness to all the deities and recite. Direct your consciousness to the mantra circle at your heart and recite. Alternately direct your consciousness to the *Hūṃ* and to the crescent moon, bindu, and nāda. Like sending forth the king's messengers, the crucial aspects of worship are inviting forth all the jinas and jinaputras with rays of light, having them repeatedly dissolve, and supplicating the deities.

"Furthermore, rays of light descending and circling from the mouth to the secret places of the male and female deities of the self- and front visualizations gather together, [244] in a mass of five-colored light, all the empowerments, blessings, and siddhis of the enlightened body, speech, mind, qualities, and activities of all the jinas and jinaputras of the three times.[186] Imagine again and again that they dissolve into you and your implements of practice. This is the crucial aspect of *accomplishment*, symbolizing the acquisition and accumulation of pleasures and wealth.

"Again immeasurable rays of light are emitted from the mantra garland at your heart, and like sunlight striking drops of dew, they completely purify all the vices, obscurations, karma, mental afflictions, and habitual propensities in the mindstreams of all beings in the three realms. Then all appearances are transformed into the nature of buddhafields and palaces, and all mundane beings are transformed into the nature of male and female deities. With one voice, and with their minds in the state of one taste, they chant in majestic union the sounds of mantras, like the sound of an agitated beehive. As a result, imagine that all the realms of the universe shake and tremble. This is the *great accomplishment*.

"Then, even if you have many different things to do, visualize the four kinds of activity like this: In the morning, the time of pacification, imagine that you emanate [245] immeasurable rays of white light to the ten directions from the mantra garlands in the hearts of the self- and front visualizations, making offerings pleasing to all the jinas and jinaputras and arousing their mindstreams. All the empowerments, blessings, siddhis, facets of primordial consciousness, and attributes of the ornamental wheels of the inexhaustible

186. In this visualization, the mantras and light at the heart of the male deity rise to his mouth and cycle to the mouth of his consort, down to her secret place, to the secret place of the male deity, and back up to his mouth, where they continue this revolution, accompanied by the sound of the mantras.

enlightened body, speech, mind, qualities, and activities are reabsorbed in the form of a white mass of light, which dissolves into you and those generated in front of you. As a result, imagine that you have attained all the empowerments, siddhis, and powers of pacification. Again an immeasurable mass of white light is emanated to the abodes of the six classes of animate beings, totally purifying all the vices, obscurations, habitual propensities, karma, mental afflictions, and suffering of all sentient beings in the three realms. Imagine that they all, without exception, become embodiments of primordial consciousness deities. This is the visualization of *pacification*.

"In the afternoon, the time of enrichment, imagine that you emanate immeasurable rays of yellow-colored light, reabsorbing in the form of a mass of yellow light the vital essence and quintessence of the four elements; the vitality and merit of all sentient beings in the three realms; all the empowerments, blessings, and siddhis of the enlightened body, speech, mind, qualities, and activities of the jinas and jinaputras of the three times; and all the vitality, merit, and power of all the devas, vidyādharas, ṛṣis, and siddhas, which all dissolve into you. [246] This is the visualization of *enrichment*.

"In the evening, the time of power, imagine that you emanate immeasurable rays of red light, like the color of ruby, drawing in all the jinas and jinaputras of the ten directions and the four times in the form of red light. They dissolve into you and subjugate all the gods, demons, and humans, all male and female beings, and every single one of the eight classes of haughty nonhuman beings. They are brought before you, where all the mighty power of all these terribly ferocious beings is overwhelmed. Then imagine that from their mouths they cough up their hearts' vitality, as they solemnly swear to be your servants and slaves, and they dissolve into the soles of your feet. Again rays of dark-red light emanate from the hearts of the self- and front visualizations, placing a half vajra on the tops of the heads of all these haughty beings, signifying that they must not transgress their samayas. If they abide by their samayas and engage in enlightened activities, this will protect them from danger and become a crown jewel for all their needs and desires. If they transgress their words and oaths, [247] it will turn into a meteorite lightning bolt that shatters their heads into small pieces, and it will become a black iron scorpion that delights in their heart's blood and torments them. This meditation on their accomplishing enlightened activities without transgressing their oaths is the visualization of *power*.

"At dusk, the time of wrathfulness, visualize yourself as the deity and imagine various weapons and sorcerer's substances emanating from your body like a violent hailstorm, expelling and dismembering all malevolent enemies, material and immaterial, and malevolent beings, like water extinguishing sparks of fire. Then innumerable small wrathful beings, iron scorpions, and garuḍas are emanated, totally devouring the mound of their flesh, blood, and bones, incinerating them in a blazing ball of fire, and dispersing them with a razor-like wind, such that not even a trace of them remains. Then imagine that their consciousnesses are liberated to a realm in which delusion is unknown. This is the visualization of *wrathfulness*.

"Occasionally imagine immeasurable rays of light being emanated and then reabsorbing, in the form of a mass of light like billowing rainbow clouds, all the empowerments, blessings, and siddhis of the enlightened body, speech, mind, qualities, and activities of all the jinas and jinaputras of the three times. [248] Repeatedly visualize them dissolving into yourself and your implements of practice. Then immeasurable rays of light emanate from your heart, striking the hearts of the jinas and jinaputras. All the buddhas are connected to you with strands of light rays, and all the nonconceptual facets of primordial consciousness in their mindstreams are transferred to your own mindstream. Without letting your consciousness be distracted elsewhere, recite the mantras without interrupting them with human words, and diligently apply yourself to practice without letting your meditation cushion grow cold.

"All appearances are displays of your personal deity; all sounds are empty sounds of the nature of mantras; all thoughts are displays of the real nature of enlightened mind. Transforming them into the path in this manner constitutes the three kinds of transformation, and they are indispensable on the path of *mahāyoga*. Stabilizing them in the ultimate nature of awareness is worship, and enhancing them by means of your conduct is practice. This is the essential nature of the yogic practice. Training like this in mental visualization is called *relative* and *provisional*. Skill in the transformations of emanating and reabsorbing rays of light is the most important, quintessential point of the practice, so hold on to this as the most crucial thing to know.

"Establishing saṃsāra and nirvāṇa as great emptiness [249] is the *vase empowerment*. Recognizing precious spontaneous actualization as the self-emergent kāyas and facets of primordial consciousness is the *secret empowerment*. The revelation of pristine awareness, the nonconceptual primordial consciousness of ultimate reality, is the *wisdom empowerment*. Mastering the fruition in yourself is called the *word empowerment*. These are the actual four empowerments, devoid of a bestower and a recipient.

"Furthermore, visualizing your body as the deity is the *vase empowerment of the body*. Expressing your speech as the mantra is the *secret empowerment of speech*. Not letting your mind be separated from the confidence of primordial consciousness is the *wisdom–primordial-consciousness empowerment of the mind*. Realizing the nonduality of the deity and your own appearance is the *word empowerment*. Just this is the simultaneous perfection of the four empowerments.

"By clinging to the true existence of all the physical worlds and their sentient inhabitants, with their three realms and all their sensory objects, deluded beings grasp at objects as being autonomous. Ascertaining all these external appearances to be displays of ultimate reality, suchness, is called the *assembly of the three realms displayed as enlightened body, speech, and mind*. As for confession, ignorance of the ultimate is what is called *vice* or a *habitual propensity*, and *obscurations* are so designated because they obscure the intrinsic nature of the ground. In reality, not even the slightest trace of so-called vices, obscurations, or habitual propensities exists, [250] so what method could there be for confessing them? Determining the meaning of the two kinds of identitylessness, then realizing the mode of existence of the ground, is called *confession* and *purification*. As substitutes for that, *confession with your mind*, *confession with material goods*, and *confession by uttering words* are methods for averting obstacles to your spiritual practice. These are taught as *intermediate confessions*.

"In this regard, there is no better way to perfect the accumulations of merit and knowledge than by engaging in the *gaṇacakra* of transforming your food and drink into the path through visualization, with your body as the maṇḍala of the buddhas, your food and drink as the gaṇacakra, and your fingers as offering goddesses.

"To enhance your practice sessions and your meditative experiences and realizations, for the gaṇacakra offer the entire universe with all its sensory objects, recognizing this not as something prepared, but as a self-emergent gaṇacakra. A single syllable *Raṃ* is emitted from your heart as your personal deity. Flames burst forth from it, incinerating all the stains of the habitual propensities of conceptual grasping at true existence. The syllable *Yaṃ* emanates, setting the air in motion and casting out all the pollution and contamination of impurities. The syllable *Khaṃ* emanates, giving rise to water, which dissolves all things into emptiness and then merges them with the absolute space of the physical worlds and their sentient inhabitants, dispersing them.

"Again imagine the syllable *A* emerging from absolute space [251] and transforming into a skull cup of primordial consciousness as vast as the absolute space of phenomena. It is white on the outside and red on the inside, and it rests on the surface of a hearth with wind and fire beneath it. Inside, in its center and in the four cardinal directions, all three realms of the physical worlds and their sentient inhabitants transform into a mountain of human flesh in the center, a mountain of elephant flesh in the east, a mountain of horse flesh in the south, a mountain of peacock flesh in the west, and a moun-

tain of pheasant flesh in the north. Visualize them all as being vast in breadth and height, oily, impressive, lustrous, powerful, and filled with vitality.

"Again imagine a mountain of excrement in the center, an ocean of urine in the southeast, bone marrow in the southwest, white and red bodhicitta in the northwest, and a swirling ocean of various kinds of blood in the northeast.

"A white *Oṃ* dissolves into the human flesh, melting it into the ambrosia of enlightened body. A blue-black *Hūṃ* dissolves into the great flesh in the east, melting it into the ambrosia of enlightened mind. A yellow *Trāṃ* dissolves into the great flesh in the south, melting it into the ambrosia of enlightened qualities. A red *Hrīḥ* dissolves into the great flesh in the west, melting it into the ambrosia of enlightened speech. A green *A* dissolves into the great flesh in the north, melting it into the ambrosia of enlightened activity. They take on the colors of white, blue, yellow, red, and green respectively.

"A blue *Mūṃ* dissolves into the excrement, a white *Māṃ* [252] dissolves into the urine, a yellow *Laṃ* dissolves into the bone marrow, a red *Pāṃ* dissolves into the bodhicitta, and a green *Taṃ* dissolves into the rakta, endowing them with the power and vital essence of the five facets of primordial consciousness.

"From beneath, *Yaṃ* causes the air to stir and *Raṃ* makes the fire blaze, melting the ambrosias in the skull like ghee and bringing them to a full boil. Spilling over, they pervade all the realms of the three kāyas of the buddhas, covering them with light rays like the colors of the rainbow and vapor like rainbow clouds. From this expanse, imagine that clouds of all the desirable outer, inner, and secret offerings and inexhaustible ornamental wheels, like the clouds of offerings of Ārya Samantabhadra, arise unimpededly with increasing power for all the buddhafields until the three realms of saṃsāra are empty. From this great ocean of ambrosia of the primordial consciousness of bliss and emptiness, the buddhas, bodhisattvas, gurus, personal deities, ḍākinīs, and guardians draw the vital essence of the ambrosia through the vajra tubes of their tongues. As they experience it, imagine that their minds are satisfied with the taste of bliss and emptiness; the accumulations of all sentient beings, including yourself and others, are perfected; all your obscurations are purified; and you all effortlessly achieve the supreme siddhi.

"As for all other offerings, [253] from the expanse of billowing clouds of fragrance and light emerge various kinds of offering substances, various kinds of symbolic substances, various kinds of substances for practice, various kinds of substances for the fulfillment ritual, substances that correspond to the classes of guardians of the doctrine and local gods, deer, livestock, water dwellers, species of birds and other winged creatures, animals with paws, hoofed animals, household goods, armor, weapons, ornaments, food, nourishment, drink, foods to lick, and foods to suck. All these attractive objects spread forth like particles of dust and like mist enveloping the sky. Imagine them covering the sky like masses of clouds, and offer them as a fine rain descending upon the earth.

"For the practice of liberation,[187] the true realization that the entire universe of saṃsāra and nirvāṇa is none other than your own appearances is called the *great fortress of the view*. Not wavering from the experience of the nature of the ground is called the *great highway of meditation*. What is called the *life force of the visualization* entails visualizing these external inanimate worlds in such a way that it is impossible for enemies and malevolent beings to survive once this visualization has merely descended upon the nature of their life force, life, and vitality. Such visualization is critical for not missing your target. [254] A crucial point for achieving irreversible results is applying diligent attention to the task of liberating your enemies by visualizing all the inner inhabitants of the universe as being perfected in the enlightened body, speech, mind, qualities, and activities of your personal deity. Especially profound points for avoiding being harmed are never departing from the divine pride of your personal deity visualized as the Great Glorious One and directly visualizing the Supreme Son Kīla.

"In particular, simply by directly visualizing effigies of your enemies placed inside an incarceration box[188]—the black dungeon of Karma Yama shaken by the din of the five poisons—like bugs that have fallen into a fire, there is no escape for them. For example, the ritual for bringing someone back from beyond the grave is similar in meaning to the practice of liberation by way of the transmissions on the enemy's life force, purification, and abode, although they entail different techniques.

"Here is the method for trapping someone in an incarceration box: Visualize in front of you a celestial palace with no doors or seams and with no way to escape other than out the top. Inside it, instead of an effigy, place a drawing of a person with joined palms. This direct meditation and the one for those who have departed from this life are similar.

"To summon your enemies, visualize that, from your heart as your personal deity, countless messengers emanate carrying hooks, [255] nooses, iron chains, and bells, sent forth like a violent, black wind that destroys the cos-

187. Tib. *bsgral las*. The wrathful activity of taking a being's life and liberating that being to a higher state of existence.

188. Tib. *'brub khung*. A triangular ritual container, often made of metal, black on the outside and red on the inside, and sometimes marked with skulls. It is visualized in various ways: as the absolute space of ultimate reality, as the miserable states of existence, as the womb of the consort, and as a prison.

mos. As a result, imagine that the life, life force, and vitality of your enemies and malevolent beings are inexorably summoned and become nondual with the effigy, like one body of water merging into another. Alternatively, the consciousness of someone who has departed is drawn in, like a fish on a hook, by light rays from the heart of the self- and front visualizations, which dissolve repeatedly into the drawing of that person. These two techniques are similar. Repeatedly imagine that the entire life, life force, and vitality of your enemy converge—like iron filings attracted to a magnet—in the form of the syllable *Nṛiḥ* on the tip of a kīla and dissolve into the intervening space between the sun and the moon of your seat, as your personal deity. Alternatively, imagine that they are drawn up from the aperture in the kīla and dissolve into the hearts of Heruka and his consort dwelling in its bulbous handle, thereby increasing their power and might. This is the *transmission on the life aspect*.

"In a similar way, for the six destinations of one who has passed away, you may bring forth the appearances of the six realms of existence in the forms of the six seed syllables of the six classes of living beings. Then, from the seed syllable at your heart, as your personal deity, emanate rays of red light, thereby gradually incinerating and transforming these appearances. [256] This is called the *transmission on the life of the six classes*.

"Ultimately, to manifest primordial consciousness, pristine awareness, is to restore yourself as the deity. To represent this, emanate countless *Hūṃ* syllables from your heart as you visualize yourself as your personal deity, completely filling the entire domain of saṃsāra and nirvāṇa. All the buddhas and buddhafields, together with the three realms of the physical worlds and their sentient inhabitants, dissolve into the *Hūṃ* syllables like salt dissolving into water or camphor dispersing into the air. Then they are all reabsorbed, dissolving into yourself such that you become the Great Glorious One of all of saṃsāra and nirvāṇa. This meditation constitutes the restoration of your being.

"The restoration of the kīla ultimately refers to the manifestation of the great wisdom of realizing identitylessness and gaining confidence within yourself. To represent this in relative terms, directly visualize the Supreme Son Kīla and emanate from him kīla replicas, like sparks emerging from fire. They completely fill all of saṃsāra and nirvāṇa, and, as before, all phenomena of the two kinds are reabsorbed and merge into the visualized Supreme Son Kīla, like salt dissolving into water. As a result, all the might, power, and strength of all of saṃsāra and nirvāṇa is drawn in and perfected. [257] This visualization is the relative path.

"For the restoration of the rūdra: Ultimately, the three realms of all the physical worlds and their sentient inhabitants are none other than the outer, inner, and secret rūdras[189] themselves, but this is obscured by ignorance. This is something to determine by means of investigation with great wisdom, and then to know as it is in reality. To represent it, directly visualize an effigy as your actual enemies and malevolent beings. From it black light is emanated, and the life force, life, vitality, merit, and possessions of all your enemies and malevolent beings are drawn in and merge with the light, like a water drop touched with the tip of a red-hot spike. Imagine them dissolving into the effigy. These three kinds of restoration are indispensable.

"Then, for the actual liberation, just by agitating the aggregates, elements, and sense bases of your enemies with the tip of the blade of the kīla—like churning butter from milk—the essential nature of the enemy's vitality turns into a shimmering white syllable *Nṛi*. This is completely drawn inside the tip of the kīla—like sucking up a water drop—and it dissolves into the kīla. Imagine that the kīla is filled to the brim, like a sack filled with yogurt. Again, with the mere agitation of their aggregates, elements, and sense bases, the essential nature of their life and merit turns into a shimmering green *Nṛi*. [258] This is completely drawn into the tip of the kīla, and all their taints and faults are purified through the kīla's aperture. Imagine that their consciousnesses emerge from the crowns of their heads and dissolve into you. Again imagine rays of white light emanating from the tip of the kīla, utterly purifying all the vices, obscurations, karma, and mental afflictions of your enemies and malevolent beings. This visualization is called the *transmission on purification*.

"In a similar way, with the vase water, the ambrosial blessings of the deities of the maṇḍala, gradually you completely purify all the causes for rebirth among the six classes of sentient beings—namely, karma, mental afflictions, and habitual propensities. This, too, is called the *transmission on purification*.

"At the time of actual liberation, when the kīla strikes the hearts of your enemies and malevolent beings, their consciousnesses turn into white bindus marked with the syllable *A*, and—as if they were being sucked up through a straw—they are drawn up through the aperture in the kīla. Then all their afflictive and cognitive obscurations are completely purified, like removing stains from a white crystal. From the lower globe of the kīla, the enlightened view of the nirmāṇakāya is transferred to their mindstreams. From its bulbous handle, the enlightened view of the saṃbhogakāya is transferred to their mindstreams; and from its upper globe, the enlightened view of the

189. Here the term *rūdra* refers to conceptual grasping by which one reifies the distinctions of outer, inner, and secret phenomena.

dharmakāya is transferred to their mindstreams.[190] [259] They dissolve into the heart of the deity generated in front of you, such that they achieve buddhahood in the expanse of the enlightened view of the four kāyas and the five facets of primordial consciousness. This visualization, in which they are elevated from their own abode, is the technique of the *transmission on the abode*.[191]

"In a similar fashion, to lead the deceased from where they are residing, all the appearances of the six classes of beings, the instantaneously arising miserable abodes, and all the habitual propensities, karma, and mental afflictions of saṃsāra are utterly purified and emerge as the appearances of a nirmāṇakāya buddhafield—as if roughly arousing someone from sleep. With the first *Phaṭ*, they are transferred to the enlightened view of the nirmāṇakāya; with the second, they are transferred to the enlightened view of the saṃbhogakāya; and with the third, they are transferred to the enlightened view of the dharmakāya. As a result, a pristine buddhafield appears in full measure. The meditation of recognizing awareness, achieving confidence, perfecting your strength, and achieving stability is called the technique of the *transmission on the abode*.

"Finally, all the aggregates, elements, and sense bases of your enemies and malevolent beings become forms of flesh and blood. These are offered to the mouth of your personal deity, thereby drawing the remains of saṃsāra into absolute space. The aggregates, elements, and sense bases of the deceased are held in the form of a nametag,[192] which is incinerated in the flames of primordial consciousness. Consequently, the residue of saṃsāra converges into the five facets of primordial consciousness. So this technique is similar to the previous one.

"If the one who is visualized in this way is alive, once he is liberated, [260] all the actions to guide him will definitely succeed. If you lack the three essential points of the fortress, highway, and vitality, whatever wrathful activities you perform will be like children's games and your goals will not be accomplished. Ultimately, in the great incarceration box of emptiness, the wisdom of realizing identitylessness liberates, like a sharp weapon, the rūdra of dualistic grasping at the physical worlds and their sentient inhabitants into

190. In this practice, the mindstream of the slain enemy is progressively liberated to each of the three kāyas as it travels through the three parts of the kīla.

191. Tib. *gnas lung gi cho ga.*

192. Tib. *ming byang.* A paper depicting an image and name of a person, into which that person's consciousness is invoked.

nonobjective identitylessness. Then the manifested primordial consciousness, pristine awareness, is aroused as the enlightened view of the three kāyas, and you proceed to the supreme state of liberation, the attainment of perfect enlightenment; and the residue of saṃsāra is withdrawn into absolute space.

"Self-grasping is the cause of the vital force and life of impure saṃsāra and the miserable states of existence, so the realization of identitylessness is the *transmission on the life of saṃsāra*. The nonconceptual primordial consciousness of ultimate reality dispels the taints of afflictive and cognitive obscurations into absolute space. This cleansing is the *purification transmission* on the removal of the habitual propensities of those two obscurations. Relatively speaking, through the teaching on the practice of liberation, liberation is possible. But all enemies and malevolent beings are self-appearances—delusive apparitions of thoughts. Their liberation, too, is an appearance of conceptualization, so this is the meaning of the ability to liberate them; and their liberation is also merely the *appearance* of their being liberated. *Summoning*, in addition, [261] is taught as gaining mastery over appearances.

"As for binding, ultimately you are bound by the cord of awareness. Relatively speaking, from the hearts of the self- and front visualizations, red light emanates in the form of cords that completely tie up and firmly bind the life force, life, and vitality as well as the body, speech, and mind of your enemies and malevolent beings. All their strength and ability to rise and move about is constrained and subdued, and you imagine them as if they were corpses cast upon a plain.

"As for isolating your enemies from their *daemons*,[193] ultimate reality is the method for isolating inborn primordial consciousness from the habitual propensities of ignorance—with which it has been melded—and for causing primordial consciousness to become manifest. Relatively speaking, place two feathers upon an incarceration box and imagine them as the owl-headed protector *piśācī*[194] and the crow-headed piśācī, with women's bodies, wings, and feathers. Imagine that they emit a noxious odor that overwhelms the gods of your enemies and malevolent beings, causes them to fall unconscious, and drives them away. The two piśācīs send out cries and begin to fight on top of the incarceration box, their wings fluttering, causing all the daemons who guard your enemies to faint, and leaving your enemies and malevolent beings stranded. [262] The two piśācīs emanate innumerable terrifying repli-

193. Tib. *lhan cig skyes pa'i lha*. A god that accompanies an individual from birth, serving as that person's protector, similar to the concept of *daemon* in classic Greek mythology.

194. Skt., Tib. *phra men*. One of eight flesh-eating protector deities with a bird's head and a woman's body or with a carnivorous animal's head and a man's body.

cas, which flail their wings, clawing the enemies and ripping them with their beaks. When the enemies are devoured, they are banished into the darkness inside a mountain on an island on the far side of the ocean. Imagine that they are so dazed that they cannot return. While reciting the mantra, flail them with a feather and fumigate them with substances. This is the way to expel them with substances, mantras, and samādhi.

"Ultimately, entering a state of intoxication is taught as the way to arouse a sense of violent delight before dispelling mental afflictions, karma, and habitual propensities. Relatively speaking, you unify all the karmic energy of all beings of the three realms, which, in the form of blackness, enters through the tips of the ring fingers of your enemies and malevolent beings. This form then passes into their vitality channels, and you imagine that they become intoxicated by the power of its movement and pass out. This visualization is the crucial point of samādhi. Wrathful mantras such as *Jva la pa ya* are the crucial point of the mantra, and fumigation with intoxicating incense is the crucial point of the substance.

"Pulverization in the mortar demonstrates that ultimately, by the great power of nondual skillful means and wisdom, the rūdra of the view of the self is released, to the point of vanishing altogether. Relatively speaking, all the forms, [263] aggregates, elements, and sense bases of your enemies and malevolent beings are gathered in the mortar of the secret space of the wrathful goddess Black Röljé. The supreme skillful means, the vajra pestle of [her consort,] the wrathful Blazing Pulverizer, hammers them so that they are pulverized into fine particles. Know that imagining this is the core of the samādhi, the mortar and pestle are the essential substances, and the mantra *Ta thā ya* and so forth is the essential mantra.

"By apprehending for yourself the dharmakāya, pristine awareness that is present in the ground, siddhis of the four kāyas and the five facets of primordial consciousness are achieved effortlessly. This is ultimate reality. Transforming siddhis into the spiritual path in dependence upon substances is taught as skillful means and as an auspicious act. In reality, even though you have mastered the dharmakāya, pristine awareness that is present in the ground, residual appearances and mindsets of saṃsāra may still linger. By achieving and perfecting the power of confidence, they vanish into ultimate reality. Relatively speaking, the remains of the gaṇacakra are offered to the illusory guests, the guardians of the remains. This is taught simply as skillful means and as an auspicious act.

"Just as the aggregations of karma and mental afflictions and the array of thoughts of the three times are vanquished by the power of natural liberation, by summoning your enemies and malevolent beings to the torma and annihilating them with the visualization techniques, their life and merit dissolves into you, their consciousness [264] dissolves into the heart of your principal personal deity, and their flesh, blood, and bones become ambrosia. They are gobbled up by the assembly of haughty guardians of the teachings, and they obey your commands to act. This visualization is taught as relative.

"Mundane existence that occurs in the natural order of dependent origination consists of displays of empty awareness, ultimate reality. The Great Mother who realizes the reverse order of the twelve links of dependent origination, the twelve aspects of emptiness, is the experience of the absolute space of the dharmakāya. This is ultimate reality. The inexhaustible tormas visualized as wish-fulfilling ambrosia are offered to the Earth Mātṛkās, who are commanded to engage in the enlightened activities of protecting the doctrine.[195] This is relative.

"As for the doctrine, the source of all the Dharmas of scripture and of realization is the nature of being of suchness, ultimate reality. All misconceptions, vices, and afflictive thoughts are confined in the incarceration box of equality, the emptiness of saṃsāra and nirvāṇa, and they are overwhelmed by the power of the displays of primordial consciousness. This is ultimate reality. Imagine that in the space of the black wind from the underlying ground, the blazing mouth of the triangular metal structure[196] of the belly of the Lord of Death, Karma Yama, suddenly gapes open. Innumerable emanations of the enlightened activities of all the jinas of the three times [265] instantly and inexorably summon all the damsis, *gab*s,[197] and demons, like dust blown away by the wind. As soon as they are cast inside the incarceration box, its lid closes over them, so there is no chance of their escape. Swooning into a state of bliss, they remain for a hundred eons, with no discursive thoughts arising in their mindstreams. Imagine vīras and vīrās emanated by the jinas dancing upon the incarceration box and overcoming the roots of all types of afflictions so that they can never arise again. This is relative.

"Ultimately, virtue has never been committed, the object of dedication is not established as real, and the one who dedicates is not established as real. With one taste in the displays of great, pervasive ultimate reality, there is no dedication that is established apart from leaving all collections of merit and knowledge in a self-emergent, spontaneously perfected state. Relatively

195. Tib. *ma mo brtan ma*; Skt. Mātṛkā-sthāvarā. The twelve Earth Mātṛkās were subjugated by Guru Padmasambhava and sworn to protect the Buddhadharma.

196. Tib. *gru gsum lcags khang.*

197. Tib. *sgab.* A demon that works in stealth.

speaking, all the collections of merit you have accumulated during the three times are unified, and you should dedicate them—just as all the jinas of the three times have dedicated them and will dedicate them—as causes for the attainment of the omniscient state of perfect enlightenment for all beings, without bias in time or space. [266]

"As for prayers, no object of prayers is established in reality apart from gaining mastery over the self-emergent, original state of the protector. Relatively speaking, you should pray that all beings may attain the state of enlightenment of perfect omniscience.

"Ultimately, the essence of auspiciousness is the perfection of all the sublime qualities of the great equality of originally pure ultimate reality, such as serenity, coolness, lucidity, and freedom from contamination. Accordingly, all the jinas and jinaputras of the ten directions arise from the absolute space of phenomena as beautiful appearances of the rūpakāya. They perform auspicious dances in the sky, and with the melodious speech of Brahmā they utter verses of auspiciousness. Their minds are mercifully set on granting the glories of such benefits to all beings. A rain of various lovely, auspicious flowers falls from their hands. This visualization is taught as being of the nature of relative skillful means.

"Ultimately, in the signless dharmakāya, the emanation and reabsorption of displays of all of saṃsāra and nirvāṇa are not established as real. Relatively speaking, the stage of generation—without the mistake of slipping into reification—dispels the extreme of an eternalist view. [267] The stage of generation, involving objects of attention with signs, is taught as a method for manifesting objectless, originally pure, enlightened view, free of conceptual elaboration, and as a method for realizing the three realms of saṃsāra to be like an illusion and a dream. So just as the pure appearances of primordial consciousness deities previously arose in their natural order from their causal syllables, they return to the state of ultimate reality, suchness.

"Alternatively, all the displays of buddhafields are reabsorbed into the palace; the palace is reabsorbed into the assembly of deities; the entire assembly of deities is reabsorbed into the absolute space of the principal deity; the principal deity is reabsorbed into the mantra circle; the mantra circle is reabsorbed into the *Hūṃ*; and the *Hūṃ* is reabsorbed into the crescent, which is reabsorbed into the bindu, which is reabsorbed into the nāda. Then the nāda is reabsorbed into the absolute space of phenomena. By remaining as long as you can in meditative equipoise in the state of pervasive emptiness, free of conceptual elaboration, the deities of meditative equipoise are withdrawn into absolute space.

"Ultimately, there is nothing for your own awareness to generate or visualize as the divine displays of original primordial consciousness. In this regard, instantaneously from the state of the absolute space of phenomena, emptiness free of conceptual elaboration—like the sudden appearance of a rainbow even though no rainbow exists in the sky, [268] or like the sudden appearance of bubbles in water in which no bubbles exist—in that very moment, from that empty absolute space, you suddenly visualize yourself as an assembly of primordial consciousness deities. Rays of light emanate from your three places, drawing in all the inexhaustible ornamental wheels of the enlightened body, speech, mind, qualities, and activities of all the jinas and jinaputras of the ten directions in the form of the syllables of white *Oṃ*, red *Āḥ*, and blue *Hūṃ*. As a result, imagine that your body is clothed in tightly woven vajra armor, which cannot be pierced or destroyed. Never being separated from divine pride is called the *path of relative skillful means*.

"Ultimately, there is no invocation or coming and going of the deities. By manifesting the self-emergent face of the absolute space of the ground as the spontaneous displays of the three kāyas, thoughts of ignorance are banished into oblivion. In general, all enemies and malevolent beings are nothing other than displays of your own mind's thoughts, and deities fabricated by thoughts arise as appearances to liberate you. For example, you may prepare a powder of various grasses, wood, flowers, minerals, flesh, and blood intended as a remedy for an illness. With the healer's firm intention to benefit, [269] and the patient's unwavering conviction that it will relieve the pain of the illness, an appearance of benefit definitely arises.

"Relatively speaking, out of anxiety about being harmed by enemies and malevolent beings, and in response to enemies and malevolent beings arising as aggressors, you emanate countless rays of light from your heart as your personal deity. They invoke terrifying forms of the jinas and jinaputras of the ten directions and the three times from the absolute space of phenomena. With weapons and sorcerer's substances, they apply themselves to the tasks of summoning and liberating all evil enemies and malevolent beings. This is analogous to taking revenge on your enemy by setting an army against him. Likewise, these beings fill all the realms of the universe, inexorably surrounding your enemies and malevolent beings, like deer driven into an enclosure, and you imagine them being violently killed and mutilated [by the jinas and jinaputras]. Like a king arousing and summoning his troops and giving them their wages, you imagine tormas becoming the inexhaustible ambrosia of primordial consciousness of the nature of mountains of flesh and oceans of blood, and you dedicate the merit.

"As for reversal, ultimately, to manifest primordial consciousness, pristine awareness, [270] all enemies and malevolent beings of mental afflictions are reverted to intangible, nonobjective displays of ultimate reality. In accordance with this method, from the heart and all the other places of the self- and front visualizations, emanate a malodorous mass of flames and assemblies of wrathful beings with iron scorpions, various weapons, and sorcerer's substances spreading everywhere throughout all the realms of the universe. These wrathful beings and their assistants liberate all your enemies and malevolent beings, hacking them up with various weapons. Many garuḍas and iron scorpions devour them, their remains are incinerated in a blaze of fire, and they are dispersed by a razor-like wind. Their consciousnesses are liberated into absolute space, in which delusion is impossible, leaving not even a trace behind. This visualization is taught as a relative path of skillful means.

"Ultimately, the wisdom that knows reality as it is and perceives the full range of phenomena, along with great primordial consciousness, incinerates all mental states and mental factors like the conflagration at the end of the eon. Like burning kindling in a fire, adventitious impurities are incinerated in the state of pristine awareness that transcends causality. To illustrate this, first *Bhrūṃ* transforms, becoming in the center an indigo flame of the nature of the primordial consciousness of the absolute space of phenomena, in the east [271] a white flame of the nature of mirror-like primordial consciousness, in the south a yellow flame of the nature of the primordial consciousness of equality, in the west a red flame of the nature of discerning primordial consciousness, and in the north a blazing dark-green flame of the nature of the primordial consciousness of accomplishment.

"For pacification, imagine a circle; for enrichment, a square; for power, a semicircle; for wrathfulness, a triangle; and for spontaneous actualization, an octagon. Moreover, imagine for pacification a white palace of fire; for enrichment, a yellow palace of fire; for power, a red palace of fire; for wrathfulness, a green or blue-green palace of fire; and for spontaneous actualization, an indigo or a multicolored palace of fire. Understand that the essential nature of all these is primordial consciousness, though their forms are palaces in the nature of flames.

"In their center, imagine the morning time of pacification as the nature of a white assembly of deities, the afternoon time of enrichment as a yellow assembly of deities, the evening time of power as a red assembly of deities, and dusk, the time of wrathfulness, as the nature of a green assembly of deities.

"Imagine the essential nature of all the substances to be burned in the process of pacification as the undefiled ambrosia of primordial consciousness, taking the form of these substances, which are offered to the mouths of the deities. As a result, the minds of the entire assembly of deities are delighted with the taste of bliss and emptiness. [272] Then white-colored rays of light emanate from their bodies, completely clearing away all diseases, demons, vices, obscurations, karmas, mental afflictions, and habitual propensities of your own mindstream and those of the beings you are visualizing, like the sun shining upon frost. Repeatedly imagine them being totally purified, without even a trace being left behind. This is the visualization for pacification.

"For enrichment, visualize the entire assembly of radiant deities, invite all the jinas and jinaputras of the three times in the form of your special deity,[198] and imagine them dissolving into this assembly. Imagine the essential nature of all the substances to be burned as the immeasurable, undefiled ambrosia of the primordial consciousness of bliss and emptiness taking the form of each of these substances. With this offering to the mouths of the assembly of deities, their minds are delighted with the taste of bliss and emptiness, and all their majesty, power, and abilities expand greatly. Emanating blazing rays of light, they draw in all the compassion, blessings, empowerments, siddhis, facets of primordial consciousness, and enlightened qualities of the entire assembly of the jinas, bodhisattvas, gurus, personal deities, dharmapālas, gods of wealth, and treasure holders, without exception. And they draw in all the life, merit, radiance, power, and abilities of all gods and demons, the eight classes of haughty gods and demons, and all the beings of the three realms of the universe.

"With these dissolving into you and the visualized deities, [273] repeatedly imagine that your life, merit, wealth, empowerments, siddhis, power, and abilities all grow and are greatly enriched. Imagine that all the empowerments, blessings, and siddhis of the deities generated in front of you also dissolve into you in the form of a yellow mass of light, such that your vitality, merit, wealth, power, and creative abilities are enriched and stabilized.

"For power, all the substances to be burned are displayed in the form of each of these substances, and their essential nature is bliss and emptiness, the vital essence of the ambrosia of undefiled primordial consciousness. The mere sight of this brings fulfillment, the mere touch of it brings satisfaction, and the mere experience of it has the ability to liberate. With this offering to the mouths of the primordial consciousness deities, their minds are intoxicated by the taste of the primordial consciousness of bliss and emptiness. The radiance, majesty, power, and enormous might of their bodies blaze up, reabsorbing in the form of rays of red light all the power, empowerments, and siddhis of the jinas and jinaputras of the ten directions and the four times, as well as all the guardians of the doctrine, dharmapālas, gods of wealth, and

198. Tib. *lhag pa'i lha*. Synonymous with "personal deity" (Tib. *yi dam*).

treasure holders. Dissolving all this into yourself, imagine that you possess the power of mastery over both saṃsāra and nirvāṇa.

"Further, all the compassion, blessings, [274] and siddhis of the deity generated in front of you dissolve into yourself in the form of rays of red light. From your heart and the hearts of the deities generated in front of you, immeasurable rays of red light are emanated in forms like hooks and nooses. All the enjoyments, wealth, and abodes of the gods, demons, and humans of the three realms and the three worlds, of male and female beings, and of the eight classes of gods and demons, yakṣas, gods of wealth, and treasure holders are inexorably brought under your control and placed in front of you. Consequently, overwhelmed by the majesty and unbearably glorious radiance of your body and that of the deity generated in front of you, they agree to be your servants and to work on your behalf, swearing to assist you forever. As a sign of their oaths, vajras appear on the crowns of their heads. Having received the vitality of their solemn samayas, imagine that an unimpeded flow of a torrential rain of all manner of enjoyments descends upon your dwelling. With the use of such visualizations you should become skillful in the transformations of the objects of subjugation.

"On occasions for wrathfulness, the substances to be burned are visualized as being of the essential nature of the combined flesh, blood, life force, life, and vitality of your enemies and malevolent beings. They are forcefully summoned and put into the incarceration box. And when they are finally scooped up with the ritual ladle, all the life force, life, physical forms, vitality, and breath of these enemies [275] is ladled up, like fruit scooped up by the handful. Then repeatedly imagine the clear, pale soles of the enemies' feet dissolving into the mouths of the visualized deities in the midst of the fire, like a pebble thrown into a pond. Even in the case of a murdered person, imagine his body and consciousness indivisibly dissolving into the mouth of your personal deity. As you count the number of scoops and offer them into the fire, with the essential point of visualizing this intently, the murdered person will certainly not take birth among demons or malevolent spirits.

"By engaging in the visualizations of pacification for others, know that the essential point is drawing the mind of the deceased into the expanse of your personal deity. By repeatedly performing burnt offerings in these ways, you have the advantage of accomplishing the four types of enlightened activity, which are taught as relative.

"Imagining that the celestial palace of your own body is filled with the entire assembly of deities of the maṇḍala, like an overflowing mound of sesame seeds, with the ritual ladles of your hands, offer all your food and drink as displays of the ambrosia of the primordial consciousness of bliss and emptiness. This is the unsurpassed burnt offering of transforming food and drink into the spiritual path.

"Ultimately, accurately realizing and manifesting the primordial consciousness and qualities of ultimate reality, the sugatagarbha, is the vase empowerment of the body. [276] Manifesting precious, spontaneously actualized absolute space by means of pervasive, all-seeing great wisdom is the secret empowerment of speech. Manifesting ultimate reality, nonconceptual absolute space, is the wisdom–primordial-consciousness empowerment of the mind. Manifesting all the qualities of the kāyas, facets of primordial consciousness, paths, and fruitions, which are unsought and spontaneously perfected, is the fourth empowerment of the word, or the unsurpassed supreme siddhi.

"As the method for this, a mass of white light marked by *Oṃ* emanates from the absolute space of the bodies of all the deities generated in front of you. Entering your body through the crown of your head, it blesses your body as the nature of the immutable vajra body, and causes the state of a matured vidyādhara to manifest. All the secret empowerments, blessings, and siddhis of speech as a mass of red light marked by *Āḥ* dissolve through your throat into your voice, blessing your voice as unimpeded vajra speech, and causing the state of a vidyādhara with mastery over life to manifest. All the empowerments, blessings, and siddhis of the mind as indigo light marked by *Hūṃ* dissolve into your heart, blessing your mind as undeluded vajra mind, and causing the state of a *mahāmudrā* vidyādhara to manifest. [277]

"Once again, five-colored rays of light, like a mass of rainbows, emanate from the five places of the deities in front of you and dissolve into your own five places, utterly purifying the two obscurations and all habitual propensities. Blessing you with all the inexhaustible ornamental wheels of their enlightened body, speech, mind, qualities, and activities, this causes the state of a spontaneously actualized vidyādhara to manifest. In short, this visualization that you have achieved all the supreme and mundane siddhis without exception is taught as relative.

"Ultimately, all such paths taught as skillful means of the stage of generation are self-appearing and naturally complete in the ground awareness, the great freedom from extremes. All bodily and verbal activities of the path of skillful means of the stage of generation are features of the dharmakāya, the pristine awareness that is present in the ground. Taking a metaphor for each one, they are taught simply in terms of the field of experience of the mind caught up in activities and actors. Know that they have no reality apart from that. Until now, under the influence of ignorance, the qualities of the ground have been reduced to an ethically neutral state, which is of no benefit or harm. If you know how they are perfect in this way, this perfection is made manifest, so this is an unsurpassed feature that distinguishes the yāna of the Great Perfection. [278] By recognizing the skillful means aspect of the stage of generation in the absolute space of wisdom, you know that the *Tantra of the Union of Interrelated Wisdom and Skillful Means* is none other than this.

"Here is a method for transferring your impure body, speech, and mind into the realm of the three primordial consciousness vajras. Small-minded people cannot accept pristine space, the great mystery of all the buddhas, absolute space free of all extremes of conceptual elaboration, in which ultimately there is no body. But practicing the following method eventually liberates you into the realm of the essential nature: Instantly transform your own body into red Vajrayoginī, with a blazing curved flaying knife in your right hand subjugating all the three realms, and a marked skull cup in your left hand. As such, you display the three realms as the ambrosia of enlightened body, speech, and mind. With your legs in an advancing posture, you are a youthful maiden of sixteen years, your body beautifully adorned with the signs and symbols of enlightenment. The braids in your hair are adorned with five kinds of precious substances and beautified with a diadem. Your head is wreathed in various flowers.

"With a countenance both slightly peaceful and slightly wrathful, your body, in the midst of a blazing mass of rainbow fire, [279] is visualized as appearing and yet not established as real. Its essential nature is empty and primordially not established in any way. But to forcefully counteract the delusion of clinging to it as a material composite, its emptiness is presented as the lucidity of the body, even though there is no emptiness inside it. While imagining lucidity within its center as a means to subdue the energy-mind in emptiness, visualize your hollow body as a pavilion of light. In its center is a hollow channel, a tube of light, which is white on the outside, symbolizing bliss; red on the inside, symbolizing luminosity; and blue like azurite[199] in between, symbolizing emptiness. Its interior is empty and unobstructed, symbolizing bodhicitta. It is as long as an average-sized arrow shaft, and its surface has no width at all. Its upper end, at the cakra of great bliss at the crown of the head, is temporarily open; and its lower end, below the navel, is firmly closed like a bamboo joint. Its characteristics are that it is as straight as the trunk of a plantain tree, as thin as a lotus petal, as clear as a sesame oil lamp, and as shiny as teak tree sap. As sheer emptiness, it abides in the essential nature of the dharmakāya.

"On its right is the red *rasanā* channel, red on the outside and white on the

199. Tib. *mthing zhun.*

inside. On its left [280] is the white *lalanā* channel, white on the outside and red on the inside. The lower ends of both are inserted into the *avadhūti*, the central channel, below the navel. Visualize their upper ends curving around the back of your ears and opening out through both nostrils. Know that these three symbolize the three kāyas.

"The *five stacked cakras* in the central channel have secondary channels: In the first cakra distinctly visualize thirty-two secondary channels; in the second, sixteen secondary channels; in the third, eight secondary channels; in the fourth, sixty-four secondary channels; and in the fifth, twenty-eight secondary channels.[200] Ultimately, however, all of saṃsāra and nirvāṇa is pervaded by the emptiness of the central [channel]. The rasanā represents the primordial consciousness of its clear nature, and the lalanā stands for the great primordial consciousness of omnipresent compassion.[201] All the aggregates, elements, and sense bases are emptiness, which is primordially unestablished and nonabiding. The placement of emptiness in the center is taught as a basis for purification, but it is certainly not established as being real.

"The three kāyas are revealed as the three channels in the way of primordially self-emergent great emptiness. The nine yānas are revealed as remedies to purify in absolute space the obscurations of ignorance, karma, and mental afflictions. Accordingly, while recognizing the karmic energies as being of the nature of karma, the mental afflictions, and habitual propensities, [281] you clear out the residual energies by means of the ninefold expulsion.

"For this, imagine that all the karma, mental afflictions, vices, obscurations, and habitual propensities aroused by the affliction of hatred are expelled through your right nostril in the form of smoke-colored air and disappear into space. Clear these three times.

"Imagine that all the karma, mental afflictions, vices, obscurations, and habitual propensities aroused by the affliction of attachment are expelled in the form of dark red air, and clear these out three times through your left nostril.

"Imagine that all the karma, mental afflictions, vices, obscurations, and habitual propensities aroused by the affliction of delusion are expelled in the form of indigo air and disappear into space like a rainbow. Clear these out three times through both nostrils equally, and imagine that all illnesses, demons, vices, obscurations, and habitual propensities, together with the material aggregate of flesh and blood, disappear into space in the form of minute particles, like soil shaken from a cloth.

200. These are the crown, throat, heart, navel, and genital cakras, respectively.

201. These three symbolize the dharmakāya, saṃbhogakāya, and nirmāṇakāya, respectively.

"Imagine that in the domain of the channels, vital energies, and bindus, all the causes that delude you endlessly in saṃsāra, together with their seeds and habitual propensities, are expelled as fragments of blackness and disappear into space. Recognize this purification [282] of the body as the sublime, quintessential means for clearing out negative actions and malevolent beings.

"Then, in terms of the vital energy of meditative equipoise and the vital energy of the postmeditative state, ultimately the space of wisdom is apprehended in the great clear light, pristine awareness, the primordial consciousness of all the jinas. Leaving your body, speech, and mind in a state of inactivity is the unsurpassed, supreme technique for inserting the energy-mind into the central channel.

"In this technique, with your body in the sevenfold posture of Vairocana, imagine in the space in front of you and level with the tip of your nose the synthesized essential nature of all the empowerments, blessings, and siddhis of the enlightened body, speech, mind, qualities, and activities of all the jinas and jinaputras of the ten directions and the four times in the form of light blue air, like a covering of mist. Imagine that from your nostrils the vital energy of blessings and primordial consciousness is drawn in like a blue silken thread or wafting incense smoke. Imagine that it swirls completely into the lower end of the central channel by way of the rasanā and lalanā channels. And in the central channel, like an inflated balloon, all the channel knots become completely untied.

"Imagine that the quintessence of the vital energies dissolves into the five secondary channels, and the residues swirl into the lower end of the central channel. During each session, rotate your torso three times [283] and press down, uninterruptedly drawing up a continuous stream of gentle energy, and hold it as long as you can. This is the vital energy of meditative equipoise.

"Alternatively, inside the central channel at the level of your heart, visualize a smooth, round bindu of five lights, and in its center imagine a clear, shimmering white syllable *A*, pale like a full moon. In the lower end of the central channel, imagine the energies of the five facets of primordial consciousness in the form of a vajra swastika. As in the previous case, imagine that the quintessence of the energies dissolves into the syllable *A* and the bindu, while the residue dissolves into the variegated vajra swastika, which is the basis of the energies. By sustaining this visualization, the energies will be inserted into the central channel, and the energies of primordial consciousness will rest in their own place.

"In the postmeditative state as well, ultimately, you do not depart from the domain of your own pristine awareness, free from delusion with respect to appearances or the mind. Those who lack such a crucial point should continually press down their vital energy below the navel and never forget to do so, including during such activities as eating, sleeping, walking, and sitting. This is the vital energy of the postmeditative state, and it is especially profound to achieve stability in it.

"Ultimately, primordial consciousness that knows reality as it is actualizes the center[202] that is present in the ground, and primordial consciousness that perceives the full range of phenomena extinguishes the karmic energies in their own place [284] and causes the energy of primordial consciousness to rest in its own place. The flaming up of *caṇḍālī*[203]—great, empty awareness, devoid of activity, the fire of primordial consciousness, the union of bliss and emptiness, which blazes as a display of the power of the five facets of primordial consciousness—arouses delight in the maṇḍala of self-appearing primordial consciousness. Once all the deluded karma, mental afflictions, and habitual propensities of ignorance are naturally purified, you achieve in yourself the great confidence of the originally pure dharmakāya. This is the ultimate caṇḍālī.

"Relatively speaking, visualize the essential nature of the vajra of the skillful means of great bliss in the form of the syllable *Haṃ* at the upper end of the central channel of emptiness. At its lower end visualize the essential nature of the wisdom of great emptiness in the form of a cone. When [the central channel] is touched by the creative power of pristine awareness of the essential nature of discerning primordial consciousness, in the form of blessings and the vital energies of primordial consciousness, the caṇḍālī flame of primordial consciousness consequently bears four characteristics: the color red, the essential nature of bliss, the nature of luminosity, and being hot to the touch.

"Visualizing it as sharp and darting, with its tip as the nature of wisdom, flickering many times, apply these four essential points: inhale slowly, fill the navel, churn the stomach, and shoot the residue up like an arrow. Through this, the flame blazes in the navel cakra and suffuses it, incinerating all karma, mental afflictions, and habitual propensities so that none remain. [285] The flame grows and totally engulfs all the cakras of the *dharmacakra* at the heart, incinerating all karma, mental afflictions, and habitual propensities without remainder.

"Spreading upward, it totally suffuses the cakra of the wheel of enjoyment at the throat, burning to a crisp all karma, mental afflictions, and habitual

202. Tib. *dbu ma*; Skt. *madhyama.*

203. Tib. *gtum mo.*

propensities. Increasing further in size, it totally fills and suffuses the entire cakra of great bliss at the crown of the head, burning to a crisp all karma, mental afflictions, and habitual propensities. Flaming up again, it strikes the syllable *Haṃ* at the crown, increasing the experience of the primordial consciousness of bliss and emptiness, in which skillful means and wisdom are united. The ambrosia of the primordial consciousness of bliss and emptiness from the bindu descends in a continuous stream, filling and suffusing all the secondary channels of the cakra of great bliss and making immeasurable offerings that please the body maṇḍala of the sugatas. Their minds being delighted with the taste of bliss and emptiness, the two accumulations are completed and the two obscurations are purified. Consider that you receive the vase empowerment of the body and that the great primordial consciousness of ecstasy arises in your mindstream.

"Again the overflow of the ambrosia descends, pervading all the secondary channels of the cakra of enjoyment at the throat and making offerings that please the speech maṇḍala of the sugatas. [286] Imagine that their minds are delighted with the taste of bliss and emptiness, the accumulations are completed, the obscurations are purified, you receive the secret empowerment of speech, and the primordial consciousness of supreme ecstasy arises in your mindstream.

"Again the ambrosia, descending to your heart, pervades all the secondary channels of the dharmacakra at the heart, making offerings that please the mind maṇḍala of the sugatas. Imagine that their minds are delighted with the taste of bliss and emptiness, the accumulations are completed, the obscurations are purified, you receive the wisdom–primordial-consciousness empowerment of the mind, and the primordial consciousness of extraordinary ecstasy arises and is experienced in your mindstream.

"Again the ambrosia, descending to your navel, fills and pervades all the secondary channels of the cakra of emanation at the navel and makes offerings that please the maṇḍala of the enlightened qualities of the sugatas. Imagine that their minds are delighted with the taste of bliss and emptiness, the accumulations are completed, the obscurations are purified, you receive the precious word empowerment, and the primordial consciousness of connate ecstasy arises and is experienced in your mindstream.

"Again the ambrosia, descending to your secret place, pervades all the secondary channels of the cakra of sustaining bliss and makes offerings that please the maṇḍala of the enlightened activities of the sugatas. Imagine that the undefiled joy of the ambrosia of bliss and emptiness is generated, the caṇḍālī fire of primordial consciousness [287] is conjoined with great warmth, the blessing energy of primordial consciousness generates power, the accumulations are completed, the obscurations are purified, and you simultaneously receive all the empowerments and siddhis of the inexhaustible ornamental wheels of the enlightened body, speech, mind, qualities, and activities [of the sugatas]. Imagine that inconceivable primordial consciousness arises and is experienced in your mindstream.

"Again the ambrosia of great bliss descends to the base of the flaming cone, such that you experience the great primordial consciousness of bliss and emptiness. Then imagine that the nature of the blessing energy of primordial consciousness, the caṇḍālī fire of primordial consciousness, and the ambrosia of the primordial consciousness of bliss and emptiness grow and burst into flame, completely engulfing all the channels and elements of the body. Then all obstacles, demons, malevolent beings, thoughts, and habitual propensities are incinerated, like tiny insects consumed in the conflagration at the end of the eon.

"Finally, the central channel together with the fire grows larger, such that all three realms of the physical worlds and their sentient inhabitants are included within the central channel, and all concepts of grasping at the physical worlds and their sentient inhabitants along with all karma and mental afflictions are burned to a crisp. Imagine that they all become of the nature of emptiness. The entire central channel together with all the fire abides as it did previously, [288] and while focusing your consciousness on this, count many full breaths of air.

"Alternatively, with yourself as Vajrayoginī, visualize a red cone at your navel, together with a bindu and nāda, and a white upside-down syllable *Haṃ* at the crown of your head. From the space at the tip of your nose, draw in through each nostril a blue mist of blessing energies, like silken threads of primordial consciousness, which pass through the channels of rasanā and lalanā and unite at the lower end of the central channel. Agitating the bindu in the cone, the flame of wisdom–primordial-consciousness blazes up, incinerating all karma, mental afflictions, and habitual propensities. All knots in the channels are loosened by the vital energies so that they dissolve naturally. Consider that the fire fills the cakras, and your entire body is suffused with great warmth.

"Throughout the network of channels within the body a white bindu rests atop each knot and a red bindu rests beneath each one. All the major, medium, and small channels are filled with the fire energy, whereupon the bindus merge indivisibly. All qualities of meditative experiences and realization are further enhanced. The entire interior of the central channel is suffused with the flame, and a continuous stream of the ambrosia of the undefiled primordial consciousness of bliss and emptiness of the melted bindu [289] of the *Haṃ* syllable strikes the cone. Imagine that as a result, the fire and ambrosia blaze nondually, such that the facets of primordial consciousness of the four ecstasies of bliss and emptiness suddenly arise in your mindstream and become immutably stable. Retain the breath many times in accordance with the duration of your meditation session.

"At all times and in all situations, do not forget the increase of the caṇḍālī flame of primordial consciousness in the central channel and all the cakras, and continuously focus your consciousness on holding your vital energy down beneath the navel. This is the crucial point for the postmeditative state, and this will also cause the warmth of bliss to blaze mightily.

"Some people take the following as the foundation and train in the yoga of space: Noisily sucking in three times, imagine that everything, right down to the last bit of space, is drawn into your mouth, and your belly is entirely filled with a blueness. Your belly encompasses all-pervasive space, so all of space is fathomed inside your abdomen. Suddenly and completely release this space, indivisible with your energy-mind, and remain in this meditative equipoise for as long as you can.

"Again suck in all the air, imagining it in the aspect of the color green, such that all air moving through space, together with its quintessence and vital essence, completely fills your abdomen. [290] Again, with a sucking sound, imagine inhaling all the water in the aspect of the color white, such that water, together with its vital essence and power, completely fills your belly. Then imagine inhaling all the earth of the three realms in the aspect of the color yellow with a sucking sound, leaving not even a trace of a remainder and totally filling your abdomen. Again suck in all the fire in the aspect of red light, and imagine that the quintessence and vital essence of the fire of the phenomenal world, together with the warmth of bliss, completely fills your belly. The sublime path of the yoga of the displays of the vital essence of the elements is placing the fire and the ultimate nature of mind in the state of nondual uniform pervasiveness.

"In reality, the central channel is emptiness; the fire and vital energy are the primordial consciousness that knows reality as it is and perceives the full range of phenomena. The syllable *Haṃ* is the skillful means of great bliss. The cone is the essential nature of the wisdom of emptiness. The cakras are the five facets of primordial consciousness. The five aggregates are the five sugatas. The five elements are the five consorts. The eight faculties are the eight male bodhisattvas, and the eight objects are the eight female bodhisattvas. The four extremes pertaining to existence and nonexistence[204] are the four gatekeepers, and all assemblies of thoughts are the spontaneously actualized assemblies of noble vīras [291] and yoginīs of absolute space, which vanish into emptiness.

"Thus, the support is the channels, what moves is the vital energies, and the displays are the essential nature called *bodhicitta*. They are perfected as natural expressions of ultimate reality, the sugatagarbha, so this is called the *Great Perfection of the four modes of existence*. Accurately knowing the manner in which they are perfected is called the *Great Perfection of the path of ultimate reality*. By establishing with discerning wisdom the ethically neutral existence of the Great Perfection that is present in the ground, you accurately know the nature of existence. Consequently, you progress through the grounds and paths all at once, and exactly this is the genuine Great Perfection of the complete, definitive path.

"In this way, the qualities of training with the channels, bindus, and vital energies cause the siddhi of the fruitional Great Perfection to become manifest, and you achieve mastery over the eight common siddhis. Moreover, the *Tantra of the Purificatory Yoga of the Channels, Vital Energies, and Bindus* is none other than this."

At this point Bodhisattva Vajra of Pristine Awareness made a vast prayer:

O excellent! Excellent, Bhagavān!
The empty vajra pierces jewels.
Empty Rāhula conquers the sun and moon.
Empty flames burn up kindling. [292]
The empty movement of air disperses material things.
Empty space conquers the physical worlds and their sentient
inhabitants.
Empty ultimate reality conquers phenomena.
The buddhas conquer māras.
The Saṅgha conquers false views.
May the view of emptiness be realized
with the precious truth of emptiness.
May the meaning of the Great Perfection be realized
with the precious view of emptiness.
By the power of the Great Perfection,
may saṃsāra be dredged from its depths.

204. Tib. *mu bzhi*; Skt. *catuṣkoṭi*. The four philosophical extremes (Greek *tetralemma*) are existence, nonexistence, both, and neither.

The Synthesis and Names of the Great Perfection

Then he continued, "O Teacher, Bhagavān, even if one correctly knows the nature of the Great Perfection of saṃsāra and nirvāṇa—the great expanse that totally subsumes the inexhaustible ornamental wheels of the enlightened body, speech, mind, qualities, and activities of the jinas and jinaputras of the three times, the great quintessence of all the ḍākinīs and vīras—in what is this synthesized, in what is it subsumed, and what are its names? Teacher, please explain!"

He replied, "O Vajra of Pristine Awareness, this is synthesized in first simply determining the mode of existence of the ground as discussed previously, then ascertaining emptiness as the ground emptiness, the great Madhyamaka. Therefore, the knowledge that all the kāyas, [293] facets of primordial consciousness, buddhafields, and their displays, along with all of saṃsāra, nirvāṇa, and the path, are not other than the nature of the ground itself is called the *Great Perfection of saṃsāra and nirvāṇa*. To beings who have not gained liberation within themselves, the ground appears as the nature of saṃsāra. Clinging to it, they become deluded. By turning away from delusional mental engagement with self-concepts and signs, and by establishing the ground by means of analytical great wisdom, you come to know the characteristics of the ground as they are. The synthesis of the pristine space of the ground is profound insight into the nature of the ground itself as the skillful means of the path and fruition and as all the avenues of wisdom.

"In what is it subsumed? No matter how the various reflections of planets and stars may appear in the ocean, they are not other than the ocean itself, so they are subsumed in the ocean. All appearances of the physical worlds, their sentient inhabitants, and sensory objects are not other than space itself, so they are subsumed in space. Likewise, you should know the way in which all of saṃsāra, nirvāṇa, and the path is not other than the nature of the expanse of the absolute space of phenomena, for this is simply the pristine domain of the absolute space of phenomena.

"How is it to be named? [294] All the names in the realms of saṃsāra and nirvāṇa are determined to be names of the sugatagarbha. In particular, it is called by all the names of all the phenomena that cause the path to become manifest. Since it is the unsurpassed transference and entrance to the experience of the fruition—the state of precious bodhicitta—it is called *bodhicitta*. All authentic realities are included in precious bodhicitta, so it is *reality*. Just as the ocean is ascertained as the source of all rivers and streams, it is ascertained as the ultimate source of all dharmas, so it is *ultimate*. It is free of all flaws and defilements, so it is *pure*. Since all of saṃsāra, nirvāṇa, the path, and the fruition is perfected in the absolute space of phenomena, it is *perfect*. All the phenomena of saṃsāra and nirvāṇa are determined by means of discerning wisdom, so that the wisdom of realizing identitylessness is made manifest. Pervasive, all-seeing great wisdom manifests the nature of existence; confidence is achieved within yourself; and by holding your own ground, the three realms of saṃsāra are dredged from their depths. Rather than regarding this as being like dream appearances disappearing into the space of awareness, or like illusory apparitions dissolving into the space of awareness, [295] by the might of the great mind, the three realms of saṃsāra are liberated as displays of the three kāyas. So this is called *citta*.[205]

"These teachings, far more secret than any mystery, are of the nature of the synthesis of the mystery of the mind of all the buddhas, so they are called *secret*. As for the way to follow the path to the nature of this ground sugatagarbha, it is not for the following people:

- Those who are not suitable vessels
- Those who are not drawn to Mahāyāna Dharma but are attracted to the Hīnayāna
- Those whose minds are generally unfit, whose mindstreams are prone to spiritual sloth and distractions, and who idle away their lives, delighting in conversation and friends and devoting their lives to that
- Those who wander about in mobs like birds and dogs in search of food
- Those with many opinions, coarse minds, and little fortitude, and those who say out loud whatever comes to mind
- Those who yearn and strive for riches, fame, profit, and devious conduct in this life and who, even though they are told about death, take no heed of it
- Those who, for their whole lives, are repulsed by the Dharma, deeds of spiritual people, and the Three Jewels
- Those who, when the Dharma is explained to them, merely retort, 'I know that; I've heard that,' [296] while holding false views concerning the Three Jewels
- Those who, even when the words of Dharma are explained to them, regard them as misleading lies
- Those who listen to the Dharma from their guru and behave with great faith and reverence while in his presence, but who steal the wealth of his followers when they are out of his sight
- Those with degenerated samayas who revile and slander their guru

205. This etymologizes "ultimate bodhicitta" (Tib. *don dam byang chub kyi sems*): reality (*don*), ultimate (*dam*), pure (*byang*), perfect (*chub*) citta (*sems*).

and all his followers and friends, as well as express deplorable, wrong views
- Evil enemies of the teachings who listen to the Dharma from their guru, but engage in conduct that damages the reputation of their guru and spiritual friends and brings harm to the teachings
- Those who trust nothing, whose minds are easily changed, and whose opinions vacillate

"With bad karma, they are not suitable vessels for the secret mantra. They will have no karmic connection with the profound secret mantra in all their lives, for they are people with bad karma whose mindstreams have been influenced by evil māras and damsis. Even if they were taught the Dharma of secret mantra, it would be of no benefit but would rather act as a cause for them to fall into Vajra Hell. So it is very secret.

"As for the time, inappropriate occasions for teaching and listening to the Dharma are when:
- Walking in the marketplace or in crowds
- Working
- Urinating or defecating
- Joking or quarreling
- Pompously carrying a parasol, [297] a staff, or a weapon
- Giving teachings other than those you have heard
- Fingering your rosary, performing circumambulations, wearing a cap and shoes, working, or engaging in conversation

"It is inappropriate to teach Dharma on those occasions. If people gather without faith, they too will fall into hell, so it is wrong to give teachings even upwind of such people who are not suitable vessels or on such inappropriate occasions. So they should be hidden like stolen property, as a solemn, hidden secret.

"In general, the primordially enlightened, undeluded, unfluctuating dharmakāya, the sugatagarbha, pervades the mindstreams of all sentient beings of the three realms. Just as all the planets and stars in the ocean are not other than the ocean and are pervaded by the ocean, all the phenomena of saṃsāra are pervaded by ultimate reality. However, under the influence of ignorance, by nature it remains concealed, so this is the concealed secret. Being endowed with these two great secrets, it is called *secret*.

"All the delusive mind states and appearances of all sentient beings of the three realms are overcome in absolute space, which transcends causality, so it is called *mantra*. All the intellectual ideologies of the eight yānas are overcome in the state of the dharmakāya, which is free of signs. [298] Since this is the great primordial consciousness, pristine awareness, free of extremes, it is called *mantra*.

"Here are the characteristics of this clear-light Great Perfection, the unsurpassed secret mantra, which is just this pristine awareness that is present in the ground:

- Invulnerability
- Indestructibility
- Reality
- Incorruptibility
- Stability
- Total unobstructability
- Utter invincibility
- Liberating sentient beings
- Terrifying
- Frightening
- Shattering all knowledge mantras
- Overcoming all knowledge mantras
- Commanding all deeds of knowledge mantras
- Accomplishing that which has not been accomplished
- Sustaining that which has been accomplished
- Fulfilling all desires
- Protecting all sentient beings
- Serenity
- Expansiveness
- Setting straight all beings
- Stupefying
- Accomplishing all deeds
- Overcoming all others' deeds
- Routing all grahas
- Liberating all grahas
- Summoning all bhūtas
- Liberating all bhūtas

"As it is endowed with these qualities, it is called *vajra*. [299] As for the term *yāna*, even when there is delusion, all the vices, obscurations, and miseries of all sentient beings do not worsen it, so it is self-upholding.[206] At the time of enlightenment, all the facets of primordial consciousness and qualities of

206. Tib. *rang theg pa*.

the realms of the buddhas do not correct or improve it. Thus, since all that is good and bad upholds itself, it is called *yāna*.[207]

"Upon establishing all self-concepts and delusive appearances as being of the empty nature of ultimate reality, the wisdom of realizing identitylessness is revealed, and you realize the state of emptiness free of conceptual elaboration. This realization is the most sublime of all states of consciousness, so it is called *wisdom*. As it transcends knowledge and the objects of knowledge, it is called the *perfection of wisdom*.[208]

"Now the unrevealed clear-light nature of the minds of sentient beings is identified, and you ascertain saṃsāra and nirvāṇa as displays of this clear light. So it is called the *clear light*. The ultimate, indestructible *vajra* is of the nature of the unified essence of all the jinas of the three times, so it is called the *essence*.[209]

"Because it transcends all the karma, mental afflictions, and habitual propensities of saṃsāra, it is called *saṃsāra and nirvāṇa*. [300] Since all the phenomena included in saṃsāra and nirvāṇa are fully included in the displays of the suchness of ultimate reality, it is said to be *complete*. Because all the causes of saṃsāra, nirvāṇa, and the path and their effects are totally perfected in the expanse of great, pervasive ultimate reality, it is called *consummation*.[210]

"As it does not fall to the extreme of birth, it is free of birth. As it does not fall to the extreme of aging, it is free of aging. As it does not fall to the extreme of decline, it is free of decline. And as it does not fall to the extreme of death, it is free of death. That which is free of these is given the name *youthful*. The spontaneous displays of the great inner luminosity of the ground itself are not separate from the ground, so the name *vase* is given. For example, all the reflections of the planets and stars are not separate from the expanse of the ocean, and all the physical worlds and their sentient inhabitants are not separate from the expanse of space. All the Dharmas of the path, the various experiences of joyful and painful sensations, the displays of the fruitional kāyas and facets of primordial consciousness, the causal virtues of accumulating

207. This etymologizes "secret mantra Vajrayāna" (Tib. *gsang sngags rdo rje'i theg pa*): secret (*gsang*) mantra (*sngags*) vajra (*rdo rje*) yāna (*theg pa*).

208. This etymologizes "perfection of wisdom" (Tib. *shes rab kyi pha rol tu phyin pa*): wisdom (*shes rab*) perfection (*pha rol tu phyin pa*).

209. This etymologizes "clear light vajra essence" (Tib. *'od gsal rdo rje snying po*): clear light (*'od gsal*) vajra (*rdo rje*) essence (*snying po*).

210. This etymologizes "complete consummation of saṃsāra and nirvāṇa" (Tib. *'khor 'das 'ub chub*): saṃsāra and nirvāṇa (*'khor 'das*), complete (*'ub*) consummation (*chub*).

merit, and all their resultant appearances of joy are, without differentiation, perfected in the ground sugatagarbha itself, so it is called *kāya*.[211] [301]

"The mode of existence of the dharmakāya, pristine awareness that is present in the ground, cannot be fathomed by the intellect. It cannot be analyzed by the mind, it transcends objects of articulation, and it subsumes everything, so it is known as the *bindu*. Whatever aspects of saṃsāra and nirvāṇa appear, they are of one taste in the fundamental, original, primordial ground, so it is called *sole*.[212]

"The great expanse of the pervasive, real nature of all of saṃsāra and nirvāṇa, free of a center and periphery, dissolves into its inner luminosity, and the state of vivid, great primordial consciousness is naturally clear, so it is called the *clear light*. The ultimate *vajra* of the nature of indestructibility, the essential nature of the unified essence of all the jinas of the three times, is called the *essence*.[213]

"Because it is not confined to any region and does not fall to any extreme, it is called the *middle*. Because it views saṃsāra and nirvāṇa as apparitions of the mind and because it knows that emanations are, as it were, sent forth outside by the one dwelling within, it is called *mahāmudrā*.[214] All these, too, are simply facets of the ground.

"Even when the ground is reduced to an ethically neutral state, all displays of the kāyas and facets of primordial consciousness are nothing other than self-emergent, naturally perfect, inner displays of the ground itself. So this is called the *Great Perfection of the time of the ground*. [302]

"As for the Great Perfection of the time of the path, when pristine awareness that is present in the ground becomes manifest, it dissolves into unmodified, ordinary mental states and appearances; so ordinary mental states and appearances are perfected.

"Since ultimate reality does not lend itself to the extreme of nihilism, the extremists' view of eternalism is perfected; since it is not apprehended as the extreme of the eternalist view, it perfects the mind that is drawn to the view of nihilism. Even if suffering, its source, its cessation, and the path are held to be autonomous objects, by realizing personal identitylessness—realizing

211. This etymologizes "youthful vase kāya" (Tib. *gzhon nu bum pa'i sku*): youthful (*gzhon nu*) vase (*bum pa*) kāya (*sku*).

212. This etymologizes "sole bindu" (Tib. *thig le nyag gcig*): bindu (*thig le*), sole (*nyag gcig*).

213. This etymologizes "clear light vajra essence" (Tib. *'od gsal rdo rje'i snying po*): clear light (*'od gsal*) vajra (*rdo rje*) essence (*snying po*).

214. This etymologizes "mahāmudrā" (*phyag rgya chen po*).

that you do not exist from your own side—the Śrāvakayāna is perfected. By realizing the nature of all appearances and mindsets of the three realms as dependently related events, the Pratyekabuddhayāna is perfected. By ascertaining that appearances are not other than the mind, the Cittamātrayāna is perfected. By realizing the meaning of the two types of identitylessness, the perfection of wisdom is perfected. By sealing saṃsāra and nirvāṇa with bodhicitta, the Bodhisattvayāna is perfected; and by that very realization of saṃsāra and nirvāṇa as great emptiness becoming the universal ground of all Madhyamakas, these yānas are all perfected.

"By not mixing up your actions and conduct with ordinary behavior, the Kriyāyāna is perfected. [303] By behaving such that your view and conduct are nondual, the Caryātantrayāna is perfected. By recognizing the view as being of greatest importance, the Yogayāna is perfected. By realizing the nonduality of the deity and your own appearances, the whole of the Mahāyogayāna is perfected. By realizing the nonduality of absolute space and primordial consciousness, the whole of the Anuyāna is perfected. By letting all that appears to the mind vanish without modification, just as it is, the mind division of Atiyoga is perfected. And by realizing the nonduality of absolute space and pristine awareness, the expanse division yāna is perfected in the dharmakāya, pristine awareness that is present in the ground.

"The realization of just how all the phenomena of those yānas are perfected is called the *secret pith instruction yāna*. Since this is the great, universal ground of all the yānas, and since all grounds and paths are simultaneously perfected, it is called the *supreme yāna of the Great Perfection*, which synthesizes the essence.

"Other yānas are merely facets of the Great Perfection, and those who adhere to their own yānas are certainly limited, like taking a drop from the ocean and thinking that it is the ocean.

"The *vinaya*[215] and the Śrāvakayāna are for the least of those with inferior faculties, [304] the Pratyekabuddhayāna is for the middling of those with inferior faculties, and the Bodhisattvayāna is for the best of those with inferior faculties. The Kriyāyāna is for the least of those with middling faculties, the Upāyayāna is for the middling of those with middling faculties, and the Yogayāna is for the best of those with middling faculties. Mahāyoga is for the least of those with superior faculties, Anuyoga is for the middling of those with superior faculties, and the three divisions of Atiyoga are for the best of those with superior faculties.

215. Tib. *'dul ba*. The teachings concerning the ethical discipline of the Buddha's monastic and lay disciples.

"Within the latter, the mind division yāna is taught to the least of those with the best of superior faculties, the expanse division yāna is taught to the middling of those with the best of superior faculties, and the secret pith instruction division yāna is taught to the best of those with the best of superior faculties.

"In accordance with each individual's own faculties and merit, it is taught that an individual may proceed along the grounds and paths to liberation. However, even though there are no differences of quality or magnitude in the fundamental minds of sentient beings, one speaks as if there were differences in the quality of their faculties due to their domination by self-grasping and their resultant failure to realize the meaning of identitylessness. The succession of yānas is taught as a path of gradual progression, like walking up a staircase. Know that it is not as if some individuals were on the ground floor, utterly incapable of ascending due to a closed skylight; nor is it as if some were up above from the outset, so that they need not descend, like planets and stars that have risen into the sky. Rather, by the power of your previous training, whatever yāna you encounter, your karmic momentum for it will gradually be aroused. [305]

"O Vajra of Pristine Awareness, in this real nature of the originally pure Great Perfection, called the *dharmakāya, pristine awareness that is present in the ground*, seven wisdoms are naturally perfected:

1. Because the one nature of all phenomena included in the world of saṃsāra and nirvāṇa, as the display of the suchness of ultimate reality, is veiled by afflictive and cognitive obscurations, it is reduced to an ethically neutral ground. Instead of the mind deludedly succumbing to dualistic grasping, by investigating and analyzing the nature of existence of phenomena, you recognize their nonobjective, open nature. This is called *discerning wisdom*; it realizes the emptiness of every single phenomenon that seems to appear from its own side.
2. In the end, stabilization in the mindstream that ascertains the identitylessness and emptiness of all phenomena of saṃsāra and nirvāṇa is called the *wisdom of realizing identitylessness*. This utterly dissolves grasping at the reality of appearances.
3. Truly knowing the manner in which all the phenomena of the path and fruition are naturally perfected in the ground itself is called the *wisdom that knows reality as it is*.
4. Just as planets and stars appear in the ocean due to the lucidity and clarity of the water, [306] all physical worlds, their sentient inhabitants, and sensory objects appear from the lucidity and clarity of space, and all of saṃsāra and nirvāṇa would not appear without that lucidity and

clarity. And just as reflections do not appear without the lucidity and clarity of a mirror, the appearances of all of saṃsāra and nirvāṇa would not occur without the lucidity and clarity of the ground. By reifying this lucidity and clarity, appearances occur. Truly realizing this is an unsurpassed feature of the Great Perfection.

As an analogy, the planets and stars in the ocean are not different from the water, and all the physical worlds and their sentient inhabitants are not different from space. Likewise, there is nothing in all of saṃsāra and nirvāṇa that is not unified with and pervaded by primordial consciousness, the pristine awareness of ultimate reality. This is called *pervasive, all-seeing great wisdom*, and it perceives all of saṃsāra and nirvāṇa as being like reflections of the moon in water. Realizing this with great wisdom, you abide in this profundity within yourself.

5. By apprehending the ground itself as the ground,[216] the saṃsāra of impure karma is released into absolute space, and your own face of the dharmakāya is perceived. This is called the *wisdom of release*.[217] By totally disengaging from all activity, you dwell in inactivity. [307]
6. The *wisdom of unification* is so designated because it forcefully unifies all clinging to the appearances of saṃsāric, impure, dualistic grasping with great purity and equality. Then there is the recognition of the equal nonexistence of all objects of hope and fear as well as the good and the bad.
7. By realizing that all phenomena are unimpeded, shifting events emerging from the one great emptiness, the whole delusion of saṃsāric, impure karma and mental afflictions is totally vanquished and incinerated; and this is called the *wisdom of vanquishing*. Then you actualize emptiness and achieve the depths of confidence.

"O son of the family, great wisdom is like the conflagration at the end of the eon, which destroys the cosmos. Like dry grass burned in a fire, all karma, mental afflictions, habitual propensities, and delusive appearances are incinerated in ultimate reality, which transcends causality. Great wisdom is like the sun rising in the sky, utterly dispelling all the darkness of ignorance. Great wisdom is like space, for it comprehends all sublime phenomena, like the physical worlds and their sentient inhabitants. In the first instant, blind sentient beings are tormented and entrapped in the sufferings of saṃsāra

216. The meaning here is that by apprehending the state of your practice, i.e., by recognizing the ground (Tib. *sa*) you stand upon, you are ready to proceed further in practice.

217. Tib. *sgrol ba'i shes rab.*

and the miserable states of existence, and mental afflictions and habitual propensities are like a sack of poison. [308] In the next instant, simply by identifying great wisdom, they become equal in fortune to the dharmakāya, Samantabhadra, and they become worthy of the homage, worship, and devotion of myriad living beings, including the gods. They become fields of merit and the foremost of assemblies. This destroys eons of impure karma, and it is ultimate.

"Relatively speaking, it is said there are seven conflagrations at the end of the eon, which destroy the cosmos. There are seven pure energies of primordial consciousness:

1. The *dispersive energy* courses through each of the domains of the mental states and appearances of impure saṃsāra, and it dissolves into emptiness your clinging to them as permanent, stable, and immutable. It extends to all appearing objects and enables you to recognize their lack of true existence.
2. All of saṃsāra and nirvāṇa is permeated by the ground, and the *pervasive energy* causes this ground to become manifest. By leaving it in its own state, without meditation, your own essential nature is actualized.
3. The *directing energy of wisdom* is so designated for it directs the avenues of the impure mind to emptiness, the great center. This sustains your own natural state in a great, intellect-transcending ineffability. [309]
4. The *apprehending energy of skillful means* embraces ultimate reality, free of conceptual elaboration, in the great primordial nature that transcends the intellect, and it merges continuously with a state of ineffability.
5. The *energy that destroys the cosmos* is so designated for, in the end, it dissolves all these appearances into great, nonobjective, originally pure ultimate reality and annihilates them, propelling them into the great extinction of phenomena, beyond the intellect.
6. The *merciless karmic energy of the eon* is so designated for, due to the all-pervasive movement of this energy of primordial consciousness, the vitality of saṃsāra is severed and sent into the absolute space of nirvāṇa. Mental states and appearances arise as emptiness, and finally they are propelled into absolute space, where delusion is unknown.
7. The *fire-accompanying energy* is so designated for it utterly eradicates the darkness of ignorance and totally incinerates all karma, mental afflictions, and habitual propensities. Banishing mental afflictions and discursive thoughts into absolute space, the vitality of omniscience courses through you as primordial consciousness.

"So the seven great energies of pure primordial consciousness slay the karmic energies right where they are. By the movement and resting of the energies of primordial consciousness in their own place, you swiftly reach the state of omniscient, perfect enlightenment.

"In this way, [310] the luminosity of the essential nature, emptiness, is called *wisdom*, and its power of self-illumination is called *vital energy*. This illustrates how the whole range of paths and fruitions is perfected in the dharmakāya, pristine awareness that is present in the ground. So that you may recognize the supremacy of the yāna of the clear-light Great Perfection, the essential points of this one yāna are repeated again and again; otherwise, they would not be correctly realized. That is why they are taught in this way. Consequently, future disciples will fathom these essential points and all doubts will be vanquished. This is called the essential nature, or core, of meditation, the razor that cuts off error, the sole eye of primordial consciousness, and the view of the vast expanse of space. Know this!

"As for the blind who are ignorant of this, the reason why they do not ascend beyond the higher realms, regardless of how much they meditate, is that they do not recognize or know the originally pure ground, the all-pervasive nature of being. Ignorance is the delusive ground of the three realms, so they do not transcend saṃsāra. Accurate knowledge of the nondual, one taste of the great, original, primordial ground of saṃsāra and nirvāṇa is called [311] *primordial consciousness, pristine awareness.* Know that all the collections of virtue that are generated from this ground will ripen solely as the resultant omniscience of perfect enlightenment!"

Phase 5: Determining Secret Dualistic Grasping and Revealing the Way of Natural Liberation

The Process of Delusion in Impure Saṃsāra

Bodhisattva Vajra of Pristine Awareness then commented, "O Teacher, Bhagavān, over lifetimes from beginningless time up to the present, with the cause of ignorance and the contributing condition of dualistic grasping, blind sentient beings of the three realms continuously, incessantly cling to delusive cycles in the endless abodes of saṃsāra. Dominated by the collective contaminations of habitual propensities within the shell of ignorance, they are oppressed by great burdens of suffering. But by the power of wisdom and primordial consciousness, the shell of habitual propensities is opened up.

"Before one awakens from the slumber of ignorance, one reifies the delusive sense of experiencing the miseries of saṃsāra and the miserable states of existence—which were never really experienced. It is laughable how one clings to experiences! Why? While the bases of designations are not established as real, different names are designated upon objectless emptiness, and in that way one deceives oneself. Ha ha!

"All appearing phenomena [312] are like mirages taken to be water, or like an illusory festival that one takes to be permanent and fixates on as if it were one's own possession. Former appearances vanish and later ones arise, with no enduring presence, but because one doesn't notice this, one is bewildered. Ha ha!

"Not recognizing how appearances arise and transform, with no stability, one takes pride in one's accumulated possessions, as if they were one's eternal wealth. Ha ha!

"When one sees saṃsāra and nirvāṇa as the open, nonobjective nature of great emptiness, all the buddhas and buddhafields that are misconstrued as sentient inhabitants and objects in the physical worlds fall into an abyss. Ha ha!

"When one sees that all physical worlds and their sentient inhabitants, with all their sense objects, are totally groundless and rootless like a dream and an illusion, and when one sees that they seem to exist even though they do not, and that they simultaneously emerge and vanish in an instant like a flash of lightning, saṃsāra is blown away by the wind. Ha ha!

"Not recognizing the fact that over beginningless lifetimes, one's own nature has never wavered for even an instant from the originally pure absolute space of phenomena, one appears to come and go and move [313] about in saṃsāra. Ha ha!

"Not recognizing the fact that over beginningless lifetimes, one's own appearances arise to oneself—and apart from them, there has never been even an iota of any sensory object—one takes appearances, which one experiences with clinging attachment, as being other than oneself. Then one is constantly deluded by adopting hopes and fears. Ha ha!

"When one encounters one's own face as the great, original, primordial ground, one awakens to the unimpeded nonobjectivity of all faults and habitual propensities. Ha ha!

"When one sees the absolute space of the ground, free of conceptual elaboration, the aid and injury brought about by gods and demons and by friends and enemies vanish without a trace. Ha ha!

"When the darkness of not knowing the absolute space of the ground is replaced by knowledge, enlightenment is not achieved by virtue of meditation, nor does one wander in saṃsāra because of not meditating. Ha ha!

"When the ground dharmakāya, the Omnipresent Lord Samantabhadra, becomes manifest, one effortlessly reaches the kingdom of the dharmakāya. Ha ha!

"When one gains mastery over primordial consciousness, pristine awareness free of extremes, without needing to view or consider all the beings of the three realms, and without needing to exert strenuous effort, one simultaneously awakens to ultimate reality, absolute space that transcends causality. Ha ha! [314]

"When one gains mastery over primordial consciousness, pristine awareness free of extremes, every single one of the innumerable maṇḍalas of the buddhas is perfected and actualized as one taste, without convergence or divergence. Ha ha!

"When the pure, uniform displays of saṃsāra and nirvāṇa and the dharmakāya—pristine awareness that is present in the ground—are perceived, one instantly becomes perfectly enlightened, without reliance upon the stages of the grounds and paths. Ha ha!

"By hearing the sound of the words of this great vajra laughter, one will fathom the real space of pristine awareness and realize these vast and profound points."

How to Follow the Path of the Great Perfection

Bodhisattva Vajra of Pristine Awareness then asked, "O Teacher, Bhagavān, Omnipresent Lord, Immutable Sovereign, Original Buddha of the ground, how does one follow the path of your nature that is called the Great Perfection? Teacher, please explain!"

He replied, "O son of the family, here is the way to follow the path of my nature, the Great Perfection: To proceed along the grounds and paths to liberation in this life, first you must know the reasons for the difficulty of obtaining a precious human life of freedom and opportunity, and those reasons must be firmly imprinted in your mindstream. In terms of the demarcation between saṃsāra and nirvāṇa, [315] if you do not practice Dharma right now, you will not encounter the grounds and paths to liberation later on; and even if you meet with them, you will find it difficult to know how to put them into practice. It is difficult to encounter a guru, or sublime spiritual mentor, who can introduce you to pristine awareness. It is very difficult to have the freedom to practice, and it is hard to assemble all the necessities of life and requisites for practice. Except for right now, the methods for gaining freedom from the dungeon of saṃsāric miseries will not come again. Once you recognize this, you must enter the Dharma as your path.

"Recognizing that the time of death is unpredictable, consider that the thunderbolt of death may strike at any time and in any situation, and that you are now on the verge of being cast away from the human realm to some other realm. Bearing in mind all the miseries you will experience then, command your own mind: 'Today I will leave everything behind, including my parents, relatives, home, and possessions, and they will remain just as they are. From now on, I will not even hear their names, I will not see even a fraction of them, and I will never return there again. When it comes time for me to depart, I will have no choice but to go where for eons I will be tossed about by waves of suffering, [316] without the slightest bit of happiness, and I will be brought before the agents of the Lord of Death. A great hurricane of the winds of karma will push me from behind, the faces of my relatives, children, and spouse will be covered with tears, and their terrible cries of lamentation will aggravate my misery. Unable to let them go, when I desperately, pathetically proceed alone, with no companion, to an unknown destination, who will accompany me? Who will help carry the burden of my misery? Who will come to my rescue? Who will take on for me that unbearable suffering? What benefit will there be from the nonvirtuous, evil karma I have accumulated for the sake of my children, relatives, and friends? They will never recall my kindness.'

"Considering the examples of yourself and others, if in this life you don't even set out on the path to liberation, whatever you do will have no benefit whatsoever. The time of your death is unknown. If everyone, including children, the young, and the old, must die, and if there is no way of determining when you will die, then without procrastination you should quickly know why you need to practice the profound pith instructions on the sublime, supreme yāna for gaining liberation in one lifetime. And you must apply yourself to them assiduously.

"If you ignore death, the thought of the Dharma will subside, and you will fall under the domination of spiritual sloth, distractions, amusements, and hankering for material gain. [317] In that way your life will pass in vain, and you will slip into death as an ordinary being, then fall into endless saṃsāra. Recalling impermanence and death and considering these points again and again is the unsurpassed fundamental basis of the path to liberation. Without this, you will succumb to detrimental karma and situations as if you were blind and crippled, so that even if you have a Dharma practice, it will be feeble and will naturally unravel like a knot in a horse's tail. So know this!

"Knowing those two points and applying them to your mindstream, you should reflect upon karma and its consequences. Bearing in mind that the consequence of hatred is hell, just count the number of deeds you have committed that were motivated by hatred! Do you sense that you will be a guest in hell? Bearing in mind that the consequence of attachment is the preta realm, just look at your own attachment. If you count the number of deeds you have committed under its influence, do you see that you will be a guest in the realm of pretas? Bearing in mind that the consequence of delusion is the animal realm, if you examine the various foul deeds generated by that cause, you will find that you have been pursuing the path leading to a visit to the animal realm. Do you understand that where you dwell is definitely within saṃsāra? [318] Actions motivated by envy lead to the realm of asuras, and if you reflect upon the ways you have accumulated karma motivated by thoughts of envy, you will see that the guests of the asuras pursue the causes of that realm, and they return to their own realm again and again. Do you understand?

"Evil, nonvirtuous deeds motivated by the three poisons of the afflicted mind include the three bodily nonvirtues of killing, stealing, and sexual misconduct; the four verbal nonvirtues of lying, slander, idle gossip, and abuse; and the three mental nonvirtues of avarice, malice, and false views. The power of all these is generated by their causal motivations, and in this way the appearances of the three miserable states of existence emerge.

"In particular, if your samayas degenerate regarding the roots of secret mantra practice—namely, your guru and spiritual friends—you must fall to the excruciating realm known as Vajra Hell, so bear in mind that it is crucial to know these samayas.

"If you think that no faults are incurred for those who do not know them, you are mistaken. Those who are ignorant of them do not recognize whether or not their samayas have degenerated, [319] so they do not take the opportunity to confess and purify them. Such people constantly incur great faults, and the consequences of their evil deeds, stemming from their ignorance and lack of awareness, manifest in their own time. This is like losing all your accumulated food and possessions because you are ignorant of the presence of a thief. There is not the slightest difference between this and knowingly being robbed of them by a bandit in broad daylight. Likewise, in terms of the karmic consequences and experiences of suffering, there is not even the slightest difference between those who are knowledgeable and those who are not. Those who know the samayas immediately understand when an infraction occurs, and by confessing it, they either purify it or diminish its harm. Those who do not know the samayas are unaware of infractions when they occur, so they continue to compound all their faults, downfalls, and broken samayas. By so doing, the infractions grow and increase, and they are never purified.

"O son of the family, until you reach the state of the great, intellect-transcending extinction into ultimate reality, examine the manner in which karma ripens, without its ever simply disappearing, and unerringly practice adopting virtues and abstaining from vices. [320] Recognize the tremendous importance of this, and guard it as you do your own life. In particular, you must bear in mind the importance of abstaining from even the subtlest of vices and nonvirtues. If you do not, and you become confused with regard to nonvirtuous conduct, the power of evil deeds will gradually grow. Eventually, due to the subtle relations between actions and their results, various contaminations of habitual propensities will combine, and enormous consequences will emerge and inexorably carry you away. Therefore, knowledge of the significance of actions and their consequences is like an eye that enables you to see the path.

"Upon considering the nature of suffering in saṃsāra, recognize that saṃsāra is like a fire pit, like a viper's nest, and like a land of cannibals, without the slightest opportunity for happiness, and apply yourself to the pursuit of liberation. Bear in mind the indispensability of generating this attitude before engaging in Dharma practice. For those who do not train their minds in this way, even if they try to implement the profound practical instructions, as soon as there are difficulties and little things like hunger and thirst, they give up and fail to carry the practice through to its culmination. Once you have first trained in the four thoughts that turn the mind, it is vital that you bear them in mind constantly, without forgetting them, at all times and in all situations. Doing so is the unsurpassed crown jewel of all Dharma practitioners. [321]

"Now, for the main practice, genuine knowledge and realization of the one taste of all of saṃsāra and nirvāṇa in the ocean of the original ground is called the *view of the vast expanse of space*, and this entails the manifestation of your own nature as the dharmakāya, devoid of signs. As for meditation, throughout beginningless lifetimes in saṃsāra, the original, primordial ground, Samantabhadra, has pervaded the mindstreams of all sentient beings, just as sesame oil pervades sesame seeds. However, under the influence of dualistic grasping and clinging to true existence, the mind becomes dimmed, as if by darkness, and deluded. But now, apart from identifying your own nature, there is nothing whatsoever on which to meditate, and you thereby gain freedom for yourself. As a result of holding your own ground, freedom is experienced in the domain of pristine space, unstructured and unmodified by the intellect, and you are infinitely immersed in great, self-emergent, primordial rest. This is like space merging with space.

"Previously, your intellect demarcated outer from inner and grasped at them as being distinct. Now, ascertaining that there is no outer or inner, you come upon the nature of great, all-pervasive openness, which is called *meditation free of the intellect and devoid of activity*. In such a meditative state, motionlessly rest your body [322] without modifying it, like a corpse in a charnel ground. Let your voice rest unmodified, dispensing with all speech and recitations, as if your voice were a lute with its strings cut. Let your mind rest without modification, naturally releasing it in the state of primordial being, without altering it in any way. With these three, dispensing with activities of the body, speech, and mind, you settle in meditative equipoise that is devoid of activity. For that reason, this is called *meditative equipoise*.

"Whenever you engage in any kind of physical or verbal activity, such as eating, lying down, walking, sitting, or going about in the marketplace or among crowds of people, maintain the constant awareness of ascertaining all things as displays of the nonduality of saṃsāra and nirvāṇa, without ever losing the power of this view. Never waver from the state of manifest pristine awareness, devoid of action, in which you retain the confidence of meditation. Abstain from the vices of nonvirtuous actions as if they were poison, never allowing your conduct to slip into carelessness.

"For your physical conduct, act slowly and serenely, firmly and resolutely, like a clay statue. When walking, move deliberately, taking each step in an easygoing manner. Let your demeanor be like that of a lion, without swiveling your head or glancing quickly to the right or left. When rising, get up slowly, not abruptly, [323] and when eating, chew and swallow deliberately, not like a yak gobbling grass. When conversing with others, abstain from flippant speech, and speak gently and slowly. Adjust your speech so that you express the truth, speaking pleasantly and deliberately, without disturbing the minds of others. Let your mind be calm, subdued, and spacious, without succumbing to emotional vacillations. The way to bring your mind to the Dharma is by having kind thoughts and great altruism, while speaking and behaving without deviousness or self-aggrandizement.

"In particular, as a sign of your own great defects, you may see everyone as being flawed, without perceiving anyone as being faultless. This perception is like that of someone who has ingested *datura*[218] and sees everything as snakes, or someone with a bile disorder who sees a conch as yellow. People you see and experience as being different from yourself are invariably perceived as being imperfect, while you see no faults in those who are close to you, such as your brothers, sisters, nephews, and uncles, whom you invariably regard as being good. This is tantamount to seeing your own side as divine and the other side as demonic. Enough of that! View everyone as being flawless, [324] and recognize all defects as your own. This is a crucial aspect of conduct.

"When you possess status and prestige, do not disregard all those who are weak, powerless, impoverished, or timid. If you fail to behave amicably with everyone, there is the possibility that misfortune will eventually befall you, and others will rise up against you in anger. As conditions degenerate, everyone in a position of royalty, power, and wealth eventually falls to an inferior position and poverty. Upon examining this matter, it is crucial that you bear malice toward no one.

"When high status, prestige, and affluence come your way, adopt a sense of humility and overcome any sense of pride. When you encounter misfortune and terrible surroundings, do not let your inner strength wane, but bring forth confidence in your view and meditation, and release your consciousness without an object, as if you were an idiot. Moreover, knowing appearances to be like illusions and dreams is another crucial aspect of your conduct. On occasions of joy and happiness, avoid self-conscious pride; and at times of

218. Tib. *dha dhu ra*; Skt. *dhattūra*. A toxic, hallucinogenic species in the nightshade family.

hunger, cold, and thirst, bring forth the strength of your mind and the confidence of the view.

"Do not utter words of abuse or slander toward anyone, [325] but devote yourself to equanimity. But do not flatter others either. Instead, remain at rest, for the end result of both reviling and glorifying others is that when those you have praised offend you, you will want to put them down, and when those you have insulted support you, you will be compelled to commend them. Then others will ridicule you, and your own flaws will become apparent.

"If you deny the excellent qualities of your enemies and opponents and instead speak of their faults, even though everyone knows of their talents and virtues, others will become disgusted with you and think of these defects as your own. Since your abusive words inflict no harm upon your enemies, dispense with them. Moreover, by extolling the virtues of your friends and relatives, who have their own flaws, everyone will despise and ridicule you. So the importance of avoiding this is another crucial aspect of your conduct.

"As a result of lying, you will fall into disgrace, and everyone will despise you as if you were dog meat. No matter what you say, people will take it to be a lie, and you will not be accorded the status of a human being. If you steal or break an oath, even though others may pretend not to know about it, secretly they will all come to gossip about it and vilify you for it. So abstain from such conduct.

"If you engage in disgusted, adversarial contempt or abuse toward any guru or teacher, [326] your path to liberation will be blocked, and this will become an enormous weight pulling you down to the miserable states of existence. As taught in the tantras, scriptures, and pith instructions, do not succumb to the slightest bit of such behavior, even at the cost of your life and body. This is the root of the Dharma, so bear it in mind as something of the greatest importance.

"By being attracted and addicted to talking and gossiping and seeing benefit in savoring words, your life may be spent in vain, and for the most part such talk becomes the basis for bickering, disputation, and irritation. This is pointless, so dispense with such entertainment and apply yourself to meditation. Even if you had a galaxy of food and wealth, you would never be satisfied. So for the duration of this human life, which is but a momentary dream, be content simply that you are not dying of starvation, regardless of how much food you have, and be satisfied with being protected from the elements, regardless of the quality of your clothes. For the most part, food and clothing are detrimental objects of attachment, which at the time of death lead to rebirth as a demon. They are called *possessions* because they possess you to take birth in miserable states of existence and saṃsāra, so even their name indicates their causal influence.

"Friends venture forth into the Dharma, taking their own measure of things, without heeding anyone's advice. No one but a qualified guru can provide them with counsel that will be of lasting benefit to them, [327] so heed your guru's guidance as a lifelong samaya.

"Think of beings who constantly strive with great diligence and courage, enduring all manner of hardships, in tasks that propel them along endlessly in saṃsāra. With them in mind, willingly accept the hardships involved in applying yourself to methods that bring eternal bliss. Abandon what is easy. Let your body and vitality be targets. Sacrifice your flesh and blood as food. If you do not constantly apply yourself to generating courage and fortitude, arouse yourself by thinking 'I will die in a while.' Whatever Dharma you practice, attend to the benefit of all sentient beings and apply yourself wholeheartedly to arduous virtues, without showing off or using pretense in order to gain others' admiration or praise.

"As for your samayas and vows, be guileless. Do not disparage the Dharma or individuals. The conduct of Dharma practitioners is to treat everyone impartially, without fawning on those in high positions or denigrating those in low positions. Do not deceive others. Do not offend the faithful. Do not beguile the minds of those applying themselves to virtue. Do not partake of food and wealth meant for those practicing in meditative retreat. [328] By diligently applying yourself to practice, without letting the practical instructions you have received fade away, qualified gurus will not rebuke you. By being completely candid about your samayas and vows, gods and guardians will not rebuke you. By saturating your life with the Dharma, without pretense or hypocrisy, you will have no cause to rebuke yourself. This is the practice of the buddhas, and their followers should maintain it as the best of practices.

"For the duration of this fleeting human life, there is no time or leisure for pursuing such things as high status, power, or wealth. Abstain from self-praise and pretense motivated by the desire for fame and status, and hold in your heart the awareness of your own mortality. Never forsaking the precious Three Jewels is the sublime foundation and root of the practice. Modify your physical and verbal conduct in these ways, and be on guard not to fall into carelessness. Attend to this, realize it, and adhere to it! This is the crucial guidance for your conduct in between sessions. Carrying through with the practice of meditative equipoise and postmeditative practice in the above manner until you die is the sublime essence of the practice.

"The essential point of conduct is not to forsake the view in the midst of your daily activities. Even though you strive in cultivating physical and verbal virtues and accumulate an enormous amount of merit, if you discard the practice of the profound view and meditation, [329] when you face death you will do so as an ordinary person, and your practice will have sustained and furthered saṃsāra. As a result, you may experience merely temporary joys of gods and humans, but the fruits of liberation will remain beyond reach, and because of that failure you will remain in bondage.

"Therefore, once you have achieved the stability of confidence in the profound view and meditation, virtuous qualities of the body and speech that can be seen or heard cannot replace the authentic view and meditation. For example, when the lion, king of beasts, haughtily gazes out over the snowy mountains, no other creature can challenge him. Similarly, you must recognize the importance of not allowing the view and meditation to be lost as you come under other influences. If you lose the view in the midst of your daily activities, know that this is like a king losing his realm to someone else.

"If you forsake proper conduct in favor of the view, you will fall under the influence of negligence, which is like succumbing to māras and rūdras; and out of your addiction to the activities of saṃsāra, a great current of negative actions will emerge, resulting in false views regarding the Three Jewels and disregard for the moral consequences of your behavior. As you fail to implement the ultimate view and meditation, you will not even have the means to accumulate merit for attaining the state of gods or humans. [330] This is like veering from a path on which you are seeking healing medicinal herbs and running into a plant that is poisonous to the touch. In this case, it is said that friends turn into māras. It is the profound view that cures the terrible, chronic disease of the sufferings of saṃsāra, but if it leads your mind to paths of iniquity, it will cause you to experience the endless miseries of saṃsāra.

"The remedy for ignorance is knowledge, and the remedy for saṃsāra is the view and meditation; however, when they are not implemented and your mind becomes filled with misconceptions and behavior contrary to the Dharma, the understanding of emptiness goes awry, and there is no remedy for it. So it is crucial for you to know this.

"In summary, at all times and in all situations, let your behavior be calm, subdued, and conscientious, and continuously guard your samayas and vows. Avoid negative, nonvirtuous deeds as if they were poison. With no other virtue to practice, apply yourself assiduously to the profound view and meditation, striving in this essential practice for your whole life. By constraining your mind as if you had come into the presence of a judge of the highest court, recognize the importance of restraint. Until you reach the state of extinction into ultimate reality, you must rightly avoid the bad and adopt the good in terms of actions and their consequences.

"Until you acquire the four kinds of great, fearless confidence[219] that are indications of having attained liberation, [331] suffering will result from nonvirtue and joy will result from virtue. This can be known by investigating and carefully reflecting upon the nature of saṃsāra and delusion, since you have been constantly addicted to experiencing the cycle of delusive experiences during beginningless lifetimes right up to the present.

"Even though you may have an ocean of knowledge acquired from hearing the Dharma, if you have no practice of profound meditation, you are like a person who returns empty-handed from an island of jewels, and you will die as an ordinary person and continue wandering in saṃsāra. Therefore, with diligent meditation apply yourself to the essential practice.

"When you are engaging in practice like this, whether there arises an unprecedented, soothing sense of bliss, or a pristine sense of luminosity, or a nebulous nonconceptuality, if you take any of these to be genuine meditation and cling to it as the fulfillment of your hopes, if you regard these as areas of danger and block them, or if you alter them with your mind, such hopes and fears will lead you astray. In contrast, once you have recognized the nature of meditative experiences, then by letting them be in their own state, without attachment, craving, rejection, [332] or affirmation, they will vanish altogether, like mist disappearing into the sky, and primordial consciousness, pristine awareness, will become manifest.

"You may perceive various disagreeable forms of gods and demons, different kinds of pleasant and unpleasant sounds, assorted foul odors and disagreeable tastes, and diverse kinds of tactile sensations. You may have nightmares and at times wake up in a panic. These experiences may bring forth various types of distress in your heart and mind. Due to your diet, environment, or trauma, illnesses may arise, and merely as a result of coming into contact with soil, rocks, wood, or weapons, you may contract afflictions that are difficult to heal. Outer upheavals, including sores, leprosy, and ulcers, as well as bad omens of apparitions created by gods or demons, may arise. Any of the 404 classes of illness of wind, bile, phlegm, and combinations of these may arise, and—as if the entire might and strength of your mind had seeped away into them—inexpressible suffering may occur. These are called the *inner upheavals of physical illnesses*.

"With respect to objects of the mind, you may experience unhappiness, attachment, hatred, craving, unbearable suffering, delight, [333] clinging to the experience of emptiness and luminosity, a sense of sheer vacuity in which appearances and the mind cease, paranoia in which everything you see or

219. Tib. *gding chen po bzhi.* The four kinds of great confidence are described at VE 462. See also CM 445, VS 604, GD 298.

feel is out to harm you, or the pride of thinking 'There is no yogin on earth who has a view and meditation like mine!' Under the influence of anger and malice, you may disturb the minds of others and afterward feel remorse. You may feel that everything you have done is wonderful and consequently feel free to do whatever you like. Such indeterminate experiences of joy and sorrow are called the *secret upheavals of mental joys and sorrows*. Know that all such sensations are deceptive experiences that occur as signs along the path. Without attachment, craving, rejection, affirmation, hope, fear, or modification, leave them as they are. By doing so, they will release themselves. Hold this knowledge to be of the highest importance.

"If your meditative experiences lead to illness and you compound this by attributing it to demonic influence, no matter how much you devote yourself to magic rituals for dispelling obstacles or to medical treatments, they will only harm you, without bringing any benefit. However hard you try, you will not benefit even the slightest bit. Eventually, if the sentry of identifying meditative experiences is lost, this might lead you to go insane, pass out, faint, or become as stupid as an animal, [334] or it might lead to your own death.

"In the past there have been many faithful students who kept their samayas and vows, and there have always been gurus who became siddhas. So they knew the various dispositions and faculties of specific students, and they led them to the state of Buddha Vajradhara in one lifetime and with one body. Nowadays, even when they are not led astray by anyone, students invariably fail to keep their samayas, they have little faith or reverence, and they are barbaric and prone to false views. And blind teachers hanker after meditative experiences and give teachings that lead their students to meditate with objectification and cling to views and meditation. Consequently, instead of identifying the mere occurrences of pleasure, pain, comfort, and distress as meditative experiences, because of their ignorance of the differences between outer and inner upheavals, they attribute them to demonic influences, thus misleading their own students. Such illegitimate teachers are certain to become māras for their students.

"There are also outer upheavals that arise solely due to people's specific constitutions and faculties, without there being any inner upheaval. Inner upheavals may also arise without there being any outer or secret upheavals. Or secret upheavals may arise by themselves, [335] without any outer or inner upheavals. Thus, it is especially crucial to know how to distinguish among them.

"Currently, in this degenerate era, when the teachings of the Buddha have fallen into decline, some teachers give instructions to sustain awareness of the movements of the mind. But since even they have no meditative experiences and realizations in such practice, the lives of all such teachers and their disciples are vainly spent in that pursuit, and eventually they die as ordinary people. This has happened many times. Some teachers remain absorbed in a relaxed, gentle state of joy, telling others that this is the culmination of the view and meditation—and they get stuck there. Other teachers have a sense of luminosity in which visions of gods and demons arise, they gain confidence in a steady vividness of the mind and appearances, and they teach this to others. Some gain confidence in a clear, nonconceptual sense of vacuity, devoid of mindfulness, in which appearances are impeded, and they teach this to others. Others gain confidence in an unimpeded, unstructured state of consciousness and present this to others as the best view and meditation. Those who identify the view and meditation in such ways do not rise above the three realms, for they have not realized the view of emptiness. [336] They are imprisoned by that failing, and consequently they do not see the path to liberation and omniscience.

"Some people idle away their whole lives by being addicted to ragged books and oral explanations, so when death suddenly comes upon them, they lack even the slightest trace of fearless confidence, for they have been fixated solely on hearing and teaching and have taken pride in their affluence and status in this life. For both those who become entranced for their whole lives by delusive appearances and mindsets, and those who become captivated by the knowledge gained from hearing and by teaching, there is no qualitative difference in the objects of their craving, just as there is no difference between being bound by fetters of gold or fetters of rope. Everything that you cling to acts solely as a cause for the bondage of your own mindstream.

"First you should come to know the critical points and accounts concerning the vast view and meditation. In the end, having sincerely dedicated yourself to essential practice, you will reach the state of liberation without getting caught up in pitfalls and errors. In this way, hearing [the Dharma] goes right to the core. Otherwise, if your pride and sense of self-importance increase due to hearing teachings many times and understanding them, everything you see will become an object for false views and invalid denials and superimpositions. Not even the slightest faith or reverence will arise in your mindstream, and you will be filled with the pomposity of thinking 'There's not a single person like me!' Contemptuous of others, you will abuse them. [337] When you hear or witness other renowned people teaching, the power of fierce pride will arise, and out of a sense of envy you will falsely superimpose faults upon them, while denying their actual excellent qualities. For such people, learning becomes a poison, and the foundation is laid for rebirth in miserable states of existence.

"Therefore, from the very beginning scrutinize such teachers and avoid them. Do not depend upon them. Regard as a buddha any guru from whom you have received as little as a single verse of instruction, and do nothing to displease your guru even for an instant. If you do displease your guru, you are abandoning all the jinas of the three times, so no meditative experiences, realizations, or enlightened qualities will arise in your mindstream. Even if merit is accumulated, its fruits will not arise. Even if you engage in practices involving deities and their maṇḍalas, you will actualize nothing but demons and spirits who cause you to break your samayas. The seeds of liberation will dry up and bear no fruit. The trunk of omniscience will rot and its leaves will not grow. Once you have received an empowerment and as few as three lines of guidance from someone, even from a non-Buddhist Sāṃkhya, revere him as the foremost of gurus and never withdraw your reverence.

"When you are sitting, [338] you may take refuge in the Three Jewels by imagining your guru on the crown of your head. When you are walking, visualize your guru on your right shoulder and imagine that you are circumambulating him. This is far superior to circumambulating all the jinas of the three times.

"When you eat and drink, visualize your guru at your throat, and imagine your food as ambrosia. That way, whatever you eat will become a gaṇacakra offering and a fire offering.

"When you are meditating and when you are lying down, visualize your guru at your heart. By merging your mind with his, you will experience the nonconceptual primordial consciousness of ultimate reality, and extraordinary realizations will arise in your mindstream. When you are practicing, if you imagine yourself as being of the nature of the deity and protector, you will not mistakenly reify the stage of generation, and a myriad of supreme and common siddhis and enlightened activities will arise. Thus, depending upon a sublime guru without violating this relationship is the supreme core of spiritual conduct."

Bodhisattva Vajra of Pristine Awareness then commented, "If all the path and fruitional Dharmas were originally, primordially, and completely present in pristine awareness, all sentient beings should certainly have come to the view of the Great Perfection. So what is the difference [between buddhas and sentient beings]? Teacher, please explain!" [339]

He replied, "O Vajra of Pristine Awareness, it is not like that. There is no difference between all buddhas and all sentient beings except that the former are aware and the latter are not. So all sentient beings apprehend their own appearances as being other than themselves and thus remain deluded. All buddhas perceive the purity and equality of saṃsāra and nirvāṇa and are thus enlightened. Therefore, pristine awareness is the great, primordial, originally pure ground, and it recognizes saṃsāra and nirvāṇa as displays of purity and equality. The ultimate reality of pristine awareness that reveals this nature is inconceivable primordial consciousness."

Liberation by Taking Primordial Consciousness, Pristine Awareness, as the Path

Bodhisattva Vajra of Pristine Awareness then commented, "O Teacher, Bhagavān, if one takes primordial consciousness, pristine awareness, as the path, how is liberation attained? What advantages are there in this?"

He replied, "O Vajra of Pristine Awareness, once you have gained mastery over primordial consciousness, pristine awareness, if you meditate uninterruptedly, you will attain liberation in this life and with this body, and you will become a buddha. If a person who had accumulated much karma from the five deeds of immediate retribution and another person who had practiced the stage of generation for his whole life were both to identify pristine awareness simultaneously and meditate upon it—since the ultimate nature of mind is not contaminated by faults or virtues—there [340] wouldn't be even a moment's difference in the times of their enlightenment. This is my solemn promise as Samantabhadra.

"If a person who had engaged in nonvirtuous, evil conduct in this life and another person who had accumulated merit for his whole life were both to identify pristine awareness simultaneously and practice it—since awareness transcends cause and effect—there wouldn't be even a moment's difference in the times of their enlightenment. This is my solemn promise as Samantabhadra.

"If a person who had cultivated profound dhyānas in this life and another person who had fallen under the influence of distraction for his whole life were both to identify pristine awareness simultaneously and practice it—since there are no distinctions of good or bad in awareness—there wouldn't be even a moment's difference in the times of their enlightenment. This is my solemn promise as Samantabhadra.

"If a person who had trained in generating bodhicitta and dedicated himself to the welfare of others for his whole life and another person who had applied himself to deeds injurious to others for his whole life were both to identify the nature of pristine awareness simultaneously and practice it—since pristine awareness is liberated in itself, without reference to activities—there would not be the slightest difference in the times of their enlightenment. This is my solemn promise as Samantabhadra. [341]

"If a person who had tried to control his mindstream for his whole life and another person who had applied himself to the ten nonvirtues for his whole life were both to identify pristine awareness simultaneously and practice it—since pristine awareness does not rely upon other contributing conditions—there wouldn't be even a moment's difference in the times of their enlightenment. This is my solemn promise as Samantabhadra.

"If a person who had practiced generosity for his whole life and another person who had been a thief for his entire life were both to identify the nature of pristine awareness simultaneously—since there is nothing that can help or harm pristine awareness—there wouldn't be even a moment's difference in the times of their enlightenment. This is my solemn promise as Samantabhadra.

"If a great evil-doer who had killed a hundred people and a hundred horses in a single lifetime and another person who had devoted his whole life to circumambulations and prostrations were both simultaneously to identify ground pristine awareness, the great liberation from extremes, and to devote themselves to essential practice—since primordial consciousness, pristine awareness, is devoid of modification or transformation—there would not be the slightest difference in their attainment of enlightenment. This is my solemn promise as Samantabhadra.

"If a person who had spent his life reciting the words of the Buddha and the commentaries and another person who had broken his oaths and lied for his whole life were both to identify pristine awareness and practice it, the state of liberation [342] would not be even the slightest bit further away for one than for the other. This is my solemn promise as Samantabhadra.

"If a person who, through training and progressing along the grounds and paths, had reached the bodhisattva ground of Very Joyful[220] and another person who had not entered this yāna in this life were both to identify for themselves the ground pristine awareness that is free of extremes and were to practice and cultivate it together, there wouldn't be even a moment's difference in the times of their enlightenment. This is my solemn promise as Samantabhadra.

"If a person who had acquainted himself throughout his life with the path pristine awareness and another person who had never seen the entrance to the Dharma were simultaneously to identify the ground pristine awareness, the great freedom from extremes, and were to ardently practice it, there would not be even the slightest difference in the time it would take them to attain enlightenment. This is my solemn promise as Samantabhadra.

"If a person who had dedicated his whole life to constructing temples

220. Tib. *rab tu dga' ba*; Skt. *pramuditā*. The first āryabodhisattva ground.

and stūpas and to protecting the lives of others and another person who had devoted his entire life to taking the lives of others as a butcher were both to identify the ground pristine awareness, the great freedom from extremes, and persistently apply themselves to practicing it, there would not be even the slightest difference in their attainment of enlightenment. This is my solemn promise as Samantabhadra.

"The point of all this is that all delusive activities, like actions in a dream, are never performed; [343] however, by clinging to the true existence of the mere appearances of activities, you see that which does not exist as being existent. Since those actions neither help nor harm the ground pristine awareness, the great freedom from extremes, they make no difference with respect to attaining enlightenment.

"No one is benefited by good deeds, so, like space, they do not exist as something good. No one is harmed by bad deeds, so they are of the nature of space—nonobjective, intangible, and all-pervasive. The reason that they appear to exist in this way is that through ignorance of the ground, which is your own mode of existence, you wander endlessly in saṃsāra, solely as a result of outwardly clinging to other objects. So once you have become aware of this situation, you attain confidence within yourself and gain mastery over yourself. This is enlightenment, which is like an insane person regaining his senses. In this analogy, until you come to your senses and gain control of your mind, there is no way for your behavior to be anything but insane, no matter what you do. Likewise, until pristine awareness identifies itself and achieves confidence within itself, there is no way that good or bad deeds can make you into a buddha. So know this!

"O Vajra of Pristine Awareness, [344] these qualities are inexpressible! The advantages of identifying pristine awareness and uninterruptedly meditating on it for six months are a hundred, a thousand, even ten thousand times greater than the advantages of performing physical prostrations and circumambulations for purifying obscurations. The advantages of identifying the dharmakāya, pristine awareness that is present in the ground, and uninterruptedly meditating on it for six months are a hundred, a thousand, even ten thousand times greater than the advantages of devoting yourself to great acts of generosity for your whole life. The advantages of identifying the dharmakāya, pristine awareness that is present in the ground, and uninterruptedly meditating on it for six months are far more than ten thousand or a hundred thousand times greater than the advantages of filling this great galaxy with stūpas and holy images made of the seven types of precious substances and making offerings and devotions to them.

"The merit of identifying the dharmakāya, pristine awareness that is present in the ground, and practicing it for six months is ten thousand or a hundred thousand times greater than the merit of spending your whole life reading the sūtras and reciting mantras and so forth. If you identify the dharmakāya, pristine awareness that is present in the ground, and practice it for six months, the advantages are a hundred, a thousand, or even ten thousand times greater than the advantages of practicing the profound stage of generation for your whole life. [345] If you identify within yourself the dharmakāya, pristine awareness that is present in the ground, and practice it uninterruptedly for six months, the merit is far more than a hundred or a thousand times that of generating bodhicitta for all sentient beings and devoting yourself to their welfare for your whole life. If you identify the dharmakāya, pristine awareness that is present in the ground, and practice it uninterruptedly, day and night, for six months, the merit is far more than ten thousand or a hundred thousand times that of constantly applying yourself to the ten virtuous deeds for your whole life.

"O Vajra of Pristine Awareness, if you wish to release all the beings of the three realms simultaneously from the ocean of suffering of mundane existence, identify the dharmakāya, pristine awareness that is present in the ground, and practice it uninterruptedly. If you wish to fathom all the inexhaustible ornamental wheels of the enlightened body, speech, mind, qualities, and activities of the jinas and jinaputras of the three times, identify the dharmakāya, pristine awareness that is present in the ground, and practice it uninterruptedly. If you wish to perfectly attain all the grounds, paths, and sublime qualities of the nine successive yānas, identify the dharmakāya, pristine awareness that is present in the ground, [346] and practice it uninterruptedly.

"If you wish to manifestly attain the state of the dharmakāya, the original protector, in this very life and with this very body, identify the dharmakāya, pristine awareness that is present in the ground, and practice it uninterruptedly. If you wish to revel in the great purity and equality of saṃsāra and nirvāṇa, identify the dharmakāya, pristine awareness that is present in the ground, and practice it uninterruptedly. If you wish to completely perfect the qualities of the ten perfections,[221] identify the dharmakāya, pristine awareness that is present in the ground, and practice it uninterruptedly. If you wish to simultaneously perfect all the facets of primordial consciousness of knowledge, compassion, and power, identify the dharmakāya, pristine awareness that is present in the ground, and practice it uninterruptedly.

221. The ten perfections include the six perfections of generosity, ethical discipline, patience, enthusiasm, meditation, and wisdom, along with skillful means, aspirational prayer, power, and primordial consciousness.

"Even if you do not meditate on the sublime qualities of what you have identified, you will undoubtedly become enlightened within seven lifetimes. Know that the advantages of identifying pristine awareness for yourself are ten million or a hundred million times greater than those of having a vision of three thousand buddhas and hearing their teachings all at once.

"O Vajra of Pristine Awareness, the vast, single taste of the womb, the mystery of the mind of all the buddhas and of Samantabhadrī—the absolute space of phenomena, [347] free of all origination, cessation, and abiding—is none other than this pristine space. All of saṃsāra, nirvāṇa, and the path is of one taste in the nature of space, and space is the essential nature of all of saṃsāra and nirvāṇa. Space is the universal ground of the totality of saṃsāra and nirvāṇa. Upon recognizing and fathoming space as all the displays of saṃsāra and nirvāṇa, and upon realizing that they are not other than space, you will fathom this space. This experience of space is called the *yoga of space*. Upon realizing everything as great emptiness, fathoming emptiness as space itself is the real essence of the meaning of emptiness. This is the meaning of *possessing primordial consciousness, manifest pristine awareness*."

Then the entire gathering of disciples, including Bodhisattva Vajra of Pristine Awareness, expressed this prayer with one voice and with one mind:

> *Kye*! May ultimate reality, free of conceptual elaboration,
> the spontaneous actualization of the dharmakāya,
> and the glory of the kāyas and facets of primordial consciousness
> be witness to the realization of this prayer!
> By the force of knowledge, compassion, and power, [348]
> may there be blessings that this prayer is realized without interferences!
>
> *Hūṃ*. With the wisdom of realizing identitylessness,
> may we authentically realize
> the originally pure, all-pervasive dharmakāya—
> the absolute space of the great purity and equality of saṃsāra and nirvāṇa,
> free of the eight extremes of conceptual elaboration—
> and emptiness endowed with the three doors of liberation.
>
> Due to the circumstance of grasping at the self,
> a name is imputed upon a nonexistent basis of designation.
> With discerning wisdom,
> may we realize this as great identitylessness.

In the great, pervasive ground of absolute space,
the physical worlds and their sentient inhabitants arise due to
deluded ego-grasping.
With discerning wisdom,
may we realize this as great emptiness.

With discerning wisdom,
may we realize the phenomena of causes and effects
and all appearances of benefit and harm by gods and demons
as great nonobjectivity.

With discerning wisdom,
may we realize buddhas and sentient beings
and all objectification and reification of hopes and fears
as great identitylessness.

With discerning wisdom,
may we realize the apparitions of the eight collections of
consciousness
and all appearances of sensory objects
as great identitylessness.

As the subjective and objective phenomena of the world [349]
are like the ten analogies of illusion,
with the wisdom of realizing identitylessness
may we comprehend them as great nonobjectivity.

With the wisdom that perceives the full range of phenomena
and knows reality as it is, may we know
the great expanse that totally encompasses
the Dharmas, paths, and fruitions of the yānas.

May we realize the authentic view
of awakening to enlightenment
in the display of the purity and equality of saṃsāra and nirvāṇa,
the originally pure, primordial ground.

Thus, saṃsāra, nirvāṇa, and the path
are like displays of reflections in the ocean.
May the great nonduality, bodhicitta, manifest,
and may we reach the supreme path.

With no meditation, free of any object of attention,
with the nonduality of a subject and object of observation,
and free of clinging to negation and affirmation,
may we abandon activity and reach the supreme path.

Once the obscuring veils of ignorance
have been removed from the face of the dharmakāya, the
original, primordial ground,
may we reach the foremost of paths
with great primordial consciousness, pristine awareness.

May we swiftly reach the foremost of paths,
in which we acquire confidence and
mastery in the great nonmeditation of ultimate reality,
free of the effort of progressing in the training.

Once the body, speech, and mind have entered the vajra
womb,[222] [350]
and the kāyas and the eye of great primordial consciousness
have been freed of muddled, habitual contaminations,
may there arise the vision of the direct perception of ultimate
reality.

Due to the sublime qualities of the vision of direct perception,
may we experience the benefits
of the sublime ground of Very Joyful
and the ground and path of a matured vidyādhara.

With the growth of meditative experiences and realizations,
as a result of all impure appearances being transmuted
into the lucidity of the pure space of pristine awareness,
may we achieve progress in meditative experience.

By the power of progress in meditative experience,
may we cross over to the fifth ground known as Difficult to
Cultivate,[223]

222. This refers to your body, speech, and mind becoming the vajra body, vajra speech, and vajra mind of a buddha.

223. Tib. *sbyang dka' ba*; Skt. *sudurjayā*. The fifth āryabodhisattva ground.

and may we attain all the sublime qualities of the ground and path
of a vidyādhara with mastery over life.

Once pristine awareness has ripened to its vital essence,
may pristine awareness reach its consummate state,
in which the phenomenal world is purified
as the great displays of the kāyas and buddhafields.

Due to the virtues of reaching consummate awareness,
may we cross over to the eighth ground known as Immovable,[224]
and may we attain all the sublime qualities of the ground and path
of a mahāmudrā vidyādhara. [351]

Once all appearances of phenomena have been extinguished
in great, intellect-transcending ultimate reality,
may we attain confidence and hold our ground,
and may we proceed to the path of no more training.

By the power of the intellect-transcending extinction into ultimate reality,
may we cross over to the great tenth ground known as Cloud of Dharma,[225]
and may we swiftly attain the sublime qualities of the ground and path
of a spontaneously actualized vidyādhara.

Thus, may we come to the culmination, in this very life,
of the essential Dharma of this swift path,
and before long, may we quickly attain
the state of a buddha.

May the primordial consciousness that knows and perceives
come ablaze in great, pervasive ultimate reality,
and may the three realms of saṃsāra be totally
transformed into the nature of the three kāyas.

May all impure, delusive phenomena

224. Tib. *mi g.yo ba*; Skt. *acalā*. The eighth āryabodhisattva ground.

225. Tib. *chos kyi sprin*; Skt. *dharmameghā*. The tenth āryabodhisattva ground.

be released right now
into the space of great, primordial purity,
like the dissolution of illusory phantoms.

May the mental states and appearances of all sentient beings
be dissolved into the great, inner, original space of pristine
  awareness,
like dreams vanishing into absolute space,
and may we become enlightened as a youthful vase kāya.[226]

Then the revealer of the original ground said, "O Vajra of Pristine Awareness, when ordinary beings make prayers, first they should invoke all the buddhas as their witnesses. At the end, for their prayers to be realized, they should repeat the words of truth.[227] Moreover, if potent mantras are recited fewer than seven times, it is very difficult for them to be effective. On the other hand, if prayers are made and the words of truth are uttered either before a physical representation of the objects of refuge, in the presence of your guru, in the midst of an assembly of many Saṅgha members, [352] on the thirtieth day of the lunar month, or at the time of a solar or lunar eclipse, they will be realized."

226. According to the dictionary *Bod rgya tshig mdzod chen mo* (p. 2432), this term (Tib. *gzhon nu bum pa'i sku*; Skt. *kumārakalaśakāya*) is unique to the Great Perfection tradition. It refers to the awareness of Samantabhadra, which is of the oceanic nature of the kāyas and facets of primordial consciousness with six qualities: (1) externally luminous consciousness is withdrawn into itself, and the great, internally luminous, original, ground absolute space appears to itself, (2) it transcends the ground, (3) it differentiates, (4) it is liberated upward, (5) it does not arise from something else, and (6) it dwells in its own place.

According to Gyatrul Rinpoché, this state of enlightenment is likened to a vase, for, as the sole bindu, it encompasses all of saṃsāra and nirvāṇa, while transcending the three times. It is called "youthful," for it is not subject to aging or degeneration, and it is called a "kāya," for it is the aggregate of the inexhaustible enlightened body (kāya), speech, mind, qualities, and activities of all the buddhas.

227. Tib. *bden brjod*. This is a genre of prayers, rather than one specific prayer or text.

Phase 6: Teachings on the Essential Points of Practice and Their Key Distinctions

THEN Bodhisattva Vajra of Pristine Awareness asked, "O Teacher, Bhagavān, when practicing this unsurpassed, supreme yāna, the profound and secret Great Perfection, are there or are there not pitfalls and obstacles that lead one astray? If there are, Teacher, please explain what they are!"

He replied, "O Vajra of Pristine Awareness, when you first establish the profound view, there is the danger of mistaking understanding for realization. Why? *Understanding* is just taking in the oral explanation of your teacher. This is like memorizing the words of a textbook without examining their meaning. By merely reciting what you have heard, without fathoming its meaning, you may have the conceit of thinking 'I know this,' but it has not really entered your mindstream. This is mere understanding, not realization. One who arrogantly takes it for realization is like someone who has never seen a king's treasury and has no claim to it, but who has heard others' reports about the treasury and memorized them, [353] and then thinks 'That is my treasury.' This is utterly futile.

"As for *realization*, whether it concerns explanations by your teacher or [whether it is] fathoming the real meaning of the tantras, oral transmissions, and pith instructions, or whether it is something that emerges from the expanse of your own wisdom, at first you may understand only a fraction. Then, with that as a catalyst, you repeatedly investigate and come to a subtle, precise knowledge of how all appearing phenomena are nonobjective and empty from their own side. Finally, you decisively fathom the one taste of great emptiness—the fact that all of saṃsāra and nirvāṇa naturally arises from the expanse of the ground and is not established as anything else. This is realization.

"If you lack such firm, vast, and profound wisdom of realization, free of the slightest doubt, then if the whole world, with its gods, were to insist repeatedly that saṃsāra and nirvāṇa are autonomous, permanent, stable, and immutable, this would deter you from the path of liberation. The nature of realization is that of meditation, for there is no meditation superior to realization. First you understand, then you gain experience, and finally you acquire the confidence of realization. Without this, there is nothing that deserves to be called the 'view' or 'meditation,' for there is not even a trace of them. [354] So be aware of how indispensable it is for firm realization to arise in your mindstream.

"Not knowing how to distinguish between realization and gaining confidence, many people mistake one for the other and thereby become confused. So learn how to make this distinction. *Realization* refers to correctly knowing with certainty the manner in which the nature of the grounds and paths and the triad of saṃsāra, nirvāṇa, and the path are all completely present in pristine awareness itself. There are many people who say that the knowledge of those who endure great hardships and experience myriad joys and sorrows is genuine realization, but that the knowledge of those who gain immediate insight into the nature of reality does not count as realization. That is incorrect.

"Consider this analogy: Some very devout people wishing to make a pilgrimage to the three types of holy representations in Lhasa, Samyé, and so on courageously make a long and arduous journey to these places of pilgrimage and encounter these holy icons. Some other people who were born in these pilgrimage sites also encounter these holy representations, without any hardship or display of courage. There is no difference in the encounters of these two groups of people. What they are encountering is the three types of representations, there is no difference in their encounters, [355] and in particular, people who were born in these holy places have the same unimpeded knowledge of all the outer, inner, and secret representations [as those who visit them from afar].

"Likewise, there is not the slightest difference between someone who identifies ultimate reality, the mode of existence of suchness, after experiencing many hardships, joys, and sorrows, and someone who establishes, by means of discerning primordial consciousness, the identitylessness of all the phenomena of saṃsāra and nirvāṇa, and then directly realizes and knows the mode of existence of ultimate reality. What each one needs to do is to ascertain ultimate reality, the mode of existence of suchness, and identify pristine awareness that is present in the ground. There is no difference whatsoever between these two people.

"Realizing, ascertaining, and fathoming the meaning is called the *view*. As for *acquiring confidence*, first you identify awareness, then you bring forth inactive, wonderfully spacious pristine awareness, and by practicing it uninterruptedly, finally you achieve stability within yourself. Then, without any deviation in terms of times or situations—like the absence of darkness once dawn has broken—it is said that you acquire confidence for yourself. As soon as you first gain realization, if you do not acquire confidence by applying yourself to practice, [356] even though you have identified your own essential nature, you will die as an ordinary person, and you will continue to wander in saṃsāra. Likewise, even if you possess a mountain of food but do not eat it, it will be of no use and you will die of starvation. Even though you own a castle filled with clothing, if you do not wear it, you will die from exposure to the elements. Therefore, recognize the vital importance of acquiring confidence.

"If you do not know how to distinguish between the mind and pristine awareness, you will confuse the mind for pristine awareness, which will unfortunately lead to obstacles to achieving the state of liberation. So know how to distinguish them! As for the *mind*, there are the *deluded mind that clings to appearances*, the *mind that seeks the path by way of negation and affirmation*, and the *mind that takes consciousness as the path*.

"The deluded mind that clings to appearances is the ordinary mind of sentient beings who do not seek the path and who do not see an entrance to the authentic path.

"The mind that seeks the path is said to take the mind as its path, for in this case, the mind observes the mind, thoughts are observed with a conceptual mind, and you seek the path of merely arousing pleasure and pain through intellectual fabrications and the acceptance and rejection of virtue and vice.

"As for the mind that takes consciousness as the path, the experience of unimpeded ordinary consciousness, which is the ground of the mind, [357] is not the realization of the view. As a result of such practice, outer appearances are reduced to an ethically neutral state, and since these appearances are taken to be real, reification is not counteracted. Inwardly, your own body appears to be ethically neutral, so the fixation of reifying the body is not counteracted. And since both outer and inner appearances are taken to be ethically neutral and autonomous, you do not transcend the mind, so this, too, is called the *mind*. Even if this were called 'pristine awareness'—like giving a boy's name to an unborn fetus—the characteristic of ascertaining pristine awareness in itself would not have been realized. Unawareness is failing to realize saṃsāra and nirvāṇa as great emptiness. The terms *awareness* and *unawareness* are known conventionally by way of their respective functions.

"*Pristine awareness* first establishes everything included in the phenomenal world of saṃsāra and nirvāṇa as emptiness. The reflections of the planets and stars in the ocean have no existence apart from the ocean, yet they are of the same nature as the displays of the ocean. Likewise, rainbows in the sky have no existence apart from the sky, yet those appearances are of the same nature as the displays of the sky. In the same manner, pristine awareness is actualized by correctly recognizing that things appear even though nothing exists from the side of the appearances, and that all appearances of the physical worlds and their sentient inhabitants have no existence apart from the ground sugatagarbha, [358] while those appearances are of the same nature as the displays of the ground sugatagarbha.

"Like the dawn breaking in the sky, without need for meditation, you comprehend saṃsāra and nirvāṇa as being totally subsumed within great enlightenment. Without need for investigation, there is your own awareness, without grasping, that all of saṃsāra and nirvāṇa is like the reflection of the planets and stars in the ocean. Without need for modification, there is natural liberation in the absolute space of the ground, the great purity and equality of saṃsāra and nirvāṇa. Without need for objectification, there is a spacious dissolution into the great expanse, with no object, obstruction, or intentionality. In this way you experience and gain mastery over the inexhaustible ornamental wheels of the enlightened body, speech, mind, qualities, and activities of the jinas and jinaputras of the three times.

"Ultimately, simply by identifying the dharmakāya, pristine awareness that is present in the ground, you gain power over the life force of saṃsāra and nirvāṇa. This is not a discussion of receiving empowerment through such things as water and symbolic pictures that are used as methods to awaken the mind. Rather, you know you have obtained the empowerments of the jinas and jinaputras and the oral transmissions of all the writings that emerge from primordial consciousness, pristine awareness. [359] Thus, you have already simultaneously obtained all empowerments and oral transmissions. Therefore, recognize the importance of not mistaking the mind for pristine awareness.

"If you do not know how to distinguish between mentation and wisdom, you will confuse mentation for wisdom, as a result of which you are in danger of wasting your entire life. So know how to distinguish them! *Mentation* is the mind of every sentient being, which serves as the basis for the emergence of all conceptions. It is the lucid, clear nature of the unimpeded appearance of objects to the mind, and it is just this that transforms all appearances into their referential objects. You may identify unimpeded mentation, this whirring consciousness, as being of the essential nature of meditation. However, since this ethically neutral consciousness of mentation is the basis of saṃsāra, even if you achieve stability in it, this will lead you only to the two higher realms of existence and not higher. So mentation does not transform into wisdom.

"Since mentation does not become wisdom, all positive and negative karmas lead solely to saṃsāra, and they never act as causes for liberation. So it is crucial to recognize the importance of not becoming absorbed in this. It is a disaster for all those meditators who remain solely in this state without ever transcending it. [360] It is from this that errors arise, stemming from the nature of all meditative experiences of vividness, from the nature of all ethically neutral states, and from various, miscellaneous extrasensory perceptions of seeing visions of gods and demons. All those who take this alone as being the path will remain endlessly deluded in saṃsāra; they are not even moving in the direction of liberation and omniscience.

"*Wisdom* is a subsequent knowledge that establishes everything included in the phenomenal world of saṃsāra and nirvāṇa as being empty, identityless, and nonobjective. This is called the *wisdom that realizes identitylessness with respect to that which has always been unreal and empty*. Due to this powerful method, all appearances and mindsets are gradually extinguished in absolute space, just as all land is saturated by the moisture of the ocean.

"The emergence in your mindstream of the great wisdom that realizes identitylessness, like salt dissolving in water, calms all appearing phenomena in the ocean of the original ground. The emergence in your mindstream of the wisdom that realizes identitylessness, like warmth suffusing ice, calms all subjective and objective phenomena in the original, primordial ground, absolute space. [361] The emergence in your mindstream of the wisdom that realizes identitylessness, like the wind carrying camphor, extinguishes saṃsāra in the great wind of reversion.[228] In the mind of a person in whom the wisdom that realizes identitylessness has arisen, all appearances do seem to exist, but in the depths of that person's mind they are known to be like illusions and dreams, so they are released as being identityless. For a person in whom the wisdom that realizes identitylessness has arisen, whatever may be craved or grasped, deep down that person has acquired confidence in identitylessness.

"In the mind of a person in whom the wisdom that realizes identitylessness has arisen, all the taproots of saṃsāra disintegrate. Thus, the wisdom that realizes identitylessness ascertains saṃsāra and nirvāṇa as great emptiness. The great wisdom that experiences reality knows how all the sublime qualities of the path and the fruition are perfected. With great, omnipresent, all-seeing wisdom, you experience the dharmakāya, pristine awareness that is present in the ground. With the wisdom that knows reality as it is, you know ultimate reality, the mode of existence of suchness. With the wisdom that perceives the full range of phenomena, [362] you perceive the taproots of all the phenomena of saṃsāra, and you perceive and experience all the

228. The analogy here is of a wind that reverses the natural sequence of saṃsāra as characterized by the twelve links of dependent origination.

inexhaustible ornamental wheels of the enlightened body, speech, mind, qualities, and activities of the jinas and jinaputras of the three times. In reality, when you fathom the vastness and depth of the great wisdom that realizes identitylessness, this is nothing other than a natural expression of the essential nature of pristine awareness.

"O Vajra of Pristine Awareness, if you do not know how to distinguish between conditioned consciousness and primordial consciousness, you may think conditioned consciousness is primordial consciousness and consequently circle about in delusion. So learn how to distinguish between them! *Conditioned consciousness* is the naturally present radiance and clarity of the unimpeded objects that emerge in the expanse of mentation, which, when they enter the sense doors, are bound by self-grasping. When looking out through the sense doors, that which appears as seeing, hearing, feeling, experiencing, and contacting external sensory appearances is called *conditioned consciousness*.

"Insofar as conditioned consciousness individually apprehends and recognizes names and things, and arouses the three closely held feelings of pleasure, pain, and indifference, all things appear to be separate and distinct. They are given individual names, and things are apprehended as being distinct. This acts as the basis, from which emerge thoughts of attachment to your own side and aversion to the other's side. [363] The good is apprehended as being good and is made into an object of hope, thus proliferating thoughts of yearning. The bad is apprehended as being bad, and this serves as a basis from which various thoughts of anxiety arise.

"What is called *mentation* manifests as the consciousness of appearances, it turns into appearing objects, and it causes appearances to be made manifest. From the very moment that a thought and a subject arise, what is called *mind* merges nondually with appearances and vanishes.

"*Primordial consciousness* is the natural glow of the ground, and it expresses itself as the five facets of primordial consciousness. Specifically, in the manifest state of the ground, great primordial consciousness, which has been forever present, abides as the aspect of lucidity and clarity, like the dawn breaking and the sun rising. It is not blank like an unimpeded darkness that knows nothing. All appearances are naturally present, without arising or ceasing. Just as heat is naturally present in the nature of fire, moisture is present in the nature of water, and coolness is present in the nature of wind, due to the unimpeded power in the nature of primordial consciousness, there is total knowledge and total awareness of all phenomena, without its ever merging with or entering into objects. [364] Primordial consciousness is self-emergent, naturally clear, and free of outer and inner obscuration; it is the all-pervasive, radiant, clear infinity of space, free of contamination.

"What are the causes and conditions by which conditioned consciousness is transformed into primordial consciousness? They are accurately knowing how thoughts of the phenomena of saṃsāra and nirvāṇa emerge—including the eight aggregates of conditioned consciousness and sensory appearances—and realizing the manner in which they are naturally perfect as displays of the kāyas and facets of primordial consciousness in the nature of ultimate reality. Then, from the time that you identify the dharmakāya, pristine awareness that is present in the ground, your conditioned consciousness is transmuted into displays of primordial consciousness. Then, regarding conditioned consciousness, by the illusory display of concepts of the self alone, primordial consciousness takes on the guise of conditioned consciousness, like a pile of stones being mistaken for a man. The transformation of this into primordial consciousness is like recognizing a scarecrow for what it is, instead of seeing it as a man. In this way, the correct realization of the mode of being of conditioned consciousness transforms it into primordial consciousness. It is not that conditioned consciousness must vanish into absolute space and primordial consciousness must arise from somewhere else. Instead, know that it just seems that way because of the functions of self-grasping and identitylessness.

"Conditioned consciousness is what makes the first moment of knowledge emerge in the aspect of the object, [365] just as various images of planets and stars emerge in the ocean. What arises is closely held by conceptual consciousness; it is bound by reification, and you thereby become deluded. Knowledge of the reasons for this brings you to primordial consciousness.

"O Vajra of Pristine Awareness, if you do not know how to distinguish between the substrate and the dharmakāya, you may take the substrate and the substrate consciousness as the path, in which case you will not transcend the three realms. Why? The *actual substrate* is something immaterial, devoid of thought, a space-like vacuity and blankness in which appearances are suspended. Know that you enter this state in deep, dreamless sleep, when you faint, and when you are dying. As a result of engaging in conceptual negation and affirmation, the substrate is aroused. Understand that if someone takes this as sublime meditation and stabilizes it, this can lead to dementia, stupor, and total ignorance. There are some teachers who identify this as the great, intellect-transcending extinction into ultimate reality. If you get stuck there, it is certain that you will be cast into existence in the realm of gods who are devoid of discernment.[229]

"Someone with an experience of vacuity and clarity who directs his attention inward may bring a stop to all external appearances [366] and come to a state in which he believes there are no appearances or thoughts. This

229. This is included in the formless realm.

experience of luminosity from which one dares not part is the substrate consciousness. This is aroused by the power of being bound by the fetters of meditation, but some teachers think it is the clear light. Others think it is the pristine awareness of nonmeditation, and yet others identify it as the insertion of the energy-mind into the central channel. In reality, it is the substrate consciousness, so if you get stuck there, you will be cast into the formless realm, without coming even a bit closer to the state of liberation. With the substrate and the substrate consciousness you observe your own mind, but you do not recognize or know saṃsāra and nirvāṇa as your own appearances.

"The *dharmakāya* is spontaneously actualized as the essential nature of the purity and equality of saṃsāra and nirvāṇa. It is emptiness, the infinity of space; its display is groundless and rootless. It is great, unobstructed non-objectivity. The facets of primordial consciousness and enlightened qualities of the buddhas do not enhance it; the terrible vices, obscurations, and miseries of sentient beings do not impair it. Not becoming good or bad, it is the great, immutable, originally pure, [367] all-pervasive absolute space of the ground. Once its mode of existence is determined, identifying its manifest state within yourself is simply holding your own ground. It is very deluded to think that the dharmakāya did not exist previously and that it newly comes into existence.

"The realm in which the absolute space of the dharmakāya manifests is nondual with space. All phenomena included in saṃsāra and nirvāṇa are naturally present in the emptiness of ultimate reality, absolute space that is free of the extremes of conceptual elaboration. It is called the embodiment of the totality of all facets of primordial consciousness and qualities as perfect, spontaneously actualized displays. Thoroughly fathoming the mode of being of this dharmakāya, Samantabhadra, is realization. By experiencing this state, you know that just as all the reflections of stars and planets in the ocean are displays of the ocean itself, and just as all the physical worlds and their sentient inhabitants are displays of one space, all of saṃsāra and nirvāṇa consists of displays of the one dharmakāya. They are all great, unimpeded effulgences of the dharmakāya.

"Just as the reflections of planets and stars in the ocean are subsumed in the ocean, and just as all the physical worlds and their sentient inhabitants are subsumed in space, so are saṃsāra, nirvāṇa, and the path all subsumed in the one dharmakāya. Experiencing this reality, [368] dwelling in it, entering the womb of the nature of existence, coming to the nature of being within yourself, and ascertaining this to be free of good and bad and of benefit and harm is the experience of realization by which you acquire confidence. And this is enlightenment.

"O Vajra of Pristine Awareness, if you do not know how to distinguish between what is and what is not the path, there is the danger that you may be led astray to what is not the path, and, unfortunately, not actualize the genuine path. So learn how to distinguish between them! The path of the perfection of wisdom consists of correctly realizing the view, the essential point of emptiness, and simply taking this knowledge as the path. Once you have realized the meaning of great emptiness, you know the nature of the whole of saṃsāra, nirvāṇa, and the path, and you experience absolute space. This is called the *pristine awareness of the Great Perfection*. The lucid, clear ground, free of contamination, is taken as the path. If you take consciousness as the path, you are taking aspects of consciousness as the path. If you take the displays of the ground, the purity and equality of saṃsāra and nirvāṇa, as the path, this is taking the essential nature as the path. It is called the *authentic path*.

"What is called *viewing discursive thoughts with discursive thoughts* is not the path. With respect to discursive thoughts, you may engage in such evaluations as denying and affirming and adopting the good and rejecting the bad, and finally regard merely unstructured consciousness as the ultimate view and meditation. [369] But that is not the path. Even if you take the creative expressions of the mind and the essential nature of the mind as the path, since the mind is the basis of delusion, you will certainly not transcend the three realms. So that is not the path.

"O Vajra of Pristine Awareness, if you do not know how to distinguish between mastering the ground and drifting off to an ethically neutral state, you will mistakenly fall under the influence of the ethically neutral state, and you will remain as deluded as you were before.

"Why? In the absence of a name, there is no basis for the appearance of the name. In the absence of a phenomenon, there is no basis for the appearance of the phenomenon. In the absence of benefit or harm, there is no basis for the appearance of benefit and harm. In the absence of saṃsāra and nirvāṇa, there is no basis for the appearance of saṃsāra and nirvāṇa. In the absence of sensory objects, there is no basis for the appearance of sensory objects. You may establish that all such bases are nonexistent and know them to be nonexistent. But if you regard the referents of those bases of appearances to be nonexistent, you have succumbed to a nihilistic view. For if not even the bases of appearances or objects existed, there would be no referents of appearances. *Mastering the ground* means realizing the clear, empty nature, free of conceptual elaboration, of the bases of appearances and their referents.

"This ground is present in the mindstreams of all sentient beings, but it is tightly constricted by dualistic grasping, and it is regarded as external, firm, and solid. This is like water in its natural, [370] fluid state freezing in a cold wind. It is due to dualistic grasping at subjects and objects that the ground, which is naturally free, becomes frozen into the appearances of things. So meditators who do not even know how dualistic grasping operates—however puffed up they may be—*reduce the ground to an ethically neutral state*. Therefore, however much they may meditate, they will not become enlightened.

"O Vajra of Pristine Awareness, if you do not know how to distinguish between delusion and liberation, you will go astray by mistaking delusion for liberation, resulting in your not attaining the great state of liberation. It is like this:

"There are three types of *delusion*: delusion in your mindstream, delusion regarding the path, and the delusion of going astray:

1. *Delusion in your mindstream* refers to the minds of all beings having become deluded by the ignorance of dualistic grasping, which prevents them from seeing the entrance to the path.
2. There are many kinds of *delusion regarding the path*. Specifically, you may spend your whole life observing and modifying discursive thoughts, which cause you to hold closely to various joys and sorrows. Some who do this become so deluded that they become delirious, like an irrigation canal that becomes blocked and overflows with swirling water. Some are deluded by taking a soothing sense of well-being as the best of meditations. Others fixate on a sense of luminosity [371] and deludedly take that to be the most sublime of meditations. Some people cling to various obsessions with divine and demonic apparitions stemming from their experience of luminosity. Holding themselves to be supreme, they proceed to teach this to others; and driven by arrogance and conceit, they waste their lives in the pursuit of material gain. Even if they meditate, it is for that purpose. Even if others try to correct them, they do not accept this, and they cannot turn away from the path they are treading. Others take nonconceptuality and a blank sense of vacuity to be the foremost of meditations; and becoming absorbed in that, they spin around in a cycle of delusion. Still others, due to their ignorance of the view, devote their entire lives to the mere vacuous luminosity of consciousness. They are all said to be deluded with respect to the path.
3. As for the *delusion of going astray*, some people, before coming to the culmination of the path, take meditative experiences and views and meditations involving reified objects as the pinnacle of meditation, and they get stuck there. They then face death as ordinary people, and they suffer the delusion of having gone astray.

"There is also *becoming deluded in error*. What is this? First you establish the emptiness of all phenomena included in the universe of saṃsāra and nirvāṇa; and after recognizing this, you think 'I have realized [372] saṃsāra and nirvāṇa as great emptiness, so now I don't need to engage in the relative Dharma of accumulating merit, nor do I need to meditate,' and you proclaim these empty words to others. There are many such people who then waste their entire lives in distractions and spiritual sloth, and they face death as ordinary people. Others, after they have similarly recognized the nature of emptiness, think 'Now there is nothing whatsoever for me to practice,' and they proclaim the superiority of their views. After misleading others with rituals and liturgies, when they die, they are caught by the ripening of their karma, and they step into the abyss of the miserable states of existence. That is a mistake.

"Some become satisfied by just hearing about and understanding emptiness, and they discard all practices of meditation as if they were clots of spittle. Maintaining that there is no need to guard all their samayas or vows, even if they were to have a direct vision of the Buddha, they would be snared by false views and misconceptions, without even a trace of faith or reverence. As for their involvement in negative actions, they would experience no qualms even about the urge to kill a human being; if they felt the need to eat their father's flesh, they would do so as if it were ambrosia. They take delight in material wealth acquired by cheating others; they partake of nonvirtue as if it were medicine, and they reject virtue as if it were poison. [373] Training in emptiness with such negative actions is like veering from a path on which you are seeking healing medicinal herbs and running into a plant that is poisonous to the touch. If emptiness becomes a cause for such negative actions, it is reduced to a demonic meditation, and in this life you are deluded as a māra and a malevolent rūdra.

"Generally speaking, once you have realized emptiness, if all accumulations of meritorious, virtuous karma were nonexistent and unnecessary, then all nonvirtuous karma, material acquisitions, attachments, hatreds, and cravings should likewise be abandoned. However, if you reject all deeds of virtue and vice, and passively dwell in the state of emptiness, you brave guys might possibly do okay. But if you reject virtue and pursue nonvirtue, don't you see that your mindstreams become demonic and diabolical?

"If you recognize that, with respect to emptiness, virtue and vice do not exist, then lie down and rest on your bed, with no virtue or vice! If you are correct in your knowledge that virtue does not exist and in your refusal to engage in virtue, there is no point in engaging in vice, either. So release yourself in nonaction and remain there! If you know that vice does not exist, what is the point of indulging in it? If you think that vice does not exist and that engaging in evil conduct is emptiness, then since all sentient beings [374] have just such an attitude and behavior, they should all have realized emptiness. Do you get it?

"Do you understand that people who engage in vice, evil, and nonvirtuous deeds are in the depths of nihilism?[230] If you truly realize the view of emptiness, you will see all acts of virtue and vice as being like children's games, so what is the point of pursuing them?

"In this way, once you have seen that all appearances are like illusions and dreams, if you completely release yourself into inactivity, just this is the conduct of emptiness. However, upon ascertaining the nonexistence of virtue, someone may develop false views regarding the Dharma; and understanding that vices do not exist, he may continuously engage in nonvirtuous behavior. In the end, the lords of hell will rise from the depths of nihilism and punish that person terribly for a long time. When such a person is endlessly tormented in the great dungeon of misery, what will he do then?

"If you say there are benefits to virtue in this lifetime, but add that virtue does not truly exist, or you dismiss it with indifference, or if you say there are disadvantages to evil, but you do not really take it seriously and hold to wrong views, then when you finally die, you will remember its drawbacks and you will tremble with fear. All the possessions and friends you have accumulated will be left behind, you will be terrified of the agents of the Lord of Death, [375] and out of unbearable fear at the miseries of hell, your eyes will fill with tears. How tragic it will be when you claw at your chest and cannot avoid going to hell! At that time it will be too late to feel regret and too late to recall the drawbacks of evil; so consider, what will bring benefit now? Do you understand that you are going into battle after losing confidence in emptiness?

"Without succumbing to such delusions and false paths, know the utmost importance of realizing emptiness and practicing until you reach the grounds and paths to liberation. Having simply identified pristine awareness, some people lack even a trace of any meditation while claiming that they have actualized the extinction into ultimate reality and that there is nothing more to enlightenment than this. That is an enormous mistake! The qualities of realization mature through the power of gradual practice. Here is how you must reach the state of liberation:

1. First, through the power of identifying pristine awareness and practicing single-pointedly, an ineffable state occurs during all meditation sessions, and this is called the *pristine awareness of identifying*.
2. Next, by the power of earnest meditative practice from the time you get

230. Tib. *med pa'i phug.*

up in the morning until you fall asleep at night, [376] never waver for even an instant from that state of awareness. This is called the *pristine awareness of the expanse.*

3. Finally, by the power of ardent meditation, pristine awareness uninterruptedly gains confidence within itself, and this is called the *ongoing current of contemplation* or *pristine awareness in which confidence is acquired.*

"Again, by the power of unimpeded meditation, thoughts of self-grasping turn into empty pristine awareness, and the ground of saṃsāra is seen to be empty. The clinging of dualistic grasping is immediately released, and the appearances of yourself and others vanish into absolute space. All hatred for your enemies, attachment to your friends, hope for good things, fear of bad things, obsession with wealth, and craving for the five sensory objects vanishes into absolute space. You dwell, like space, without activity in the infinite expanse of ultimate reality, and this is *certain liberation.*

"If someone says, 'I have been extinguished into ultimate reality,' since such words and thoughts are of the intellect and mentation, this reveals that no such extinction has occurred. If the appearances of illness arise for such a person, this indicates that illness and the location of the illness have not been extinguished. If there are appearances of hunger and thirst and of being warm and cold, they are indications of self-grasping. [377]

"If someone says, 'Even though I have no attachment, hatred, or obsessive craving, I act as if I did,' such duplicity of pretending they have something they really don't indicates that no extinction has occurred. There is no reason why they would engage in such pretense, so this indicates that they have not been released into great, intellect-transcending ultimate reality. Those who seek out and grasp at material possessions demonstrate that they are not liberated. Even if they maintain that they are liberated, the fallacy of their assertion is revealed by examining the signs. Those who say they are liberated whether or not they meditate and who have not progressed in the slightest beyond all ordinary types of activity reveal the falsity of their own words, and they become objects of great derision for wise people who possess sublime qualities.

"Visionary experiences vanish like mist, without imparting the slightest benefit or harm. Realization is like space, for it has immutably come to the nature of reality. Whether or not you are liberated is revealed by examining the signs of both. The measure of liberation can be understood through your dreams:

1. Superior people purify their dreams in the clear light and become thoroughly integrated with it.

2. Middling people recognize their dreams as dreams and are able to engage in various types of emanations and transformations. [378]
3. The least of people find that the stream of negative dreams produced by habitual propensities is cut, and they have only good dreams.

"When sleep arises as the clear light, you acquire confidence in terms of the enlightened view of the dharmakāya. When you acquire mastery over the displays of emanation and transformation in your dreams, you can transform your own appearances into displays of the saṃbhogakāya. When you have only good dreams, without a single bad one, you are definitely released as a nirmāṇakāya. These are taught as methods for investigating your own degree of spiritual maturation.

"The state of extinction into ultimate reality is one in which all appearances of things have dissolved into great, intellect-transcending ultimate reality. Thus, you do not mentally engage for even an instant in the affairs of saṃsāra but remain inactive. This is definite liberation. Strive diligently in the practice of profound meditation until you meet the criteria of liberation!

"Even if you have heard many teachings and know many treatises of the sūtras and tantras, if your mindstream is not liberated by great meditative experience, there is not the slightest benefit, and you must continue wandering in saṃsāra. Thus, liberating your own mindstream is the vast treasury of all learning, the great treasure of wisdom and great primordial consciousness, and the most sublime of all meditations. [379] So recognize the indispensability of striving in essential practice. Hold fast to it! Rely upon it! Realize it!

"If you derive no benefit for your own mindstream, and focus on the many implications of the words you have heard, your life will be spent in vain. Moreover, you will have a hard time finding anyone to teach, for you will only generate powerful pride and conceit in others, making it very difficult for them to receive any benefit. Even if you acquire enormous prestige and notoriety, this human life is like an episode in a dream and like a visit to the marketplace. So do not be beguiled, for the time of death is coming and there is no time for pursuing prestige and fame.

"Some people, when their lives are at an end, do not notice the occurrence of portents of death, such as advanced age, the loss of physical strength, and the decline of their mental powers. Even so, they praise themselves, thinking 'I am great; I am good.' Still attached and clinging to greatness and prestige, their craving does not cease. When you analyze this, feel compassion for such people who do not see the futility of wasting their lives in the pursuit of status and honor.

"Do not rely upon anyone, but entrust yourself to the Three Jewels. Do not cling to other affairs, but apply yourself to the sublime Dharma. [380] Do not cherish other hopes, but place all your hopes in the state of liberation. Do not waste the rest of your life, but embrace it in essential practice. You do not really achieve fame by working for it, so yearn for the kingdom of the dharmakāya. Without deceiving yourself, apply yourself to a genuine spiritual practice for dying. This is the only time you will attain a human life, so make sure that it is meaningful. Now is the only time you will encounter such profound practical instructions, so do not throw them away, but put them into practice!

"Without deceiving yourself, never forget death. When you go to the next world, you will do so without friends or relatives, so dispense with activities for protecting your family. When you run into death, since you must leave your body and possessions behind, and since there is no way for your friends and relatives to accompany you, utterly sever craving for and attachment to anything. For those who uphold the lineage, these are highly cherished, quintessential pith instructions pointing out the supreme path for attaining liberation in this lifetime. So put them into practice! Fuse them inseparably with your mind! If you lack these vital points, you will not attain liberation in this life, [381] so guard them as the very essence of practical advice.

"O Vajra of Pristine Awareness, if you do not know how to distinguish between buddhas and sentient beings, you may mistake sentient beings for buddhas. Deluded, ignorant fools who do so run the risk of wasting their human lives. Why? *Buddhas* are so designated because they have cleansed the stains of ignorance in absolute space and fully increased all facets of primordial consciousness and enlightened qualities. Infinitely pervasive like space, such beings are free of the eight extremes of conceptual elaboration, are endowed with the three doors of liberation, and are enlightened in the great bliss of equality. The dharmakāya, free of signs and names, is open and unobstructed. Free of change within the three times, it has no fundamental ground.

"Apart from that, do not think that buddhas have bodies! If you thought so, buddhas would have to have parents, and then wouldn't you regard them as sentient beings who have fallen to the extreme of birth? Do not think that buddhas have a self! If you thought so, wouldn't you regard them as sentient beings bound by the ignorance of being single individuals? Do not think that buddhas have realms, [382] with inhabitants, called buddhafields. If you thought so, wouldn't you regard them as sentient beings bound by dualistic grasping?

"Do not think that buddhas have eyes! If you thought so, wouldn't you regard them as sentient beings with visual consciousness? Do not think that buddhas have ears! If you thought so, they would seem to have auditory consciousness together with sounds, and wouldn't you regard them as sentient beings having the same? Do not think that buddhas have noses! If you thought so, wouldn't you regard them as sentient beings involved in olfactory dualistic grasping? Do not think that buddhas have tongues! If you thought so, wouldn't you regard them as sentient beings involved in gustatory dualistic grasping? Do not think that buddhas have bodies! If you thought so, wouldn't you regard them as sentient beings involved in tactile dualistic grasping?

"Do not think that buddhas arose in the past! If you thought so, wouldn't you regard them as sentient beings who have fallen to the extreme of death? Do not think that buddhas will arise in the future! [383] If you thought so, wouldn't you regard them as deluded beings who are subject to birth? Do not think that buddhas exist in the present! If you thought they existed somewhere, wouldn't you regard them as permanent, immutable beings?

"Do not think that buddhas are teachers with disciples! If you thought so, wouldn't you regard them as sentient beings who reify themselves and others? Do not think that buddhas are favorably or unfavorably influenced by receiving homage, offerings, and service! If you thought so, wouldn't you regard them as beings who have prejudicial clinging concerning the good and the bad? Do not think that buddhas have individual locations in the east, south, west, north, or intermediate directions! If you thought so, wouldn't you regard them as sentient beings with identifiable distinctions?

"In short, if any buddhas were like sentient beings, they would come when beckoned; if they were served as masters, they would be directly seen just as masters are, and you would have to hope that they would respond as such. [384] But you should understand something from the fact that however you might call upon them and revere them, not even an atom comes into existence. If buddhas were established in any of the three times, they would have to be produced by the intention to manifest themselves, and they would be established by the power of meditation. In that case, since they would have to be first nonexistent and then freshly established, that would indicate that there would be an impulse of intention and an object of meditation. This demonstrates that they are not established in any of the three times.

"A *sentient being* is one who grasps at and is bound by grasping at a personal identity. Grasped objects foster grasping at the identities of phenomena. Then obsessive clinging and holding to them proliferates an unbroken chain link of discursive thoughts, and one is dazed by roaming in cycles of delusion.

"Through the power of practicing single-pointedly and with great fortitude, ultimately, the contaminated psycho-physical aggregates vanish, right down to the level of atoms. Then the complete signs of having actualized perfect buddhahood occur, including such events as roaring sounds, earthquakes, being enveloped in light, and the simultaneous entrance of the sun and moon into the mouth of Rāhula.[231] Now the profound, swift path to enlightenment as a great transference rainbow body in one life and with one body simultaneously completes [385] all the collections of merit and knowledge, without having to accumulate great collections of merit for many countless eons. If you do not know the entrance to the secret shortcut of direct crossing over, it is difficult to transfer impure mental states and appearances into absolute space. So you should know the practical guidance on directly transferring all mental states and appearances into the absolute space of the clear light, ultimate reality."

231. This refers to an eclipse.

Phase 7: How to Follow the Path of the Great Clear Light, Direct Crossing Over

The Path of Direct Crossing Over to Spontaneous Actualization

Bodhisattva Vajra of Pristine Awareness then commented, "O Teacher, Bhagavān, having been propelled by karmic energies over many eons, there is no guarantee that we will attain a life in which we have the conscious intention to accumulate collections of merit and knowledge and to dispel obscurations. Therefore, since all the necessary conditions are assembled right now, Teacher, please reveal the profound guidance in the swift path of liberation in one life and with one body!"

He replied, "O Vajra of Pristine Awareness, from beginningless time until now, the power of a great many negative thoughts and deeds has endlessly propelled you through saṃsāra. On this occasion, through the confluence of having accumulated good karma and having made fine prayers, [386] you have now attained a human body and have encountered the Dharma. Therefore, if you do not strive at this time, it will be difficult for you to attain such a body in the future, and it will be difficult for you to master the profound path. Even though you have a little karma from the accumulation of merit, with the continuation of negative karma from constantly engaging with miserable, delusive appearances, there is no telling what the results of this will be after many eons. So you should attain liberation in this very lifetime. Carefully examine this point and realize it!

"To follow the profound, swift path of enlightenment in this lifetime, these methods and circumstances must be assembled:

- Directly see your guru as a buddha and do not displease him for even an instant.
- Apply yourself to meditation, worship and accomplishment, offerings, receiving empowerments, and merging your mind with that of your guru.
- Regard your companions as vīras and ḍākinīs, and unflaggingly cultivate faith and reverence for them, while avoiding all contempt, false views, disdain, scorn, ridicule, physical abuse, and deceit, as if they were poisons.

- Regard all beings as your own parents [387] and, out of compassion and bodhicitta, constantly cultivate the attitude of directing all your actions to the service of others.
- Recognize how all the appearances of this life are devoid of essence, like dreams and illusions.
- Think 'This body of mine in this lifetime is something I have for only a few years or months. It is not permanent, and there is no way of knowing when death will come.' And consider 'Whatever I do now on behalf of my spouse and relatives, once I am dead, no one will remember what I have done for them.' To illustrate this utter lack of benefit for yourself, just look at the way in which you do not recall the kindness of your own parents and other relatives who have cared for you!

"In short, recognizing that all the affairs of this life are as pointless as children's games, know that you must take care of yourself. Many people, such as your parents, relatives, and friends, may tell you, 'If you don't strive in worldly activities, you will go hungry! You will be left out in the cold! And you will be weak and pitiful! You must apply yourself to worldly activities for your own sake and for that of your family.' Longing for your happiness and well-being, they will instruct you in ways that will give rise to endless suffering. [388]

"Like the blind leading the blind, there are plenty of teachers who offer bad advice with the best of intentions. However, considering that no one but a qualified guru can instruct you in methods leading to ultimate, eternal bliss, take responsibility for yourself, and recognize the importance of not taking just anyone's advice.

"Even though you wish to accomplish some benefit while accumulating negative deeds for the sake of your parents and family, consider how this actually casts both yourself and others into endless miserable states of existence. Consider 'Now that this body of mine has emerged from my parents' flesh and blood, with the hope that benefit and happiness for them both may arise from this, I shall offer them the first fruits of the harvest, and I shall dress them in the best of garments. As they have brought me up with great affection, if I can now realize eternal bliss, the omniscient state of perfect enlightenment, there will be great significance to my parents' care of my body. They will accrue vast merit, I shall repay my parents' kindness and render service to my guru, and something of great significance will be accomplished for the sake of sentient beings.' Recognizing this, entrust your innermost heart to the Dharma. Roam about from one solitary place of retreat to another. [389] Be content with mere sustenance, without regard to the quality of your food. Be content merely to have protection from the rain and wind, without regard to the quality of your habitation, and apply yourself to essential practice.

"If you overeat, discursive thoughts will increase, and you will succumb to spiritual sloth and distractions. If you place a priority on beautiful, fine clothes, you will fall under the influence of luxuries, and you will want to show off in public. If you drink alcohol, your mind will become addled, and as an ordinary meditator you will become bewildered. If you become infatuated with red, white,[232] sweet, and rich foods, you will risk wasting your whole life in the pursuit of them, while neglecting any thoughts of virtue.

"Therefore, outwardly have no luxuries. Inwardly, have no acquisitions, have no hope in others, and have no thoughts of others giving you anything. Even if you were to die right now, like a little bird alighting on a treetop, cling to nothing in the past and regard it without nostalgia. Have no boss above you, no servant beneath you, and no companions at your own level.

"There are those who first leave behind their family and homeland and move abroad, where they take up with women and sire bastards. They live on earnings from reciting prayers for the dead and for warding off danger. If they hear even a word of praise, their minds become filled with pride and arrogance, [390] and puffing up their chests, they praise themselves and abuse others. When they hear even a word of disparagement, their minds fill with hatred and anger, and they go looking for a fight. Not even knowing that they may die right now, they tell others that they have extrasensory perception. They beat their gums in proclaiming the loftiness of their view. Like stray dogs, they are frantically attached to their territory. Like demons roving about a village, they constantly delude themselves with magic rituals. Their lives are wasted in the pursuit of material acquisitions and eminence and renown as meditators; and without devoting themselves to retreat for a year or even a month, when they meet death, they do so as ordinary beings.

"The wise do not divulge the faults of others, but rather disclose their own defects. On the other hand, those who spend their lives fixated on attachments and aversions, without considering their own failings, allow their life principles to be carried away by demons and their minds to be possessed by māras. So you must reject such evil conduct and meditate.

"While not devoting themselves the slightest bit to their own spiritual practice, people who disparage and revile others who are applying themselves to virtue come under the influence of māras and damsis. So they abandon the Dharma. Even if they are practicing the Dharma, when many of their friends get together, they become depressed by this and retreat into solitude with the

232. Red and white foods refer to meat and dairy products.

earnest desire to practice the Dharma. When they are living alone, they wander everywhere, [391] like calves separated from their mothers. Like weasels burrowing into holes in the ground, they cannot stay where they are. Like stray dogs in search of food, they restlessly roam about in town. Attracted to conversation and chitchat, they seek out someone to talk to, thereby interfering with others' spiritual practices. Having many plans, even if they have identified their own essential nature, they have no confidence in meditation and think instead of going on pilgrimages. When they are actually wandering on pilgrimages, they wish they were staying in one place or else they yearn to be back home. Those unfortunate ones are making nothing of this life or their future lives. They do not follow the practical advice they have received.

"Their hearts are inflamed with envy at others' eminence, and without considering the exhaustion of their own merit, they revile those who are meritorious. Lacking contentment, their thoughts filled with all the things they want and need, they are heedless of their own total inability to do anything and instead boss others around. They have a hard time exerting themselves enough to tie their own belts and shoelaces; but—without noticing that—they are not impressed even if others move mountains, and they order them to do even more. When they see others wearing their cast-off clothing and eating their leftovers, [392] they respond with stinginess; but—heedless of that—even when others give them a mountain of food and possessions, they are still not satisfied. Such corrupt people are despised and rejected by everyone, so they have certainly not been engaging in spiritual practice.

"Some people do have thoughts of the Dharma, and whenever they have time, they devote themselves to verbal and physical virtues. Taking delight in emulating others, people who get carried away by such behavior rack up as many relative virtues as they can. But when they encounter a little hardship and hunger and cold, they abandon those virtues. Such people are cut off from engaging in the ultimate Dharma practice. Their strong emotional vacillations are like fleeting rays of sunlight through the clouds, and their busy frenzy is like a winter gale. All their companionships are of short duration, and everyone rejects them. Such people invariably forsake their practice, for they are constitutionally incapable of pursuing it.

"People wishing to engage in pure spiritual practice who go to strict masters and try inordinately to please them sacrifice their own personal freedom to someone else. As a result, they run the danger of blocking their own progress on the path of liberation. [393]

"It is a mistake to cultivate a Dharma relationship with a guru who is temperamental, for such a person is a friend who will cast you into hell. It is a mistake to cultivate a relationship with a guru who has many needs and desires, for there is the danger that you may lose the life force of your solemn samayas. It is a mistake to cultivate a relationship with a guru who is manipulative and who has no regard for the hardships and emotional well-being of others, for your samayas will degenerate and you will fall into hell. It is a mistake to cultivate a relationship with a guru who is involved in a lot of activities, for you will be cast into hell because of your inability to serve him effectively.

"It is a mistake to cultivate a relationship with a guru who, out of self-centeredness and desire for notoriety, is enamored with those of high status and disdains those of low standing, with no regard for the emotional well-being of his disciples. Following such a guru, you will come to have false views and then fall into hell. It is a mistake to cultivate a relationship with a guru who has false views, who spends little time in meditation, who applies himself to the eight concerns of this life, or who lacks the wisdom derived through learning and reflection. Following such a guru, you will not progress beyond inferior views.

"At the outset, spend a long time examining what others say of a guru and what you observe for yourself. Then, if you rely upon one who is impeccable and replete with sublime qualities, he will show you the path of liberation, and you will not succumb to any faults or downfalls. From the time that you devote yourself to the teacher, do not have any false views about him, [394] even if he kills a hundred men and a hundred horses in one day. Even if he tells you to kill, to steal, and to take up with women, if you do not do so without hesitation, you will fall into Avīci Hell.[233] Thus, the jinas and jinaputras have said many times that you should obey the guru's instructions. It is of the utmost importance to rely upon a sublime guru in this way and strive in essential practice for your whole life, without wasting the guidance you have received. So recognize this!

"If disciples are not examined, they may become māras for their teacher, which is like throwing your practical advice into a river and like giving your food and possessions to an enemy. The best of disciples are those in whom the following qualities are present:

- Disillusion and disgust with the affairs of this life
- Unwavering faith in the Three Jewels
- Great compassion
- Little avarice
- Delight in generosity
- No envy
- Candor

233. Tib. *mnar med*. The "Unremitting Hell," the worst of the hot hells.

- Courage and fortitude
- Dependability
- Single mindedness
- Firm resolve

"If such disciples are accepted and given guidance, they will undoubtedly accomplish something of great significance.

"If disciples with the following qualities are given practical advice, eventually they will definitely become māras for the teacher:

- Obsession with saṃsāra
- Little faith or reverence [395]
- Duplicity and deceitfulness
- No compassion
- Great avarice
- Envy
- Hatefulness and irritability
- Emotional instability and fickleness
- Crudeness, with no courage or fortitude
- Strong distraction and spiritual sloth
- Attraction to entertainment and obsession with those of high status
- Great satisfaction with oneself but no interest in others
- Shallowness
- Penchant for divisive speech
- Fondness for dishonesty and gossip

"Examine disciples and investigate them accordingly, reject those who are unworthy vessels, and devote yourself to those who are worthy."

The Special Preliminary Practices

"Now, to practice the instructions on the great clear light, direct crossing over, if you do not first engage in the profound preliminary techniques, there will be a great many obstacles and pitfalls to your practice. Therefore, at the stage of the preliminaries, apply yourself to the *differentiation of saṃsāra and nirvāṇa*[234] with respect to your body, speech, and mind.

"First, for the outer differentiation, go to a solitary and wild place where there are no people and reflect 'In order to free all beings of the three realms

234. Tib. *'khor 'das ru shan*. The direct crossing over preliminary practices of differentiating saṃsāra from nirvāṇa with respect to your body, speech, and mind.

from the ocean of suffering of mundane existence, [396] I shall differentiate saṃsāra from nirvāṇa with respect to my body, speech, and mind. And I shall bring all beings to the state of omniscient, perfect enlightenment.'

"Then apply this to your own mind in the following way: 'When I am beset with a virulent, unbearable, fatal disease, my mind will be filled with terrible anguish, and I will groan in agony and writhe on the ground. My loved ones will give me all kinds of advice and call a doctor. The doctor will then come, examine my pulse, and tell me the disease is incurable. I will be told I must quickly have many rituals done on my behalf, for I am on the verge of losing everything, and I will agree. My family will advise me to have a divination done by a psychic and to have an astrologer make his own prognosis. When the messengers eventually return from making those requests, my family and I will ask what they said. The psychic and astrologer will say that rituals must be done for me, so I must act quickly. But then, hearing that all psychics and astrologers are so deeply at odds with one another that they are of no use, I will fall into intense despair.

"'Imagining many rituals being done, [397] I finally fall on my bed, unable to rise. My lips and face twitch, my eyes turn upward, and whatever I drink comes out my nose. Quivering on my bed, I beg to be lifted from the depths into which I have fallen. With anxiety and clinging to my human environment, I ask to be taken outside and to be consoled. I am then carried outside, but the whole earth seems deserted, and by simply casting my eyes on my surroundings, I sense I will not be here for long. My mind is then overwhelmed with unbearable grief.

"'Once again, out of attachment to my own home and family, I am tormented by the thought that I am about to be separated from them. I then ask to be taken back indoors, and when I am laid on my bed, all my relatives recognize that I am dying. They gather around me and take hold of my head and limbs. Clinging to my body, their faces are covered with tears. I hear them wailing and moaning. I see with my very eyes that the envoys of the Lord of Death are coming to take me away. When the agents of Yama come before me and prepare to lead me away, I am unable to let go of my beloved children and wife and [398] all my dear brothers and other relatives, even though it is inevitable.

"'The time will have come—even though I cannot bear to leave them—when I have no choice but to go where I will not see or meet them again. I have to make my way alone to an unknown destination, with no friends or companions, leaving behind my cherished body, clothes, ornaments, food, wealth, and home. By imagining that this occasion has come upon me now, forcefully arousing a sense of dread, and acting in every way as if this were happening, I train for the transitional phase[235] of dying. By doing so, I will certainly turn away from clinging to the appearances of this life.'

"Then imagine that all external appearances dissolve into your consciousness, bringing forth a vision of a pale, shimmering light. This dissolves into an increasing radiance; and now imagine a reddish luminosity like a flash of lightning. Then, as that dissolves into darkness, a gloom overtakes your mind like the appearance of pitch blackness. Then there is death, and by training for the time you will die, you will turn away from obsessive clinging.

"Then bring to mind a space-like radiance and luminosity, and remain in meditative equipoise for as long as you can, in a state of pervasive, luminous emptiness. This is the experience of the ground clear light. [399] Then cover your eyes with a loosely woven blindfold and remain in meditative equipoise focused on the appearances of the five lights. This is training in the appearances of the transitional phase of ultimate reality. Then bring to mind the visions of the transitional phase of becoming, imagine that you unimpededly go wherever you think of going, and remain in this state for a while.

"Finally, imagine that many terrifying agents of Yama catch you around the waist with lassos, strike you with various weapons, and draw you helplessly into the dark. A fierce gale of karma pushes you from behind until you come before Yama, Dharmarāja. In the presence of Dharmarāja, the great workmen—Attachment, bearing the head of a monkey; Delusion, bearing the head of a bull; and Hatred, bearing the head of a snake—hold a scale that weighs the pebbles of karma, a mirror that reflects good and evil, and a book of accounts that records the numbers of good and evil deeds.

"They are surrounded by innumerable workmen bearing heads that change shape. In front of them on your right is a white, coarisen son of the gods,[236] and on your left is a black māra who accompanies you. [400] The two of them in succession report to Dharmarāja on the nature of your virtues and vices. The black māra wins his case, and finally Dharmarāja commands that the white and black pebbles of karma be put on the scale. The deva and māra weigh them, the bull-headed creature examines them, and the black pebbles prove to be heavier. Examining the mirror, they see that evil is predominant. Upon looking at the accounts, it appears that nonvirtuous deeds are far more prevalent. Consequently, Dharmarāja immediately commands, 'In this life this person has avoided positive, virtuous deeds as if they were poison and has adopted negative vices as if they were medicine. Let these deeds fully ripen now! Take this person to the hot hells!'

235. Tib. *bar do*, Skt. *antarabhāva*. Any one of the six transitional phases of living, dreaming, meditation, dying, ultimate reality, and the transitional phase of becoming.

236. Tib. *lha'i bu*; Skt. *devaputra*. This deva is coarisen with yourself.

"As if they were taking convicts to prison, the workmen all shout together in voices like a thousand peals of thunder, 'Kill! Kill! Mutilate! Mutilate!' and drive many beings to hell. There you are surrounded by an unbroken, seamless, burning metal ground. The space around you is entirely filled with flickering flames.

"In the Resuscitation Hell, hostile beings regard each other as deadly enemies and battle to the death with various weapons; and then they are resuscitated. [401] In the Black Line Hell, lines are drawn on your body, which is then dismembered with a burning metal saw. In the Confinement and Destruction Hell, you are placed in a burning metal mortar and pulverized with a red-hot pestle. In the Wailing Hell, you suffer by being trapped inside a blazing metal building with no doors. In the Shrieking Hell, you are forced into a two-story, blazing metal building and are incinerated there. In the Hot Hell, you are run through with a blazing metal trident. In the Scorching Hell, you are immersed in molten iron, copper, and bronze. In Avīci Hell, you are incinerated with a torch of flaming iron.

"Imagine taking on all the sufferings of those hells, and really act out the various cries and expressions of those experiencing them. Experiencing such terror and despair is the differentiation with respect to the mind. The differentiation with respect to the body entails physically writhing on the ground, rising up, and flailing your limbs. Vocally wailing and screaming is the way of achieving the differentiation with respect to the speech.

"In the cold hells, the ground all around you is frozen and you are crushed under a blizzard. There are eight cold hells called the Blistering Hell, the Bursting Blisters Hell, the Achu Hell, the Wailing Hell, [402] the Chattering Teeth Hell, the Splitting like a Lotus Hell, the Splitting like a Blue Lotus Hell, and the Splitting like a Great Lotus Hell. Imagine taking upon yourself the miseries of the eight cold hells, the ephemeral and neighboring hells, and so forth. Act out the expressions and cries of beings there, constantly rolling on the ground and moving about in various ways as if you were in agony. Practice to the point that you actually feel that you are taking on such suffering.

"Likewise, act as if you were experiencing the hunger and thirst of the pretas; the enforced labor, slaying, and so on of animals; the birth, aging, sickness, and death of humans; the conflicts of the asuras; and the death and downfall of the devas. Physically crouch down, jump, run, get up, move around, sit, move your limbs, and so on; make various sounds; and mentally imagine taking on various experiences of joy and sorrow. Experiencing this is the phase of training for the intermediate period.

"Cultivate a spirit of emergence and a sense of disillusionment with respect to saṃsāra until you are nauseated like a person with hepatitis being offered cooked food. This will cause you to turn away from craving for saṃsāra and apply yourself to the sublime Dharma for the time being, and ultimately it will cause saṃsāra to be dredged from its depths. [403]

"If you do not bring the visions of the intermediate period to mind and experience them, a spirit of emergence will not arise from the depths of your being. As a result of not taking these experiences to heart, even though you hear accounts of the sufferings of dying and saṃsāra, you will regard them merely as conditions somewhere else, and there will be only the remotest chance that you will apply their significance to your own mindstream. But if you bring them to your own mind and train in these appearances, their significance will certainly come to you. So appreciate the importance of this mind training!

"When you have finished training in repeatedly bringing all these appearances of saṃsāra to mind, instantly transform your appearances and imagine this outer physical world as absolute space, emptiness free of conceptual elaboration. Being of this nature, imagine the whole earth as being free of all rough surfaces such as jagged mountains, rugged and rocky ravines, and thorn trees. Imagine its surface to be soft and even like the palm of a young woman and expansive like the sky, such that when you step down it gives way, and when you lift up it rebounds. Aromatic fragrances waft from verdant hills of medicinal herbs. Blossoming lotuses of various colors cover the entire ground. [404] Checkered patterns of rainbows and lattices of light rays cover the sky. Clouds of offerings of sensory objects billow up and float in the sky like summer mist rising from the ocean.

"Imagine purifying springs, ponds bearing ambrosia imbued with eight excellent qualities, wish-fulfilling trees, beautiful, exquisite birds of various species, different kinds of intelligent forest creatures, and emanated retinues of male and female bodhisattvas adorned with the signs and symbols of enlightenment, who are calm, fresh, lucid, and free of contamination. Imagine youthful beings like sixteen-year-olds adorned with beautiful, attractive ornaments and garments casually strolling on the ground.

"In the center of an unimaginable assembly of innumerable, invincible lotus blossoms, imagine yourself upon a Dharma throne as the Bhagavān, Buddha Śākyamuni, your body radiant with light like a golden mountain drenched by a hundred thousand suns. You sit with your legs in the *vajrāsana* position. Your right hand touches the earth, and your left is in the mudrā of meditative equipoise. Bearing a calm and smiling countenance, [405] you are clothed with the three kinds of robes. You are adorned with the thirty-two excellent signs and eighty symbols of enlightenment.

"From the tip of every one of your body hairs, inconceivable, countless trillions of light rays are emitted, pervading everywhere throughout the three realms. At the tip of each light ray, a great ray of light takes on the form of various individual sentient beings, with their races, languages, and customs, and dispels the ignorance of each one, like the sun dispelling darkness. This subdues their mindstreams by revealing the Dharma, and draws them into spiritual practice. Imagine everyone transforming into manifestations of male and female bodhisattvas, filling to overflowing the buddhafield you have created, and listening to the Dharma. You recite the *Heart Sūtra* and so forth, and explain the Dharma.

"Imagine that they all come to know great, ultimate absolute space, and as the illusory fictions of the phenomenal world dissolve into the original, primordial ground, the absolute space of Samantabhadra, they become enlightened and the entirety of the three realms of saṃsāra becomes empty. By settling in meditative equipoise in that awareness, you establish the circumstances for purifying your buddhafield. In the meantime, by engaging in the conduct of the Three Jewels, [406] you are seen as the teacher of all beings, and outer, inner, and secret obstacles are dispelled.

"Finally, you emanate your buddhafield, with its teacher and circle of disciples, and you experience your own goal of the dharmakāya. By the very force of this, the goals of others will be accomplished with the power of great blessings. This is called the *outer differentiation of the body, speech, and mind.*

"Next is the *inner differentiation of the body, speech, and mind.* At the crown of your normal body imagine the white seed syllable *A* of devas in the form of an orb of dim light. Imagine the causes of birth as a deva, along with the associated karma, mental afflictions, and habitual propensities, converging in the form of dim white light and dissolving into that seed.

"At your throat visualize as before the seed syllable *Su* of asuras in the form of a yellow orb of light, and imagine the causes of birth as an asura, along with the associated karma, mental afflictions, and habitual propensities, converging in the form of greenish-yellow light and dissolving into the *Su*.

"At your heart visualize the seed syllable of humans in the form of a light blue *Nṛi*. Rays of light are emitted from it, drawing in all the causes of birth as a human, along with the associated karma, mental afflictions, and habitual propensities. Imagine them dissolving into the *Nṛi*.

"At your navel visualize the seed syllable of animals, a dark-red *Tri*, and as before, imagine all the karma, mental afflictions, and habitual propensities [407] that act as causes for rebirth as an animal being drawn in and dissolving into the *Tri*.

"At your genital region visualize rays of light being emitted from the preta seed syllable, a gray *Pre*, drawing in all the karma, mental afflictions, and habitual propensities that act as causes for rebirth as a preta, together with the miseries associated with such a rebirth, and imagine them dissolving into the *Pre*.

"At the soles of your feet imagine light emanating from the hell seed syllable, a shimmering black *Du*, retracting in the form of black light all the karma, mental afflictions, vices, obscurations, and habitual propensities in the minds of all sentient beings that act as causes for rebirth in hell, together with the miseries of such a rebirth. Imagine that all these dissolve into this seed, leaving not even a residual trace behind. These are what are to be purified.

"Then, at your crown imagine the essential nature of the bodies of all the buddhas as a white *Oṃ*, blazing with greater brilliance than the light of a hundred thousand suns. The light emanated from this syllable draws in all the inexhaustible ornamental wheels of the bodies of the jinas and jinaputras of the three times in the form of a mass of white light, which dissolves into the white *Oṃ*.

"At your throat imagine the seed syllable of enlightened speech as a red *Āḥ*, which emanates light as before, drawing in all the inexhaustible wheels of the speech of all the jinas and jinaputras of the three times in the form of a mass of red light, [408] which dissolves into the *Āḥ*.

"At your heart imagine the seed syllable of enlightened mind as an indigo *Hūṃ*, which blazes with light and emanates light rays, drawing in all the inexhaustible wheels of the enlightened mind, qualities, and activities of the jinas and jinaputras of the three times in the form of a mass of indigo light, which dissolves into the *Hūṃ*.

"Then, from these three vajra-essence purifying syllables, imagine white, red, and blue light rays blazing forth strongly like flames, completely burning up all the seeds of hell, together with its habitual propensities. Recite *Oṃ Āḥ Hūṃ*, and imagine these syllables likewise burning up saṃsāra in both the reverse order and the forward order of its origination. Do not let your consciousness be distracted elsewhere, do not interrupt this with human speech, and recognize the importance of meditating and reciting without letting your meditation cushion grow cold.

"At the conclusion, as the mass of light grows larger, it totally incinerates illnesses, malevolent spirits, vices, obscurations, habitual propensities, and the material aggregates of flesh and blood. Then visualize your body as a rainbow or as an empty appearance, a mass of light like a reflection in a mirror, and utter the vajra recitation of the three seed syllables one hundred thousand times for each of the seed syllables to be purified, along with one extra set, making a total of seven hundred thousand recitations. [409]

"By meditating like this without distraction and reciting single-pointedly without interruption by idle chatter, signs arise in the waking state, meditative experiences, or dreams. These signs include a sense of pristine space; extraordinary meditative experiences and realizations; ascending to the peak of a mountain that reaches to the heights of the sky; flying in the sky; pus, blood, and lymph oozing from your body; many parasites emerging from your body; intentionally burning up buildings; seeing buddhafields; and having visions of deities. These arise as signs of having purified all illnesses, malevolent spirits, vices, and obscurations.

"So the practice called *differentiation* is like this: Your own ground, which is the displays of the spontaneous actualization of the three kāyas, is contaminated and mixed with the taints of habitual propensities of the three realms. Once saṃsāra is purified in absolute space and the three kāyas are actualized, this is differentiation. When the seeds that produce the body are incinerated and the vajra body is actualized, this is called the *differentiation of body*. When mantras are recited verbally and vajra speech is actualized, this is called the *differentiation of speech*. The severance of the mental stream of delusive conceptualization with the meditation on the [stage of] generation is called the *differentiation of mind*. [410] This is analogous to winnowing grain, throwing away the chaff, and keeping the kernels.

"By inwardly performing such a differentiation, in the short term, habitual propensities and obscurations are purified, and there will be no obstacles or interferences to your life and spiritual practice. Ultimately, you will become a buddha, as your body, speech, and mind manifest as the three vajras.

"After that has been completed, perform the secret differentiation of saṃsāra and nirvāṇa with respect to your body, speech, and mind. First, saṃsāra and nirvāṇa are to be differentiated with respect to your body as follows: All the inexhaustible ornamental wheels of the enlightened body, speech, mind, qualities, and activities of all the buddhas, bodhisattvas, gurus, jinas, and jinaputras of the ten directions and the three times dissolve into you in the form of a mass of five-colored light. Imagine that they completely clear away all illnesses, malevolent spirits, vices, obscurations, habitual propensities, and material aggregates, and that you expand into the nature of all-pervasive space. Remain for a while in this meditative equipoise.

"Then join your palms above the crown of your head while spreading out your elbows. Press the heels of your feet together and stand with your knees spread out to the sides. Imagine that your body instantly transforms into a blazing, three-pronged, meteorite vajra, like a rainbow appearing in the sky. [411] Understand that the upper central prong symbolizes the primordial consciousness of the essential nature of emptiness, the upper right prong symbolizes the primordial consciousness of the nature of luminosity, and the upper left prong symbolizes the primordial consciousness of all-pervasive compassion. Understand that the lower central prong symbolizes the dharmakāya, the lower right prong symbolizes the saṃbhogakāya, and the lower left prong symbolizes the nirmāṇakāya. Visualize the natural radiance of primordial consciousness in the form of a blazing mass of fire, and remain in meditative equipoise without distraction for as long as you can.

"When you can no longer stand like that, while maintaining the same visualization as before, alternate between lying on your back and sitting in the squatting position. By diligently meditating like this for a sustained period, all demons and obstructive forces will see your body as a blazing vajra, and they will not be able to come within seven yojanas of you. Ultimately your body will take on the enlightened nature of the vajra body.

"Second, for the differentiation of speech, first there is the practice of *sealing*. For the *external sealing* of appearances, imagine that from your mouth an indigo syllable *Hūṃ* successively [412] sends out white, yellow, red, and green *Hūṃ*s, completely filling and pervading the whole of space. Imagine all the elements of earth, water, fire, and air transforming into the nature of *Hūṃ*, without leaving even a trace of the elements behind.

"For the *internal sealing* of your own body, imagine all the external *Hūṃ*s converging one by one and entering your mouth. The whole interior of your body is filled with *Hūṃ*s, and your entire body, from the top of your head to the soles of your feet, consists of *Hūṃ*s, right down to the atomic level. Imagine your body in the indigo wrathful and ferocious form of Vajrapāṇi. Imagine that your right hand holds a vajra and your left hand holds a serpent noose. You stand powerfully and haughtily, with your legs spread wide apart, in the midst of a blazing fire of primordial consciousness. Everything that has been sealed externally and internally takes on the pleasing sound of the gently melodious *Hūṃ*. This leads to the realization of the illusion-like nature of appearances, and its purpose is to liberate your body as having no inherent nature.

"Then, as for developing your creative power, you do so regarding outer appearances[237] as follows: From your mouth, a powerful, sharp, darting, indigo *Hūṃ*, one cubit in length, shoots forth like a lightning bolt, striking all physical objects, such as mountains, boulders, and stones, and thoroughly penetrating each one. [413] While you imagine that you are transforming everything into empty space, leaving not even a trace behind, powerfully and harshly recite *Hūṃ*. Then rest without focusing on anything at all.

237. Tib. *phyi snang ba la rtsal sbyang ba.*

"Then developing your creative power regarding your own inner body[238] is as follows: Imagine that an indigo *Hūṃ*, one cubit in length, emerges from your body in its ordinary state. Penetrating straight into the exterior and interior of your body, it pierces in every direction, leaving no spot untouched. Imagine your body disintegrating into nothingness, and recite *Hūṃ* many times in a fierce, harsh voice. If, as a result, the flesh of your body tingles and goose bumps arise, these are signs of having developed your creative power with respect to your body. The purposes of this are to realize the lack of inherent existence of appearances, to subdue the demon of reification, and to powerfully realize emptiness.

"Then cultivating pliability[239] is as follows: While sitting cross-legged on a comfortable cushion, imagine a dark-blue *Hūṃ* at your heart. From it a strand of light rays composed of many dark-blue *Hūṃs* like chain links issues forth from your mouth and coils clockwise around the base of a meditative support in front of you, such as a stick. [414] When the first *Hūṃ* that emerged is standing on top of the meditative support, directly focus your attention on it, and slowly and melodiously chant the sound of *Hūṃ*. Then forcefully concentrate on the strand of *Hūṃ*s gradually unraveling from the meditative support, and imagine it finally drawing back into your heart. Then relax. Then alternately visualize white, yellow, red, and green *Hūṃ*s. Repeated training of this sort will dispel obstacles that make your channels dysfunctional in the short term, and ultimately it will provide you with mastery over your energy-mind.

"Once again visualize yourself as indigo, wrathful, and ferocious Vajrapāṇi, your right hand holding aloft a meteorite vajra, your left hand in the threatening gesture and holding a serpent noose. From the *Hūṃ* at your heart, *Hūṃ*s are emitted like swirling particles of dust in the sunlight. All appearances of saṃsāra and nirvāṇa, including the physical worlds, their sentient inhabitants, and all sensory objects, dissolve into the *Hūṃ* syllables, like salt dissolving into water, leaving not even a trace behind. Imagine drawing them back in again. They now enter your mouth and fill your body, causing it to increase in size until it pervades the entire domain of space. Visualize *Hūṃ*s emanating throughout all of saṃsāra and nirvāṇa, [415] completely pervading it like a covering of mist. On occasion transform them into white, yellow, red, and green forms. Recognize the importance of not letting your attention be distracted elsewhere. In the short term, this practice will make

238. Tib. *rang lus la rtsal sbyang ba.*

239. Tib. *mnyen btsal ba.*

you invulnerable to all interferences. Its final aim is to dissolve your body into minute particles and to liberate your awareness as the dharmakāya.

"Then comes entering the path:[240] Imagine your body transforming into a blazing white syllable *Hūṃ*, one cubit above the ground, tilting this way and that way. Imagine yourself gradually moving throughout all the realms of the six types of beings in the galaxy, each with its Mount Meru, four continents, and subcontinents. Then, like an arrow shot by a powerful archer, you successively proceed to Abhirati in the east, Śrīmat in the south, Sukhāvatī in the west, Karmaprasiddhi in the north, and Ghanavyūha in the center.

"Imagine that you behold the five families of buddhas and receive teachings, prophecies, and empowerments from them. While visualizing this, recite *Hūṃ* beautifully, slowly, and melodiously. This serves the needs of sentient beings [416] and allows for the final accomplishment of the purification of the buddhafields.[241] By doing so, those aims will finally be accomplished. In the short term it also has the effect of bringing about a sense of disillusionment, disgust, and revulsion toward all activities of saṃsāra.

"By applying yourself in these ways to the practice of *differentiation of speech*, your speech will become enlightened displays of vajra speech. When all verbal defects vanish and you attract others with the sweetness of your voice, these are the signs of purification.

"Now for the differentiation of mind, go to a very remote, solitary place where there are no disturbances to dhyāna. Then, in order to dispel the great, disturbing, obstructive forces that may arise from physical disturbances brought on by the preceding practices, first of all settle in your natural state: Motionlessly relax your body in whatever way is comfortable, like an unthinking corpse in a charnel ground. Let your voice be silent, like a lute with its strings cut. Rest your mind in an unmodified state, like the primordial presence of space. Remain for a long time in these three ways of resting. This pacifies all illnesses due to disturbances of the elements and unfavorable circumstances, and your body, speech, and mind naturally calm down. The ultimate purpose of this practice is to experience the dharmakāya, free of activity. [417]

"Then, for restoration,[242] position your body in the sevenfold posture of Vairocana, direct your gaze over the tip of your nose, and rest in meditative

240. Tib. *lam du gzhug pa*.

241. All the buddhafields are naturally pure, but this practice helps to purify your vision of them.

242. Tib. *sor gzhug pa*. The second definition of *so* in the *Bod rgya tshig mdzod chen mo* is "*rang sa'm rang tshugs thub pa'i rten gzhi dang nus pa*," translated as "your own state, or a

equipoise, letting your thoughts just be, without intervention. Then assume the bodhisattva gaze, with your eyes directed about six feet in front of you, and remain with a sense of limitless consciousness. Then assume a wrathful gaze, standing powerfully and haughtily, with your legs spread wide apart. Point your right hand to the sky in a threatening gesture, point your attention in the same direction, and bellow out, 'Ha ha!' Reach out with your left hand in a threatening gesture, point it to the sky, and wrathfully bellow out, 'Hee hee!' Then rest, without directing your attention to any appearances. This will empower your awareness in the great confidence in ultimate reality.

"By differentiating saṃsāra and nirvāṇa in these ways, you will become a suitable vessel for the unsurpassed secret, and your body, speech, and mind will transform into the nature of the three vajras. Reinforce these external, internal, and secret differentiations of the body, speech, and mind by practicing for no less than eighty days, [418] and not merely for a day or two. As explained previously, it is imperative that you practice until you experience all the signs and qualities of having dispelled the problems and defects of your body, speech, and mind and of having purified vices and obscurations. So practice this for a long time."

How to Engage in the Main Practice

"Now, for the stages of the main practice, first of all, upon determining the ground by way of cutting through,[243] the first moment of impure consciousness took on the aspect of a mental object, a subsequent thought fastened onto it, and delusion set in. Now, in contrast, in direct crossing over, the initial moment of consciousness is transformed into an appearance of clear light, and by experiencing the very nature of consciousness, all impure appearances dissolve into absolute space and vanish. Knowing how this occurs is the indispensable, sublime point of direct crossing over, so recognize it!

"If you do not recognize this vital point, however much you meditate, you will go astray on the path of dualistic grasping, and you will not progress along the grounds and paths to liberation. But once you have truly realized in this way how all of saṃsāra and nirvāṇa is none other than your own appearances, all mental states and appearances of impure saṃsāra will be forcefully transformed into displays of the clear light, ultimate reality. [419] So this

self-sufficient basis and power" (p. 2952). Thus, this practice is aimed at restoring yourself by entering into such a state.

243. Tib. *khregs chod.* The first of the two major phases in the practice of the Great Perfection, aimed at gaining direct, sustained realization of the essential nature of the mind.

is the practical guidance on the great transference. By truly recognizing the entrance to this path with the wisdom of realizing identitylessness, the expansive eye of wisdom reveals originally pure ultimate reality, transcending mental investigation, which is absolute space, free of conceptual elaboration. Unlike nebulous, obscure meditations and intellectual fabrications, with the eye of wisdom you directly see precious, spontaneously actualized absolute space, which is the real nature of the expanse of clear light.

"To practice these instructions, at the outset you must bind your posture, for if this is not done, the space of awareness, bindus, and vital energies will be dispersed in the channels and elements of the body, and they will not manifest, just as the limbs of a snake will not appear unless he is squeezed.[244] The posture is therefore of tremendous importance.

"First, the lion's posture is as follows: Join the soles of your feet in front of you. Plant your vajra fists on the ground between your legs and look up into the sky. This is the dharmakāya posture and gaze.

"For the saṃbhogakāya posture, plant your knees and elbows on the ground and support your cheeks with your palms. [420] Point the soles of your feet outward and gaze directly in front of you. However, if appearances of the clear light do not manifest, alternately turn your gaze to the left and right and up and down. Rest your gaze wherever these appearances are the clearest.

"For the nirmāṇakāya posture, plant the soles of your feet on the ground, press your knees against your chest, and clasp your knees with both hands while interlacing your fingers. Straighten your spine and gaze downward.

"Here is the significance of these postures: With the dharmakāya posture, the soles of the feet are joined in order to keep the afflictive vital energies in their own place. The vajra fists are placed on the ground to cut off the pathways of the afflictions. The gaze is directed upward to open the vision of primordial consciousness.

"With the saṃbhogakāya posture, pointing the soles outward causes the vital energies to flow easily. Pressing your knees against your chest balances the heat and cold elements of the body. Pointing your knees and elbows at the ground blocks the impure apertures. Supporting your cheeks with your palms equalizes bliss and emptiness. By directing your gaze straight in front of you, primordial consciousness settles in its own luminosity.

"With the nirmāṇakāya posture, [421] the soles of your feet press on the air maṇḍala in order to suppress the power of the karmic vital energies. By

244. Tibetan lore considered a male snake's hemipenes, which can be everted by applying pressure, to be his "limbs."

pressing together the fire maṇḍala of the thighs and the fire maṇḍala of the belly, the impure vital energies of saṃsāra are extinguished in their own place. By pressing together the water maṇḍala of the knees and the fire maṇḍala of the palms, the heat and cold elements of the body are equalized. By pressing together the fire maṇḍala of the palms and the fire maṇḍala of the armpits, cold disorders are dispelled.[245] By pressing together the water maṇḍala of the backs of the hands and the water maṇḍala of the throat, heat disorders are dispelled. By gazing downward, the eye of omniscience is opened. Whether you look straight ahead or turn your gaze upward, the eye of omniscience is still opened, so there is no difference. You may direct your gaze wherever you find the greatest clarity.[246]

"Moreover, it is not necessary to use all three postures. Rather, you may stay in any one of the postures that facilitates the arising of the clear light and that you find comfortable and suitable. If you like variety, you may shift from one posture to another and from time to time apply yourself to other spiritual practices. If you want nothing complicated, strive in meditation continuously throughout the day and night. [422] Those who can meditate only during the day and not through the night should constantly practice throughout the day. The practice is to have three special sessions during the night and to intermittently train in the dying process.[247]

"The vital point regarding the sense doors is that you look with your eyes partially open, not suddenly opening them wide, for that will dull your vision, and it will prevent the appearances of the clear light from manifesting. So do not rigidly fix your gaze. The vital point for the vital energies is that you practice breathing gently through your mouth, via a small opening between your lips and teeth, and pause for a moment once the breath has been exhaled.

"As for the object of your gaze, in the beginning, for about one month, during the daytime direct your gaze one cubit away from the sun. Then practice during the night to clear away any problem of heat increasing in the eyes from the sun.[248] In order to achieve stability in the clear light, gaze at the moon in the same way.

245. This line refers to an alternate form of the nirmāṇakāya posture in which the arms are crossed over the knees with the palms at the armpits.

246. These eight paragraphs compare with CM 429–31.

247. This refers to the preceding practice of imagining the dying process as a preparation for the main practice of direct crossing over.

248. Although the improper daytime practice of gazing near the sun may impair your vision, it is said that the nighttime practice of gazing at the moon may actually enhance

"At night if you gaze at a flame, by looking above it with your eyes half open, at first you will see only something like an orange haystack. After a while, visions will appear in the space of awareness, and bindus will arise in the form of quivering lines. Finally, beautiful, lucid visions of bindus will appear clearly and abundantly in the space of awareness. [423] Rest with your body unmoving, like a corpse in a charnel ground; keep your voice silent, avoiding all vocalization; and do not exhale through your nose but slowly breathe through your mouth, without impeding or forcing the respiration. This is the stabilization regarding the vital point of freeing the channels and vital energies from control and effort. Abide motionlessly in a state in which consciousness experientially emerges as clear light, without the mind being modified in any way. Wherever you are, by keeping the body straight, all the channels and vital energies will be straight, and once the mind has dissolved into empty pristine awareness, you will be stabilized in that state.[249]

"The explanation of the channels and bindus of the path according to this yāna is called *ati anu*,[250] so you should come to know them correctly. The mouth is the aperture through which coarse, impure mental afflictions and energy-mind manifest; and the nose is the aperture for subtle afflictions and energy-mind. Here is how they move: In the lungs, channels the width of a straw of wheat are filled with the *exhaled and inhaled energy*. If they increase, heat disorders arise; if they decrease, cold disorders occur; and if the energy flows smoothly, there is a balance of the heat and cold elements of the body. In one day there are 21,600 breaths, [424] which serve as the mounts for the mind's discursive thoughts. Therefore, even though there are profound methods for forcefully constraining the energy-mind by retaining and manipulating the channels and the breath, there are great obstacles to such practices, and there are many ways to go astray.

"The six lamps[251] of the ground of the nature of existence are the avenues through which primordial consciousness arises, and the eyes are the apertures through which primordial consciousness manifests. The ears are the apertures

---

your vision. Most important is to carefully monitor and adjust your practice to avoid damaging your eyesight.

249. These three paragraphs compare with CM 431–32.

250. *Ati anu* means the *anu* aspect of the atiyoga path, with *ati* referring to the practice of the Great Perfection and *anu* referring to practice with the channels, vital energies, and bindus.

251. The use of the term *lamp* (Tib. *sgron me*) is a metaphor, for the essential nature of these lamps is luminosity.

of subtle and hidden primordial consciousness, and they are the pathways by which consciousness apprehends appearances. Due to them, sounds are purified. Through the apertures by which primordial consciousness manifests, the clear light that illuminates darkness is purified. Dream appearances are the avenues for the manifestation of stainless vision. By familiarizing yourself with the clear light, emanation, and transformation, the appearances in the transitional phase of becoming can be emanated and transformed. From that you can emanate a pristine nirmāṇakāya buddhafield and familiarize yourself with transforming the appearances of the intermediate period.[252]

"Here, in order to experience the visions of the kāyas and facets of primordial consciousness, there are the three kinds of lamps of the vessel. The quintessence of the body is the *citta lamp of the flesh* at the heart, inside of which is the soft white lamp of the channels, the quintessence of the channels called the *hollow crystal kati channel.* It is a single channel, one-eighth the width of a horsehair, with two branches that stem from inside the heart [425] like the horns of a wild ox. These curve around the back of the ears and come to the pupils of the eyes. Their root is the heart, their trunk is the channels, and their fruit is the eyes. The quintessence of the apertures is called the *fluid distant lasso lamp*.

"So those are three kinds of lamps of the vessel. Although the three kinds of lamps of the vessel are given three names, in reality they refer to the same thing, just as the name of the fruit is given to the root, trunk, and fruit. Thus, in the context of the path, they are simply called the *fluid distant lasso lamp*.[253]

"As for the three kinds of lamps of the vital essence, the *lamp of the pristine space of awareness* is the quintessence of the five outer elements. The transmutation of residues into the five-colored lights of the empty essential nature of the quintessence is called the *space of awareness*; and because it purifies the reification of contaminations, it is called *pristine*. The element appearing as space, transformed into its quintessence, is indigo or light blue. The element appearing as water, transformed into its quintessence, is white or gray. The element appearing as fire, transformed into its quintessence, is red or brown. The element appearing as earth, transformed into its quintessence, is yellow, pale yellow, or dark yellow. The element of air, transformed into its quintessence, appears as green, tan, or light green. In whatever color the impure visions initially appear, [426] when they shift to the space of awareness, they continue to appear in that same color.

252. These two paragraphs compare with CM 421–23.

253. These two paragraphs compare with CM 423.

"As for the visions in the space of awareness, at first they are of the nature of things such as the sun, the moon, and a flame, bearing all five colors and filled with rainbow patterns in the space of awareness, like brilliant brocade. This rainbow weave arises as vertical and horizontal images. Beginners may achieve stability in this by gazing for a month at the sun through a crystal during the daytime, by gazing at the moon during the nighttime, and by gazing at a flame in the morning and evening.

"In the beginning, shifting, quivering images arise, after a while they become more stable, and finally they remain motionless. At that time, look out a window and disengage from the flaws of enjoying or not enjoying the beauty or lack of beauty of the visions of light. Then a whitish blue emerges that is not that of the external sky. Even so, know that it is important to rest in this state without attraction or aversion to its qualities.

"To transmute the five inner elements into their quintessences, the element of the quintessence of the mind is transmuted into indigo and appears as such. The element of the quintessence of the blood is transmuted into the color white and appears as such. The element of the quintessence of the flesh is transmuted into the color yellow and appears as such. [427] The element of the quintessence of warmth is transmuted into the color red and appears as such.[254] And the element of the quintessence of the breath is transmuted into the color green and appears as such.

"As for the *lamp of the empty bindus*, these five quintessences appear in round forms, so they are called *bindus*. Although they are spherical, without corners, in your vision they appear like the concentric circles that arise from a stone thrown into a pond.[255] In the expanse that is filled with the lights of the five quintessences, inside the *hollow crystal kati channel* abides an image of an indestructible bindu. By gazing with the eye of wisdom, the interior of this channel manifests and arises in the form of outer appearances. Without grasping at them, your own channels will illuminate themselves. If you grasp at the visions in the space of awareness as being external and awareness as being internal, you will fall into the error of dualistic grasping.

"In the domain of this pristine space of awareness, the radiance of awareness called *vajra strands*[256] appears like moving, floating threads of gold. That is the initial phase. After a while the vajra strands appear like pearls threaded

254. *The Essence of Clear Meaning* states instead that the quintessence of blood is red and that of warmth is white (CM 426).

255. These five paragraphs compare with CM 424–26.

256. Tib. *rdo rje lu gu rgyud*. Lit. "vajra lamb-strings," alluding to the appearances of grazing sheep.

on a string, and finally they emerge in the form of latticework and pendants. They are the basis from which the two kinds of lamps of vital essence arise, [428] and they are called the *lamp of self-emergent wisdom*, which is your own pristine awareness, the sugatagarbha.

"The four lamps of the path of appearances are the fluid lasso lamp, the lamp of the pristine space of awareness, the lamp of the empty bindus, and the lamp of self-emergent wisdom. The four lamps of the yogic path are combined in one. Know that synthesizing them and then applying yourself to practice is of the utmost importance.[257] If you practice in this way—unlike the mentally constructed, obscure meditation of cutting through—the real nature of the clear light will directly appear to your senses, and this is therefore called the *vision of the direct perception of ultimate reality*."

How the Four Visions Gradually Arise

"This is not like meditating on autonomous, anthropomorphic deities who are strenuously conjured up by the mind, as in the stage of generation. This alone is the teaching for achieving stability in the great experiential displays of the kāyas and facets of primordial consciousness, thereby liberating the actual three kāyas within yourself.

"This path is superior to the ordinary kinds of transference involving the three recognitions,[258] in which you visualize shapes and colors and propel yourself aloft, as it were. This path has the distinction of being the great transference by which you transform all appearances and mindsets of saṃsāra and nirvāṇa into the absolute space of ultimate reality. [429]

"By continuously practicing single-pointedly in that way, the potency of the vase empowerment enters the material constituents of your body, so that you have no wish to move your body. Through the potency of the secret empowerment permeating your speech patterns, you have no wish to speak; and through the potency of the wisdom empowerment entering your mental continuum, your attention remains wherever you place it. This is actual śamatha without signs, in that all coarse and subtle conceptions are calmed in the ocean of the original ground, so it is *quiescent*; and since awareness remains without fluctuation in its own state, it is *still*.[259]

257. These three paragraphs compare with CM 427–28.

258. Tib. *'du shes gsum*. Recognizing the channels as the path, your own consciousness as the traveler on the path, and a buddhafield as your destination.

259. This etymologizes "śamatha" (Tib. *zhi gnas*): quiescent (*zhi*), still (*gnas*).

"By transforming appearances and mindsets into displays of the kāyas and facets of primordial consciousness, there is an exceptional vision of the clear-light appearances of ultimate reality, so this is called *vipaśyanā*. From the impure state of saṃsāra, you come to truly know the real nature of cutting through, the nature of existence of suchness, and thus you see the truth of ultimate reality. By achieving a great, unprecedented vision of ultimate reality, this is the ground of Very Joyful. With this first vision of direct crossing over, you acquire the confidence of never returning to saṃsāra, so you implicitly achieve the first ground of the sūtra path. [430] On the mantra path, all delusive appearances and mindsets come to maturation in the nature of the clear light, ultimate reality; unawareness is transformed into awareness, and you implicitly achieve the ground in which pristine awareness holds its own place. At this time, even if you die and your practice is interrupted, you will be reborn as a nirmāṇakāya, and you will have embarked on the path of liberation. The outer signs are that the appearances in the space of awareness are majestic and stable, as if the curtain on them had been opened, and bindus appear, ranging from the size of fish eyes to thumb rings.

"Here is how progress in meditative experience occurs: Initially, vital energy fills the interior of your body from your heart up to your throat, or various sorts of illnesses or disagreeable pains will definitely occur. Randomly moving throughout the exterior and interior of your body, and not staying in one place for long, these disturbances arise due to the potency of the vital energy of primordial consciousness affecting the ascending wind. After a while they increase, and your throat may become sore and blocked so that food is obstructed and coughed up. You may lose your appetite, have trouble breathing, or lose your voice.

"Then they may increase further, and disturbances may arise from the potency of the vital energy of primordial consciousness affecting the life-sustaining wind. [431] You may consequently experience mood swings from joy to sorrow and from desire to hatred.

"With the potency of the vital energy of primordial consciousness affecting the descending wind, urine and feces are blocked and cannot be excreted when the disturbances increase, and they are expelled constantly when the disturbances subside.

"With the potency of the vital energy of primordial consciousness affecting the pervasive wind, your body becomes swollen when these disturbances increase, and when they decrease, your bodily flesh withers as if you were becoming a corpse.

"With the potency of the vital energy of primordial consciousness affecting the fire-accompanying wind, sweat emerges from your body and great heat arises when the disturbances increase. When they subside, you get goose bumps, your complexion deteriorates, and you shiver with cold.

"Finally, all the winds combine and enter the channels and elements of your body, and sharp pains arise in all the channels. Movements of the winds permeate your whole body, inside and outside, giving rise to various illnesses such as complex heat and cold disorders. Your body becomes swollen, boils and sores appear, dire illnesses arise, medications and divinations go awry, [432] bad omens appear, and individual channels and joints become painful. Gout, rheumatoid arthritis, and lymph disorders may arise, you may become lame, blind, deaf, or mute, or you may pass out. Know that various random kinds of afflictions may arise in your body.

"You may engage in various kinds of behavior, acting coquettishly or shamelessly, like someone afflicted with a disease. In short, know full well that due to the functions of the channels, winds, and elements, these physical afflictions will not be the same for everyone, so there is no single criterion for recognizing them.

"As for your speech, you may find yourself singing various songs and melodies, babbling, speaking offensively, behaving contrary to your speech, not living in accord with your words and acting contrary to them, and speaking uncontrollably as if your words were uttered by an insane person. Such speech is nonsensical and random, so recognize this!

"As if your mind were insanely agitated, your attention may ramble aimlessly, without your being able to remedy or alter it in any way. [433] Due to the disorders in your heart and life-force channel, at times you may weep, groan, sigh, exhale forcefully, or need to be constantly on the move, unable to remain in one place. Your environment may seem so miserable that you do not want to stay where you are, and you may continuously experience a wide range of confused emotions. So recognize this! You may have various sorts of visions of gods and demons or random sensations of hunger, thirst, heat, cold, and so on. These are the outer signs of the appearances of the clear light.

"At the beginning stage, remain motionlessly with your face completely covered, and bindus will appear, from the size of the spots on dice up to the size of thumb rings. At times the visions in the space of awareness, together with the bindus, will not be evident, but the radiance of awareness will appear in forms called *vajra strands*. At times the bindus in the space of awareness will not arise; then they will fluctuate in size, and they will become unclear, no matter how much you exert yourself. On occasion the visions in the space of awareness will repeatedly appear in the expanse of clear light in spherical forms of five-colored lights. [434] These are the signs of gaining familiarity with the practice.

"At this time, even if your life comes to an end, you will go directly to a nirmāṇakāya buddhafield, with no intermediate period. By gaining greater familiarity with this practice, visions in the space of awareness will appear resplendently, like loosely woven cloth, and they will appear in the sky in the form of dangling latticework and pendants. All sorts of images may appear in these visions in the space of awareness, such as stūpas, lotuses, white conches, wheels, vajras, jewels, swastikas, swords, and spear tips, images like stacks of books, and various forms of syllables and animals. Everything that appears consists of visions in the space of awareness, so know that it is important not to mistake them for bindus. Bindus will appear in round shapes, gradually growing from the size of thumb rings to the size of cups on up to the size of round shields.

"At the beginning stage, the lights of pristine awareness, called *vajra strands*, no broader than a hair's width and radiant like the sheen of gold, appear to move to and fro, never at rest, like hairs moving in the breeze. Then as they stabilize a little bit, [435] they become clear and lustrous, temporarily wavy, and they slow down somewhat, appearing like deer running across a mountainside. Then, as you become somewhat more accustomed to the practice, they appear like strung pearls, and they slowly circle around the peripheries of the bindus in the space of awareness, like bees circling flowers. Their clear and lustrous appearance is an indication of the manifestation of awareness. Their fine, wavy shapes indicate liberation in dependence upon the channels, and their moving to and fro indicates liberation in dependence upon the vital energies. Due to the qualities of purifying the bindus, the presence of bindus on the curves of the strands indicates that you will be liberated.

"By the power of meditation, the vajra strands appear in the form of latticework and pendants, transparent like crystal, glowing like gold, and like garlands strung with medium-sized crystals. The sign of having thoroughly familiarized yourself with the practice is that they appear indeterminately, but they remain stable, without moving or vibrating. In this case, the name of the cause is also given to the result, and these are the *vajra strands, the radiance of pristine awareness*. They are the radiance of pristine awareness, so they gradually become as stable as pristine awareness itself. But they are not the actual, self-emergent lamps of pristine awareness and wisdom. [436]

"Once the beginner's phase has passed, the visions in the space of awareness become beautiful, clear, and stable, and they take on various divine forms. Although they may increase and decrease before a single inner sign has arisen, the appearances of such outer signs are premature, like a *dzaki* flower that blooms out of season. So this does not constitute progress in terms of meditative experiences and realizations.

"Even when the inner signs occur, the outer bindus in the space of awareness may be indistinct. This happens to some people with a dominant water element, and the elements of their channels are such that their meditative experiences and realizations mature at a slow pace.

"If progress in meditative experience and reaching consummate awareness are misidentified, even if visions occur that would seemingly indicate the *extinction into ultimate reality*, in fact you have in no way transcended your ordinary stream of consciousness. Indeed, you are proceeding in the opposite direction, contrary to the tantras, so this is an enormous error. It is important to know this.

"Even if vague outer signs and vivid images present themselves, recognize the importance of the emergence of the inner signs. Although visionary experiences may appear to your inner consciousness, if the outer signs are unclear, this indicates that you will not be able to gaze at the clear light for sustained periods, and there will be obstacles. [437] Know this as well. When visionary experiences homogeneously arise inwardly, the visions of cutting through are aroused, causing the meditative experiences of direct crossing over to be disrupted. However, if the visions have not matured into the clear light, the potency of the clear light has not been perfected. If the visionary experiences stop, the visions of light will not develop, and this indicates that the eye of primordial consciousness has not engaged the eye of wisdom.[260] Therefore, you should constantly strive in the practice.

"When encountering this situation, some people develop their minds with meditative experiences, then travel to many regions, and finally succumb to adversities. Consequently, they get stuck there and do not achieve liberation. Some people encounter images of the body, speech, and mind of buddhas—that are actually illusory displays of māras, gods, and demons—and due to visions from the potency of meditation, words of Dharma appear to them as written letters, and they are consumed by the desire to write them down. Out of lust, they consort with women, and consequently they claim to be treasure revealers. There are many such people who bring ruin to themselves and others.

"Having extrasensory perception and visions in dreams, some people perceive good and bad things in themselves and others, and they leave such things as handprints in rocks and other objects. Signs may manifest due to

260. The eye of wisdom sees the appearances of bindus and vajra strands that arise in the space of awareness simply due to attention to the visions of light, whereas during meditative equipoise the eye of primordial consciousness sees the displays of bindus in the space of awareness as they increase, stabilize, and become continuous (VE 442–43).

apparitions of gods and demons, causing them to declare themselves to be siddhas. They then take consorts [438] and exert control over those around them. Laying the foundations for prestige and great deeds, they spend their whole lives in constant, relentless striving. Those who spend their lives tricking others with magic rituals to dispel obstacles and who wander around begging and seeking wealth without satiation are possessed by māras and demons. Even if they become renunciates and gurus with great followings, they are deludedly involved in the eight mundane concerns and the negative conduct of māras.

"Some people take meditative experiences to be illnesses and regard conducive circumstances as demonic. When they receive medical treatment and perform rituals, they become confused by all kinds of divinations and diagnoses, and they become overwhelmed by their speculations. Upon noting bad dreams and evil omens, fantasies arise even more forcefully, and these outer upheavals are apparitions of gods and demons. All the 404 kinds of illnesses in the body, including disorders of wind, bile, phlegm, and combinations of them, are inner upheavals as bodily pain. If you regard them as being truly existent, you fall into error, and you will either die or deludedly fall under the influence of objective adversities.

"Some people go through various kinds of unbearable miseries and delightful and ecstatic experiences, all of them arising as secret upheavals called [439] *joys and sorrows*. If you cling to them and reify them, you will stray into error, and you will not attain liberation. From misery and discomfort and pain in the life force within the heart, people sigh and feel like weeping, and everything they see and feel seems to be of the nature of suffering. Then they restlessly yearn to escape to some place where there will be no human intruders; and when they come to such a place of solitude, they yearn for companionship and to move around. Overcome by desires and cravings, they find they cannot remain in solitude, and they scramble after anything that will bring them pleasure. This is falling into error, so recognize it!

"Frightened by suffering, your body, speech, and mind may become agitated, impelling you to become active, and this is a great mistake. Some people become depressed at the miserable pain in the life force within their hearts, and when they wander out of despair from one village to another, this seems to help. Then when they settle in their own homeland and so on, before many days have passed, uneasiness arises again, just as it did before, and they wish to be on the move again. Such people wind up squandering their whole lives in this way. [440]

"Some people's minds are filled with doubt and vacillation, wondering whether they can ever come to certainty, and they waste their lives by repeatedly traveling to many lands.

"Some are carried away by viewing their teacher's counsel as being wrong, and they fall into false views. Others take their own meditative practice to be harmful, and they constantly feel regret and wonder what to do. They think that it might help if they were to go to some other famous spiritual teacher. These days there is not a single spiritual teacher who is well versed in the nature of this path, the manner in which meditative experiences arise, and so forth. But fearing that their reputation will decline, [such ignorant teachers] cannot admit that they do not know and are unfamiliar with such things.

"Some of them teach things that are their own mental fabrications, then tell others that their meditation is wrong. Others say, 'Your guru doesn't know how to teach, so you have been proceeding on a false path. Do this instead. . . .' Teaching that their own level of instruction is all you need, they heap praise upon it.

"There are a great many who pompously declare that they can transfer their realization to others, [441] saying, 'I shall grant you my realization, our minds will merge, and you will simultaneously perfect all the grounds and paths.' If that were possible, the buddhas would have transferred their state of realization to sentient beings, and saṃsāra would already be empty. In particular, if the minds of all the buddhas' śrāvaka and pratyekabuddha disciples received the buddhas' realizations by their minds merging with the buddhas', why wouldn't they ascend higher and higher, far surpassing the Hīnayāna? Do not place credence in pretentious assertions about transferring one's realization.

"Some people think they have no craving for the eight mundane concerns. Others who have not developed their minds in the slightest become obsessed with various visions they experience. Such spiritually blind people never critically examine the way they wander about in delusion, then claim they have reached the state of the extinction into ultimate reality and think that their own delusions have vanished. Accomplished scholars scorn such attitudes and demolish them with their weapons of scriptural authority and logic. So individuals who enter this path [442] should be careful in this regard.

"In other Dharma practices, even if you succeed, you will not achieve the highest state of liberation in this very lifetime. Consequently, māras will not be envious or angry, so they will not create obstacles for you. If you come to the culmination of this path, you may achieve liberation in one lifetime and with one body. In this case the might of the terrifying Lord of Māras is dredged up, the māras are aroused to envy and aggression toward those advancing toward the state of enlightenment, and they are sent out to create obstacles. They then create problems and manifest illusory apparitions of misleading phenomena to lead people astray.

"By practicing single-pointedly, without succumbing to such obstacles, the appearances of light increase, and as soon as you settle in meditative equipoise, all appearances become totally pervaded by light and bindus, with no intervals between them.

"Ordinary phenomena that appear by looking at impure phenomena with the eyes are seen with the eyes of the flesh. The appearances of bindus and strands arise in the space of awareness simply due to attention to the visions of light. They are derivative of the manifestation of wisdom, so it is said that they are seen with the eye of wisdom. During meditative equipoise, the displays of bindus in the space of awareness increase, stabilize, and become continuous, [443] and it is said that they are illuminated by the eye of primordial consciousness.

"The consciousness that manifests the visions of the clear light during the initial phase is called the *eye of wisdom*. Wherever the eye of primordial consciousness, free of taints, is directed, it illuminates whatever it sees until the visions of absolute space, bindus, clear light, and kāyas are seen.

"Then, due to the sharp pinnacle of primordial consciousness, free of fluctuations in the clarity of the eye of wisdom, all appearances—whether in meditative equipoise or otherwise—transform into displays of light and rainbow bindus with ever-increasing clarity. In the end, appearances of earth and rock vanish and dissolve into the continuous, omnipresent displays of visions of light. That is the sign that you have acquainted yourself with this practice. Impurities have been transformed into the essence, the essence has been transformed into the five lights, and they are actualized. That is the sign by which you can know that you have perfected the potency of progress in meditative experience. At this juncture, the larger bindus cover the sky and earth, while the smaller ones variously appear as small as grains of mustard and in aggregates of five. Within the visions in the space of awareness appear the doors, roof, Dharma wheel, crowning parasol, strings of bells, and silk hangings of a palace. [444]

"Individuals who embark on such a profound, swift path, who have the fortune of converging their karma and prayers, will experience the spherical images of the first phase even at the time of death. At that time, they will pass away as nature nirmāṇakāyas.[261] Finally, once this potency has reached perfection and nothing appears other than the fivefold aggregates of bindus, they will be liberated as saṃbhogakāyas, without experiencing the intermediate period.

261. Tib. *rang bzhin sprul pa*. The term "nature" refers to the manifest nature, which is the second quality of pristine awareness, and this is the path form of the saṃbhogakāya, so this kind of nirmāṇakāya is a reflection of the saṃbhogakāya.

"To present this explanation in terms of the grounds and paths, when you come to the stage called *progress in meditative experience* on the path of direct crossing over, this stage is identified with the fifth ground on the sūtra path, called Difficult to Cultivate. These meditative experiences are unbearably painful, and under their influence you experience craving and confusion. Therefore, when you come to this stage, since it is very difficult to follow the path to its culmination, it is called Difficult to Cultivate. On the mantra path, all the appearances of birth and death in saṃsāra are cut off, and you do not perish. This is the achievement of the state of a *vidyādhara with mastery over life*.

"Then the appearances of *reaching consummate awareness*, in which pristine awareness matures into its vital essence, are as follows: The upper portions of the kāyas appear in the midst of all the fivefold aggregates of bindus, while the lower portions of the kāyas appear in forms of clouds of light, so the kāyas appear to be divided in half. By practicing continuously at this point, [445] eventually the kāyas will appear in their entireties. The white, solitary kāya, replete with the ornaments of a saṃbhogakāya, is Vairocana, the blue kāya is Vajrasattva, the yellow kāya is Ratnasaṃbhava, the red kāya is Amitābha, and the green kāya is Amoghasiddhi. By continuing in constant practice, the kāyas eventually appear in the form of male and female deities in union, and they arise together with their retinues of four male and four female bodhisattvas.

"As a result of further, continuous practice, assemblies of the five buddha families appear in spacious, vast palaces, beautifully adorned with all manner of ornaments, clothed in various silks, blazing with rays of light, and adorned with bindus and minute spheres.

"By the power of increasing familiarity, in the expanse of the outer palace and the inner blazing volcano palace constructed of three tiers of skulls appear maṇḍalas of wrathful herukas. The deities and consorts embrace in union, and single male deities appear dressed in fresh elephant skins tied with belts of human skin with lower garments of tiger skins, [446] each bearing weapons. They appear in all sizes, the larger ones as vast as the sky, and the smaller ones as tiny as peas. The entire universe appears to be filled and totally pervaded with rainbow light and blazing fire. Objects as small as the head of a pin are filled and illuminated with kāyas and all their ornaments. This marks the perfection of the potency of reaching consummate awareness.

"The mark of your speech at this point is that your voice is soothing and enchanting, like songs sung by the children of *kumbhāṇḍas*.[262] In addition,

262. Tib. *grul bum*. A type of yakṣa.

various words of Dharma, legends, and knowledge of linguistics, poetry, and composition naturally emerge. Appearances arise as symbols and as scriptures, and the meaning of all oral transmissions and pith instructions flows forth like the current of a river. Words of melodious songs and so on inspire others' perceptions of the world, and their minds are blessed.

"The physical signs are that your body, like an image in a mirror, and like a reflection in a transparent and luminous expanse, appears as clear mudrās of the five buddha families, as various reflections, as light as cotton, and with no sense of materiality. [447] As an indication that parasites on the body have been released into the clear light, your body will be free of lice and nits. White hair turns dark, bright white new teeth grow in, your muscles become youthfully strong, and wrinkles clear away. Simply by laying eyes on you, the perceptions of others shift, and they experience faith and reverence. As the warmth of primordial consciousness blazes, any concern for clothing is discarded, there is no longer any sense of being cold, and you experience continual, blissful warmth. Casting off all thoughts of food, you can live for months and years on the food of samādhi—the power of bliss and emptiness. In each pore of your body are displayed unimaginable abodes of sentient beings as well as buddhafields, and this shows that you have achieved mastery of miraculous emanations.

"With your mastery of incarnation and emanation, you manifest an inconceivable number of emanations in an unimaginable range of abodes of sentient beings, and in a single instant you guide an inconceivable number of sentient beings [along the path]. You manifest an inconceivable number of emanations in an unimaginable number of buddhafields, where you make myriad offerings, receive empowerments, and open up an inconceivable number of avenues of samādhi. [448] Such transformations are displayed in your own and others' fields of experience, and you send forth and disclose unimaginable emanations and miraculous displays.

"Because you have pristine perception, appearances arise as displays of buddhafields, and due to the pristine purity of the ultimate nature of mind, the universe arises as displays of kāyas. Due to the pristine purity of your voice, sounds arise as wheels of Dharma. Pure appearances pervasively arise as displays of these three pristine purities, without even a trace of impure appearances.

"Having mastered union, the many avenues of impure saṃsāra are purified and can be united with the great bliss of absolute space. Having mastered liberation, simply by focusing your awareness you can bring to a state of liberation even someone who has committed the five deeds of immediate retribution. Having achieved mastery over the elements, you can transform all things into gold, silver, and so on; and phenomena are mastered such that you can transform water into fire, fire into water, and so forth.

"Having mastered the *āyatanas*[263] of the five generic emblems,[264] you can transform your body into the five elements, [449] have your body take on the shape of other creatures, and manifest yourself in various emanated forms.

"Having mastered all stages of birth, dying, and aging, when you want to transcend the three worlds, you will become enlightened in the absolute space of the dharmakāya, Samantabhadra. This occasion is called *enlightenment in great, unimpeded openness*,[265] without reliance upon any of the virtues, vices, causes, or effects of all your lifetimes. Without reliance upon the quality of your karma or the appearances of the intermediate period, all mental states and appearances naturally awaken by themselves, like the dawn breaking in the sky, and there is no death.

"Reaching the state of *consummate awareness* on the path of the Great Perfection means that you implicitly attain what is called the *eighth ground* of the sūtra path, and you also implicitly achieve the state of a *mahāmudrā vidyādhara* on the path of development. Moreover, because of the inconceivable differences among people's constitutions and faculties, there is a corresponding inconceivable array of meditative experiences. Thus, they are not uniform, and there are no definite criteria for them. The foregoing descriptions are simply metaphoric and symbolic. You must examine this with awareness and ascertain that all appearances [450] are of the nature of meditative experiences. So recognize this!

"O Vajra of Pristine Awareness, by practicing in this way, enthusiastic, courageous individuals do not need to be concerned with such issues as the acuity of their faculties, the quality of their karma, or their age, as is the case on other paths. It is solely due to their enthusiasm and courage that they are said to be of superior faculties. Therefore, when those who integrate the Dharma with their lives, without becoming frustrated in their meditative practice, experience the outer and inner appearances of reaching consummate

263. These āyatanas presumably refer to the five "signs" (Tib. *mtshan ma*; Skt. *nimitta*) that eventually arise by meditating on the generic emblems of the five elements of earth, water, fire, air, and space. These practices are discussed in B. Alan Wallace, *The Bridge of Quiescence: Experiencing Tibetan Buddhist Meditation* (Chicago: Open Court, 1998), in the chapter "Quiescence in Theravāda Buddhism."

264. Tib. *zad pa lnga*. These correspond to the kasiṇas, which are explained in detail in the Pāli canon and Theravāda commentaries, such as Buddhaghoṣa's *Path of Purification*.

265. Tib. *zang thal chen por sangs rgyas pa*.

awareness, without confusing one for the other, all phenomena will appear only as lustrous light, and no ordinary appearances will ever arise again.

"Finally, like a full moon, the appearances of all kāyas and bindus gradually decrease in number. From your bone palace[266] a white mass of light, like a billowing cloud, emerges in the space in front of you. In its midst appears an aggregate of five bindus, in the center of which appears Vairocana with his consort, adorned with saṃbhogakāya ornaments and surrounded by four similar deities in union. Above, below, and all around these kāyas, white vajra strands arise in the form of dangling latticework and pendants, like rosaries of clear crystals. [451] Then threads of light, white like the moon, billow forth from the hearts of these kāyas and penetrate down into the point between your eyebrows. For either seven or five days, the threads of light appear as ornaments of stacked bindus like upside-down conch bowls. Finally, they dissolve into the point between your eyebrows, transforming your body into a mass of light. You thereby receive the immutable-vajra empowerment of the body.

"At this point, even if you die, without experiencing an intermediate period, you will be transferred to the central buddhafield called Ghanavyūha and achieve it firmly. Here the entire ground is composed of precious crystal. It is so vast and all-pervasively immense that it rivals the dimensions of space itself. Its surface is smooth and even, like the face of a mirror. When you step down it gives way, and when you lift up it rebounds. As the soles of your feet touch the surface of the ground, the primordial consciousness of bliss and emptiness blazes. Aromatic fragrances waft from hills covered with medicinal plants, and the whole ground is completely covered with brilliant lotuses of various colors. The sky is crisscrossed with lattice patterns of rainbow-colored light, and within it appear forms of rainbow canopies, parasols, [452] victory banners, and pennants.

"It is completely surrounded by a great moat of water with eight excellent qualities. On its shores are pebbles of various precious substances, turquoise meadows, and golden sand. On the inner periphery are forests of wish-fulfilling trees that are not very dense but are very expansive. In the groves around its ponds are flocks of birds that are emanations of buddhas, white like the color of conch, yellow like gold, red like coral, green like emerald, and blue like lapis lazuli, as well as other colors such as black, tan, and variegated. Their beautiful forms are pleasing to behold, and their lovely voices proclaim the words of sublime Dharma as they circle around the ocean and alight on

266. The Tibetan term here (*dung khang*) literally means "conch abode," but it refers to the skull.

the wish-fulfilling trees. In the rivers are innumerable charming, enchantingly beautiful goddesses emanated by daughters of devas, nāgas, gandharvas, and *kiṃnaras*,[267] who constantly make clouds of offerings and render service.

"In the center of this buddhafield [453] is a square palace with doors on each of its four sides, brought forth from the self-appearance of primordial consciousness. Its east side is composed of crystal, its south side is composed of gold, its west side is composed of ruby, and its north side is composed of emerald. Its roof is of lapis lazuli, and its exterior and interior are spacious and luminous. Its interior floors are made entirely of precious rainbow crystal. When the light of the sun and moon streams through its windows, the floors are covered in rainbow light and bindus. Jeweled latticework and pendants hang from its walls, and parasols, victory banners, pennants, and silk ribbons flutter in the wind, giving rise to words of sublime Dharma, to which herds of lovely deer are listening. This vast, spacious palace is beautifully adorned with thresholds, Dharma wheels, and ornaments of the sun and moon on top. It is exquisitely designed and is replete with all ornaments.

"In its center, a broad, high, jeweled throne supported by eight lions is adorned with rainbows and a mass of light. Upon its lotus, sun, and moon seat sits Bhagavān Vairocana, adorned with all the saṃbhogakāya ornaments, [454] who is of the nature of the purified aggregate of form and the embodiment of the primordial consciousness of the absolute space of phenomena. He is surrounded by an immeasurable assembly of tenth-stage bodhisattvas, and he continuously turns the wheel of Dharma. Recognize the importance of occasionally bringing this buddhafield to mind, even while you are still on the path.

"O Vajra of Pristine Awareness, when you, as a follower of this path, finally go beyond that stage, red-colored light emerges from your throat and spreads into the sky in front of you. In the midst of this light a fivefold aggregate of bindus arises, in the center of which appears Amitābha with his consort, surrounded by four male and four female bodhisattvas. Between them are red vajra strands in patterns of latticework and pendants, like rubies strung together. From the hearts of these kāyas appear threads of red light, which strike your throat in the form of garlands of bindus, like upside-down ruby bowls, and stack up there. They appear to dissolve into your throat for twenty-one, seven, or five days. You thereby receive the secret-vajra empowerment of unimpeded speech, [455] and you acquire confidence.

"At this time there is a discontinuity, a shift of appearances, and in an

267. Skt., Tib. *mi 'am ci*. Lit. "man or what?"—a human-bird chimera. One of the eight classes of haughty gods and demons.

instant the entire ground, vast and spacious, is composed of ruby. When you step down it gives way, and when you lift up it rebounds. The whole ground is completely covered with brilliant lotus blossoms of various colors. The entire environment in all directions is completely surrounded by inconceivable buddhafields. There are self-appearing ambrosial ponds with jewel pebbles, golden sand, turquoise meadows, wish-fulfilling trees, ambrosial springs, rainbow canopies, and various parasols, victory banners, and pennants. Unimaginable offering goddesses are continuously making offerings and rendering service, and in the center of all this is a palace composed of ruby.

"Its inner walls are white in the east, yellow in the south, red in the west, and green in the north. Its roof is blue and blazes with blue light, and it is fully adorned with ornaments and fine attributes. In its center is a lotus, sun, and moon seat on a jeweled throne supported by eight peacocks. [456] Upon it sits Bhagavān Amitābha, red in color and adorned with all the saṃbhogakāya ornaments and garments, who is of the nature of the purified aggregate of recognition and the embodiment of discerning primordial consciousness. He is turning the wheel of Dharma for an immeasurable congregation of tenth-stage bodhisattvas. You are instantly transported into their midst and attain a firm and confident state.

"Then, when you move beyond that point, indigo light emerges from your heart into the space in front of you like a billowing cloud, and in its midst arises a fivefold aggregate of vast, spacious indigo bindus. In their center is the principal deity Akṣobhya with his consort, surrounded by four male and four female bodhisattvas. All manner of ornaments adorn them, and latticework and pendants of blue vajra strands arise in the spaces between them like blue beryl garlands. Indigo light billows forth from the hearts of these kāyas, penetrating down into your own heart, where bindus stack up in a column like upside-down lapis lazuli bowls. [457] They appear to dissolve into your heart for ten days or longer. You thereby receive the wisdom–primordial-consciousness empowerment of undeluded enlightened mind, and you acquire confidence.

"Even if there is an interruption at this time, without experiencing an intermediate period, your appearances will shift, and you will experience the eastern buddhafield of Abhirati, as vast as absolute space itself. Its surface is smooth and lucid, like the face of a mirror. Its color is blue like lapis lazuli, and it is crisscrossed with lattice patterns of rainbow light. Verdant hills of medicinal plants are beautifully adorned with various flowers, wish-fulfilling trees, lakes of water with eight excellent qualities, golden sand, turquoise meadows, jewel pebbles, and unimaginable goddesses making offerings, singing praise, and rendering service.

"In the midst of the sky and intervening space adorned with all manner of lovely ornaments is a square palace with four doors. Its exterior is indigo in color like lapis lazuli and blazes with light. Its interior is radiant and luminous with the colors of the five facets of primordial consciousness. In its center is a jeweled throne supported by eight elephants, and seated upon its lotus, sun, and moon seat is [458] Bhagavān Akṣobhya, indigo in color and adorned with all the saṃbhogakāya ornaments, who is of the nature of the purified aggregate of consciousness and the embodiment of mirror-like primordial consciousness. One of his hands touches the earth, while the other is in the mudrā of meditative equipoise. Around him is assembled a Saṅgha of innumerable bodhisattvas, who are listening to the teacher's Dharma while bowing their heads in respect. As your appearances shift to this, you will attain liberation.

"When you move beyond that point, yellow light emerges from your navel into the space in front of you like a billowing cloud. Immediately, the whole ground becomes luminous with yellow light like the color of gold, and all other phenomena arise as displays of yellow light. In the midst of this mass of light, a fivefold aggregate of large bindus arises like a round shield, and in its center is Ratnasaṃbhava with his consort, surrounded by four male and four female bodhisattvas. Latticework and pendants of yellow vajra strands arise in the spaces between them like amber garlands. From the hearts of these kāyas, yellow light billows forth, penetrating down into your own navel. [459] In this continuum of light, bindus appear to stack up in a column like upside-down golden bowls for five or seven days, until finally they dissolve into you. You thereby receive the vajra empowerment of primordial consciousness, free of signs and words, in which all sublime qualities are perfected.

"Even if there is an interruption at this time, without experiencing an intermediate period, your appearances will shift, and you will experience the precious buddhafield of Śrīmat, as vast as absolute space itself, in which the whole ground is like the color of refined gold. Its surface is smooth and even. It is filled with verdant hills of medicinal plants and blanketed with various flowers, ambrosial ponds, purifying springs, and myriad clouds of offerings of such things as wish-fulfilling trees. In its center is a palace emanated by primordial consciousness. Its exterior is like the color of precious gold, and its interior bears the colors of the four kinds of enlightened activity deriving from the natural glow of the five facets of primordial consciousness. In its center is a jeweled throne supported by eight supreme horses, and seated upon its lotus, sun, and moon seat is Bhagavān Ratnasaṃbhava, whose body is adorned with the signs [460] and symbols of enlightenment and with all the saṃbhogakāya ornaments, and who is of the nature of the purified aggregate of feeling and the embodiment of the primordial consciousness of equality. He is surrounded by a Saṅgha of innumerable bodhisattvas to whom he is continuously revealing the Dharma. With the emergence of these appearances, you will achieve liberation.

"When you move beyond that point, your body appears as five lights, and from it emerges a mass of dark-green light in the space in front of you. In its midst appears a fivefold aggregate of five-colored bindus of light, like a rhinoceros-hide shield. Within it is the principal deity Amoghasiddhi with his consort, surrounded by four male and four female bodhisattvas. The images of their kāyas are luminous, they are replete with all manner of ornaments, and they blaze within a magnificent mass of light. Everywhere above and below them vajra strands like turquoise garlands appear in the form of latticework and pendants. As for the upward billowing forth and downward penetration,[268] from the hearts of these kāyas green light billows forth, like the color of emerald, penetrating your secret center. In that continuum of light, bindus appear to form in a column like upside-down turquoise bowls for ten days or so, and when they are complete, they appear to dissolve into you. You thereby receive the empowerment that grants you mastery over the spontaneously actualized kāyas and displays of primordial consciousness. [461]

"At this time, even if your appearances shift, you will experience the buddhafield of Karmaprasiddhi, in which the whole ground blazes like the color of emerald. The entire environment is replete with all manner of ornaments and fine characteristics, and in its center is a palace bearing all wonderful qualities. Its exterior is green like the color of emerald, and its interior is of the clear, luminous colors of the four kinds of activities deriving from the natural glow of the five facets of primordial consciousness. In its center is a jeweled throne supported by eight pheasants, and seated upon its lotus, sun, and moon seat is Bhagavān Amoghasiddhi, whose body is green in color and adorned with all the saṃbhogakāya ornaments, and who is of the nature of the purified aggregate of compositional factors and the embodiment of the primordial consciousness of accomplishment. He is surrounded by an immeasurable assembly of tenth-stage bodhisattvas for whom he is continuously turning the wheel of Dharma. As your appearances shift to this, you will achieve liberation.

"When you receive the vajra empowerment of spontaneous, original perfection and you go beyond the final purification of the visions of meditative experience, all the maṇḍalas of the herukas in the bone palaces appear to you.

268. Tib. *yar mched pa dang mar 'jug pa.*

Rising up into the sky above, you let out a terrifying roar and appear to dance in various ways, [462] causing all realms of the universe to tremble and shake and the great earth to quake with a mighty roar. Consequently, all the physical worlds and their sentient inhabitants dissolve into the nature of light, and with a wave of your hand, your own body disappears into the realm of light.

"At this time, you will acquire the four kinds of great, fearless confidence. What are the four?

1. By arriving at the ground of your own being, the dharmakāya, the nature of the original protector, the primordial buddha, even if you have visions of buddhas filling the whole of space, you achieve the great confidence in which there is not the slightest bit of faith or reverence for them.
2. By coming to enlightenment within yourself, in which you can be neither benefited nor harmed by any other causes or effects, you achieve the great confidence in which there are no hopes for the ripening of effects from their causes.
3. By coming to the ground of your own being, which is originally free of birth, cessation, and abiding, even if you are surrounded by a thousand assassins intent on murdering you, you achieve the great confidence that is devoid of even the slightest trace of fear.
4. By experiencing the state of the originally pure primordial protector, and coming to the state that is originally free of delusion, you achieve the great confidence in which there is no anxiety concerning saṃsāra or the miserable states of existence. [463]

"Then the appearances of the bindus, kāyas, and buddhafields gradually vanish from the space of awareness, like the full moon waning to the point of disappearing into a moonless sky. Finally, pristine awareness is awakened as the ground, and you come to the nature of the dharmakāya. The fundamental root of self-grasping is destroyed, and the mind of grasping is extinguished. The cord of dualistic grasping is severed, thereby extinguishing apprehended objects. Conceptualization involving dualistic appearances is extinguished, so you expand into the uniformly pervasive nature of the purity and equality of saṃsāra and nirvāṇa. Your body becomes like a corpse abandoned in a charnel ground, so no fear arises even if you are surrounded by a thousand assassins. Your speech becomes like an echo, reverberating back all the sounds of others. Like a rainbow dissolving into the sky, your mind expands into ultimate reality, free of conceptual elaboration, a great, all-pervasive state beyond all dimensions.

"O Vajra of Pristine Awareness, an individual who has extinguished the appearances of all phenomena into the absolute space of ultimate reality has far exceeded the tenth ground of the sūtra path known as Cloud of Dharma. Such a person has implicitly reached the supreme stage of a *spontaneously actualized vidyādhara* on the mantra path.

"Still, the subtlest of latent cognitive obscurations arise, [464] and like the illumination from a flash of lightning in the sky, on occasion your body appears, for just the duration of a hand wave, as a luminous body in an expanse of light. Recognize that appearances and the mind occasionally separate, and speech and words of Dharma are sometimes uttered as they were previously. When this phase is complete, in ten days to ten months, the subtlest of cognitive obscurations vanish into absolute space. This perfects the power of primordial consciousness that knows reality as it is, and you gain mastery of the originally pure ground, the primordial dharmakāya.

"By perfecting the power of primordial consciousness that perceives the full range of phenomena, you gain mastery over the spontaneously actualized kāyas and displays of primordial consciousness. As the originally pure youthful vase kāya, you are transformed into a totally perfected buddha, and you become all-pervasive.

"Those of the most superior faculties are liberated as a great transference body, extending infinitely into the all-pervasive dharmakāya, like water merging with water, or space merging with space. Those of middling faculties attain enlightenment as a great rainbow body, like a rainbow vanishing into the sky. For those of inferior faculties, when the clear light of the ground arises, the colors of the rainbow spread forth from absolute space, and their material bodies decrease in size until finally they vanish as rainbow bodies, [465] leaving not even a trace of their aggregates behind. That is called the *small rainbow body*. When the clear light of the ground arises, the material bodies of some people decrease in size for as long as seven days. Then, finally, they leave only the residue of their hair and nails behind. The dissolution of the body into minute particles is called the *small transference*. For those of superior faculties, this dissolution of the body into minute particles may occur even during the practice of cutting through.

"O assembled disciples, including Vajra of Pristine Awareness,
listen and pay attention!
These are the extraordinary characteristics
of the spontaneously actualized youthful vase kāya:
The obscurations of ignorance are dispelled in absolute space,
so the dharmakāya surpasses the substrate.
The primordial consciousness of the inner glow manifests,

and it surpasses the brilliance of the outer radiance.
Great identitylessness manifests,
and it surpasses the appearances of the self.
The kāyas and facets of primordial consciousness manifest,
and they surpass appearances.
The perceptions of the full range of phenomena manifest,
and this primordial consciousness surpasses the mind.
You are awakened within yourself,
and this surpasses going to buddhafields.
You are freed from all extremes of conceptual elaboration,
and this surpasses the causation of dependent origination.
You are endowed with the eight freedoms,[269] [466]
and this surpasses all the paths and fruitions.
You uniformly pervade absolute space and primordial consciousness,
and this surpasses mundane existence.
These nine great, exceptional characteristics
are highly praised by all the jinas
in truly perfected buddhas."

The Essentials of Practice in the Transitional Phases

Then the entire assembly of disciples, including Vajra of Pristine Awareness, asked, "O Teacher, Bhagavān, in this era afflicted by the five dregs,[270] beings are under the power of barbarism. Some, because of poverty, waste their lives in the pursuit of food and wealth. Some succumb to distractions and spiritual sloth, and their lives are squandered in that way. Others, while seeking to defeat their enemies and protect their families, spend their whole lives constantly pursuing profit and renown. Some people get caught up in activities pertaining to the eight mundane concerns and fall under the spell of the bounties of mundane existence. Others are overcome by māras and obstacles, so their meditations veer off into ordinary mental states. Because

269. The eight freedoms (Tib. *rnam thar brgyad*; Skt. *aṣṭauvimokṣa*) are (1) not viewing that which has form as form, (2) recognizing the absence of inner form and not viewing outer forms, (3) not viewing the sense base of boundless space, (4) not viewing the sense base of boundless consciousness, (5) not viewing the sense base of nothingness, (6) not viewing the sense base of neither discernment nor nondiscernment, (7) not viewing the pleasantness of the dispersal of obscurations, and (8) not viewing the cessation of discernments and feelings.

270. Tib. *snyigs ma lnga*; Skt. *pañcakaṣāya*. Degenerate lifespans, mental afflictions, sentient beings, times, and views.

of the paucity of favorable circumstances and the abundance of unfavorable circumstances, very few reach the state of liberation. If they are not liberated, they must proceed into the transitional phases, so Teacher, please explain precisely the essentials of practice in those states!" [467]

The Teacher replied, "O Vajra of Pristine Awareness and you other assembled disciples, listen! The essential nature of the *transitional phases* is simply this ordinary, lucid, clear, fresh, unstructured, uncontaminated consciousness of the present moment. How is this so? By failing to realize this, you must wander endlessly in saṃsāra, but by realizing it, you are brought to nirvāṇa. This very consciousness, being free throughout the three times, does not become enlightened; and since it is not freed, it does not [truly] wander in saṃsāra. Rather, it remains in between—in an ethically neutral state—and this is the defining characteristic of a sentient being.

"The emergence of sentient beings out of ignorance of the ground is like the sun. The emergence of conceptual mental processes from the mind is like the rays of the sun. The emergence of appearances from mental processes is like the light of the sun. The manifestation of the radiant and clear essential nature of the mind is like the eyes. As for the etymology of *mind*, this term refers to the mental activity that takes place because of appearances. Thus, the ground of the mind naturally arises as the essential nature of the transitional phases.

"As for the etymology of *transitional phase*, this term refers to the arising of unstable, delusive, dream-like appearances in the intervals after a prior state of existence [468] and before a later state of existence occurs. Here are the classifications of the transitional phases:

1. The grasping transitional phase of living
2. The contemplative transitional phase of meditation
3. The delusive transitional phase of dreams
4. The gradual transitional phase of dying
5. The inconceivable transitional phase of ultimate reality
6. The karmic transitional phase of becoming

"First, the *transitional phase of living* is like a little bird on a treetop, for in this transitional phase you cannot remain for long before you must move on to another world. By pondering the nature of this process, you abandon the attitude of preparing to remain in this world for a long time. Then, like a bee in pursuit of nectar, you first cut through mistaken notions by means of hearing and pondering the Dharma; and when you are practicing, you must cut off uncertainties and hesitation as if you were a swallow entering its nest. Among birds, the swallow is especially skilled at inspection. When it first builds its nest, it carefully observes for a long time whether or not there might be disturbances or harm from other creatures. After this is determined, it builds its nest. Once its nest is built, from then on it goes straight to its nest, like an arrow, without any uncertainty or hesitation. Likewise, by first devoting yourself to a qualified teacher and [469] by acquiring broad learning and deep understanding, you should be able to proceed to the essential points of the path by your own power, without error.

"First gain a sound understanding of the view, meditation, meditative experiences and realizations, and the nature of the grounds and paths, and comprehend them through your own experience. Eventually, you will never be separated from the awareness that the appearances of this life are like dreams and illusions. Like a visitor getting what he needs in a marketplace, without satiation you will practice with zeal and great courage. Like a traveler from a distant land who has gotten what he wanted and does not lose it to enemies or thieves when he sets out on the road, do not succumb to activities involving the eight mundane concerns, such as the great obstacles of entertainment, distractions, defeating your enemies, and protecting your loved ones. Adhering to this crucial point is the sublime quintessence for all Dharma practitioners, so be aware of it!

"By practicing in this way, those of superior faculties attain enlightenment as a great transference rainbow body, without reliance upon death or their full lifespan. Those of middling faculties are liberated during the dying process, with no intermediate period, in the nature of ultimate reality. Those of inferior faculties merge the mother and child clear light in the intermediate period [470] and attain liberation.

"It is important that you occasionally train in the path of transference in the following way:

> *Aḥ*. Imagine a white syllable *A* on the crown of your head;
> immeasurable masses of light emanate from it.
> In the actual, self-appearing, great buddhafield of Akaniṣṭha,
> vast as the absolute space of phenomena,
> beautifully arranged and adorned, is a great palace.
> From an *A* in its center appears the original ground dharmakāya,
> Samantabhadra,
> indigo like a lapis-lazuli mountain.
> Naked and unadorned, he sits cross-legged upon a lotus and
> moon.
> His hands are in the mudrā of meditative equipoise, and
> he blazes with the light of the signs and symbols of
> enlightenment.

The displays of myriad buddhafields are all present in this kāya.
Like a dream instantly dissolving into the space of pristine
awareness,
your appearances and mindsets, being of one taste,
are indivisibly transferred to the absolute space of the great bliss
of Akaniṣṭha.

"With the syllable *A*, the three realms of all physical worlds and their sentient inhabitants dissolve into that buddhafield, becoming indivisible with it. Uttering '*A*,' recognize this and bring it to mind. Uttering '*A*,' imagine that you acquire great confidence.

"To the east imagine the vast and spacious buddhafield of Abhirati, white and luminous like a full moon, the color of conch, filling the entire sky without leaving any space. To the south imagine the vast and spacious buddhafield of Śrīmat, like the color of gold, blazing throughout the entire sky, [471] earth, and everything in between. To the west imagine the vast and spacious buddhafield of Sukhāvatī, red like the color of ruby. To the north imagine the buddhafield of Karmaprasiddhi, like the color of emerald, with dimensions equal to the absolute space of phenomena.

"Imagine yourself as a bodhisattva imbued with the power and might of primordial consciousness. Starting from the east, imagine that you proceed to these buddhafields like an arrow shot by a powerful archer, and imagine that three times you circumambulate the tathāgatas who are the lords of the buddha families. You make prostrations and immeasurable offerings, and you receive empowerments, hear teachings, and receive oral transmissions and blessings. Imagine that you then return to the buddhafield of Ghanavyūha in the center, where the dharmakāya, the buddha of the original ground, is present in the space in front of you. These are the teachings called *transferring your own appearances to a buddhafield and entering therein*. In the intermediate period, when you recognize that you have died, simply by bringing this to mind, the appearances of the intermediate period will shift to those of a buddhafield, [472] and you will achieve liberation.

"Second, the *transitional phase of meditation* is like the situation of an exhausted person taking a rest. Why? During their lifetimes in beginningless saṃsāra, beings wander aimlessly, like rabid stray dogs, throughout the states of existence of the three realms, without a moment's rest. Here is a way to recognize this situation and bring forth a sense of disillusionment and disgust.

"Examine the delusive causes and conditions in the past, and recognize how they have established a foundation of ignorance, and how you then became possessed by the great demon of dualistic grasping—which has crazed you and left you with no self-mastery or stability. Then take control of your energy-mind, and establish confidence on the basis of firm mindfulness and introspection. Let your awareness hold its own ground, and strive in the practice of meditation. Just this provides relief from delusion on the basis of meditation.

"At this point, you are like someone suffering from hunger and thirst who comes upon food and drink and insatiably partakes of them until he is full. Similarly, people of superior, middling, and lesser faculties may be likened to calves, which first live on milk, and with further growth live on both grass and milk, and finally forgo milk and live on grass alone. [473] In a similar progression, first you arrest and subdue the discursive thoughts aroused by your energy-mind, and then you release your thoughts and let them manifest. This phase of alternating concentration with release is like the period when a calf lives on milk. If it stayed in this phase and did not encounter grass, it would surely die of malnutrition. Likewise, if you do not encounter the manifest path, you will not transcend the lower states of mundane existence, and you will continue wandering there.

"Once consciousness has manifested and you practice single-pointedly, if you remain in that state and do not eventually encounter all-pervasive awareness—originally pure ground pristine awareness itself, the Great Perfection free of extremes—you will not transcend the three realms of mundane existence, and you will be cast back into the ocean of saṃsāric miseries, as you were before. This is analogous to the time when a calf needs both grass and milk and dies of starvation if it does not get either one.

"Once you have ascertained saṃsāra and nirvāṇa as great emptiness and have identified the dharmakāya, pristine awareness, disengage from all types of activities until you reach the state of omniscient, perfect enlightenment. Practicing by way of naturally settled conduct, free of activity, is like a calf living on grass alone, without reliance upon milk. [474] If you remain at the point where you have merely identified pristine awareness, you will be like someone who does not eat or satisfy his hunger and thirst, even though he has food. Such a person will surely die. Likewise, if your practice does not encompass death, you will be involved in hopes and fears concerning all good and bad things of the present. If this happens, you will be deluded throughout endless saṃsāra by dualistic appearances of yourself and others and by thoughts that cling to hopes and fears concerning the good and the bad. So recognize this!

"Therefore, you must bear in mind the utmost importance of practicing with zeal and great courage until the state of liberation and omniscience has manifested. Both living and meditation are called *transitional phases*, for both take transitional states of consciousness as their basis.

"Third, the delusive *transitional phase of dreaming* appears in the following way: Although some people may say that daytime appearances arise as dream appearances, from the primordial beginning of time, the face of the ground—absolute space, free of the eight extremes of conceptual elaboration, the displays of the kāyas and facets of primordial consciousness—has been veiled by ignorance. Then, possessed by the intoxicating demon of the three realms of saṃsāra, [475] the great fiend of karmic energies has allowed the grasping inner mind to act as the primary cause and outer grasped objects to act as the contributing conditions. Then, due to the reification of the appearances of the five senses, daytime appearances emerge; and once they have dissolved into the space of awareness, dream appearances emerge. The appearances of this life and all that follows indicate the fallacy of the notion that daytime appearances are true and dream appearances are false.

"In terms of the causes and conditions of both daytime appearances and dream appearances, that which serves as the cause is the subliminal consciousness that misapprehends identityless, dependently related events as bearing their own identities. That which has the capacity to give rise to lucid, clear objects serves as the contributing condition. From the confluence of these causes and conditions, connections in the manner of nondual sequences bring forth delusive appearances that do not actually exist.

"With the understanding of this as the basis, train in regarding all appearances as dreams; then identify dream appearances themselves. In doing so, if you acquire confidence by growing accustomed to pristine awareness holding its own ground, the appearances of the intermediate period will be cut off, and you will gain mastery over the great bounty of ultimate reality.

"Fourth, what is called the *transitional phase of dying* is like falling into the hands of an evil assassin, and it refers to the period from the time you are struck by a terminal illness until your breath ceases. [476] At first, when you are struck by an illness, carefully check to see whether or not your feces have stopped emitting vapor. Check your vision by placing your fist on your forehead to see whether the form of your space vitality has vanished,[271] like the sun descending behind a mountain peak; and note whether the hum in your ears has disappeared. Then apply yourself to ritual practices and so on for the sake of accumulating merit.

"If that does not help, take a good friend who has not broken his samayas with you to a solitary place free of other people and disturbing influences. At your heart visualize a large white syllable *A*, with twenty-one white *A*'s

271. With this practice you place your fist on your forehead, and if you can see right through it, with no interval between the left and right sides of your vision, then "the form of your space vitality" has vanished.

stacked on top of it. Recite *A* twenty-one times, and as you do so, imagine the *A*'s merging upward, until, with the sound of *Phaṭ*, the topmost white *A* merges into the great bliss of Akaniṣṭha, the expanse of space of Buddha Samantabhadra of the original ground. Then, as a result of resting in this uniform pervasiveness, vapor may rise from your Brahmā aperture or your breath may stop, both of which are signs of achieving liberation in space.

"If you cannot achieve transference that way, lie down in the lion's posture, direct your attention to your eyes, and steadily focus your eyes on the space in front of you. Then imagine your body, mind, and all appearances simultaneously fading into the form of a five-colored mass of light. [477] By taking this appearance of light as your path and settling there in meditative equipoise, your breath may come to a stop and you may achieve liberation with no intermediate period.

"Alternatively, have your companion say three times in a loud voice, 'O friend, in the space one cubit above the top of your head sits the Bhagavān, the original ground dharmakāya, Samantabhadra—the buddha who dwells in neither of the extremes of mundane existence or liberation—whose body is indigo in color, naked, and adorned with the signs and symbols of enlightenment. Merge your consciousness with the nonconceptual primordial consciousness of his mind.' Each time this is said, have your companion utter the sounds *Hi Ka* three times. By doing so, if your eyes roll upward, that is the measure of success.

"If you do not die with that, when your breath goes out and the appearances of external objects fade away, have your companion insert a hollow bamboo or paper tube into your ear and say into it three times, 'O friend, when the white and red phases of dissolution arise for you, that is the reversal of saṃsāra. Merge with the absolute space of the ground, free of conceptual elaboration, the originally pure primordial ground, and transfer there!' He should also utter the sound *Phaṭ* three times.

"If your breath does not cease by that means either, [478] have your companion say, 'Friend, dissolve your consciousness into a white syllable *A*, and, like an arrow shot by a powerful archer, transfer it from your Brahmā aperture to the realm of pristine space.' This counsel will bring greater clarity to the dying process, for it is like a message sent by a king.

"If you derive no benefit in those ways, either from the transference by your own power or by the assistance of someone else, the sign of the pervasive wind escaping is the deterioration of the complexion and radiance of your body. The sign of the fire-accompanying wind escaping is the loss of all bodily warmth in the limbs and so on, so that you become as cold as a stone. The sign of the descending wind escaping is the outflow of all the vital essences of the body. The signs of the ascending wind escaping are the expulsion of the breath, food, and drink that have been taken in through the mouth and their emergence from the nose, and drooling of saliva and mucus.

"Due to interference between the vital energies of the channels and elements and the blood, various delusive appearances arise. Eventually the blood converges in the life-force channel, the vital energies are expelled, and awareness collapses into the center of the heart. Now you have come to what is called the *separation of the energy-mind.*

"Up to that point, [479] consciousness gradually dissolves into an appearance of a white vision like a flash of lightning. The sign that the white vision is dissolving into the red emergence is the appearance of a red vision like the rising sun. After that, the sign that the red emergence is dissolving into the dark attainment is a vision of darkness like twilight. When you fall unconscious in that state, you have died.

"It is very important to recognize the stages of dissolution at these times, as if you were a lovely woman gazing at herself in a mirror. Those of superior faculties follow the instructions on entering into the clear light. Those of middling faculties reverse the impure appearances and mindsets of saṃsāra back into displays of the clear light, ultimate reality. It is also crucially important that those of lesser faculties recognize the stages of dissolution and then establish confidence in the clear light that emerges at that point.

"Depending on their faculties, some remain unconscious in that state for six hours, twelve hours, one full day, or two or three days. However long you stay there, that is the phase when you dissolve into the actual substrate that emerges at that point.

"Following that is the *dissolution of the dark attainment into the clear light.* As an analogy, just as the space inside a jar is united with the space outside, [480] without even a speck of any appearance of a self, a radiant, clear expanse arises like all-pervasive space, free of contamination—like dawn breaking in the sky. At this time, people who are already very familiar with ground pristine awareness by means of cutting through and who have acquired confidence in this will recognize the meeting of the pristine awareness in which they have previously trained—which is like a familiar person—and the clear light that emerges later on. There they must hold their own ground, like a king sitting upon his throne.

"For those who have taken cutting through as their path, without knowing direct crossing over or gaining success in its practice, this occasion is a critical juncture, like conducting heart surgery.[272] Once they have recognized

272. Tib. *snying la gser thur 'dren pa.* This refers to the ancient Tibetan medical practice of inserting a golden tube into the heart region to withdraw excess fluid.

pristine awareness, if they can establish confidence, this is called *liberation in the clear light of the dharmakāya during the dying process.* It is like surviving after removing fluid from the heart. If they do not recognize pristine awareness or establish confidence, they will endlessly wander in delusive saṃsāra, like perforating the heart with a golden tube, in which case death is certain. The number of days you remain in meditation in the clear light of the dying process corresponds to the stability and duration of your present practice. Those who have achieved stability of practice lasting throughout the day and night [481] may achieve stability lasting seven human days at death. But for those who have not entered the path, the clear light will not appear for longer than the time it takes to eat a bowl of food.

Fifth is the *transitional phase of ultimate reality*. For those who see the entrance to the great clear light, direct crossing over, and then apply themselves to the practice intermittently, knowledge arises simply by their own appearances, which is called *dissolution into the spontaneously actualized clear light*. Wherever you look, you see everything completely filled and pervaded by a great radiance of light, like brocade filled with rainbows. This is like a sprout of rice, and thereafter like the emergence of a bundle of rice, numerous bindus appear, ranging in size from those as small as fish eyes to those as expansive as the sky, and they pervade and fill everything.

"Like the ripening of rice seedlings, first in the midst of one large bindu, the principal deities Vairocana and his consort appear, surrounded by four male and four female bodhisattvas. From the hearts of these deities white light billows forth, too brilliant to behold, penetrating the crown of your head. Upon it, bindus appear to stack up like upside-down conch bowls. [482] This is called the *open path of Vairocana*. Simultaneously with it appears the path to the animal realm, which is blue and faintly luminous.

"When you come to this point, the child clear light in which you have trained previously and the subsequently arising mother luminosity converge. As a result, like a child unhesitatingly crawling onto its mother's lap, when your consciousness enters into the clear light, you will achieve liberation in the great bliss of union.

"If you fail to recognize the clear light at that point and are therefore not liberated, all appearances transform into displays of red light. In the midst of this light, the principal deity Amitābha with his consort, surrounded by four male and four female bodhisattvas, appears inside a bindu extending from the earth to the sky. From the hearts of these kāyas red light billows forth, penetrating your throat, in which bindus are stacked up like upside-down ruby bowls. Simultaneously there arises a pale red pathway to the preta realm, devoid of any luster. At this time, those who recognize their own appearances merge and transform into kāyas and brilliant light, [483] and if they acquire confidence without being distracted elsewhere, they will achieve liberation.

"If you fail to recognize these [appearances] and therefore are not liberated, all appearances become completely veiled and pervaded by a dark-blue light, in the midst of which appears the principal deity Akṣobhya with his consort, surrounded by four male and four female bodhisattvas. They are adorned with the signs and symbols of enlightenment and in saṃbhogakāya attire. From their hearts dark-blue light billows forth, too brilliant to behold, penetrating your heart, in which bindus are stacked up like upside-down lapis lazuli bowls. Simultaneously, below this arises a path of black light, devoid of any luster, leading to the realm of hell beings. At this time as well, if your consciousness merges into the absolute space of the kāyas and you hold your own ground with confidence, you will achieve liberation in the buddhafield of Abhirati.

"If you are not liberated at that point, all appearances transform and emerge into displays of yellow light, in the midst of which appears a vast, expansive yellow bindu, like a rhinoceros-hide shield. Inside it appears a variegated lotus, sun, and moon seat, upon which sits Bhagavān Ratnasaṃbhava, his body the color of refined gold, adorned in saṃbhogakāya attire. [484] Embracing his consort, their glory and aura are too brilliant to behold. On their right is Bodhisattva Samantabhadra, on their left is Bodhisattva Ākāśagarbha, in front of them is Bodhisattvī Mamālema, and behind them is Bodhisattvī Dhūpema, blazing with light like sun shining on refined gold. From the hearts of these kāyas yellow light billows forth, penetrating your navel, where yellow bindus stack up like upside-down amber bowls. Simultaneously, below them arises the white pathway of the devas, devoid of luster. If you recognize Ratnasaṃbhava in this open path and merge your awareness with him, you will gain mastery over the southern buddhafield of Śrīmat, and you will achieve liberation.

"These are called the *paths of union with the four facets of primordial consciousness*. In the first instant of this very secret, unsurpassed, swift path there is recognition; in the second, you acquire confidence; and in the third, you achieve liberation.

"You may not be able to bear to look at and focus on the luminous path of purity; and if you can't, by merging with the four impure paths and focusing on them, you will take birth in those states of existence. Until you perfect the power of progress in meditative experience, [485] the open path of Amoghasiddhi will not appear. And from the time that the power of progress in meditative experience has been perfected to the phase of reaching consummate awareness, enlightenment will be achieved without an intermediate period, and those visions will not appear.

"Then the appearances of the kāyas and bindus decrease, and from your bone palace all the maṇḍalas of displays of the herukas disperse and spread into the sky, like sparks from a fire. From each one of them countless others are emanated, pervading and filling all the realms of the universe. Rays of light beam forth from their eyes like the light from a hundred thousand suns and moons. With their mouths gaping open and their teeth bared like the moon, their mustaches aflame, and lightning flashing from their eyebrows, they are replete with charnel ground attire. In the midst of flames like the conflagration at the end of the eon, they hold aloft various weapons and bellow forth *Hūṃ Phaṭ* and the words 'Strike! Kill!' like the simultaneous roaring of a thousand peals of thunder. Creatures with various heads brandish weapons and dance around. When seeing these appearances of terrifying kāyas and hearing their wrathful roars, the assemblies of Yama, the Lord of Death, are intimidated and terrified. [486]

"If you recognize all these as direct appearances of the emanated peaceful and wrathful maṇḍalas of the vajra city of your aggregates,[273] and have the power to unite with them nondually, you will achieve liberation in the Blazing Volcano Charnel Ground of Akaniṣṭha.

"For those who have succeeded in the training and have become acquainted with all the peaceful and wrathful appearances of lights and bindus appearing as the path of the great clear light, direct crossing over, seven days of meditation will arise as seven weeks. By the power of this extended period, recognition and liberation will certainly be theirs. For those who have not seen the entrance to the path of the clear-light Great Perfection, and for those who have seen it but have not practiced or succeeded in the training due to their lack of confident recognition or due to spiritual sloth, distraction, and indulgence in amusements, the lights and bindus will appear no longer than the duration of an eclipse. So it goes without saying that they will not have time to recognize them or gain liberation.

"When all such peaceful and wrathful appearances vanish into absolute space, you will recall all the types of Dharma you have heard in the past, but you will forget them as soon as you remember them. Moreover, during this phase innumerable types of Dharma appear that you have never before heard or understood, [487] and as soon as they do, they are forgotten. For the most part, people experience the visions of the clear light for a short time, and they remain in this state only briefly. For those with faith, reverence, and great adoration for their gurus, as soon as they remember their guru the

273. This refers to your own body, which is the locus of the three vajras of the body, speech, and mind.

self-appearing teacher may appear as their guru and show them the way to liberation; and they may indeed attain liberation.

"Those who have broken their samayas with respect to their vajra guru or who have committed deeds of immediate retribution descend into a fathomless abyss. After their outer breath has ceased and before their inner breath has stopped, with no demarcation between life and death, they fall to Vajra Hell with no intermediate period. Those who have not broken their samayas with respect to their guru or vajra family and who have succeeded well in their practice of cutting through and direct crossing over ascend into a fathomless expanse. After their outer breath has ceased and before their inner breath has stopped, with no demarcation between life and death, they are naturally liberated, with no intermediate period. Like space dissolving into space, they become enlightened in the original ground dharmakāya.

"For everyone else, the following appearances of the intermediate period are inevitable. Nowadays, [488] among the tantras, oral transmissions, and pith instructions, it is especially important to examine, investigate, and properly understand the teachings on how the transitional phases arise, and then to apply them to your own experience. So comprehend this!

"After the inconceivable transitional phase of ultimate reality is completed, this is the way you go astray in the sixth *karmic transitional phase of becoming*. Moved by karmic energies, your consciousness is unable to go to the absolute space of phenomena, the vajra seat,[274] or your future mother's womb. Except for those two destinations, however, it moves freely and unimpededly through all concrete, material things such as earth, stone, mountains, boulders, and trees. It is complete with a self-appearing, empty form just like your previous physical form, and all your senses are present. Thus, objects appear just as they are, and you have mastery of various kinds of paranormal abilities. You are endowed with clairvoyance with which you can see various beings similar to yourself, and you are aware of the thoughts of attachment and anger in the minds of others.

"At times, when you are in the presence of humans, you hear their conversations, but those people neither hear nor answer your responses. You may become upset, thinking that they are all mad at you. [489] Even when you are with your spouse, he or she gives you no food. Noting that you cast no

274. In this context, the "vajra seat" refers to buddhahood or to any of the buddhafields, to which the being in this transitional phase of becoming does not have access. In addition, until the transitional phase has run its course, such a being cannot go to his or her future mother's womb, either.

shadow in the sunlight, show no reflection in a mirror, leave no tracks in sand, soft earth, or liquid, and so on, you feel perplexed, and it dawns on you that you have died. This brings you immeasurable fear and misery.

"When you see those who have gone for refuge to the guru making devotions, you may note that they are conducting the rituals improperly, that they have no practice of the stage of generation or stage of completion, and that they have many other faults, such as breaking their samayas and vows. Thinking that you have been duped by these people and that you will be cast into a miserable state of existence, false views may arise. Ardently yearning to adopt a body quickly, you rove about in all directions, looking for an entrance to a womb. But until the time of the intermediate period has run its course, you do not see or find an entrance to a womb.

"After each period of seven days has passed, the appearances of the prior conditions for your death arise, producing immense suffering. You hear four terrifying sounds: the sound of a thousand mountains crumbling to pieces, the sound of a raging ocean, the sound of a blazing bonfire, and the roaring sound of the wind. White, red, and black abysses appear, which are natural forms of the three poisons, and you experience unbearable horror that you will fall into them. [490] Horrendous, delusive appearances arise, such as soldiers and assassins chasing you, a great mountain tumbling down upon you, and a violent storm bearing down on you. At times you appear in the form of your previous body, and at times you appear in the form of your next body.

"A sign that you will be reborn either as a deva or a human is that your head turns upward. A sign that you will be reborn either as an asura or an animal is that you look horizontally; and a sign that you will be reborn as a hell being or a preta is that you look downward. A sign that you will be reborn in hell is the appearance of a stump-like pillar of black light; for a preta rebirth it is an appearance like dangling black wool; for an animal rebirth it is an appearance like an ocean of blood; for a human rebirth it is an appearance of white light; for an asura rebirth it is an appearance of green light; and for a deva rebirth it is a white light one fathom long.

"In terms of your stream of consciousness, for rebirth in a formless realm you take great delight in vacuity; for rebirth in a form realm you crave luminosity; for rebirth as a deva of the desire realm you crave joy; for human rebirth you crave objects; for rebirth as an asura you desire snow and rain; for rebirth as an animal you yearn for dark light; for rebirth as a preta you are drawn to pale red light; and for rebirth in hell you are attracted to flames. [491] All those objects appear to you to be beautiful and attractive, and you feel an irresistible attraction to them.

"If you become acquainted with these points starting right now and take them to heart, you may recognize these signs in the present, experience the dharmakāya—pristine awareness that is present in the ground—and establish confidence in it. And then the ground clear light, the originally pure dharmakāya, will appear again. This is like repairing a broken irrigation canal, and you will thereby achieve liberation.

"Alternatively, you may bring to mind the buddhafield, palace, and personal deity on which you have meditated in the past; and if you hold your ground in this, your appearances will shift to them and you will be liberated. Moreover, if you have manifested a pristine buddhafield, which brings enormous relief, and have established habitual propensities in your mind for this, upon recalling it and accurately bringing it to mind, your appearances will shift there, and you will achieve stability.

"Those who lack such habitual propensities through practice may see a beautiful mass of fire, and as soon as they come into its midst, visions of hell emerge and they suffer. By going into a lovely cave, preta appearances arise; by entering a river or a swamp, animal appearances emerge; by going into a fine rain or a fierce blizzard, asura appearances arise; and with the appearances of such things as a garden and a palace, [492] they enter rebirth as a deva.

"As for grasping at a human environment, the eastern world sector of Videha appears in the form of a fish; Godānīya appears in the form of a swan; Uttarakuru appears in the form of a crane; and Jambudvīpa appears in the form of a man and a woman in sexual union. At this time, if you block the entrance to the womb and bring to mind the preceding points, you may still achieve liberation.

"Alternatively, if you do enter a womb, in the presence of a man and woman in sexual union who are of a fine heritage and who dwell in the vicinity of an excellent spiritual mentor, where Dharma is flourishing in Jambudvīpa, which is the foremost of all the world sectors, with attraction for your mother and aversion for your father, you may unhesitatingly enter her womb by way of her anus. At that time, if you can imagine yourself in the form of your guru or your personal deity and pray to be of great service to the world, you will certainly achieve a precious human rebirth endowed with the eighteen types of freedom and opportunity. It is important to know that if you enter the womb with attraction for your father and aversion for your mother, you will be reborn as a girl.

"To practice the instructions now for purifying the intermediate period, earnestly consider, 'Alas! I have died. This appearance is the appearance of the intermediate period.' [493] Then rest for a while in a state of recognizing saṃsāra and nirvāṇa as great emptiness. Then think, 'I have really died. This is the transitional phase of becoming. Now I must engage in a method for escaping from this miserable dungeon of saṃsāra.' Then bring to mind the buddhafield of Abhirati to the east, and imagine white light, like a mass of clouds, illuminating the sky to the farthest reaches of the east.

"This buddhafield is vast and spacious and unimaginably immense. Its surface is smooth, even, radiant, and clear like the surface of a mirror. It is filled and blanketed with lotus blossoms of various colors. When you step down it gives way, and when you lift up it rebounds. The four cardinal directions and eight intermediate directions are adorned with wish-fulfilling trees. Springs of purifying ambrosia flow forth. Jewel pebbles, turquoise meadows, and golden sand surround lakes and ponds of ambrosia imbued with eight excellent qualities. In the midst of checkered patterns of rainbows, many goddesses bring forth offering clouds of sensual delights. Flocks of many exquisite emanated birds [494] with lovely voices sing melodies of the Dharma. In the sky appear images such as canopies, parasols, and silk pennants formed from rainbows.

"Imagine that in the center of this buddhafield is a palace created from the brilliant light of primordial consciousness. Vast and spacious, it is resplendent with white, yellow, red, green, and blue hues. It is well designed and is replete with all manner of lovely ornaments and qualities. In its center is a jeweled throne supported by eight elephants, on which is a lotus, sun, and moon seat. Upon it sits Bhagavān Vajrasattva, his body white in color, adorned with the signs and symbols of enlightenment and with all the saṃbhogakāya attire. This supreme, illusory kāya of primordial consciousness is surrounded by an inconceivable assembly of bodhisattvas.

"Then imagine that you ascend to this buddhafield, like an arrow shot by a powerful archer, and you circumambulate the palace three times. You confess your vices and nonvirtues. Upon your request, the gatekeeper opens the door, and you enter the palace and pay homage, make offerings, confess your vices, [495] and pray to the Tathāgata. The Tathāgata beholds you with great mercy and blesses you, makes a prophecy concerning you, and grants you empowerments, and you take your seat among the students to whom he is teaching the Dharma.

"If you succeed in the practice of transforming your appearances during the transitional phase of becoming, as soon as you recognize that you have died, by the power of the habitual propensities in which you have trained previously with the aspiration to be liberated from saṃsāra, you may recall this buddhafield and accurately bring it to mind. Then by focusing your desire to go there, you will have the fortune to arrive there, like an arrow shot by a strong archer, and you will achieve stability in this buddhafield.

"Occasionally bring to mind the buddhafield of Śrīmat to the south, in which the whole sky and earth blazes like the color of gold. In its center is Bhagavān Ratnasaṃbhava, with his body the color of refined gold. He is surrounded by an assembly of vīras and yoginīs of the jewel family. Imagine yourself arriving there and sitting before him as you did before.

"From time to time bring to mind the ruby-like buddhafield of Sukhāvatī to the west, in the center of which is red Amitābha, surrounded by an assembly of vīras and yoginīs of the lotus family. [496] Imagine that you have arrived in their presence.

"Occasionally bring to mind the buddhafield of Karmaprasiddhi to the north, which is like the color of emerald. In its center is Bhagavān Amoghasiddhi, adorned with saṃbhogakāya attire and surrounded by an assembly of vīras and yoginīs of the karma family. Imagine that you perceive the display of the buddhafield as if you were seeing it directly with your eyes, and then imagine going there like an arrow shot by a powerful archer. Imagine being there as if you were a criminal who has escaped from prison and has arrived home, and prostrate, make offerings, pray, and so on to the Tathāgata as before.

"At times imagine all appearances as the buddhafield of your personal deity. For example, imagine, as if you were seeing them with your eyes from the center of a vast region, the regions to the east, south, west, and north. To the east imagine the buddhafield of Abhirati, adorned with white flowers and with white light reaching up into the heavens. To the south imagine the buddhafield of Śrīmat, adorned with yellow flowers and with yellow light reaching up into the heavens. To the west imagine the buddhafield of Sukhāvatī, adorned with red flowers and with red light reaching up into the heavens; [497] and to the north imagine the buddhafield of Karmaprasiddhi, adorned with green flowers and with green light reaching up into the heavens. Bringing them to mind as if you were seeing them with your own eyes, generate confidence in this state and dwell there.

"The practice of occasionally imagining the appearances of going to these buddhafields as if you were an arrow shot by a powerful archer establishes potencies in your mindstream that provide enormous relief in the intermediate period. Therefore, recognize the supreme importance of succeeding in the practice of these instructions and gaining stability in your mindstream with respect to this training.

"At the time of the transitional phase of ultimate reality, either your guru or a spiritual friend whose samayas are not broken should speak to you, saying, 'O friend!' and calling out your name three times, explain, 'By dissolving the impure entrances of saṃsāra into pure ultimate reality, like the autumn sky free of the three contaminating conditions,[275] there will arise an all-pervasive, uncontaminated, lucid radiance, devoid of direction or limits. This is your original, primordial ground, your originally pure, essential nature. So recognize it! Bring forth confidence in your own consciousness! With confidence, hold your own ground! You will then become enlightened in the unmistaken absolute space of the dharmakāya, the mind of Samantabhadra.' [498] This should be said three times—specifically, three times each day for three days.

"From the third to the seventh day, that person should say, 'O friend, listen well and bear this in mind! The appearances of light, light rays, bindus, and peaceful and wrathful kāyas are said to dissolve into spontaneously actualized original purity. The residues of the elements emerge as quintessences, causing the quintessences of the five lights to ripen as vital essences. The vital essences of their bindus come to fruition as the kāyas. Without letting your consciousness become distracted elsewhere, merge with the light, like a child crawling onto its mother's lap. Merge your mind with the kāyas and the bindus!

"'Your own appearances are manifesting in the nature of the clear-light great bliss, so recognize this! Merge there, transfer there, and find confidence! Hold your own ground on the basis of this confidence, and without being distracted by anything else, if you hold your own ground without delusion, you will become enlightened as a saṃbhogakāya in the intermediate period. Do not be afraid of your own appearances as the wrathful maṇḍala. Do not be terrified of your own sounds that appear to you. Do not fear the variously appearing light rays, but remain firm in the recognition of the ground pristine awareness [499] as displays of the consummation of saṃsāra and nirvāṇa, and expand without limit.'

"Then, for six weeks [the guide] should place an image of the deceased in front of him or her and imagine hooking the consciousness of the deceased into this image nine times, and then imagine placing it inside a pod of light. Then that person should say, 'O friend, listen without distraction! You have certainly died, so recognize this!

"'In the transitional phase of becoming, you can instantly go anywhere you imagine. Inconceivable, terrifying, delusive appearances will arise, and this is called the *karmic transitional phase of becoming*. You have arrived at the border between saṃsāra and nirvāṇa, so be disillusioned and repelled by saṃsāra, whose nature is suffering, without even a moment of true happiness. These worlds of the six types of existence of devas, humans, and so

275. The three contaminations of the sky are fog, smoke, and dust.

forth are delusive appearances, like illusions and dreamscapes, so forcefully cut off craving and attachment. A world to the east of here called Abhirati is a buddhafield graced with immeasurable joys and excellent qualities. There Bhagavān Vajrasattva [500] is revealing the Dharma and bringing blessings to an immeasurable assembly of bodhisattvas. Bring this to mind!

"'You have no material aggregate of flesh and blood, so let your mental body of empty form go to that buddhafield as if it were an arrow shot by a powerful archer.'

"Uttering *Phaṭ*, that person should imagine the deceased going there like a shooting star. Uttering *Phaṭ* again, imagine the deceased arriving at the buddhafield. Uttering *Phaṭ* again, imagine the deceased recognizing the appearances of the buddhafield, achieving confidence, perfecting the power in this, and achieving stability.

"Then, leading the deceased like before, that person should say, 'To the south of here is a buddhafield called Śrīmat, which is endowed with superb joys and excellent qualities. There Bhagavān Ratnasaṃbhava is revealing the Dharma and bringing blessings to an immeasurable assembly of bodhisattvas . . .' and so on. Then the guide should say, 'Innumerable yojanas to the west of here is the immeasurably blissful buddhafield called Sukhāvatī, in which Bhagavān Amitābha of immeasurable light is revealing the Dharma . . .' and so forth. Then he should say, 'In a world to the north, countless yojanas from here, is a buddhafield called Karmaprasiddhi, [501] which is replete with displays of the kāyas and facets of primordial consciousness. There Bhagavān Amoghasiddhi is revealing the Dharma...' and so on.

"Unless the deceased has a little familiarity with the stages of generation and completion, it will be very difficult for this person to be helped by such introductions. If these words of introduction are heard by someone who is somewhat familiar with the stages of generation and completion, this person will experience the great relief of fearlessness.

"If the guide has realization of the view, when the dying person experiences the dissolution into the dark attainment,[276] the guide should imagine the dying person's consciousness as a stainless, clear, radiant white syllable *A* and should call out the dying person's name three times and say three times, 'O friend, imagine your consciousness as a stainless white syllable *A*. O friend, the Brahmā aperture on the crown of your head, which is like a vent, is the pathway to ascend upward into openness. Transport yourself through it like a shooting star!'

276. This is the phase following the visions of a white sheen and then of a red sheen when one temporarily loses consciousness.

"The guide should nondually merge his own awareness with the consciousness of the other person and remain for a while in meditative equipoise. Then he should imagine the dying person's consciousness emerging from the Brahmā aperture like a shooting star and then dissolving up into the realm of Akaniṣṭha. [502] After reciting *A* five times, he should imagine it ascending while uttering *Phaṭ* three times. If the guide is imbued with the glories of primordial consciousness and enlightened qualities, vapor rising from the Brahmā aperture of the other person is the sign of success.

"If that does not happen, [the guide should] imagine that immeasurable lights and light rays emanate from his heart, and all the maṇḍalas of the three kāyas of the buddhas completely melt and converge into five-colored masses of light. In the space one cubit above the crown of the head of the deceased, visualize Buddha Amitābha, together with an assembly of bodhisattvas. At the heart of the Tathāgata imagine a lotus and moon seat upon which sits the dharmakāya Samantabhadra, one hand span in height, naked, and devoid of accoutrements and ornaments. At his heart visualize a white syllable *A*, radiant like the moon.

"From their kāyas, masses of five-colored light spread forth like billowing clouds and enter the body, speech, and mind of the deceased. All his mental states and appearances melt into light, and his body becomes an empty pavilion of light. In its center, the masses of light converge and bless the life principle, mentation, and mind of the deceased, like placing a pillar in an empty abode of light. [503] This tube of light reaches upward to the *A* at the heart of Samantabhadra and extends downward as far as the deceased's heart, where it stops. Inside it, twenty-one white *A* syllables are stacked up from the heart to the crown of the head. Imagine them to be of the essential nature of the life principle, mentation, and mind of the deceased.

"Uttering *A Phaṭ* twenty-one times, imagine each *A* gradually merging into the syllable above, then imagine the uppermost *A* dissolving into the *A* at the heart of Samantabhadra, like a shooting star. Uttering *Phaṭ* once, imagine the emergence of the buddhafield of Sukhāvatī, just as it actually is. Uttering it a second time, imagine the deceased recognizing this buddhafield. Uttering it a third time, imagine that he perfects the power of pristine awareness and achieves stability therein. This practice of bringing the buddhafield to mind and sustaining it for as long as you can is profound and potent when applied to all types of people, superior or inferior.

"If the guide does not know the essentials of the stage of generation and has no familiarity with them, whatever he does will have no more power to benefit or protect than simply offering ordinary prayers of supplication. Therefore, the guides of the deceased should have confidence in the view and meditation, and they should train in the essentials of the stage of generation and of transference in order to accomplish the welfare of others. If they do not succeed in such practices, they are no better than hunters and bandits in guiding the deceased. [504] By deceiving others, they trap themselves, like spiders that are caught in their own webs. They pay the price of experiencing the suffering of the miserable states of existence, so this should be recognized."

The Reasons Why This Tantra Was Revealed

"This quintessential, fundamental tantra, which is the treasury of space of the sugatagarbha, with its illumination of numerous entrances to the originally pure primordial consciousness of the youthful vase kāya, provides access to the methods of natural liberation in the state of ultimate reality. The reasons why such a tantra has been revealed by me—the original ground, the Teacher Lake-Born Vajra—to my emanated circle of disciples, who are not other than myself, are as follows:

"In earlier times, the teachings of the Great Perfection shone like the sun. When sublime, supreme teachers explained them to people with good karma and fortune, first they would gain certainty by way of the view. Then they would identify pristine awareness and dispel their flaws by means of meditation. And finally, by practicing, remaining inactive, they all became siddhas and experienced the state of omniscient enlightenment. This is the unsurpassed quality of the profound path of the *Vajra Essence*.

"Nowadays however, people may meditate while having no experience or familiarity with the view, but identifying merely the natural luminosity of consciousness; they do not go beyond the ordinary, and they never achieve the fruition of omniscient enlightenment. [505] Some teachers are expert at oral explanations, but they cannot reveal the path of liberation, so it is impossible for them to bring much benefit to the minds of others.

"Thus, teachers who can explain it are gradually becoming more and more rare, and there is no one who is practicing. As a result, the teachings of the Great Perfection are lost to the point that they are becoming like a drawing of a butter lamp. This tantra has been revealed because of the dependently originated circumstances of the physical worlds and their sentient inhabitants in times such as this.

"Like the sun briefly appearing through a break in the clouds, this will not remain for long. Why? Because there are no teachers who know how to explain it, and there are few people who have the karma, prayers, and fortune to receive it. Thus, just as it has emerged from absolute space, it will reabsorb back into it."

At these words, the entire assembly of disciples including Vajra of Pristine Awareness rejoiced and offered praise. Immediately the Teacher Lake-Born Vajra dissolved into a mass of light, and the disciples also vanished into this light. The light then increased in size, pervading all phenomena, which then dissolved into light; and the light merged with space, which pervasively expanded without bounds. Then, from nonobjective, empty absolute space, these words arose: [506]

"All of you who meditate on the clear-light vajra essence, listen! This is the way to become enlightened as a display of the purity and equality of the nonduality of liberating yourself through realization and liberating others through compassion.

"*Hūṃ Hūṃ Hūṃ*. Lord of the three realms, Mahādeva; his supreme son, the basis of emanation of all the protectors, Gaṇapati;[277] the displays of the great emptiness of saṃsāra and nirvāṇa, Dhātvīśvarī; the king who masters the three realms, the dark-red Yakṣa Karttṛkā; the lord of the whole universe, Planetary Māra of the Poisonous Razor; agents of the five elements, the six pārthivas, and evil demons, together with Shulpalbar! This king of tantras, which is the essence of the life force of all the jinas of the three times, and which synthesizes the quintessence of the Sūtrayāna, Mantrayāna, and the ocean of tantras, this great *Tantra on the Self-Emergent Nature of Existence*, is entrusted to you. Care for it with your samayas!

"Grant it to sublime individuals who are suitable vessels for it, and bring them to the state of liberation and omniscience. Keep it secret from those types of people who are not suitable vessels and who harbor false views. Demolish the faculties of the enemies of these teachings who engage in false imputations and denials, and reduce them to dust. Sustain the lives of those who maintain these teachings, preserving them and causing them to flourish, [507] and provide them with conducive conditions. Engage in deeds that enhance and develop disciples, the teachings, society, and strength, like a waxing moon. *Samaya*. Sealed, sealed, sealed, the treasure is sealed, sealed in secrecy, profoundly sealed. *Ithi*."[278]

277. Tib. *tshogs kyi bdag po*. An epithet of Mahākāla.

278. This is an approximation of the ḍākinī script in the text that comes from the original terma, and which has no translation apart from the terma itself.

The Colophon

The above remained as a command for eighteen human years. At the end of that time, when the appropriate circumstances came to pass, at the meaningful request of the disciple Tsechu, the Mongolian Lama Phuntsok Tashi, and Lhajé Rikzin Zangpo, the syllables brought forth from the absolute space of the illusory matrix of the clear light by Traktung Düdjom Dorjé were written down by the Mongolian Lama Phuntsok Tashi and Lhajé Rikzin Zangpo from the region of Golok.

> By the powerful blessings of the truth of the precious Three Jewels
> and the secret mantra, Vajrayāna,
> may all the fortunate men and women who see this
> practice it correctly, maintain the lineage,
> and become perfectly enlightened as youthful vase kāyas
> in the dharmakāya, the realm of light of the original protector.

Oṃ svasti siddhi.[279]

1. In the all-pervasive, primordial, originally pure, innate nature,
the vajra cloud of the great bliss of the unimpeded union, [508]
the Lord of Kings, Traktung Düdjom, fully arises
as the self-appearing, compassionate teacher to train disciples.

2. Your mind emerges from the space of the great expanse of clear light,
the Great Perfection, which thoroughly transcends mentally fabricated meditation;
by entering the womb of ineffable great bliss,
you have merged in one taste with the pristine awareness of Guru Samantabhadra.

3. When the spontaneously actualized dance of the illusory matrix
fully emerges in the inexhaustible ornamental wheels of the buddhafields, teachers, and disciples,

279. This colophon is by Düdjom Rinpoché, who edited this text for publication.

the power to transform the universe in an instant
infinitely manifests as a wondrous, pure display.

4. Then the nāda melody of indestructible ultimate reality,
this Secret Vajra Tantra, Self-Emergent from the Nature of Existence,
the ever-so-profound essence of the awareness of Samantabhadra,
descends as a rain of Dharma that is the essence of a hundred thousand classes of tantras.

5. This is the ambrosial essence of speech of the pervasive expanse,
uncluttered by scriptural citations, syllogisms, or errors;
when well taught, these practical instructions bring enlightenment within a hand's reach in a single lifetime,
ripening as the heart's power of those of good fortune.

6. This is unlike ordinary treatises of scholars,
unlike ordinary *dohā*s of siddhas,
unlike ordinary profound teachings,
and unlike ordinary practices that are promoted enthusiastically.

7. Its words of expression are few, but its expressed meaning is profound. [509]
It is as difficult to find in the three times as the *udumbara* lotus.
Even if you were to actually meet Samantabhadra,
I swear that he would not say a single word other than these.

8. In this final era of the five dregs,
the great, synthesizing proclamation of the vajra prophecy
arises as an infallible, directly visible sign of virtue:
"The revelation of the mind of Samantabhadra has emerged!"

9. O fortunate friends who earnestly long for liberation,
do not drool over many profound things.
Know this one excellent treatise and witness total liberation.
Here the elaborations of various teachings are cut short.

10. Do not trouble yourself seeking out the meanings of words
as you do for treatises of conventional logic.

Bring forth reverence, and if you encounter the natural state
without distraction,
you will certainly achieve the primordial consciousness of the
lineage of blessings.

11. By hearing and encountering even a single word
of such precious, infallible, unique teachings as these,
if people nakedly realize the primordial consciousness of the
dharmakāya,
aren't those who maintain this correctly actual buddhas?

12. Therefore, this essential treasure, brought forth by Sampo Teji,
is superior to the essenceless, illusory wealth
of images of the dharmakāya that are priceless in the mundane
world,
and it surpasses supreme Dharma relics.

13. Like a vajra promise made in a religious ritual, [510]
those discerning ones who long familiarize themselves
with the *ati* teachings of the Great Perfection
will eventually find satisfaction—this is the power of enlightenment.

14. If it is difficult to measure the collection of subtle, positive,
compounded virtues,
who can measure the full extent of the merit
accumulated in the expanse of the absolute space of phenomena
of the three realms,
which is uncontaminated and uncompounded?

15. Innate reality is not an object of the intellect, and it is ineffable;
when it comes to the inconceivable abode of deeds of the jinas,
all emanated, elucidating volumes of expressive words
are simply methods for engaging with the dispositions of
disciples.

16. Apart from stainless deeds well done, may the adventitious delusions
of all beings concerning nonexistent appearances be naturally
dispelled;
and may the uncontrived, self-emergent nature of existence, the
original ground,
suchness that is free of elimination and acquisition, be actualized.

17. May this way of Dharma, like the disks of the sun and moon,
remain firm and all-pervasive for as long as space remains;
and may the great lion's roar of the supreme yāna
crush the brains of the jackals of misconceptions.

18. Due to the sublime truth of the all-pervasive nature of existence,
the Great Perfection,
the unsought, self-emergent, spontaneously actualized nature of
pristine awareness,
unmoving and permanent, [511]
may we actualize the auspiciousness of Samantabhadra!

These verses were brought forth as an inexhaustible treasure of sacred relics of Dharma offerings of the dharmakāya from the altruistic work of the glorious lord of men Tsewang Rikzin Nampar Gyalwedé.[280] When he was requested to stay at the wondrous, wish-fulfilling palace called the Great Radiant Akaniṣṭha Samantabhadra Palace, the flaws and errors that crept in through later redactions of this treatise were cleared out. By careful examination, a pure edition was produced, and for its publication, a few words of prayer were appended to the text. This was done by Jikdral Yeshé Dorjé, who is presumed to be a reincarnation of the great vidyādhara who revealed this treasure. May the blessed conduct of teaching and practicing this revelation of the clear-light Great Perfection cause innumerable fortunate disciples to be liberated in the inner realm of the original ground.[281]

May the Great Perfection of the Early Translation School of the
tradition of Padmasambhava,
the teachings of the profound treasure of the authoritative
teacher of the essential, definitive meaning,
never decline for as long as the world lasts,
but be preserved through teachings and practice!

Sarvadā maṅgalam!

280. This refers to Düdjom Rinpoché.

281. It appears that this colophon was composed by a student of Düdjom Rinpoché.

Table of Fives

THE FOLLOWING TABLE shows correspondences among all the fivefold enumerations in the series, showing the characteristics of each of the five buddha families. These are drawn from the following passages: CM 397–98; VS 551–56; BM 327–31; GD 151–56; VE 120–29, 308–9, 450–61.

Families	**Buddha**	**Vajra**	**Jewel**	**Lotus**	**Karma**
Directions	Center	East	South	West	North
Places	Crown	Throat	Heart	Navel	Secret
Cakras	Great bliss	Enjoyment	Dharma	Emanation	Sustaining bliss
Ecstasies	Ecstasy	Supreme	Extraordinary	Connate	Inconceivable
Empowerments	Vase (body)	Secret (speech)	Wisdom–Primordial-Consciousness (mind)	Word (qualities)	All (activities)
Seed Syllables	*Oṃ*	*Hūṃ*	*Trāṃ*	*Hrīḥ*	*Āḥ*
Jinas	Vairocana	Akṣobhya	Ratnasaṃbhava	Amitābha	Amoghasiddhi
Consorts	Ākāśa-Dhātvīśvarī	Buddhalocanā	Māmakī	Pāṇḍaravāsinī	Samayatārā
Ḍākinīs	Māmānyaśrī-Dhātviśvarī	Vajraḍākinī	Ratnaḍākinī	Padmaḍākinī	Karmaḍākinī
Buddhafields	Ghanavyūha	Abhirati	Śrīmat	Sukhāvatī	Karmaprasiddhi
Primordial Consciousnesses	Absolute space of phenomena	Mirror-like	Equality	Discerning	Accomplishment
Great Elements	Blue light	White light	Yellow light	Red light	Green light
Derivative Elements	Space	Water	Earth	Fire	Air
Vital Energies	Obscuring	Assembling	Differentiating	Vacillating	Transforming

Families	**Buddha**	**Vajra**	**Jewel**	**Lotus**	**Karma**
Aggregates	Form	Consciousness	Feeling	Recognition	Compositional factors
Conditioned Consciousnesses	Substrate	Substrate Consciousness	Afflictive Mentation	Mentation	Five Sensory Consciousnesses
Poisons	Delusion	Hatred	Pride	Attachment	Envy

Bibliography

Source Text

Düdjom Lingpa. *The Vajra Essence: From the Matrix of Pure Appearances and Primordial Consciousness, a Tantra on the Self-Emergent Nature of Existence. Dag snang ye shes drva ba las gnas lugs rang byung gi rgyud rdo rje'i snying po*. In vol. 17 of *Collected Works of the Emanated Great Treasures, the Secret, Profound Treasures of Düdjom Lingpa*. Thimphu, Bhutan: Lama Kuenzang Wangdue, 2004.

Citations

Buddhaghosa, Bhadantācariya. *The Path of Purification (Visuddhimagga)*. Translated by Bhikkhu Ñāṇamoli. Onalaska, WA: BPS Pariyatti Editions, 1999.

Dudjom Lingpa. *Buddhahood Without Meditation: A Visionary Account Known as Refining One's Perception (Nang-jang)*. Translated by Richard Barron and Susanne Fairclough. Junction City, CA: Padma Publishing, 2006.

———. *The Vajra Essence: From the Matrix of Pure Appearances and Primordial Consciousness, a Tantra on the Self-Originating Nature of Existence*. Translated by B. Alan Wallace. Alameda, CA: Mirror of Wisdom, 2004.

Dudjom Rinpoche and Dudjom Lingpa. *Sublime Dharma: A Compilation of Two Texts on the Great Perfection*. Translated by Chandra Easton and B. Alan Wallace. Ashland, OR: Vimala Publishing, 2012.

Wallace, B. Alan. *The Bridge of Quiescence: Experiencing Tibetan Buddhist Meditation*. Chicago: Open Court, 1998.

Index

not tormented, 48
realm of, 58
pride
in affluence and status, 185
of being the deity, 133, 134, 140, 148
devas from, 71
embodiment of, 79
grasping at body as, 133
of hearing many teachings, 185
in possessions, 173
primordial consciousness obscured as, 69
space reified by, 77
vajra of, 62
in your view and meditation, 184
primordial consciousness. *See* consciousness, primordial
pristine awareness. *See* awareness, pristine
Profound Practice of the Severance of Māras Tantra (*bdud gcod zab mo brtul zhugs*), 85, 89
protection, wheel of, 117
protector
great wisdom as, 62
primordial, 67, 93, 134, 253
tantric, 77
of three realms, 76
See also dharmapāla; guardians
purification
of body, speech, mind, 155
confession and, 138
of dying process, 124
enlightenment not from three countless eons of, 12
of grasping at the body, 125
of obscurations, 53, 66, 189
signs of, 226, 230, 231
spontaneously actualized, 107
of syllables of six realms, 226
symbols of, 127
Purificatory Yoga of the Channels, Vital Energies, and Bindus Tantra (*rtsa rlung thig le dag sbyor*), 160
purity, primordial, original, 6, 14n39, 187, 276
qualities, eight excellent, 7, 97, 121, 224, 248, 250, 269
quintessences, 71, 77
radiance, outer, 255
radiance of awareness, 9, 236, 239
Rāhula (gza' rgod), 77, 78, 83, 160, 213
rainbow body, 213, 254, 257
rākṣasa, 75, 83, 116, 134
rakta, 118, 127, 139
Ratnaḍākinī (rin po che mkha' 'gro), 111, 112
Ratnasaṃbhava (rin chen 'byung ldan), 110, 111n158, 124, 245, 251, 264, 270, 272
razor that cuts off error, 171
reality, nature of, 198, 209
reality, ultimate
absolute space of, 105, 129, 140n188, 174, 237, 254
apprehending energy of skillful means embraces, 170
clear light of, 62
devoid of signs, 8
direct perception of, 85
etymology of, 65n74
experience of, 19
identifying, with difficulty or ease, 198
manifesting, 59, 152
mastery of, 6
mode of existence of, 61, 198
natural sound of, 8
nature of existence as, 6
phenomena as displays of, 41
primordial consciousness of, 84, 105, 137, 144, 186
of pristine awareness, 66
reduced to ethical neutrality, 63
sugatagarbha as, 59, 152, 160
symbolic signs of, 5
transcends causality, 66, 105, 169
transcends intellect, 6, 132, 194, 209, 210
truth of, 10, 64, 238
realization
of absolute space, 96
of authentic view, 192
delusive claim of, 48

About the Translator

B. Alan Wallace is president of the Santa Barbara Institute for Consciousness Studies. He trained for many years as a monk in Buddhist monasteries in India and Switzerland. He has taught Buddhist theory and practice in Europe and America since 1976 and has served as interpreter for numerous Tibetan scholars and contemplatives, including H. H. the Dalai Lama. After graduating *summa cum laude* from Amherst College, where he studied physics and the philosophy of science, he earned his MA and PhD in religious studies at Stanford University. He has edited, translated, authored, and contributed to more than forty books on Tibetan Buddhism, medicine, language, and culture, and the interface between science and religion.

Also Available by B. Alan Wallace from Wisdom Publications

Heart of the Great Perfection
Düdjom Lingpa's Visions of the Great Perfection, Vol. 1
Foreword by Sogyal Rinpoche

"Superb. We are indebted to Wallace, and to those who inspired and assisted him, for providing us with such a rich and vital resource for coming to terms with the profundities and puzzles of the Great Perfection."—*Buddhadharma*

Buddhahood without Meditation
Düdjom Lingpa's Vision of the Great Perfection, Vol. 2
Foreword by Sogyal Rinpoche

Stilling the Mind
Shamatha Teachings from Düdjom Lingpa's Vajra Essence

"A much needed, very welcome book."—Jetsün Khandro Rinpoche

The Attention Revolution
Unlocking the Power of the Focused Mind
Foreword by Daniel Goleman

"Indispensable for anyone wanting to understand the mind. A superb, clear set of exercises that will benefit everyone."—Paul Ekman, Professor Emeritus at University of California–San Francisco

Tibetan Buddhism from the Ground Up
A Practical Approach for Modern Life

"One of the most readable, accessible, and comprehensive introductions to Tibetan Buddhism."—*Mandala*

Natural Liberation
Padmasambhava's Teachings on the Six Bardos
Commentary by Gyatrul Rinpoche

"Illuminates the most profound questions about who we are and provides a roadmap for the journey through life, death, and rebirth in great depth and simplicity."—Tulku Thondup

Also Available from Wisdom Publications

The Nyingma School of Tibetan Buddhism
Its Fundamentals and History
Dudjom Rinpoche
Translated and edited by Gyurme Dorje and Matthew Kapstein

"A landmark in the history of English-language studies of Tibetan Buddhism."—*History of Religions*

Approaching the Great Perfection
Simultaneous and Gradual Methods of Dzogchen Practice in the Longchen Nyingtig
Sam van Schaik

"An important work for its breadth and attention to detail. Van Schaik's lucid explanation of the issues and technical vocabulary in the 'seminal heart', or *nyingtig*, teachings provide the reader with an essential framework for tackling the extensive primary source material found in this work."—*Buddhadharma*

Mipham's Beacon of Certainty
Illuminating the View of Dzogchen, the Great Perfection
John W. Pettit
Foreword by His Holiness Penor Rinpoche

"A riveting and wonderful work, which gives the reader a real education in some of the most compelling issues of Buddhism, especially their impact on Dzogchen."—Anne Klein, Rice University

Original Perfection
Vairotsana's Five Early Transmissions
Keith Dowman
Foreword by Bhakha Tulku Pema Rigdzin

A beautiful, lyrical translation of the first five Dzogchen texts with crystal-clear commentary.

About Wisdom Publications

Wisdom Publications is the leading publisher of classic and contemporary Buddhist books and practical works on mindfulness. To learn more about us or to explore our other books, please visit our website at wisdompubs.org or contact us at the address below.

Wisdom Publications
199 Elm Street
Somerville, MA 02144 USA

We are a 501(c)(3) organization, and donations in support of our mission are tax deductible.

Wisdom Publications is affiliated with the Foundation for the Preservation of the Mahayana Tradition (FPMT).